SWEET & MAXWELL'S

CONSUMER LAW

STATUTES

WITHDRAWN
FROM
UNIVERSITY OF PLYMOUTH
LIBRARY SERVICES

90 034405

KT-381-097

AUSTRALIA
LBC Information Services
Sydney

CANADA and USA
Carswell
Toronto, Ontario

NEW ZEALAND
Brooker's
Auckland

SINGAPORE and MALAYSIA
Thomson Information (S.E. Asia)
Singapore

SWEET & MAXWELL'S

CONSUMER LAW STATUTES

Edited by

Malcolm Leder

*Professor of Consumer Law
and Head of School of Law
Middlesex University*

London
Sweet & Maxwell
1996

UNIVERSITY OF PLYMOUTH

2 JAN 1996

Class No.

Cont No.

LIBRARY SERVICES

Published in 1996 by
Sweet & Maxwell Limited,
South Quay Plaza
183 Marsh Wall
London E14 9FT

Computerset by Wyvern Typesetting, Bristol
Printed in England by Clays Ltd, St Ives plc

A CIP catalogue record for this book
is available from the British Library

ISBN 0 421 533803

All rights reserved.
UK statutory material is acknowledged as Crown copyright. No part of this
publication may be reproduced or transmitted in any form or by any means,
or stored in any retrieval system of any nature without prior written
permission, except for permitted fair dealing under the Copyright, Designs
and Patents Act 1988, or in accordance with the terms of a licence issued by
the Copyright Licensing Agency in respect of photocopying and/or
reprographic reproduction. Application for permission for other use of
copyright material including permission to reproduce extracts in other
published works shall be made to the publishers. Full acknowledgement of
author, publisher and source must be given.

No natural forests were destroyed to make this product; only farmed timber
was used and re-planted

© Sweet and Maxwell Limited
1996

UNIVERSITY OF PLYMOUTH

Item No.	900 3442741
Date	2 3 JAN 1998 *B*
Class No.	343.071 SW E
Contl. No.	0421 533803

LIBRARY SERVICES

PREFACE

It is a remarkable fact that, despite the prevalence of the subject in the curriculum and its popularity as a student elective, there is little choice of dedicated books giving the text of consumer legislation. Instead, many students of consumer law make do with books on, or including, commercial law statutes, with consequent wasted expenditure on unnecessary content to say nothing of the loss of subject focus.

Sweet & Maxwell are now making good this deficiency through this sourcebook in their *Statutes* series. The content of the present work by no means merely comprises commercial law statutes minus the irrelevancies. The objective, subject to considerations of space — for consumer law is far-reaching — is to include not only relevant statutes but also the chief statutory instruments which give substance to the legislative framework. EC Directives make their appearance when the implementing primary or secondary legislation is included, for the reason that in the event of conflict the provisions of national law have to be interpreted as far as possible in the light of the wording and purpose of the relevant Directive; if reconciliation cannot thus be achieved the member state may in certain circumstances have to compensate individuals for loss caused by the default in implementation under the *Francovich* principle [1991] I E.C.R. 5357, [1993] 2 C.M.L.R. 66.

The accessibility of all these materials within one volume will, it is hoped, be a useful reference resource for students preparing coursework assignments; moreover, modern assessment strategies rightly allow candidates to consult their own copies of statutory materials in the examination room, and this book should serve that purpose too. But irrespective of these points, the compiler would recommend students to acquire familiarity with primary legal sources, because the subject of law cannot be truly assimilated and remembered without that kind of first-hand experiential learning.

Conformably with the aims expressed in the preceding paragraph, this sourcebook makes no attempt to indicate the legislative history (including commencement dates) of the material, and simply gives the current text. Editorial notes are limited to the minimum necessary to help readers find their way around the book. In particular, the principal changes effected by the Sale and Supply of Goods Act 1994, which does not "stand alone", have been noted where incorporated into the amended legislation. Readers who need to know the derivation of the current provisions, or who desire annotations, are referred to the standard practitioners' texts, such as Sweet & Maxwell's *Consumer Law Encyclopedia*. The materials herein are for the most part printed in their entirety, with gaps or omissions identified as appropriate.

Discrete statues are included only where they apply to England and Wales. Nevertheless, provisions *within* statutes have *not* been excised merely because they apply solely to Scotland or Northern Ireland. For example, Part II of the Unfair Contract Terms Act 1977 (as amended) is printed, as is the new Part 1A of the Supply of Goods and Services Act 1982, which (thanks to the Sale and Supply of Goods Act 1994) for the first time makes equivalent statutory provision to the 1982 Act for Scotland. Since much consumer legislation applies *mutatis mutandis* throughout the United Kingdom, readers from Scotland or Northern Ireland will find many of their requirements met by this work.

The text is up to date as it is known to me on July 19, 1995. Thus, besides the previously mentioned Sale and Supply of Goods Act 1994, the book takes on board the important new developments represented by the Sale of Goods (Amendment) Act 1994, the General Product Safety Regulations 1994, the Unfair Terms in Consumer Contracts Regulations 1994 and the Sale of Goods (Amendment) Act 1995.

My thanks are due to the editorial staff at Sweet & Maxwell for their enthusiastic reception of this project and subsequent valuable assistance.

MALCOLM LEDER

July 1995

CONTENTS

WITHDRAWN FROM UNIVERSITY OF PLYMOUTH LIBRARY SERVICES

page

Preface v

[**Note**: the provisions of the Sale and Supply of Goods Act 1994, the Sale of Goods (Amendment) Act 1994 and the Sale of Goods (Amendment) Act 1995 are incorporated within the Sale of Goods Act 1979, with consequential amendments elsewhere as appropriate.]

Statutory Instruments

ALPHABETICAL TABLE

[**Note**: the provisions of the Sale and Supply of Goods Act 1994, the Sale of Goods (Amendment) Act 1994 and the Sale of Goods (Amendment) Act 1995 are incorporated within the Sale of Goods Act 1979, with consequential amendments elsewhere as appropriate.]

EC Directives

Factors Act 1889

(c. 45)

PRELIMINARY

Definitions
   1. For the purposes of this Act—
   (1) The expression "mercantile agent" shall mean a mercantile agent having in the customary course of his business as such agent authority either to sell goods, or to consign goods for the purpose of sale, or to buy goods, or to raise money on the security of goods.
   (2) A person shall be deemed to be in possession of goods or of the documents of title to goods, where the goods or documents are in his actual custody or are held by any other person subject to his control or for him or on his behalf.
   (3) The expression "goods" shall include wares and merchandise.
   (4) The expression "document of title" shall include any bill of lading, dock warrant, warehouse-keeper's certificate, and warrant or order for the delivery of goods, and any other document used in the ordinary course of business as proof of the possession or control of goods, or authorising or purporting to authorise, either by endorsement or by delivery, the possessor of the document to transfer or receive goods thereby represented.
   (5) The expression "pledge" shall include any contract pledging, or giving a lien or security on, goods, whether in consideration of an original advance or of any further or continuing advance or of any pecuniary liability.
   (6) The expression "person" shall include any body of persons corporate or unincorporate.

DISPOSITIONS BY MERCANTILE AGENTS

Powers of mercantile agent with respect to disposition of goods
   2.—(1) Where a mercantile agent is, with the consent of the owner, in possession of goods or of the documents of title to goods, any sale, pledge, or other disposition of the goods, made by him when acting in the ordinary course of business of a mercantile agent, shall, subject to the provisions of this Act, be as valid as if he were expressly authorised by the owner of the goods to make the same; provided that the person taking under the disposition acts in good faith, and has not at the time of the disposition notice that the person making the disposition has not authority to make the same.
   (2) Where a mercantile agent has, with the consent of the owner, been in possession of goods or of the documents of title to goods, any sale, pledge, or other disposition, which would have been valid if the consent had continued, shall be valid notwithstanding the determination of the consent: provided that the person taking under the disposition has not at the time thereof notice that the consent has been determined.
   (3) Where a mercantile agent has obtained possession of any documents of title to goods by reason of his being or having been, with the consent of the owner, in possession of the goods represented thereby, or of any other documents of title to the goods, his possession of the first-mentioned documents

shall, for the purposes of this Act, be deemed to be with the consent of the owner.

(4) For the purposes of this Act the consent of the owner shall be presumed in the absence of evidence to the contrary.

*   *   *   *   *

Disposition by seller remaining in possession

8. Where a person, having sold goods, continues, or is, in possession of the goods or of the documents of title to the goods, the delivery or transfer by that person, or by a mercantile agent acting for him, of the goods or documents of title under any sale, pledge, or other disposition thereof, or under any agreement for sale, pledge, or other disposition thereof, to any person receiving the same in good faith and without notice of the previous sale, shall have the same effect as if the person making the delivery or transfer were expressly authorised by the owner of the goods to make the same.

Disposition by buyer obtaining possession

9. Where a person, having bought or agreed to buy goods, obtains with the consent of the seller possession of the goods or the documents of title to the goods, the delivery or transfer, by that person or by a mercantile agent acting for him, of the goods or documents of title, under any sale, pledge, or other disposition thereof, or under any agreement for sale, pledge, or other disposition thereof, to any person receiving the same in good faith and without notice of any lien or other right of the original seller in respect of the goods, shall have the same effect as if the person making the delivery or transfer were a mercantile agent in possession of the goods or documents of title with the consent of the owner.

For the purposes of this section—

    (i) the buyer under a conditional sale agreement shall be deemed not to be a person who has bought or agreed to buy goods, and

    (ii) "conditional sale agreement" means an agreement for the sale of goods which is a consumer credit agreement within the meaning of the Consumer Credit Act 1974 under which the purchase price or part of it is payable by instalments, and the property in the goods is to remain in the seller (notwithstanding that the buyer is to be in possession of the goods) until such conditions as to the payment of instalments or otherwise as may be specified in the agreement are fulfilled.

*   *   *   *   *

Hire-Purchase Act 1964

(c. 53)

* * * * *

PART III[1]

TITLE TO MOTOR VEHICLES ON HIRE-PURCHASE OR CONDITIONAL SALE

Protection of purchasers of motor vehicles

27.—(1) This section applies where a motor vehicle has been bailed or (in Scotland) hired under a hire-purchase agreement, or has been agreed to be sold under a conditional sale agreement, and, before the property in the vehicle has become vested in the debtor, he disposes of the vehicle to another person.

(2) Where the disposition referred to in subsection (1) above is to a private purchaser, and he is a purchaser of the motor vehicle in good faith without notice of the hire-purchase or conditional sale agreement (the "relevant agreement") that disposition shall have effect as if the creditor's title to the vehicle has been vested in the debtor immediately before that disposition.

(3) Where the person to whom the disposition referred to in subsection (1) above is made (the "original purchaser") is a trade or finance purchaser, then if the person who is the first private purchaser of the motor vehicle after that disposition (the "first private purchaser") is a purchaser of the vehicle in good faith without notice of the relevant agreement, the disposition of the vehicle to the first private purchaser shall have effect as if the title of the creditor to the vehicle had been vested in the debtor immediately before he disposed of it to the original purchaser.

(4) Where, in a case within subsection (3) above—

(a) the disposition by which the first private purchaser becomes a purchaser of the motor vehicle in good faith without notice of the relevant agreement is itself a bailment or hiring under a hire-purchase agreement, and

(b) the person who is the creditor in relation to that agreement disposes of the vehicle to the first private purchaser, or a person claiming under him, by transferring to him the property in the vehicle in pursuance of a provision in the agreement in that behalf,

the disposition referred to in paragraph (b) above (whether or not the person to whom it is made is a purchaser in good faith without notice of the relevant agreement) shall as well as the disposition referred to in paragraph (a) above, have effect as mentioned in subsection (3) above.

(5) The preceding provisions of this section apply—

(a) notwithstanding anything in section 21 of the Sale of Goods Act 1979 (sale of goods by a person not the owner), but

(b) without prejudice to the provisions of the Factors Act (as defined by

---

[1] Part III of this Act is printed as substituted by the Consumer Credit Act 1974, s.192(3)(a), Sched. 4, para. 22 and as further amended in part by the Sale of Goods Act 1979, s.63, Sched. 2, para. 4.

section 61(1) of the said Act of 1979) or of any other enactment enabling the apparent owner of goods to dispose of them as if he were the true owner.

(6) Nothing in this section shall exonerate the debtor from any liability (whether criminal or civil) to which he would be subject apart from this section; and, in a case where the debtor disposes of the motor vehicle to a trade or finance purchaser, nothing in this section shall exonerate—

(a) that trade or finance purchaser; or

(b) any other trade or finance purchaser who becomes a purchaser of the vehicle and is not a person claiming under the first private purchaser,

from any liability (whether criminal or civil) to which he would be subject apart from this section.

Presumptions relating to dealings with motor vehicles

28.—(1) Where in any proceedings (whether criminal or civil) relating to a motor vehicle it is proved—

(a) that the vehicle was bailed or (in Scotland) hired under a hire-purchase agreement, or was agreed to be sold under a conditional sale agreement, and

(b) that a person (whether a party to the proceedings or not) became a private purchaser of the vehicle in good faith without notice of the hire-purchase or conditional sale agreement (the "relevant agreement"),

this section shall have effect for the purposes of the operation of section 27 of this Act in relation to those proceedings.

(2) It shall be presumed for those purposes, unless the contrary is proved that the disposition of the vehicle to the person referred to in subsection (1)(b) above (the "relevant purchaser") was made by the debtor.

(3) If it is proved that that disposition was not made by the debtor, then it shall be presumed for those purposes, unless the contrary is proved—

(a) that the debtor disposed of the vehicle to a private purchaser purchasing in good faith without notice of the relevant agreement, and

(b) that the relevant purchaser is or was a person claiming under the person to whom the debtor so disposed of the vehicle.

(4) If it is proved that the disposition of the vehicle to the relevant purchaser was not made by the debtor, and that the person to whom the debtor disposed of the vehicle (the "original purchaser") was a trade or finance purchaser, then it shall be presumed for those purposes, unless the contrary is proved,—

(a) that the person who, after the disposition of the vehicle to the original purchaser, first became a private purchaser of the vehicle was a purchaser in good faith without notice of the relevant agreement, and

(b) that the relevant purchaser is or was a person claiming under the original purchaser.

(5) Without prejudice to any other method of proof, where in any proceedings a party thereto admits a fact, that fact shall, for the purposes of this section, be taken as against him to be proved in relation to those proceedings.

Interpretation of Part III

29.—(1) In this Part of this Act—

"conditional sale agreement" means an agreement for the sale of goods under which the purchase price or part of it is payable by instalments, and the property in the goods is to remain in the seller (notwithstanding that the buyer is to be in possession of the goods) until such conditions as to the payment of instalments or otherwise as may be specified in the agreement are fulfilled; "creditor" means the person by whom goods are bailed or (in Scotland) hired under a hire-purchase agreement or as the case may be, the seller under a conditional sale agreement, or the person to whom his rights and duties have passed by assignment or operation of law;

"disposition" means any sale or contract of sale (including a conditional sale agreement), any bailment or (in Scotland) hiring under a hire-purchase agreement and any transfer of the property in goods in pursuance of a provision in that behalf contained in a hire-purchase agreement, and includes any transaction purporting to be a disposition (as so defined), and "dispose of" shall be construed accordingly.

"hire-purchase agreement" means an agreement, other than a conditional sale agreement, under which—

(a) goods are bailed or (in Scotland) hired in return for periodical payments by the person to whom they are bailed or hired, and

(b) the property in the goods will pass to that person if the terms of the agreement are complied with and one or more of the following occurs—

(i) the exercise of an option to purchase by that person,

(ii) the doing of any other specified act by any party to the agreement,

(iii) the happening of any other specified events; and

"motor vehicle" means a mechanically propelled vehicle intended or adapted for use on roads to which the public has access.

(2) In this Part of this Act "trade or finance purchaser" means a purchaser who, at the time of the disposition made to him, carries on a business which consists, wholly or partly,—

(a) of purchasing motor vehicles for the purpose of offering or exposing them for sale, or

(b) of providing finance by purchasing motor vehicles for the purpose of bailing or (in Scotland) hiring them under hire-purchase agreements or agreeing to sell them under conditional sale agreements,

and "private purchaser" means a purchaser who, at the time of the disposition made to him, does not carry on any such business.

(3) For the purposes of this Part of this Act a person becomes a purchaser of a motor vehicle if, and at the time when, a disposition of the vehicle is made to him; and a person shall be taken to be a purchaser of a motor vehicle without notice of a hire-purchase agreement or conditional sale agreement if, at the time of the disposition made to him, he has no actual notice that the vehicle is or was the subject of any such agreement.

(4) In this Part of this Act the "debtor" in relation to a motor vehicle which has been bailed or hired under a hire-purchase agreement, or, as the case may be, agreed to be sold under a conditional sale agreement, means the person who at the material time (whether the agreement has before that time been terminated or not) either –

(a) is the person to whom the vehicle is bailed or hired under that agreement, or

(b) is, in relation to the agreement, the buyer, including a person who at the time is, by virtue of section 130(4) of the Consumer Credit Act 1974 treated as a bailee or (in Scotland) a custodier of the vehicle.

(5) In this Part of this Act any reference to the title of the creditor to a motor vehicle which has been bailed or (in Scotland) hired under a hire-purchase

agreement, or agreed to be sold under a conditional sale agreement, and is disposed of by the debtor, is a reference to such title (if any) to the vehicle as, immediately before that disposition, was vested in the person who then was the creditor in relation to the agreement.

*   *   *   *   *

Trading Stamps Act 1964

(c. 71)

Restrictions on persons who may carry on business as promoters of trading stamp schemes

1.—(1) No person other than a company or an industrial and provident society shall carry on business as the promoter of a trading stamp scheme.

(2) [*Repealed*]

(3) If a person carried on business in contravention of subsection (1) of this section he shall be liable—

    (a) on conviction on indictment to a fine of any amount, and

    (b) on summary conviction to a fine not exceeding the prescribed sum.

(4) In this and the next following section—

"company" means a company formed and registered under the Companies Act 1985 or an existing company within the meaning of that Act, and "private company" has the same meaning as in that Act;

"industrial and provident society" means a society registered under the Industrial and Provident Societies Act 1893.

Statements required on face of trading stamps

2.—(1) No person shall after the coming into force of this section issue any trading stamp, or cause any trading stamp to be issued, or deliver any trading stamp to any person in connection with the sale of any goods, the bailment or (in Scotland) the hiring of any goods under a hire-purchase agreement or the performance of any services, unless such trading stamp bears on its face in clear and legible characters a value expressed in or by reference to current coin of the realm.

(2) As from the coming into force of this section it shall be the duty of a company or industrial and provident society carrying on business as the promoter of a trading stamp scheme to secure that all trading stamps issued under the scheme bear on their face in clear and legible characters—

    (a) in case of a company, either the name of the company or a business name registered in respect of the company under the Registration of Business Names Act 1916;

    (b) in the case of an industrial and provident society, the name of the society.

(3) A person guilty of a contravention of subsection (1) of this section or of a failure to comply with subsection (2) of this section shall on summary conviction be liable to a fine not exceeding—

    (a) in the case of an offence by a promoter of a trading stamp scheme, level 3 on the standard scale, and

    (b) in the case of an offence by some other person, level 1 on the standard scale.

Redemption of trading stamps for cash

3.—(1) If the holder of any number of redeemable trading stamps which have an aggregate cash value of not less than 25p so requests, the promoter of the trading stamp scheme shall redeem them by paying over their aggregate cash value.

(2) The holder may exercise his right under the foregoing subsection—

    (a) by presenting the stamps at any reasonable time at the promoter's registered office, or

    (b) by sending the stamps by post to that office with sufficient instructions as to the manner in which the cash value is to be paid over,

or in any other manner afforded by the promoter.

(3) The obligation under this section in the case of an aggregate cash value which includes a fraction of a new penny shall be arrived at by taking the sum to the nearest new penny below the aggregate cash value.

(4) In this section "redeemable trading stamps" means trading stamps delivered after the coming into force of this section in accordance with a trading stamp scheme on or in connection with either—

    (a) the purchase of any goods,

    (b) the bailment or (in Scotland) the hiring of any goods under a hire-purchase agreement, or

    (c) the obtaining of any services for money,

and "the holder", in relation to such a trading stamp, means the person to whom it was so delivered or any person who holds it without notice of any defect in title.

(5) Subject to the following subsection this section shall also apply to trading stamps so delivered before the date of the coming into force of this section if a cash value is stated on their face.

(6) This section shall not apply—

    (a) to trading stamps which have been so delivered before the date of the coming into force of this section and which show on their face that they were so delivered before that date, or

    (b) to trading stamps which have been so delivered not later than six months after the passing of this Act and which show on their face, instead of any reference to any kind of value to the holder, a value indicating the sum paid on the purchase or other transaction in connection with which they were delivered or some other value which, having regard to the terms of the trading stamp scheme, it would be unreasonable to take as their value for the purposes of redemption under this section.

(7) Any agreement under which the rights conferred by this section on holders of redeemable trading stamps are surrendered or modified shall be void.

Terms to be implied on redemption of trading stamps[1]

4.—(1) In every redemption of trading stamps for goods, notwithstanding any terms to the contrary on which the redemption is made, there is—

    (a) an implied term on the part of the promoter of the trading stamp scheme that he has a right to give the goods in exchange;

    (b) an implied term that the goods are free from any charge or encumbrance not disclosed or known to the person obtaining the goods before, or at the time of, redemption and that that person will enjoy quiet possession of the goods except so far as it may be disturbed by the owner or other person entitled to the benefit of any charge or encumbrance so disclosed or known;

    (c) an implied term that the goods are of satisfactory quality.

---

[1] Section 4 was substituted by the Supply of Goods (Implied Terms) Act 1973, s.16, and further amended by the Sale and Supply of Goods Act 1994, s.7 and Sched. 2.

(2) For the purposes of paragraph (c) of subsection (1) of this section, goods are of satisfactory quality if they meet the standard that a reasonable person would regard as satisfactory, taking account of any description of the goods and all the other relevant circumstances.

(2A) For the purposes of that paragraph, the quality of goods includes their state and condition and the following (among others) are in appropriate cases aspects of the quality of goods—

(a) fitness for all the purposes for which goods of the kind in question are commonly supplied,

(b) appearance and finish,

(c) freedom from minor defects,

(d) safety, and

(e) durability.

(2B) The term implied by that paragraph does not extend to any matter making the quality of goods unsatisfactory—

(a) which is specifically drawn to the attention of the person obtaining the goods before or at the time of redemption, or

(b) where that person examines the goods before or at the time of redemption, which that examination ought to reveal.

(3) As regards England and Wales, the terms implied by subsection (1) of this section are warranties.

Catalogues and stamp books to include name and address of promoter

5.—(1) Every catalogue published by or on behalf of the promoter of a trading stamp scheme which indicates (whether by reference to a stated number of filled stamp books or otherwise) the number of trading stamps required to obtain anything described in the catalogue, and every stamp book published by or on behalf of the promoter of such a scheme, shall contain a prominent statement of the name of the promoter and the address of the promoter's registered office.

(2) If the promoter of a trading stamp scheme publishes, issues or distributes a catalogue or stamp book which fails to comply with any of the requirements of this section, he shall be liable on summary conviction to a fine not exceeding level 3 on the standard scale.

Advertisements referring to value of trading stamps

6.—(1) It shall be unlawful for the promoter of a trading stamp scheme, or for any person carrying on a trade or business in which a trading stamp scheme is operated, after the coming into force of this section to issue or publish, or cause to be issued or published, an advertisement in any medium which conveys, or purports to convey, the cash value of any trading stamps—

(a) by means of a statement which associates the worth of any trading stamps with what the holder pays or may pay to obtain them, or

(b) in terms which are misleading or deceptive.

(2) A person contravening this section shall be liable on summary conviction to a fine not exceeding level 3 on the standard scale.

(3) For the purposes of this section an advertisement issued by way of display or exhibition in a public place shall be treated as issued on every day on which it is so displayed or exhibited, but in proceedings brought by virtue of this subsection in a case where the display or exhibition began before the date of the coming into force of this section, it shall be a defence to show that the defendant had taken all reasonable steps to secure that the display or exhibition was terminated before the date.

Display of information in shops

7.—(1) In the case of every shop in which a trading stamp scheme is operated—

    (a) there shall be kept posted a notice stating the cash value of the trading stamps issued under the scheme and giving such particulars as will enable customers readily to ascertain the number of trading stamps, if any, to which they are entitled on any purchase or other transaction, and

    (b) if any current catalogue has been published for the trading stamp scheme by or on behalf of the promoter, a copy of that catalogue shall be kept where it can be conveniently consulted by customers.

(2) A notice under this section shall be posted in such characters and in such a position as to be conveniently read by customers.

(3) If without reasonable excuse any of the foregoing provisions of this section are not complied with in the case of any shop, the occupier or other person having control of the shop shall be liable on summary conviction to a fine not exceeding level 1 on the standard scale.

(4) If any person pulls down any notice posted in pursuance of this section, he shall be liable on summary conviction to a fine not exceeding level 1 on the standard scale.

(5) In this section "current catalogue" means any such catalogue as is described in section 5(1) of this Act, being a catalogue which has not been superseded or withdrawn.

Offences committed by corporations

8. Where any offence under this Act committed by a corporation is proved to have been committed with the consent or connivance of any director, manager, secretary or other officer of the corporation, he, as well as the corporation, shall be deemed to be guilty of that offence and shall be liable to be proceeded against and punished accordingly.

Venue in summary proceedings

9. Summary proceedings against a person for an offence under this Act may be taken before the court having jurisdiction in the place where that person is for the time being or, in the case of a body corporate, for the time being has a place of business.

Interpretation

10.—(1) In this Act, unless the context otherwise requires, the following expressions have the meanings hereby assigned to them respectively, that is to say—

"cash value" means, in relation to any trading stamp, the value stated on such stamp;

"conditional sale agreement" means an agreement for the sale of goods under which the purchase price or part of it is payable by instalments, and the property in the goods is to remain in the seller (notwithstanding that the buyer is to be in possession of the goods) until such conditions as to the payment of instalments or otherwise as may be specified in the agreement are fulfilled;

"corporation" means any body corporate, whether incorporated in Great Britain or elsewhere;

"goods" includes vehicles, vessels, aircraft and animals, and generally includes articles and property of any description;

"hire-purchase agreement" means an agreement, other than a conditional sale agreement, under which—

> (a) goods are bailed or (in Scotland) hired in return for periodical payments by the person to whom they are bailed or hired, and
>
> (b) the property in the goods will pass to that person if the terms of the agreement are complied with and one or more of the following occurs—
>
> > (i) the exercise of an option to purchase by that person,
> >
> > (ii) the doing of any other specified act by any party to the agreement,
> >
> > (iii) the happening of any other specified event;

"to redeem" means, in relation to any trading stamps, to exchange such stamps (whether by delivering up the stamps or by suffering the same to be cancelled or otherwise howsoever) for money or for goods or for any other benefit, allowance, concession or advantage (but not including the service or repair by the seller or manufacturer of the goods upon or in connection with the purchase of which the stamps are delivered or the replacement of such goods if defective); and the expressions "redeemable" and "redemption" shall be construed accordingly;

"shop" includes any premises, and any vehicle, stall or place other than premises, on or in which any retail trade or business is carried on;

"stamp" means any stamp, coupon, voucher, token or similar device, whether adhesive or not, other than lawful money of the realm;

"stamp book" means a book or similar article in or to which it is intended that trading stamps shall be affixed;

"trading stamp" means a stamp which is, or is intended to be, delivered to any person on or in connection with either—

> (i) the purchase of any goods, or
>
> (ii) the bailment or (in Scotland) the hiring of any goods under a hire-purchase agreement,

(other than the purchase of a newspaper or other periodical of which the stamp forms part or in which it is contained) and is, or is intended to be, redeemable (whether singly or together with other such stamps) by that or some other person:

> Provided that a stamp shall not be deemed to be a trading stamp if—
>
> (a) it is delivered or is intended to be delivered to a person (in this definition called "the purchaser") on or in connection with the purchaser, or the bailment or (in Scotland) the hiring to him of any goods, and
>
> (b) it is intended to be, and is not, redeemable from any person other than—
>
> > (i) the person (in this definition called "the seller") from whom the purchaser purchased those goods, or whom bailed or hired those goods to him, or
> >
> > (ii) any person from whom the seller (whether directly or indirectly) acquired those goods, and
>
> (c) in the case where a business is carried on by six or more retail establishments, the stamp is one of a kind obtainable at no more than six of those retail establishments and not obtainable by the public elsewhere, and the arrangements under which it is redeemable are entirely separate from arrangements under which any other stamps, whether trading stamps or not, are redeemable.

and references in this definition to the purchase of goods include references to the obtaining of services for money;

"trading stamp scheme" means any arrangements for making trading stamps available for use in shops or elsewhere, together with arrangements for their redemption, and "promoter," in relation to a trading stamp scheme, includes, in a case where a person carrying on a retail trade or business assumes responsibility for the redemption of trading stamps, that person.

(2) For the purposes of this Act, a person shall be deemed to be a director of a corporation if he occupies in relation thereto the position of a director, by whatever name called, or is a person in accordance with whose directions or instructions the directors of the corporation or any of them act;

Provided that a person shall not, by reason only that the directors of a corporation act on advice given by him in a professional capacity, be taken to be a person in accordance with whose directions or instructions those directors act.

Short title, extent and commencement

11.—(1) This Act may be cited as the Trading Stamps Act 1964.

(2) This Act shall not extend to Northern Ireland.

(3) Section 1 of this Act shall come into force at the expiration of a period of six months beginning with the date of the passing of this Act, and sections 2 to 7 of this Act shall come into force at the expiration of a period of twelve months beginning with that date.

Misrepresentation Act 1967

(c. 7)

An Act to amend the law relating to innocent misrepresentations and to amend sections 11 and 35 of the Sale of Goods Act 1893.   [22 March 1967]

Removal of certain bars to rescission for innocent misrepresentation

1.   Where a person has entered into a contract after a misrepresentation has been made to him, and—

(a) the misrepresentation has become a term of the contract; or

(b) the contract has been performed;

or both, then, if otherwise he would be entitled to rescind the contract without alleging fraud, he shall be so entitled, subject to the provisions of this Act, notwithstanding the matters mentioned in paragraphs (a) and (b) of this section.

Damages for misrepresentation

2.—(1) Where a person has entered into a contract after a misrepresentation has been made to him by another party thereto and as a result thereof he has suffered loss, then, if the person making the misrepresentation would be liable to damages in respect thereof had the misrepresentation been made fraudulently, that person shall be so liable notwithstanding that the misrepresentation was not made fraudulently, unless he proves that he had reasonable ground to believe and did believe up to the time the contract was made that the facts represented were true.

(2) Where a person has entered into a contract after a misrepresentation has been made to him otherwise than fraudulently, and he would be entitled, by reason of the misrepresentation, to rescind the contract, then, if it is claimed, in any proceedings arising out of the contract, that the contract ought to be or has been rescinded, the court or arbitrator may declare the contract subsisting and award damages in lieu of rescission, if of opinion that it would be equitable to do so, having regard to the nature of the misrepresentation and the loss that would be caused by it if the contract were upheld, as well as to the loss that rescission would cause to the other party.

(3) Damages may be awarded against a person under subsection (2) of this section whether or not he is liable to damages under subsection (1) thereof, but where he is so liable any award under the said subsection (2) shall be taken into account in assessing his liability under the said subsection (1).

Avoidance of provision excluding liability for misrepresentation

3.   If a contract contains a term which would exclude or restrict—

(a) any liability to which a party to a contract may be subject by reason of any misrepresentation made by him before the contract was made; or

(b) any remedy available to another party to the contract by reason of such a misrepresentation,

that term shall be of no effect except in so far as it satisfies the requirement of reasonableness as stated in section 11(1) of the Unfair Contract Terms Act 1977; and it is for those claiming that the term satisfies that requirement to show that it does.

4.   [*Repealed*]

Saving for past transactions

5. Nothing in this Act shall apply in relation to any misrepresentation or contract of sale which is made before the commencement of this Act.

Short title, commencement and extent

6.—(1) This Act may be cited as the Misrepresentation Act 1967.

(2) This Act shall come into operation at the expiration of the period of one month beginning with the date on which it is passed.

(3) This Act does not extend to Scotland.

(4) This Act does not extend to Northern Ireland.

Trade Descriptions Act 1968

(c. 29)

An Act to replace the Merchandise Marks Acts 1887 to 1953 by fresh provisions prohibiting misdescriptions of goods, services accommodation and facilities provided in the course of trade; to prohibit false or misleading indications as to the price of goods; to confer power to require information or instructions relating to goods to be marked on or to accompany the goods or to be included in advertisements; to prohibit the unauthorised use of devices or emblems signifying royal awards; to enable the Parliament of Northern Ireland to make laws relating to merchandise marks; and for purposes connected with those matters.

[30 May 1968]

Prohibition of false trade descriptions

Prohibition of false trade descriptions

    1.—(1) Any person who, in the course of a trade or business,—
        (a) applies a false trade description to any goods; or
        (b) supplies or offers to supply any goods to which a false trade description is applied;
shall, subject to the provisions of this Act, be guilty of an offence.
    (2) Sections 2 to 6 of this Act shall have effect for the purposes of this section and for the interpretation of expressions used in this section, wherever they occur in this Act.

Trade description

    2.—(1) A trade description is an indication, direct or indirect, and by whatever means given, of any of the following matters with respect to any goods or parts of goods, that is to say—
        (a) quantity, size or gauge;
        (b) method of manufacture, production, processing or re-conditioning;
        (c) composition;
        (d) fitness for purpose, strength, performance, behaviour or accuracy;
        (e) any physical characteristics not included in the preceding paragraphs;
        (f) testing by any person and results thereof;
        (g) approval by any person or conformity with a type approved by any person;
        (h) place or date of manufacture, production, processing or reconditioning;
        (i) person by whom manufactured, produced, processed or reconditioned;
        (j) other history, including previous ownership or use.
    (2) The matters specified in subsection (1) of this section shall be taken—
        (a) in relation to any animal, to include sex, breed or cross, fertility and soundness;
        (b) in relation to any semen, to include the identity and characteristics of the animal from which it was taken and measure of dilution.
    (3) In this section "quantity" includes length, width, height, area, volume, capacity, weight and number.
    (4) Notwithstanding anything in the preceding provisions of this section, the

following shall be deemed not to be trade descriptions, that is to say, any description or mark applied in pursuance of—

    (a) *[Repealed]*

    (b) section 2 of the Agricultural Produce (Grading and Marking) Act 1928 (as amended by the Agricultural Produce (Grading and Marking) Amendment Act 1931) or any corresponding enactment of the Parliament of Northern Ireland;

    (c) the Plant Varieties and Seeds Act 1964;

    (d) the Agriculture and Horticulture Act 1964 or any Community grading rules within the meaning of Part III of that Act;

    (e) the Seeds Act (Northern Ireland) 1965;

    (f) the Horticulture Act (Northern Ireland) 1966;

    (g) the Consumer Protection Act 1987;

any statement made in respect of, or mark applied to, any material in pursuance of Part IV of the Agriculture Act 1970, any name or expression to which a meaning has been assigned under section 70 of that Act when applied to any material in the circumstances specified in that section [. . .] any mark prescribed by a system of classification compiled under section 5 of the Agriculture Act 1967 and any designation, mark or description applied in pursuance of a scheme brought into force under Section 6(1) or an order made under section 25(1) of the Agriculture Act 1970.

    (5) Notwithstanding anything in the preceding provisions of this section,

    (a) where provision is made under the Food Safety Act 1990 or the Food and Drugs Act (Northern Ireland) 1958 or the Consumer Protection Act 1987 prohibiting the application of a description except to goods in the case of which the requirements specified in that provision are complied with, that description, when applied to such goods, shall be deemed not to be a trade description.

    (b) where by virtue of any provision made under Part V of the Medicines Act 1968 (or made under any provisions of the said Part V as applied by an order made under section 104 or section 105 of that Act) anything which in accordance with this Act, constitutes the application of a trade description to goods is subject to any requirements or restrictions imposed by that provision, any particular description specified in that provision, when applied to goods in circumstances to which those requirements or restrictions are applicable, shall be deemed not to be a trade description.

False trade description

    3.—(1) A false trade description is a trade description which is false to a material degree.

    (2) A trade description which, though not false, is misleading, that is to say, likely to be taken for such an indication of any of the matters specified in section 2 of this Act as would be false to a material degree, shall be deemed to be a false trade description.

    (3) Anything which, though not a trade description, is likely to be taken for an indication of any of those matters and, as such an indication, would be false to a material degree, shall be deemed to be a false trade description.

    (4) A false indication, or anything likely to be taken as an indication which would be false, that any goods comply with a standard specified or recognised by any person or implied by the approval of any person shall be deemed to be

a false trade description, if there is no such person or no standard so specified, recognised or implied.

Applying a trade description to goods

4.—(1) A person applies a trade description to goods if he—

    (a) affixes or annexes it to or in any manner marks it on or incorporates it with—

        (i) the goods themselves, or

        (ii) anything in, on or with which the goods are supplied; or

    (b) places the goods in, on or with anything which the trade description has been affixed or annexed to, marked on or incorporated with, or places any such thing with the goods; or

    (c) uses the trade description in any manner likely to be taken as referring to the goods.

(2) An oral statement may amount to the use of a trade description.

(3) Where goods are supplied in pursuance of a request in which a trade description is used and the circumstances are such as to make it reasonable to infer that the goods are supplied as goods corresponding to that trade description, the person supplying the goods shall be deemed to have applied the trade description to the goods.

Trade descriptions used in advertisements

5.—(1) The following provisions of this section shall have effect where in an advertisement a trade description is used in relation to any class of goods.

(2) The trade description shall be taken as referring to all goods of the class, whether or not in existence at the time the advertisement is published—

    (a) for the purpose of determining whether an offence has been committed under paragraph (a) of section 1(1) of this Act; and

    (b) where goods of the class are supplied or offered to be supplied by a person publishing or displaying the advertisement, also for the purpose of determining whether an offence has been committed under paragraph (b) of the said section 1(1).

(3) In determining for the purposes of this section whether any goods are of a class to which a trade description used in an advertisement relates regard shall be had not only to the form and content of the advertisement but also to the time, place, manner and frequency of its publication and all other matters making it likely or unlikely that a person to whom the goods are supplied would think of the goods as belonging to the class in relation to which the trade description is used in the advertisement.

Offer to supply

6. A person exposing goods for supply or having goods in his possession for supply shall be deemed to offer to supply them.

Power to define terms and to require display, etc. of information

Defintion orders

7. Where it appears to the Board of Trade—

    (a) that it would be in the interest of persons to whom any goods are supplied; or

    (b) that it would be in the interest of persons by whom any goods are exported and would not be contrary to the interest of persons to whom such goods are supplied in the United Kingdom;

that any expressions used in relation to the goods should be understood as having definite meanings, the Board may by order assign such meanings either—

    (i) to those expressions when used in the course of a trade or business as, or as part of, a trade description applied to the goods; or

    (ii) to those expressions when so used in such circumstances as may be specified in the order;

and where such a meaning is so assigned to an expression it shall be deemed for the purposes of this Act to have that meaning when used as mentioned in paragraph (i) or, as the case may be, paragraph (ii) of this section.

Marking orders

8.—(1) Where it appears to the Board of Trade necessary or expedient in the interests of persons to whom any goods are supplied that the goods should be marked with or accompanied by any information (whether or not amounting to or including a trade description) or instruction relating to the goods, the Board may subject to the provisions of this Act, by order impose requirements for securing that the goods are so marked or accompanied, and regulate or prohibit the supply of goods with respect to which the requirements are not complied with; and the requirements may extend to the form and manner in which the information or instruction is to be given.

(2) Where an order under this section is in force with respect to goods of any description, any person who, in the course of any trade or business, supplies or offers to supply goods of that description in contravention of the order shall, subject to the provisions of this Act, be guilty of an offence.

(3) An order under this section may make different provision for different circumstances and may, in the case of goods supplied in circumstances where the information or instruction required by the order would not be conveyed until after delivery, require the whole or part thereof to be also displayed near the goods.

Information, etc. to be given in advertisements

9.—(1) Where it appears to the Board of Trade necessary or expedient in the interest of persons to whom any goods are to be supplied that any description of advertisements of the goods should contain or refer to any information (whether or not amounting to or including a trade description) relating to the goods the Board may, subject to the provisions of this Act, by order impose requirements as to the inclusion of that information, or of an indication of the means by which it may be obtained, in such description of advertisements of the goods as may be specified in the order.

(2) An order under this section may specify the form and manner in which any such information or indication is to be included in advertisements of any description and may take different provision for different circumstances.

(3) Where an advertisement of any goods to be supplied in the course of any trade or business fails to comply with any requirement imposed under this section, any person who publishes the advertisement shall, subject to the provisions of this Act, be guilty of an offence.

Provisions supplementary to sections 8 and 9

10.—(1) A requirement imposed by an order under section 8 or section 9 of this Act in relation to any goods shall not be confined to goods manufactured or produced in any one country or any one of a number of countries or to goods manufactured or produced outside any one or more countries, unless—

    (a) it is imposed with respect to a description of goods in the case of which the Board of Trade are satisfied that the interest of persons in the United Kingdom to whom goods of that description are supplied will be sufficiently protected if the requirement is so confined; and

    (b) the Board of Trade are satisfied that the order is compatible with the international obligations of the United Kingdom.

(2) Where any requirements with respect to any goods are for the time being imposed by such an order and the Board of Trade are satisfied, on the representation of persons appearing to the Board to have a substantial interest in the matter, that greater hardship would be caused to such persons if the requirements continued to apply than is justified by the interest of persons to whom the goods are supplied, the power of the Board to relax or discontinue the requirements by a further order may be exercised without the consultation and notice required by section 38(3) of this Act.

Misstatements other than false trade descriptions

11. [*Repealed*]

False representations as to royal approval or award, etc

12.—(1) If any person in the course of any trade or business, gives, by whatever means, any false indication, direct or indirect, that any goods or services supplied by him or any methods adopted by him are or are of a kind supplied to or approved by Her Majesty or any member of the Royal Family, he shall, subject to the provisions of this Act be guilty of an offence.

(2) If any person, in the course of any trade or business, uses, without the authority of Her Majesty, any device or emblem signifying the Queen's Award to Industry or anything so nearly resembling such a device or emblem as to be likely to deceive, he shall, subject to the provisions of this Act, be guilty of an offence.

False representations as to supply of goods or services

13. If any person, in the course of any trade or business, gives, by whatever means, any false indication, direct or indirect, that any goods or services supplied by him are of a kind supplied to any person he shall, subject to the provisions of this Act, be guilty of an offence.

False or misleading statements as to services, etc

14.—(1) It shall be an offence for any person in the course of any trade or business—

    (a) to make a statement which he knows to be false; or

    (b) recklessly to make a statement which is false; as to any of the following matters, that is to say,—

        (i) the provision in the course of any trade or business of any services, accommodation or facilities;

        (ii) the nature of any services, accommodation or facilities provided in the course of any trade or business;

        (iii) the time at which, manner in which or persons by whom any services, accommodation or facilities are so provided;

(iv) the examination, approval or evaluation by any person of any services, accommodation or facilities so provided; or

(v) the location or amenities of any accommodation so provided.

(2) For the purposes of this section—

(a) anything (whether or not a statement as to any of the matters specified in the preceding subsection) likely to be taken for such a statement as to any of those matters as would be false shall be deemed to be a false statement as to that matter; and

(b) a statement made regardless of whether it is true or false shall be deemed to be made recklessly, whether or not the person making it had reasons for believing that it might be false.

(3) In relation to any services consisting of or including the application of any treatment or process or the carrying out of any repair, the matters specified in subsection (1) of this section shall be taken to include the effect of the treatment, process or repair.

(4) In this section "false" means false to a material degree and "services" does not include anything done under a contract of service.

Orders defining terms for purposes of section 14

15. Where it appears to the Board of Trade that it would be in the interest of persons for whom any services, accommodation or facilities are provided in the course of any trade or business that any expressions used with respect thereto should be understood as having definite meanings, the Board may by order assign such meanings to those expressions when used as, or as part of, such statements as are mentioned in section 14 of this Act with respect to those services, accommodation or facilities; and where such a meaning is so assigned to an expression it shall be deemed for the purposes of this Act to have that meaning when so used.

Prohibition of importation of certain goods

Prohibition of importation of goods bearing false indication of origin

16. Where a false trade description is applied to any goods outside the United Kingdom and the false indication, or one of the false indications, given, or likely to be taken as given, thereby is an indication of the place of manufacture, production, processing or reconditioning of the goods or any part thereof, the goods shall not be imported into the United Kingdom.

Restriction on importation of goods bearing infringing trade marks

17. *[Omitted]*

Provisions as to offences

Penalty for offences

18. A person guilty of an offence under this Act for which no other penalty is specified shall be liable—

(a) on summary conviction, to a fine not exceeding the prescribed sum; and

(b) on conviction on indictment, to a fine or imprisonment for a term not exceeding two years or both.

Time limit for prosecutions

19.—(1) No prosecution for an offence under this Act shall be commenced after the expiration of three years from the commission of the offence or one year from its discovery by the prosecutor, whichever is the earlier.

(2) Notwithstanding anything in section 127(1) of the Magistrates' Courts Act 1980, a magistrates' court may try an information for an offence under this Act if the information was laid at any time within twelve months from the commission of the offence.

(3) Notwithstanding anything in section 23 of the Summary Jurisdiction (Scotland) Act 1954 (limitation of time for proceedings in statutory offences) summary proceedings in Scotland for an offence under this section may be commenced at any time within twelve months from the time when the offence was committed, and subsection (2) of the said section 23 shall apply for the purposes of this subsection as it applies for the purposes of that section.

(4) Subsections (2) and (3) of this section do not apply where—

    (a) the offence was committed by the making of an oral statement; or

    (b) the offence was one of supplying goods to which a false trade description is applied, and the trade description was applied by an oral statement; or

    (c) the offence was one where a false trade description is deemed to have been applied to goods by virtue of section 4(3) of this Act and the goods were supplied in pursuance of an oral request.

Offences by corporations

20.—(1) Where an offence under this Act which has been committed by a body corporate is proved to have been committed with the consent and connivance of, or to be attributable to any neglect on the part of, any director, manager, secretary or other similar officer of the body corporate, or any person who was purporting to act in any such capacity, he as well as the body corporate shall be liable to be proceeded against and punished accordingly.

(2) In this section "director", in relation to any body corporate established by or under any enactment for the purpose of carrying on under national ownership any industry or part of an industry or undertaking, being a body corporate whose affairs are managed by the members thereof, means a member of that body corporate.

Accessories to offences committed abroad

21.—(1) Any person who, in the United Kingdom, assists in or induces the commission in any other country of an act in respect of goods which, if the act were committed in the United Kingdom, would be an offence under section 1 of this Act shall be guilty of an offence, except as provided by subsection (2) of this section, but only if either—

    (a) the false trade description concerned is an indication (or anything likely to be taken as an indication) that the goods or any part thereof were manufactured, produced, processed or reconditioned in the United Kingdom; or

    (b) the false trade description concerned—

        (i) consists of or comprises an expression (or anything likely to be taken as an expression) to which a meaning is assigned by an order made by virtue of section 7(b) of this Act, and

        (ii) where that meaning is so assigned only in circumstances specified in the order, the trade description is used in those circumstances.

(2) A person shall not be guilty of an offence under subsection (1) of this section, if by virtue of section 32 of this Act, the act, though committed in the United Kingdom would not be an offence under section 1 of this Act had the goods been intended for despatch to the other country.

(3) Any person who, in the United Kingdom, assists in or induces the commission outside the United Kingdom of an act which if committed in the United Kingdom, would be an offence under section 12 of this Act shall be guilty of an offence.

Restrictions on institution of proceedings and admission of evidence

22.—(1) Where any act or omission constitutes both an offence under this Act and an offence under any provision contained in or having effect by virtue of Part IV of the Weights and Measures Act 1985 or Part V of the Weights and Measures (Northern Ireland) Order 1981—

    (a) proceedings for the offence shall not be instituted under this Act, except by virtue of section 23 thereof, without the service of such a notice as is required by subsection (3) of section 83 of the said Act of 1985 or, as the case may be, paragraph (3) of Article 46 of the said Order of 1981, nor after the expiration of the period mentioned in paragraph of that subsection or, as the case may be, that paragraph; and

    (b) sections 35, 36 and 37(1) and (2) of the said Act of 1985 or, as the case may be, of Article 24 of the said Order of 1981, shall, with the necessary modifications, apply as if the offence under this Act were an offence under Part IV of that Act or, as the case may be, Part V of that Order, or any instrument made thereunder.

(2) Where any act or omission constitutes both an offence under this Act and an offence under the food and drugs laws, evidence on behalf of the prosecution concerning any sample procured for analysis shall not be admissible in proceedings for the offence under this Act unless the relevant provisions of those laws have been complied with.

(2A) In subsection (2) of this section—

"the food and drugs laws" means the Food Safety Act 1990, the Medicines Act 1968 and the Food Safety (Northern Ireland) Order 1991 and any instrument made thereunder;

"the relevant provisions" means—

    (i) in relation to the said Act of 1990, section 31 and regulations made thereunder;

    (ii) in relation to the said Act of 1968, so much of Schedule 3 to that Act as is applicable to the circumstances in which the sample was procured; and

    (iii) in relation to the said Order, Article 31 and regulations made thereunder, or any provisions replacing any of those provisions by virtue of section 17 of the said Act of 1990, paragraph 27 of Schedule 3 to the said Act of 1968 or Article 16 of the said Order.

(3) The Board of Trade may by order provide that in proceedings for an offence under this Act in relation to such goods as may be specified in the order (other than proceedings for an offence failing within the preceding provisions of this section) evidence on behalf of the prosecution concerning any sample procured for analysis shall not be admissible unless the sample has been dealt with in such manner as may be specified in the order.

Offences due to fault of other person

23. Where the commission by any person of an offence under this Act is due to the act or default of some other person that other person shall be guilty of the offence, and a person may be charged with and convicted of the offence by virtue of this section whether or not proceedings are taken against the first-mentioned person.

Defences

Defence of mistake, accident, etc

24.—(1) In any proceedings for an offence under this Act it shall, subject to subsection (2) of this section, be a defence for the person charged to prove—

(a) that the commission of the offence was due to a mistake or to reliance on information supplied to him or to the act or default of another person, an accident or some other cause beyond his control; and

(b) that he took all reasonable precautions and exercised all due diligence to avoid the commission of such an offence by himself or any person under his control.

(2) If in any case the defence provided by the last foregoing subsection involves the allegation that the commission of the offence was due to the act or default of another person or to reliance on information supplied by another person, the person charged shall not, without leave of the court, be entitled to rely on that defence unless, within a period ending seven clear days before the hearing, he has served on the prosecutor a notice in writing giving such information identifying or assisting in the identification of that other person as was then in his possession.

(3) In any proceedings for an offence under this Act of supplying or offering to supply goods to which a false trade description is applied it shall be a defence for the person charged to prove that he did not know, and could not with reasonable diligence have ascertained, that the goods did not conform to the description or that the description had been applied to the goods.

Innocent publication of advertisement

25. In proceedings for an offence under this Act committed by the publication of an advertisement it shall be a defence for the person charged to prove that he is a person whose business it is to publish or arrange for the publication of advertisements and that he received the advertisement for publication in the ordinary course of business and did not know and had no reason to suspect that its publication would amount to an offence under this Act.

Enforcement

Enforcing authorities

26.—(1) It shall be the duty of every local weights and measures authority to enforce within their area the provisions of this Act and of any order made under this Act.

(2) Every local weights and measures authority shall, whenever the Board of Trade so direct, make to the Board a report on the exercise of their functions under this Act in such form and containing such particulars as the Board may direct.

(3), (4) [*Repealed*]

(5) Nothing in this section shall be taken as authorising a local weights and measures authority in Scotland to institute proceedings for an offence.

Power to make test purchases

27. A local weights and measures authority shall have power to make, or to authorise any of their officers to make on their behalf, such purchases of goods, and to authorise any of their officers to secure the provision of such services, accommodation or facilities, as may appear expedient for the purpose of determining whether or not the provisions of this Act and any order made thereunder are being complied with.

Power to enter premises and inspect and seize goods and documents

28.—(1) A duly authorised officer of a local weights and measures authority or of a Government department may, at all reasonable hours and on production, if required, of his credentials, exercise the following powers, that is to say,—

   (a) he may, for the purpose of ascertaining whether any offence under this Act has been committed, inspect any goods and enter any premises other than premises used only as a dwelling;

   (b) if he has reasonable cause to suspect that an offence under this Act has been committed, he may, for the purpose of ascertaining whether it has been committed, require any person carrying on a trade or business or employed in connection with a trade or business to produce any books or documents relating to the trade or business and may take copies of, or of any entry in, any such book or document;

   (c) if he has reasonable cause to believe that an offence under this Act has been committed, he may seize and detain any goods for the purpose of ascertaining, by testing or otherwise, whether the offence has been committed;

   (d) he may seize and detain any goods or documents which he has reason to believe may be required as evidence in proceedings for an offence under this Act;

   (e) he may, for the purpose of exercising his powers under this subsection to seize goods, but only if and to the extent that it is reasonably necessary in order to secure that the provisions of this Act and of any order made thereunder are duly observed, require any person having authority to do so to break open any container or open any vending machine and, if that person does not comply with the requirement, he may do so himself.

(2) An officer seizing any goods or documents in the exercise of his powers under this section shall inform the person from whom they are seized and, in the case of goods seized from a vending machine, the person whose name and address are stated on the machine as being the proprietor's or, if no name and address are so stated, the occupier of the premises on which the machine stands or to which it is affixed.

(3) If a justice of the peace, on sworn information in writing—

   (a) is satisfied that there is reasonable ground to believe either—

      (i) that any goods, books or documents which a duly authorised officer has power under this section to inspect are on any premises and that their inspection is likely to disclose evidence of the commission of an offence under this Act; or

      (ii) that any offence under this Act has been, is being or is about to be committed on any premises; and

   (b) is also satisfied either—
      (i) that admission to the premises has been or is likely to be refused
         and that notice of intention to apply for a warrant under this subsec-
         tion has been given to the occupier; or
      (ii) that an application for admission, or the giving of such a notice,
         would defeat the object of the entry or that the premises are unoccu-
         pied or that the occupier is temporarily absent and it might defeat
         the object of the entry to await his return,
the justice may by warrant under his hand, which shall continue in force for a
period of one month, authorise an officer of a local weights and measures authority or of a Government department to enter the premises, if need be by force.
In the application of this subsection to Scotland, "justice of the peace" shall
be construed as including a sheriff and a magistrate.

(4) An officer entering any premises by virtue of this section may take with
him such other persons and such equipment as may appear to him necessary;
and on leaving any premises which he has entered by virtue of a warrant under
the preceding subsection he shall, if the premises are unoccupied or the occupier
is temporarily absent, leave them as effectively secured against trespassers as
he found them.

(5) If any person discloses to any person—
   (a) An any information with respect to any manufacturing process or trade
      secret obtained by him in premises which he has entered by virtue of
      this section; or
   (b) any information obtained by him in pursuance of this Act; he shall be
      guilty of an offence unless the disclosure was made in or for the pur-
      pose of the performance by him or any other person of functions under
      this Act.

(5A) Subsection (5) of this section does not apply to disclosure for a purpose
specified in section 38(2)(a), (b) or (c) of the Consumer Protection Act 1987.

(6) If any person who is not a duly authorised officer of a local weights and
measures authority or of a Government department purports to act as such under
this section he shall be guilty of an offence.

(7) Nothing in this section shall be taken to compel the production by a
solicitor of a document containing a privileged communication made by or to
him in that capacity or to authorise the taking of possession of any such document which is in his possession.

Obstruction of authorised officers

29.—(1) Any person who—
   (a) wilfully obstructs an officer of a local weights and measures authority
      or of a Government department acting in pursuance of this Act; or
   (b) wilfully fails to comply with any requirement properly made to him
      by such an officer under section 28 of this Act; or
   (c) without reasonable cause fails to give such an officer so acting any
      other assistance or information which he may reasonably require of
      him for the purpose of the performance of his functions under this Act,
shall be guilty of an offence and liable, on summary conviction to a fine not
exceeding level 3 on the standard scale.

(2) If any person in giving any such information as is mentioned in the preceding subsection, makes any statement which he knows to be false, he shall be
guilty of an offence.

(3) Nothing in this section shall be construed as requiring a person to answer any question or give any information if to do so might incriminate him.

Notice of test and intended prosecution

30.—(1) Where any goods seized or purchased by an officer in pursuance of this Act are submitted to a test, then—

   (a) if the goods were seized the officer shall inform the person mentioned in section 28(2) of this Act of the result of the test;

   (b) if the goods were purchased and the test leads to the institution of proceedings for an offence under this Act, the officer shall inform the person from whom the goods were purchased, or, in the case of goods sold through a vending machine, the person mentioned in section 28(2) of this Act, of the result of the test;

and shall, where as a result of the test proceedings for an offence under this Act are instituted against any person, allow him to have the goods tested on his behalf if it is reasonably practicable to do so.

   (2)–(4) [*Repealed*]

Evidence by certificate

31.—(1) The Board of Trade may by regulations provide that certificates issued by such persons as may be specified by the regulations in relation to such matters as may be so specified shall, subject to the provisions of this section be received in evidence of those matters in any proceedings under this Act.

   (2) Such a certificate shall not be received in evidence—

   (a) unless the party against whom it is to be given in evidence has been served with a copy thereof not less than seven days before the hearing; or

   (b) if that party has, not less than three days before the hearing, served on the other party a notice requiring the attendance of the person issuing the certificate.

   (3) In any proceedings under this Act in Scotland, a certificate received in evidence by virtue of this section or, where the attendance of a person issuing a certificate is required under subsection (2)(b) of this section, the evidence of that person, shall be sufficient evidence of the matters stated in the certificate.

   (4) For the purposes of this section any document purporting to be such a certificate as is mentioned in this section shall be deemed to be such a certificate unless the contrary is shown.

   (5) Regulations under this section shall be made by statutory instrument which shall be subject to annulment in pursuance of a resolution of either House of Parliament.

Miscellaneous and supplemental

Power to exempt goods sold for export, etc

32.   In relation to goods which are intended—

   (a) for despatch to a destination outside the United Kingdom and any designated country within the meaning of section 24(2)(b) of the Weights and Measures Act 1985 or section 15(5)(b) of the Weights and Measures Act (Northern Ireland) 1967; or

   (b) for use as stores within the meaning of the Customs and Excise Management Act 1979 in a ship or aircraft on a voyage or flight to an eventual destination outside the United Kingdom; or

(c) for use by Her Majesty's forces or by a visiting force within the meaning of any of the provisions of Part I of the Visiting Forces Act 1952; or

(d) for industrial use within the meaning of the Weights and Measures Act 1985 or for constructional use;

section 1 of this Act shall apply as if there were omitted from the matters included in section 2(1) of this Act those specified in paragraph (a) thereof; and, if the Board of Trade by order specify any other of those matters for the purposes of this section with respect to any description of goods, the said section 1 shall apply, in relation to goods of that description which are intended for despatch to a destination outside the United Kingdom and such country (if any) as may be specified in the order, as if the matters so specified were also omitted from those included in the said section 2(1).

(2) In this section "constructional use", in relation to any goods, means the use of those goods in constructional work (or, if the goods are explosives within the meaning of the Explosives Acts 1875 and 1923, in mining, quarrying or demolition work) in the course of the carrying on of a business.

Compensation for loss, etc. of goods seized under s. 28

33.—(1) Where, in the exercise of his powers under section 28 of this Act, an officer of a local weights and measures authority or of a Government department seizes and detains any goods and their owner suffers loss by reason thereof or by reason that the goods, during the detention, are lost or damaged or deteriorate, then, unless the owner is convicted of an offence under this Act committed in relation to the goods, the authority or department shall be liable to compensate him for the loss so suffered.

(2) Any disputed question as to the right to or the amount of any compensation payable under this section shall be determined by arbitration and, in Scotland, by a single arbiter appointed, failing agreement between the parties, by the sheriff.

Trade marks containing trade descriptions

34. The fact that a trade description is a trade mark, or part of a trade mark, does not prevent it from being a false trade description when applied to any goods, except where the following conditions are satisfied, that is to say—

(a) that it could have been lawfully applied to the goods if this Act had not been passed; and

(b) that on the day this Act is passed the trade mark either is registered under the Trade Marks Act 1938 or is in use to indicate a connection in the course of trade between such goods and the proprietor of the trade mark; and

(c) that the trade mark as applied is used to indicate such a connection between the goods and the proprietor of the trade mark or in the case of a registered trade mark, a person licensed to use it; and

(d) that the person who is the proprietor of the trade mark is the same person as, or a successor in title of, the proprietor on the day this Act is passed.

Saving for civil rights

35. A contract for the supply of any goods shall not be void or unenforceable by reason only of a contravention of any provision of this Act.

Country of origin

36.—(1) For the purposes of this Act goods shall be deemed to have been manufactured or produced in the country in which they last underwent a treatment or process resulting in a substantial change.

(2) The Board of Trade may by order specify—

    (a) in relation to any description of goods, what treatment or process is to be regarded for the purposes of this section as resulting or not resulting in a substantial change;

    (b) in relation to any description of goods different parts of which were manufactured or produced in different countries, or of goods assembled in a country different from that in which their parts were manufactured or produced, in which of those countries the goods are to be regarded for the purposes of this Act as having been manufactured or produced.

Market research experiments

37.—(1) In this section "market research experiment" means any activities conducted for the purpose of ascertaining the opinion of persons (in this section referred to as "participants" of—

    (a) any goods; or

    (b) anything in, on or with which the goods are supplied; or

    (c) the appearance or any other characteristic of the goods or of any such thing; or

    (d) the name or description under which the goods are supplied.

(2) This section applies to any market research experiment with respect to which the following conditions are satisfied, that is to say,—

    (a) that any participant to whom the goods are supplied in the course of the experiment is informed, at or before the time at which they are supplied to him, that they are supplied for such a purpose as is mentioned in subsection (1) of this section, and

    (b) that no consideration in money or money's worth is given by a participant for the goods or any goods supplied to him for comparison.

(3) Neither section 1 nor section 8 of this Act shall apply in relation to goods supplied or offered to be supplied, whether to a participant or any other person, in the course of a market research experiment to which this section applies.

Orders

38.—(1) Any power to make an order under the preceding provisions of this Act shall be exercisable by statutory instrument, which shall be subject to annulment in pursuance of a resolution of either House of Parliament, and includes power to vary or revoke such an order by a subsequent order.

(2) Any order under the preceding provisions of this Act which relates to any agricultural, horticultural or fishery produce, whether processed or not, food, feeding stuffs or ingredients of food or feeding stuffs, fertilisers or any goods used as pesticides or for similar purposes shall be made by the Board of Trade acting jointly with the following Ministers, that is to say, if the order extends to England and Wales, the Minister of Agriculture, Fisheries and Food, and if it extends to Scotland or Northern Ireland, the Secretary of State concerned.

(3) The following provisions shall apply to the making of an order under section 7, 8, 9, 15 or 36 of this Act, except in the case mentioned in section 10(2) thereof, that is to say—

    (a) before making the order the Board of Trade shall consult with such organisations as appear to them to be representative of interests substantially affected by it and shall publish, in such manner as the Board think appropriate, notice of their intention to make the order and of the place where copies of the proposed order may be obtained; and

(b) the order shall not be made until the expiration of a period of twenty-eight days from the publication of the notice and may then be made with such modifications (if any) as the Board of Trade think appropriate having regard to any representations received by them.

Interpretation

39.—(1) The following provisions shall have effect, in addition to sections 2 to 6 of this Act, for the interpretation in this Act of expressions used therein, that is to say—

"advertisement" includes a catalogue, a circular and a price list;

"goods" includes ships and aircraft, things attached to land and growing crops;

"premises" includes any place and any stall, vehicle, ship or aircraft; and

"ship" includes any boat and any other description of vessel used in navigation.

(2) For the purposes of this Act, a trade description or statement published in any newspaper, book or periodical or in any film or sound or television broadcast or in any programme included in any programme service (within the meaning of the Broadcasting Act 1990) other than a sound or television broadcasting service shall not be deemed to be a trade description applied or statement made in the course of a trade or business unless it is or forms part of an advertisement.

Provisions as to Northern Ireland

40.—(1) This Act shall apply to Northern Ireland subject to the following modifications, that is to say—

(a) section 19(2) shall apply as if for the references to section 127(1) of the Magistrates' Courts Act 1980 and the trial and laying of an information there were substituted respectively references to section 34 of the Magistrates' Courts Act (Northern Ireland) 1964 and the hearing and determination and making of a complaint;

(b) section 26 and subsections (2) to (4) of section 30 shall not apply but it shall be the duty of the Ministry of Commerce for Northern Ireland to enforce the provisions of this Act and of any order made under it (other than the provisions of section 42 of this Act);

(c) sections 27 to 29 and 33 shall apply as if for references to a local weights and measures authority and any officer of such an authority there were substituted respectively references to the said Ministry and any of its officers.

(2)—(5) *[Repealed]*

(6) Nothing in this Act shall authorise any department of the Government of Northern Ireland to incur any expenses attributable to the provisions of this Act until provision has been made by the Parliament of Northern Ireland for those expenses to be defrayed out of moneys provided by that Parliament.

(7) *[Repealed]*

Consequential amendments and repeals

41.—(1) The enactments mentioned in Schedule 1 to this Act shall have effect subject to the amendments specified in that Schedule.

(2) [*Repealed*]

42. [*Repealed*]

Short title and commencement

43.—(1) This Act may be cited as the Trade Descriptions Act 1968.

(2) This Act shall come into force on the expiration of the period of six months beginning with the day on which it is passed.

* * * * *

Unsolicited Goods and Services Act 1971

(c. 30)

Rights of recipient of unsolicited goods

1.—(1) In the circumstances specified in the following subsection, a person who after the commencement of this Act receives unsolicited goods, may as between himself and the sender, use, deal with or dispose of them as if they were an unconditional gift to him, and any right of the sender to the goods shall be extinguished.

(2) The circumstances referred to in the preceding subsection are that the goods were sent to the recipient with a view to his acquiring them, that the recipient has no reasonable cause to believe that they were sent with a view to their being acquired for the purposes of a trade or business and has neither agreed to acquire nor agreed to return them, and either—

>   (a) that during the period of six months beginning with the day on which the recipient received the goods the sender did not take possession of them and the recipient did not unreasonably refuse to permit the sender to do so; or

>   (b) that not less than thirty days before the expiration of the period aforesaid the recipient gave notice to the sender in accordance with the following subsection, and that during the period of thirty days beginning with the day on which the notice was given the sender did not take possession of the goods and the recipient did not unreasonably refuse to permit the sender to do so.

(3) A notice in pursuance of the preceding subsection shall be in writing and shall—

>   (a) state the recipient's name and address and, if possession of the goods in question may not be taken by the sender at that address, the address at which it may be so taken;

>   (b) contain a statement, however expressed, that the goods are unsolicited,

and may be sent by post.

(4) In this section "sender", in relation to any goods, includes any person on whose behalf or with whose consent the goods are sent, and any other person claiming through or under the sender or any such person.

Demands and threats regarding payment

2.—(1) A person who, not having reasonable cause to believe there is a right to payment, in the course of any trade or business makes a demand for payment, or asserts a present or prospective right to payment, for what he knows are unsolicited goods sent (after the commencement of this Act) to another person with a view to his acquiring them, shall be guilty of an offence and on summary conviction shall be liable to a fine not exceeding level 4 on the standard scale.

(2) A person who, not having reasonable cause to believe there is a right to payment, in the course of any trade or business and with a view to obtaining any payment for what he knows are unsolicited goods sent as aforesaid—

>   (a) threatens to bring any legal proceedings; or

>   (b) places or causes to be placed the name of any person on a list of defaulters or debtors or threatens to do so; or

31

(c) invokes or causes to be invoked any other collection procedure or threatens to do so,

shall be guilty of an offence and shall be liable on summary conviction to a fine not exceeding level 5 on the standard scale.

Directory entries

3.—(1) A person shall not be liable to make any payment, and shall be entitled to recover any payment made by him, by way of charge for including or arranging for the inclusion in a directory of an entry relating to that person or his trade or business, unless there has been signed by him or on his behalf an order complying with this section or a note complying with this section of his agreement to the charge and, in the case of a note of agreement to the charge, before the note was signed, a copy of it was supplied, for retention by him, to him or to a person acting on his behalf.

(2)[1] A person shall be guilty of an offence punishable on summary conviction with a fine not exceeding the prescribed sum if, in a case where a payment in respect of a charge would, in the absence of an order or note of agreement to the charge complying with this section, be recoverable from him in accordance with the terms of subsection (1) above, he demands payment, or asserts a present or prospective right to payment, of the charge or any part of it, without knowing or having reasonable cause to believe that the entry to which the charge relates was ordered in accordance with this section or a proper note of agreement has been duly signed.

(3) For the purposes of subsection (1) above, an order for an entry in a directory must be made by means of an order form or other stationery belonging to the person to whom, or to whose trade or business, the entry is to relate and bearing, in print, the name and address (or one or more of the addresses) of that person; and the note required by this section of a person's agreement to a charge [must state the amount of the charge immediately above the place for signature, and—

(a) must identify the directory or proposed directory, and give the following particulars of it—
  (i) the proposed date of publication of the directory or of the issue in which the entry is to be included and the name and address of the person producing it;
  (ii) if the directory or that issue is to be put on sale, the price at which it is to be offered for sale and the minimum number of copies which are to be available for sale;
  (iii) if the directory or that issue is to be distributed free of charge (whether or not it is also to be put on sale), the minimum number of copies which are to be so distributed; and
(b) must set out or give reasonable particulars of the entry in respect of which the charge would be payable.][2]

(4) Nothing in this section shall apply to a payment due under a contract entered into before the commencement of this Act, or entered into by the acceptance of an offer made before that commencement.

---

[1] See the Unsolicited Goods and Services (Amendment) Act 1975, s. 3 (see p. 150 below).
[2] By the Unsolicited Goods and Services Act 1975, s. 2, from a date to be appointed the words in square brackets will be substituted by the words: "shall comply with the requirements of regulations under section 3A of this Act applicable thereto".

Contents and form of notes of agreement, invoices and similar documents

3A.—(1) For the purposes of this Act, the Secretary of State may make regulations as to the contents and form of notes of agreement, invoices and similar documents; and, without prejudice to the generality of the foregoing, any such regulations may—

(a) require specified information to be included,

(b) prescribe the manner in which specified information is to be included,

(c) prescribe such other requirements (whether as to presentation, type, size, colour or disposition of lettering, quality or colour of paper or otherwise) as the Secretary of State may consider appropriate for securing that specified information is clearly brought to the attention of the recipient of any note of agreement, invoice or similar document,

(d) make different provision for different classes or descriptions of notes of agreement, invoices and similar documents or for the same class or description in different circumstances,

(e) contain such supplementary and incidental provisions as the Secretary of State may consider appropriate.

(2) Any reference in this section to a note of agreement includes any such copy as is mentioned in section 3(1) of this Act.

(3) Regulations under this section shall be made by statutory instrument and shall be subject to annulment in pursuance of a resolution of either House of Parliament.

Unsolicited publications

4.—(1) A person shall be guilty of an offence if he sends or causes to be sent to another person any book, magazine or leaflet (or advertising material for any such publication) which he knows or ought reasonably to know is unsolicited and which describes or illustrates human sexual techniques.

(2) A person found guilty of an offence under this section shall be liable on summary conviction to a fine not exceeding level 5 on the standard scale.

(3) A prosecution for an offence under this section shall not in England and Wales be instituted except by, or with the consent of, the Director of Public Prosecutions.

Offences by corporations

5.—(1) Where an offence under this Act which has been committed by a body corporate is proved to have been committed with the consent or connivance of, or to be attributable to any neglect on the part of, any director, manager, secretary, or other similar officer of the body corporate, or of any person who was purporting to act in any such capacity, he as well as the body corporate shall be guilty of that offence and shall be liable to be proceeded against and punished accordingly.

(2) Where the affairs of a body corporate are managed by its members, this section shall apply in relation to the acts or defaults of a member in connection with his functions of management as if he were a director of the body corporate.

Interpretation

6.—(1) In this Act, unless the context or subject matter otherwise requires,—

"acquire" includes hire;

"send" includes deliver, and "sender" shall be construed accordingly;

"unsolicited" means, in relation to goods sent to any person, that they are sent without any prior request made by him or on his behalf.

(2) For the purposes of this Act any invoice or similar document stating the amount of any payment and not complying with the requirements of regulations under section 3A of this Act applicable thereto shall be regarded as asserting a right to the payment.

Citation, commencement and extent

7.—(1) This Act may be cited as the Unsolicited Goods and Services Act 1971.

(2) This Act shall come into force at the expiration of three months beginning with the day on which it is passed.

(3) This Act does not extend to Northern Ireland.

Supply of Goods (Implied Terms) Act 1973[1]

(c. 13)

*   *   *   *   *

HIRE-PURCHASE AGREEMENTS

Implied terms as to title

8.—(1) In every hire-purchase agreement, other than one to which subsection (2) below applies, there is—

    (a) an implied term on the part of the creditor that he will have a right to sell the goods at the time when the property is to pass; and

    (b) an implied term that—

        (i) the goods are free, and will remain free until the time when the property is to pass, from any charge or encumbrance not disclosed or known to the person to whom the goods are bailed or (in Scotland) hired before the agreement is made, and

        (ii) that person will enjoy quiet possession of the goods except so far as it may be disturbed by any person entitled to the benefit of any charge or encumbrance so disclosed or known.

(2) In a hire-purchase agreement, in the case of which there appears from the agreement or is to be inferred from the circumstances of the agreement an intention that the creditor should transfer only such title as he or a third person may have, there is—

    (a) an implied term that all charges or encumbrances known to the creditor and not known to the person to whom the goods are bailed or hired have been disclosed to that person before the agreement is made; and

    (b) an implied term that neither—

        (i) the creditor; nor

        (ii) in a case where the parties to the agreement intend that any title which may be transferred shall be only such title as a third person may have, that person; nor

        (iii) anyone claiming through or under the creditor or that third person otherwise than under a charge or encumbrance disclosed or known to the person to whom the goods are bailed or hired, before the agreement is made;

will disturb the quiet possession of the person to whom the goods are bailed or hired.

(3) As regards England and Wales and Northern Ireland, the term implied by subsection (1)(a) above is a condition and the terms implied by subsections (1)(b), (2)(a) and (2)(b) above are warranties.

---

[1] Sections 12–15 of this Act are printed as substituted by paras. 35 and 36 of Sched. 4 to the Consumer Credit Act 1974 (with subsequent amendments and repeals, including the consequential amendments made by the Sale and Supply of Goods Act 1994, s. 7 and Sched. 2).

Bailing or hiring by description

9.—(1) Where under a hire-purchase agreement goods are bailed or (in Scotland) hired by description, there is an implied term that the goods will correspond with the description, and if under the agreement the goods are bailed or hired by reference to a sample as well as a description, it is not sufficient that the bulk of the goods corresponds with the sample if the goods do not also correspond with the description.

(1A) As regards England and Wales and Northern Ireland, the term implied by subsection (1) above is a condition.

(2) Goods shall not be prevented from being bailed or hired by description by reason only that, being exposed for sale, bailment or hire, they are selected by the person to whom they are bailed or hired.

Implied undertakings as to quality or fitness

10.—(1) Except as provided by this section and section 11 below and subject to the provisions of any other enactment, including any enactment of the Parliament of Northern Ireland or the Northern Ireland Assembly, there is no implied term as to the quality or fitness for any particular purpose of goods bailed or (in Scotland) hired under a hire-purchase agreement.

(2) Where the creditor bails or hires goods under a hire purchase agreement in the course of a business, there is an implied term that the goods supplied under the agreement are of satisfactory quality.

(2A) For the purposes of this Act, goods are of satisfactory quality if they meet the standard that a reasonable person would regard as satisfactory, taking account of any description of the goods, the price (if relevant) and all the other relevant circumstances.

(2B) For the purposes of this Act, the quality of goods includes their state and condition and the following (among others) are in appropriate cases aspects of the quality of goods—

 (a) fitness for all the purposes for which goods of the kind in question are commonly supplied,

 (b) appearance and finish,

 (c) freedom from minor defects,

 (d) safety, and

 (e) durability.

(2C) The term implied by subsection (2) above does not extend to any matter making the quality of goods unsatisfactory—

 (a) which is specifically drawn to the attention of the person to whom the goods are bailed or hired before the agreement is made,

 (b) where that person examines the goods before the agreement is made, which that examination ought to reveal, or

 (c) where the goods are bailed or hired by reference to a sample, which would have been apparent on a reasonable examination of the sample.

(3) Where the creditor bails or hires goods under a hire-purchase agreement in the course of a business and the person to whom the goods are bailed or hired, expressly or by implication, makes known—

 (a) to the creditor in the course of negotiations conducted by the creditor in relation to the making of the hire-purchase agreement, or

 (b) to a credit-broker in the course of negotiations conducted by that broker in relation to goods sold by him to the creditor before forming the subject matter of the hire-purchase agreement,

any particular purpose for which the goods are being bailed or hired, there is an implied term that the goods supplied under the agreement are reasonably fit for that purpose, whether or not that is a purpose for which such goods are commonly supplied, except where the circumstances show that the person to whom the goods are bailed or hired does not rely, or that it is unreasonable for him to rely, on the skill or judgment of the creditor or credit-broker.

(4) An implied term as to quality or fitness for a particular purpose may be annexed to a hire-purchase agreement by usage.

(5) The preceding provisions of this section apply to a hire-purchase agreement made by a person who in the course of a business is acting as agent for the creditor as they apply to an agreement made by the creditor in the course of a business, except where the creditor is not bailing or hiring in the course of a business and either the person to whom the goods are bailed or hired knows that fact or reasonable steps are taken to bring it to the notice of that person before the agreement is made.

(6) In subsection (3) above and this subsection—
- (a) "credit-broker", means a person acting in the course of a business of credit brokerage.
- (b) "credit brokerage" means the effecting of introductions of individuals desiring to obtain credit—
  - (i) to persons carrying on any business so far as it relates to the provision of credit, or
  - (ii) to other persons engaged in credit brokerage.

(7) As regards England and Wales and Northern Ireland, the terms implied by subsections (2) and (3) above are conditions.

Samples

11.—(1) Where under a hire-purchase agreement goods are bailed or (in Scotland) hired by reference to a sample, there is an implied term—
- (a) that the bulk will correspond with the sample in quality; and
- (b) that the person to whom the goods are bailed or hired will have a reasonable opportunity of comparing the bulk with the sample; and
- (c) that the goods will be free from any defect, making their quality unsatisfactory, which would not be apparent on reasonable examination of the sample.

(2) As regards England and Wales and Northern Ireland, the term implied by subsection (1) above is a condition.

Modification of remedies for breach of statutory condition in non-consumer cases

11A.—(1) Where in the case of a hire purchase agreement—
- (a) the person to whom goods are bailed would, apart from this subsection, have the right to reject them by reason of a breach on the part of the creditor of a term implied by section 9, 10 or 11(1)(a) or (c) above, but
- (b) the breach is so slight that it would be unreasonable for him to reject them,

then, if the person to whom the goods are bailed does not deal as consumer, the breach is not to be treated as a breach of condition but may be treated as a breach of warranty.

(2) This section applies unless a contrary intention appears in, or is to be implied from, the agreement.

(3) It is for the creditor to show—

    (a) that a breach fell within subsection (1)(b) above, and

    (b) that the person to whom the goods were bailed did not deal as consumer.

(4) The references in this section to dealing as consumer are to be construed in accordance with Part I of the Unfair Contract Terms Act 1977.

(5) This section does not apply to Scotland.

Exclusion of implied terms

12. An express term does not negative a term implied by this Act unless inconsistent with it.

Remedies for breach of hire-purchase agreement as respects Scotland

12A.—(1) Where in a hire-purchase agreement the creditor is in breach of any term of the agreement (express or implied), the person to whom the goods are hired shall be entitled—

    (a) to claim damages, and

    (b) if the breach is material, to reject any goods delivered under the agreement and treat it as repudiated.

(2) Where a hire-purchase agreement is a consumer contract, then, for the purposes of subsection (1) above, breach by the creditor of any term (express or implied)—

    (a) as to the quality of the goods or their fitness for a purpose,

    (b) if the goods are, or are to be, hired by description, that the goods will correspond with the description,

    (c) if the goods are, or are to be, hired by reference to a sample, that the bulk will correspond with the sample in quality,

shall be deemed to be a material breach.

(3) In subsection (2) above "consumer contract" has the same meaning as in section 25(1) of the Unfair Contract Terms Act 1977; and for the purposes of that subsection the onus of proving that a hire-purchase agreement is not to be regarded as a consumer contract shall lie on the creditor.

(4) This section applies to Scotland only.

13. [*Repealed*]

Special provisions as to conditional sale agreements

14.—(1) Section 11(4) of the Sale of Goods Act 1979 (whereby in certain circumstances a breach of a condition in a contract of sale is treated only as a breach of warranty) shall not apply to a conditional sale agreement where the buyer deals as consumer within Part I of the Unfair Contract Terms Act 1977.

(2) In England and Wales and Northern Ireland a breach of a condition (whether express or implied) to be fulfilled by the seller under any such agreement shall be treated as a breach of warranty, and not as grounds for rejecting the goods and treating the agreement as repudiated, if (but only if) it would have fallen to be so treated had the condition been contained or implied in a corresponding hire-purchase agreement as a condition to be fulfilled by the creditor.

Supplementary

15.—(1) In sections 8 to 14 above and this section—

"business" includes a profession and the activities of any government department (including a Northern Ireland department), or local or public authority;

"buyer" and "seller" includes a person to whom rights and duties under a conditional sale agreement have passed by assignment or operation of law;

"conditional sale agreement" means an agreement for the sale of goods under which the purchase price or part of it is payable by instalments, and the property in the goods is to remain in the seller (notwithstanding that the buyer is to be in possession of the goods) until such conditions as to the payment of instalments or otherwise as may be specified in the agreement are fulfilled;

"consumer sale" has the same meaning as in section 55 of the Sale of Goods Act 1979 (as set out in paragraph 11 of Schedule 1 to that Act).

"creditor" means the person by whom the goods are bailed or (in Scotland) hired under a hire-purchase agreement or the person to whom his rights and duties under the agreement have passed by assignment or operation of law; and

"hire-purchase agreement" means an agreement, other than a conditional sale agreement, under which—

  (a) goods are bailed or (in Scotland) hired in return for periodical payments by the person to whom they are bailed or hired, and
  (b) the property in the goods will pass to that person if the terms of the agreements are complied with and one or more of the following occurs—
       (i) the exercise of an option to purchase by that person,
       (ii) the doing of any other specified act by any party to the agreement,
       (iii) the happening of any other specified event.

(2) [*Repealed*]

(3) In section 14(2) above "corresponding hire-purchase agreement" means, in relation to a conditional sale agreement, a hire-purchase agreement relating to the same goods as the conditional sale agreement and made between the same parties and at the same time and in the same circumstances and, as nearly as may be, in the same terms as the conditional sale agreement.

(4) Nothing in sections 8 to 13 above shall prejudice the operation of any other enactment including any enactment of the Parliament of Northern Ireland or the Northern Ireland Assembly or any rule of law whereby any term, other than one relating to quality or fitness, is to be implied in any hire-purchase agreement.

16. [Substitutes a new section 4 of the Trading Stamps Act 1964, s. 4 and is incorporated therein (as amended by the Sale and Supply of Goods Act 1994, s. 7 and Sched. 2).]

MISCELLANEOUS

Northern Ireland

  17.—(1) It is hereby declared that this Act extends to Northern Ireland.

  (2) [*Repealed*]

Short title, citation, interpretation, commencement, repeal and saving

  18.—(1) This Act may be cited as the Supply of Goods (Implied Terms) Act 1973.

  (2) [*Repealed*]

  (3) This Act shall come into operation at the expiration of a period of one month beginning with the date on which it is passed.

  (4) Sections 17 to 20 and 29(3)(c) of each of the following Acts, that is to

say, the Hire-Purchase Act 1965, the Hire-Purchase (Scotland) Act 1965 and the Hire Purchase Act (Northern Ireland) 1966 (provisions as to conditions, warranties and stipulations in hire-purchase agreements) shall cease to have effect.

(5) This Act does not apply to contracts of sale or hire-purchase agreements made before its commencement.

Fair Trading Act 1973

(c. 41)

An Act to provide for the appointment of a Director General of Fair Trading
and of a Consumer Protection Advisory Committee, and to confer an the Director General and the Committee so appointed, on the Secretary of State, on
the Restrictive Practices Court and on certain other courts new functions for the
protection of consumers; to make provision, in substituion for the Monopolies
and Restrictive Practices (Inquiry and Control) Act 1948 and the Monopolies
and Mergers Act 1965, for the matters dealt with in those Acts and related
matters, including restrictive labour practices; to amend the Restrictive Trade
Practices Act 1956 and the Restrictive Trade Practices Act 1968, to make provision for extending the said Act of 1956 to agreements relating to services, and
to transfer to the Director General of Fair Trading the functions of the Registrar
of Restrictive Trading Agreements; to make provision with respect to pyramid
selling and similar trading schemes; to make new provision in place of section
30(2) to (4) of the Trade Descriptions Act 1968; and for Purposes connected
with those matters.   [25th July 1973]

PART I

INTRODUCTORY

Director General of Fair Trading
   1.—(1) The Secretary of State shall appoint an officer to be known as the
Director General of Fair Trading (in this Act referred to as "the Director") for
the purpose of performing the function assigned or transferred to the Director
by or under this Act.
   (2) An appointment of a person to hold office as the Director shall not be
for a term exceeding five years; but previous appointment to that office shall
not affect eligibility for re-appointment.
   (3) The Director may at any time resign his office as the Director by notice
in writing addressed to the Secretary of State; and the Secretary of State may
remove any person from that office on the ground of incapacity or misbehaviour.
   (4) Subject to subsections (2) and (3) of this section, the Director shall hold
and vacate office as such in accordance with the terms of his appointment.
   (5) The Director may appoint such staff as he may think fit, subject to the
approval of the Minister for the Civil Service as to numbers and as to terms
and conditions of service.
   (6) The provisions of Schedule I to this Act shall have effect with respect to
the Director.

General functions of Director
   2.—(1) Without prejudice to any other functions assigned or transferred to
him by or under this Act, it shall be the duty of the Director so far as appears
to him to be practicable from time to time,—
   (a) to keep under review the carrying on of commercial activities in the
       United Kingdom which relate to goods supplied to consumers in the
       United Kingdom or produced with a view to their being so supplied,

or which relate to services supplied for consumers in the United Kingdom, and to collect information with respect to such activities, and the persons by whom they are carried on, with a view to his becoming aware of, and ascertaining the circumstances relating to, practices which may adversely affect the economic interests of consumers in the United Kingdom, and

(b) to receive and collate evidence becoming available to him with respect to such activities as are mentioned in the preceding paragraph and which appears to him to be evidence of practices which may adversely affect the interests (whether they are economic interests or interests with respect to health, safety or other matters) of consumers in the United Kingdom, and

(2) It shall also be the duty of the Director, so far as appears to him to be practicable from time to time, to keep under review the carrying on of commercial activities in the United Kingdom, and to collect information with respect to those activities, and the persons by whom they are carried on, with a view to his becoming aware of, and ascertaining the circumstances relating to, monopoly situations or uncompetitive practices.

(3) It shall be the duty of the Director, where either he considers it expedient or he is requested by the Secretary of State to do so,—

(a) to give information and assistance to the Secretary of State with respect to any of the matters in respect of which the Director has any duties under subsections (1) and (2) of this section, or

(b) subject to the provisions of Part II of this Act in relation to recommendations under that Part of this Act, to make recommendations to the Secretary of State as to any action which in the opinion of the Director it would be expedient for the Secretary of State or any other Minister to take in relation to any of the matters in respect of which the Director has any such duties.

(4) It shall also be the duty of the Director to have regard to evidence becoming available to him with respect to any course of conduct on the part of a person carrying on a business which appears to be conduct detrimental to the interests of consumers in the United Kingdom and (in accordance with the provisions of Part III of this Act) to be regarded as unfair to them, with a view to considering what action (if any) he should take under Part III of this Act.

(5) It shall be the duty of the Director to have regard to the needs of regional development and to the desirability of dispersing administrative offices from London in making decisions on the location of offices for his staff.

Consumer Protection Advisory Committee

3.—(1) There shall be established an advisory committee to be called the Consumer Protection Advisory Committee (in this Act referred to as "the Advisory Committee") for the purpose of performing the functions assigned to that Committee by Part II of this Act.

(2) Subject to subsection (6) of this section, the Advisory Committee shall consist of not less than ten and not more than fifteen members, who shall be appointed by the Secretary of State.

(3) The Secretary of State may appoint persons to the Advisory Committee either as full-time members or as part-time members.

(4) Of the members of the Advisory Committee, the Secretary of State shall appoint one to be chairman and one to be deputy chairman of the Advisory Committee.

(5) In appointing persons to be members to the Advisory Committee, the Secretary of State shall have regard to the need for securing that the Advisory Committee will include—

(a) one or more persons appearing to him to be qualified to advise on practices relating to goods supplied to consumers in the United Kingdom or produced with a view to their being so supplied, or relating to services supplied for consumers in the United Kingdom, by virtue of their knowledge of or experience in the supply (whether to consumers or not) of such goods or by virtue of their knowledge of or experience in the supply of such services;

(b) one or more persons appearing to him to be qualified to advise on such practices as are mentioned in the preceding paragraph by virtue of their knowledge of or experience in the enforcement of the Weights and Measures Act 1985 or the Trade Descriptions Act 1968 or other similar enactments; and

(c) one or more persons appearing to him to be qualified to advise on such practices by virtue of their knowledge of or experience in organisations established, or activities carried on, for the protection of consumers.

(6) The Secretary of State may by order made by statutory instrument increase the maximum number of members of the Advisory Committee to such number as he may think fit.

(7) The provisions of Schedule 2 to this Act shall have effect with respect to the Advisory Committee.

* * * * *

Powers of Secretary of State in relation to functions of Director

12.—(1) The Secretary of State may give general directions indicating considerations to which the Director should have particular regard in determining the order of priority in which—

(a) matters are to be brought under review in the performance of his duty under section 2(1) of this Act, or

(b) classes of goods or services are to be brought under review by him for the purpose of considering whether a monopoly situation exists or may exist in relation to them.

(2) The Secretary of State may also give general directions indicating—

(a) considerations to which, in cases where it appears to the Director that a practice may adversely affect the interests of consumers in the United Kingdom, he should have particular regard in determining whether to make a recommendation to the Secretary of State under section 2(3)(b) of this Act, or

(b) considerations to which, in cases where it appears to the Director that a consumer trade practice may adversely affect the economic interests of consumers in the United Kingdom, he should have particular regard in determining whether to make a reference to the Advisory Committee under Part II of this Act, or

(c) considerations to which, in cases where it appears to the Director that a monopoly situation exists or may exist, he should have particular regard in determining whether to make a monopoly reference to the Commission under Part IV of this Act.

(3) The Secretary of State, on giving any directions under this section, shall arrange for those directions to be published in such manner as the Secretary of State thinks most suitable in the circumstances.

PART II[1]

REFERENCES TO CONSUMER PROTECTION ADVISORY COMMITTEE

General provisions

Meaning of "consumer trade practice"

13. In this Act "consumer trade practice" means any practice which is for the time being carried on in connection with the supply of goods (whether by way of sale or otherwise) to consumers or in connection with the supply of services for consumers and which relates—

(a) to the terms or conditions (whether as to price or otherwise) on or subject to which goods or services are or are sought to be supplied, or

(b) to the manner in which those terms or conditions are communicated to persons to whom goods are or are sought to be supplied or for whom services are or are sought to be supplied, or

(c) to promotion (by advertising, labelling or marking of goods, canvassing or otherwise) of the supply of goods or of the supply of services, or

(d) to methods of salesmanship employed in dealing with consumers, or

(e) to the way in which goods are packed or otherwise got up for the purpose of being supplied, or

(f) to methods of demanding or securing payment for goods or services supplied.

General provisions as to references to Advisory Committee

14.—(1) Subject to sections 15 and 16 of this Act, the Secretary of State or any other Minister or the Director may refer to the Advisory Committee the question whether a consumer trade practice specified in the reference adversely affects the economic interests of consumers in the United Kingdom.

(2) The Secretary of State or any other Minister by whom a reference is made under this section shall transmit a copy of the reference to the Director.

(3) On any reference made to the Advisory Committee under this section the Advisory Committee shall consider the question so referred to them and shall prepare a report on that question and (except as otherwise provided by section 21(3) of this Act) submit that report to the person by whom the reference was made.

(4) Subject to the provisions of section 133 of this Act, it shall be the duty of the Director, where he is requested by the Advisory Committee to do so for the purpose of assisting the Committee in carrying out an investigation on a reference made to them under this section, to give to the Committee—

(a) any information which is in his possession and which relates to matters falling within the scope of the investigation, and

(b) any other assistance which the Committee may require, and which it is within his power to give, in relation to any such matters.

(5) The Advisory Committee shall transmit to the Secretary of State a copy

---

[1] Part II of the Act has *not* been repealed, but *pro tem* the Advisory Committee has been disbanded.

of every report which is made by them under this section to a person other than the Secretary of State, and shall transmit to the Director a copy of every report which is made by them under this section to a person other than the Director.

Exclusion from s. 14 in respect of certain services

15. No reference under section 14 of this Act shall be made to the Advisory Committee by the Secretary of State or by any other Minister or by the Director if it appears to him—

(a) that the consumer trade practice in question is carried on in connection only with the supply of services of a description specified in Schedule 4² to this Act, and

(b) that a monopoly situation exists or may exist in relation to the supply of services of that description.

Restriction on references under s. 14 in respect of certain goods and services

16.—(1) No reference under section 14 of this Act shall be made to the Advisory Committee by the Director except with the consent of the appropriate Minister, if it appears to the Director that the consumer trade practice in question—

(a) is carried on in connection only with the supply, by a body corporate to which this section applies, of goods or services of a description specified in Part I of Schedule 5 to this Act,

(b) *[Repealed]* or

(c) is carried on in connection only with the supply of electricity by a licence holder within the meaning of Part I of the Electricity Act 1989.

(2) This section applies to any body corporate which fulfils the following conditions, that is to say—

(a) that the affairs of the body corporate are managed by its members, and

(b) that by virtue of an enactment those members are appointed by a Minister; and in this section "Minister" includes a Minister of the Government of Northern Ireland, and "the appropriate Minister", in relation to a body corporate, means the Minister by whom members of that body corporate are appointed.

(2A) In this section "the appropriate Minister", in relation to a licence holder within the meaning of Part I of the Electricity Act 1989, means the Secretary of State responsible for matters relating to energy.

(3) The Secretary of State may by order made by statutory instrument vary any of the provisions of Schedule 5 to this Act, either by adding one or more further entries or by altering or deleting any entry for the time being contained in it; and any reference in this Act to that Schedule shall be construed as a reference to that Schedule as for the time being in force.

Reference to Advisory Committee proposing recommendation to Secretary of State to make an order

17.—(1) This section applies to any reference made to the Advisory Committee by the Director under section 14 of this Act which includes proposals in accordance with the following provisions of this section.

---

² Schedule 4 to the Act (not printed in this work) specifies *inter alia* legal, medical, dental, and accounting and auditing services.

(2) Where it appears to the Director that a consumer trade practice has the effect, or is likely to have the effect,—

    (a) of misleading consumers as to, or withholding from them adequate information as to, or an adequate record of, their rights and obligations under relevant consumer transactions, or

    (b) of otherwise misleading or confusing consumers with respect to any matter in connection with relevant consumer transactions, or

    (c) of subjecting consumers to undue pressure to enter into relevant consumer transactions, or

    (d) of causing the terms or conditions, on or subject to which consumers enter into relevant consumer transactions, to be so adverse to them as to be inequitable, any reference made by the Director under section 14 of this Act with respect to that consumer trade practice may, if the Director thinks fit, include proposals for recommending to the Secretary of State that he should exercise his powers under the following provisions of this Part of this Act with respect to that consumer trade practice.

(3) A reference to which this section applies shall state which of the effects specified in subsection (2) of this section it appears to the Director that the consumer trade practice in question has or is likely to have.

(4) Where the Director makes a reference to which this section applies, he shall arrange for it to be published in full in the London, Edinburgh and Belfast Gazettes.

(5) In this Part of this Act "relevant consumer transaction", in relation to a consumer trade practice, means any transaction to which a person is, or may be invited to become, a party in his capacity as a consumer in relation to that practice.

No such recommendation to be made except in pursuance of reference to which s. 17 applies

    18.   The Director shall not make any recommendation to the Secretary of State to exercise his powers under the following provisions of this Part of this Act except by way of making a reference to the Advisory Committee to which section 17 of this Act applies.

Scope of recommendation proposed in reference to which s. 17 applies

    19.—(1) In formulating any proposals which, in accordance with the provisions of section 17 of this Act, are included in a reference to which that section applies, the Director shall have regard—

    (a) to the particular respects in which it appears to him that the consumer trade practice specified in the reference may adversely affect the economic interests of consumers in the United Kingdom, and

    (b) to the class of relevant consumer transactions, or the classes (whether being some or all classes) of such transactions, in relation to which it appears to him that the practice may so affect those consumers;

and the proposed recommendation shall be for an order making, in relation to relevant consumer transactions of that class or of those classes, as the case may be, such provision specified in the proposals as the Director may consider requisite for the purpose of preventing the continuance of that practice, or causing it to be modified, in so far as it may so affect those consumers in those respects.

(2) Without prejudice to the generality of the preceding subsection, for the purpose mentioned in that subsection any such proposals may in particular

recommend the imposition by such an order of prohibitions or requirements of any description specified in Schedule 6 to this Act.

(3) In that Schedule, in its application to any such proposals, "the specified consumer trade practice" means the consumer trade practice specified in the reference in which the proposals are made, "specified consumer transactions" means transactions which are relevant consumer transactions in relation to that consumer trade practice and are of a description specified in the proposals, and "specified" (elsewhere than in those expressions) means specified in the proposals.

Time-limit and quorum for report on reference to which s. 17 applies

20.—(1) A report of the Advisory Committee on a reference to which section 17 of this Act applies shall not have effect, and no action shall be taken in relation to it under the following provisions of this Part of this Act, unless the report is made before the end of the period of three months beginning with the date of the reference or of such further period or periods (if any) as may be allowed by the Secretary of State.

(2) The Secretary of State shall not allow any further period for such a report except after consulting the Advisory Committee and considering any representations made by them with respect to the proposal to allow a further period.

(3) No such further period shall be tonger than three months; but (subject to subsection (2) of this section) two or more further periods may be allowed in respect of the same reference.

(4) The quorum necessary for a meeting of the Advisory Committee held for the final settling of a report of the Committee on a reference to which section 17 of this Act applies shall be not less than two-thirds of the members of the Committee.

Report of Advisory Committee on reference to which s. 17 applies

21.—(1) A report of the Advisory Committee on a reference to which section 17 of this Act applies shall state the conclusions of the Committee on the questions—

(a) whether the consumer trade practice specified in the reference adversely affects the economic interests of consumers in the United Kingdom, and

(b) if so, whether it does so by reason, or partly by reason, that it has or is likely to have such one or more of the effects specified in section 17(2) of this Act as are specified in the report.

(2) If in their conclusions set out in such a report, the Advisory Committee find that the consumer trade practice specified in the reference does adversely affect the economic interests of consumers in the United Kingdom, and does so wholly or partly for the reason mentioned in subsection (1)(b) of this section, the report shall state whether the Committee—

(a) agree with the proposals set out in the reference, or

(b) would agree with those proposals if they were modified in a manner specified in the report, or

(c) disagree with the proposals and do not desire to suggest any such modifications.

(3) Every report of the Advisory Committee on a reference to which section 17 of this Act applies shall be made to the Secretary of State, and shall set out in full the reference on which it is made.

Order in pursuance of report of Advisory Committee

Order of Secretary of State in pursuance of report on reference to which s. 17 applies[3]

22.—(1) The provisions of this section shall have effect where a report of the Advisory Committee on a reference to which section 17 of this Act applies has been laid before Parliament in accordance with the provisions of Part VII of this Act, and the report states that the Committee—

    (a) agree with the proposals set out in the reference, or

    (b) would agree with those proposals if they were modified in a manner specified in the report.

(2) In the circumstances mentioned in the preceding subsection, the Secretary of State may, if he thinks fit, by an order made by statutory instrument make such provision as—

    (a) in a case falling within paragraph (a) of the preceding subsection, is in his opinion appropriate for giving effect to the proposals set out in the reference, or

    (b) in a case falling within paragraph (b) of that subsection, is in his opinion appropriate for giving effect either to the proposals as set out in the reference or to those proposals as modified in the manner specified in the report, as the Secretary of State may in his discretion determine.

(3) Any such order may contain such supplementary or incidental provisions as the Secretary of State may consider appropriate in the circumstances; and (without prejudice to the generality of this subsection) any such order may restrict the prosecution of offences under the next following section in respect of contraventions of the order where those contraventions also constitute offences under another enactment.

(4) No such order, and no order varying or evoking any such order, shall be made under this section unless a draft of the order has been laid before Parliament and approved by a resolution of each House of Parliament.

Penalties for contravention of order under s. 22

23.   Subject to the following provisions of this Part of this Act, any person who contravenes a prohibition imposed by an order under section 22 of this Act, or who does not comply with a requirement imposed by such an order which applies to him, shall be guilty of an offence and shall be liable—

    (a) on summary conviction, to a fine not exceeding the prescribed sum;

    (b) on conviction on indictment, to a fine or to imprisonment for a term not exceeding two years or both.

Offences due to default of other person

24.   Where the commission by any person of an offence under section 23 of this Act is due to the act or default of some other person, that other person shall be guilty of the offence, and a person may be charged with and convicted of the offence by virtue of this section whether or not proceedings are taken against the first-mentioned person.

---

[3] The Orders made under this section (S.I. 1976 No. 1812, S.I. 1976 No. 1813, S.I. 1977 No. 1918) are printed below at pp. 274–278.

Defences in proceedings under s. 23

25.—(1) In any proceedings for an offence under section 23 of this Act it shall, subject to subsection (2) of this section, be a defence for the person charged to prove—

    (a) that the commission of the offence was due to a mistake, or to reliance on information supplied to him, or to the act or default of another person, an accident or some other cause beyond his control, and

    (b) that he took all reasonable precautions and exercised an due diligence to avoid the commission of such an offence by himself or any person under his control.

(2) If in any case the defence provided by the preceding subsection involves the allegation that the commission of the offence was due to the act or default of another person or to reliance on information supplied by another person, the person charged shall not, without leave of the court, be entitled to rely on that defence unless, within a period ending seven clear days before the hearing, he has served on the prosecutor a notice in writing giving such information identifying or assisting in the identification of. that other person as was then in his possession.

(3) In proceedings for an offence under section 23 of this Act committed by the publication of an advertisement, it shall be a defence for the person charged to prove that he is a person whose business it is to publish or arrange for the publication of advertisements, and that he received the advertisement for publication in the ordinary course of business and did not know and had no reason to suspect that its publication would amount to an offence under section 23 of this Act.

Limitation of effect of orders under s. 22

26. A contract for the supply of goods or services shall not be void or unenforceable by reason only of a contravention of an order made under section 22 of this Act; and, subject to the provisions of section 33 of the Interpretation Act 1889 (which relates to offences under two or more laws), the provisions of this Part of this Act shall not be construed as—

    (a) conferring a right of action in any civil proceedings (other than proceedings for the recovery of a fine) in respect of any contravention of such an order, or

    (b) affecting any restriction imposed by or under any other enactment, whether public or private, or

    (c) derogating from any right of action or other remedy (whether civil or criminal) in proceedings instituted otherwise than under this Part of this Act.

Enforcement of orders

Enforcing authorities

27.—(1) It shall be the duty of every local weights and measures authority to enforce within their area the provisions of any order made under section 22 of this Act.

(2) Nothing in subsection (1) shall be taken as authorising a local weights and measures authority in Scotland to institute proceedings for an offence.

Power to make test purchases

28. A local weights and measures authority may make, or may authorise any of their officers to make on their behalf, such purchases of goods, and may authorise any of their officers to obtain such services, as may be expedient for the purpose of determining whether or not the provisions of any order made under section 22 of this Act are being complied with.

Power to enter premises and inspect and seize goods and documents

29.—(1) A duly authorised officer of a local weights and measures authority, or a person duly authorised in writing by the Secretary of State, may at all reasonable hours, and on production, if required, of his credentials, exercise the following powers, that is to say—

    (a) he may, for the purpose of ascertaining whether any offence under section 23 of this Act has been committed, inspect any goods and enter any premises other than premises used only as a dwelling;

    (b) if he has reasonable cause to suspect that an offence under that section has been committed, he may, for the purpose of ascertaining whether it has been committed, require any person carrying on a business or employed in connection with a business to produce any books or documents relating to the business and may take copies of, or of any entry in, any such book or document;

    (c) if he has reasonable cause to believe that such an offence has been committed he may seize and detain any goods for the purpose of ascertaining, by testing or otherwise, whether the offence has been committed;

    (d) he may seize and detain any goods or documents which he has reason to believe may be required as evidence in proceedings for such an offence;

    (e) he may, for the purpose of exercising his powers under this subsection to seize goods, but only if and to the extent that it is reasonably necessary in order to secure that the provisions of an order made under section 22 of this Act are duly observed, require any person having authority to do so to break open any container or open any vending machine and, if that person does not comply with the requirement, he may do so himself.

(2) A person seizing any goods or documents in the exercise of his powers under this section shall inform the person from whom they are seized and, in the case of goods seized from a vending machine, the person whose name and address are stated on the machine as being the proprietor's or, if no name and address are so stated, the occupier of the premises on which the machine stands or to which it is affixed.

(3) If a justice of the peace, on sworn information in writing,—

    (a) is satisfied that there is reasonable ground to believe either—

        (i) that any goods, books or documents which a person has power under this section to inspect are on any premises and that their inspection is likely to disclose evidence of the commission of an offence under section 23 of this Act, or

        (ii) that any offence under section 23 has been, is being or is about to be committed on any premises, and

    (b) is also satisfied either—

        (i) that admission to the premises has been or is likely to be refused and that notice of intention to apply for a warrant under this subsection has been given to the occupier, or

(ii) that an application for admission, or the giving of such a notice, would defeat the object of the entry or that the premises are unoccupied or that the occupier is temporarily absent, and it might defeat the object of the entry to await his return, the justice may by warrant under his hand, which shall continue in force for a period of one month, authorise any such officer or other person as is mentioned in subsection (1) of this section to enter the premises, if need be by force.

In the application of this subsection to Scotland "justice of the peace" shall be construed as including a sheriff and a magistrate.

(4) A person entering any premises by virtue of this section may take with him such other persons and such equipment as may appear to him necessary and on leaving any premises which he has entered by virtue of a warrant under subsection (3) of this section he shall, if the premises are unoccupied or the occupier is temporarily absent, leave them as effectively secured against trespassers as he found them.

(5) Nothing in this section shall be taken to compel the production by a barrister, advocate or solicitor of a document containing a privileged communication made by or to him in that capacity or to authorise the taking of possession of any such document which is in his possession.

Offences in connection with exercise of powers under s. 29

30.—(1) Subject to subsection (6) of this section, any person who—

(a) wilfully obstructs any such officer or person as is mentioned in subsection (1) of section 29 of this Act acting in the exercise of any powers conferred on him by or under that section, or

(b) wilfully fails to comply with any requirement properly made to him by such an officer or person under that section, or

(c) without reasonable cause fails to give to such an officer or person so acting any other assistance or information which he may reasonably require of him for the purpose of the performance of his functions under this Part of this Act,

shall be guilty of an offence.

(2) If any person, in giving any such information as is mentioned in subsection (1)(c) of this section, makes any statement which he knows to be false, he shall be guilty of an offence.

(3) If any person discloses to any other person—

(a) any information with respect to any manufacturing process or trade secret obtained by him in premises which he has entered by virtue of section 29 of this Act, or

(b) any information obtained by him under that section or by virtue of subsection (1) of this section,

he shall, unless the disclosure was made in the performance of his duty, be guilty of an offence.

(4) If any person who is neither a duly authorised officer of a weights and measures authority nor a person duly authorised in that behalf by the Secretary of State purports to act as such under section 29 of this Act or under this section, he shall be guilty of an offence.

(5) Any person guilty of an offence under subsection (1) of this section shall be liable on summary conviction to a fine not exceeding level 3 on the standard

scale; and any person guilty of an offence under subsection (2), subsection (3) or subsection (4) of this section shall be liable—

    (a) on summary conviction, to a fine not exceeding the prescribed sum;

    (b) on conviction on indictment, to a fine or to imprisonment for a term not exceeding two years or to both.

(6) Nothing in this section shall be construed as requiring a person to answer any question or give any information if to do so might incriminate that person or (where that person is married) the husband or wife of that person.

Notice of test

31. Where any goods seized or purchased by a person in pursuance of this Part of this Act are submited to a test, then—

    (a) if the goods were seized, he shall inform any such person as is mentioned in section 29(2) of this Act of the result of the test;

    (b) if the goods were purchased and the test leads to the institution of proceedings for an offence under section 23 of this Act, he shall inform the person from whom the goods were purchased, or, in the case of goods sold through a vending machine, the person mentioned in relation to such goods in section 29(2) of this Act, of the result of the test;

and where, as a result of the test, proceedings for an offence under section 23 of this Act are instituted against any person, he shall allow that person to have the goods tested on his behalf if it is reasonably practicable to do so.

Compensation for loss in respect of goods seized under s. 29

32.—(1) Where in the exercise of his powers under section 29 of this Act a person seizes and detains any goods, and their owner suffers loss by reason of their being damaged or deteriorate, unless the owner is convicted of an offence under section 23 of this Act committed in relation to the goods, the appropriate authority shall be liable to compensate him for the loss so suffered.

(2) Any disputed question as to the right to or the amount of any compensation payable under this section shall be determined by arbitration and, in Scotland, by a single arbiter appointed, failing agreement between the parties, by the sheriff.

(3) In this section "the appropriate authority"—

    (a) in relation to goods seized by an officer of a local weights and measures authority, means that authority, and

    (b) in any other case, means the Secretary of State.

Application of Part II to Northern Ireland

33.—(1) It shall be the duty of the Ministry of Commerce for Northern Ireland to enforce in Northern Ireland the provisions of any order under section 22 of this Act.

(2) In the application of this Part of this Act to Northern Ireland:

    (a) section 27 shall not apply;

    (b) in sections 28 and 29, any reference to a local weights and measures authority shall be construed as a reference to the Ministry of Commerce for Northern Ireland, and the provisions of sections 30 to 32 shall be construed accordingly;

    (c) in section 29(3), any reference to a justice of the peace shall be construed as a reference to a resident magistrate; and

    (d) the provisions of the Arbitration Act (Northern Ireland) 1937, except the provisions set out in Schedule 3 thereto, shall apply to an arbitration under section 32 of this Act as if the arbitration were pursuant to an arbitration agreement (as defined in section 30(1) of that Act).

PART III

ADDITIONAL FUNCTIONS OF DIRECTOR FOR PROTECTION OF CONSUMERS

Action by Director with respect to course of conduct detrimental to interests of consumers

34.—(1) Where it appears to the Director that the person carrying on a business has in the course of that business persisted in a course of conduct which—

(a) is detrimental to the interests of consumers in the United Kingdom, whether those interests are economic interests or interests in respect of health, safety or other matters, and

(b) in accordance with the following provisions of this section is to be regarded as unfair to consumers,

the Director shall use his best endeavours, by communication with that person or otherwise, to obtain from him satisfactory written assurance that he will refrain from continuing that course of conduct and from carrying on any similar course of conduct in the course of that business.

(2) For the purposes of subsection (1)(b) of this section a course of conduct shall be regarded as unfair to consumers if it consists of contraventions of one or more enactments which impose duties, prohibitions or restrictions enforceable by criminal proceedings, whether any such duty, prohibition or restriction is imposed in relation to consumers as such or not and whether the person carrying on the business has or has not been convicted of any offence in respect of any such contravention.

(3) A course of conduct on the part of the person carrying on a business shall also be regarded for those purposes as unfair to consumers if it consists of things done, or omitted to be done, in the course of that business in breach of contract or in breach of a duty (other than a contractual duty) owed to any person by virtue of any enactment or rule of law and enforceable by civil proceedings, whether (in any such case) civil proceedings in respect of the breach of contract or breach of duty have been brought or not.

(4) For the purpose of determining whether it appears to him that a person has persisted in such a course of conduct as is mentioned in subsection (1) of this section, the Director shall have regard to either or both of the following, that is to say—

(a) complaints received by him, whether from consumers or from other persons;

(b) any other information collected by or furnished to him, whether by virtue of this Act or otherwise.

Proceedings before Restrictive Practices Court

35. If, in the circumstances specified in subsection (1) of section 34 of this Act,—

(a) the Director is unable to obtain from the person in question such an assurance as is mentioned in that subsection, or

(b) that person has given such an assurance and it appears to the Director that he has failed to observe it,

the Director may bring proceedings against him before the Restrictive Practices Court.

Evidence in proceedings under s. 35

36.—(1) For the purposes of section 11 of the Civil Evidence Act 1968, section 10 of the Law Reform (Miscellaneous Provisions) (Scotland) Act 1968 or section 7 of the Civil Evidence Act (Northern Ireland) 1971 (each of which relates to convictions as evidence in civil proceedings), proceedings under section 35 of this Act shall (without prejudice to the generality of the relevant definition) be taken to be civil proceedings within the meaning of the Act in question.

(2) Where in any proceedings under section 35 of this Act the Director alleges such a breach of contract or breach of duty as is mentioned in section 34(3) of this Act, a judgment of any court given in civil proceedings which includes a finding that the breach of contract or breach of duty in question was conunitted,—

(a) shall be admissible in evidence for the purpose of proving the breach of contract or breach of duty, and

(b) shall, unless the contrary is proved, be taken to be sufficient evidence that the breach of contract or breach of duty was committed.

(3) For the purposes of subsection (2) of this section no account shall be taken of a judgment given in any civil proceedings, if it has subsequently been reversed on appeal, or has been varied on appeal so as to negative the finding referred to in that subsection.

(4) In subsection (1) of this section "the relevant definition" means section 18(1) of the Civil Evidence Act 1968, section 17(1) of the Law Reform (Miscellaneous Provisions) (Scotland) Act 1968 or section 14(1) of the Civil Evidence Act (Northern Ireland) 1971, as the case may be.

Order of, or undertaking given to, Court in proceedings under s. 35

37.—(1) Where in any proceedings before the Restrictive Practices Court under section 35 of this Act—

(a) the Court finds that the person against whom the proceedings are brough (in this section referred to as "the respondent") has in the course of a business carried on by him persisted in such a course of conduct as is mentioned in section 34(1) of this Act, and

(b) the respondent does not give an undertaking to the Court under subsection (3) of this section wbich is accepted by the Court, and

(c) it appears to the Court that, unless an order is made against the respondent under this section, he is likely to continue that course of conduct or to carry on a similar course of conduct,

the Court may make an order against the respondent under this section.

(2) An order of the Court under this section shall (with such degree of particularity as appears to the Court to be sufficient for the purposes of the order) indicate the nature of the course of conduct to which the finding of the Court under subsection (1)(a) of this section relates, and shall direct the respondent—

(a) to refrain from continuing that course of conduct, and

(b) to refrain from carrying on any similar course of conduct in the course of his business.

(3) Where in any proceedings under section 35 of this Act the Court makes such a finding as is mentioned in subsection (1)(a) of this section, and the respondent offers to give to the Court an undertaking either—

(a) to refrain as mentioned in paragraphs (a) and (b) of subsection (2) of this section, or

(b) to take particular steps which, in the opinion of the Court, would suffice

to prevent a continuance of the course of conduct to which the complaint relates and to prevent the carrying on by the respondent of any
similar course of conduct of his business,

the Court may, if it thinks fit, accept that undertaking instead of making an
order under this section.

**Provisions as to persons consenting to or conniving at courses of conduct
detrimental to interests of consumers**

38.—(1) The provisions of this section shall have effect where it appears to
the Director—

    (a) that a body corporate has in the course of a business carried on by that
body persisted in such a course of conduct as is mentioned in section
34(1) of this Act, and

    (b) that the course of conduct in question has been so persisted in with
the consent or connivance of a person (in this and the next following
section referred to as "the accessory") who at a material time fulfilled
the relevant conditions in relation to that body.

(2) For the purposes of this section a person shall be taken to fulfil the relevant
conditions in relation to a body corporate at any time if that person either—

    (a) is at that time a director, manager, secretary or other similar officer of
the body corporate or a person purporting to act in any such capacity, or

    (b) whether being an individual or a body of persons, corporate or unin-
corporate, has at that time controlling interest in that body corporate.

(3) If, in the circumstances specified in subsection (1) of this section,—

    (a) the Director has used his best endeavours to obtain from the accessory
such an assurance as is mentioned in the next following subsection and
has been unable to obtain such an assurance from him, or

    (b) the accessory has given such an assurance to the Director and it appears
to the Directory that he has failed to observe it,

the Director may bring proceedings against the accessory before the Restrictive
Practices Court.

(4) The assurance referred to in subsection (3) of this section is a satisfactory
written assurance given by the accessory that he will refrain—

    (a) from continuing to consent to or connive at the course of conduct in
question;

    (b) from carrying on any similar course of conduct in the course of any
business which may at any time be carried on by him; and

    (c) from consenting to or conniving at the carrying on of any such course
of conduct by any other body corporate in relation to which, at any
time when that course of conduct is carried on, he fulfils the relevant
conditions.

(5) Proceedings may be brought against the accessory under this section
whether or not any proceedings are brought under section 35 of this Act against
the body corporate referred to in subsection (1) of this section.

(6) Section 36 of this Act shall have effect in relation to proceedings under
this section as it has effect in relation to proceedings under section 35 of this
Act.

(7) For the purposes of this section a person (whether being an individual or
a body of persons, corporate or unincorporate) has a controlling interest in a
body corporate if (but only if) that person can, directly or indirectly, determine
the manner in which one-half of the votes which could be cast at a general
meeting of the body corporate are to be cast on matters, and in circumstances,

not of such a description as to bring into play any special voting rights or restrictions on voting rights.

Order of, or undertaking given to, Court in proceedings under s. 38

39.—(1) Where in any proceedings brought against the accessory before the Restrictive Practices Court under section 38 of this Act—

    (a) the Court finds that the conditions specified in paragraphs (a) and (b) of subsection (1) of that section are fulfilled in the case of the accessory, and

    (b) the accessory does not give an undertaking to the Court under subsection (3) of this section which is accepted by the Court, and

    (c) it appears to the Court that, unless an order is made against the accessory under this section, it is likely that he will not refrain from acting in one or more of the ways mentioned in paragraphs (a) to (c) of subsection (4) of that section,

the Court may make an order against the accessory under this section.

(2) An order of the Court under this section shall (with such degree of particularity as appears to the Court to be sufficient for the purposes of the order) indicate the nature of the course of conduct to which the finding of the Court under subsection (1)(a) of this section relates and shall direct the accessory in relation to the course of conduct so indicated, to refrain from acting in any of the ways mentioned in paragraphs (a) to (c) of subsection (4) of section 38 of this Act.

(3) Where in any proceedings under section 38 of this Act the Court makes such a finding as is mentioned in subsection (1)(a) of this section, and the accessory offers to give to the Court an undertaking either—

    (a) to refrain from acting in any of the ways mentioned in paragraphs (a) to (c) of subsection (4) of that section, or

    (b) to take particular steps which, in the opinion of the Court, would suffice to prevent him from acting in any of those ways,

the Court may, if it thinks fit, accept that undertaking instead of making an order under this section.

Provisions as to interconnected bodies corporate

40.—(1) This section applies to any order made under section 37 or section 39 of this Act.

(2) Where an order to which this section applies is made against a body corporate which is a member of a group of interconnected bodies corporate, the Restrictive Practices Court, on making the order, may direct that it shall be binding upon all members of the group as if each of them were the body corporate against which the order is made.

(3) Where an order to which this section applies has been made against a body corporate, and at a time when that order is in force—

    (a) the body corporate becomes a member of a group of interconnected bodies corporate, or

    (b) a group of interconnected bodies corporate of which it is a member is increased by the addition of one or more further members,

the Restrictive Practices Court, on the application of the Director, may direct that the order shall thereafter be binding upon each member of the group as if it were the body corporate against which the order was made.

(4) The power conferred by subsection (3) of this section shall be exercisable—

(a) whether, at the time when the original order was made, the body corporate against which it was made was a member of a group of interconnected bodies corporate or not, and

(b) if it was such a member, whether a direction under subsection (2) of this section was given or not.

Concurrent jurisdiction of other courts in certain cases

41.—(1) In any case where—

(a) the Director could bring proceedings against a person before the Restrictive Practices Court under section 35 or section 38 of this Act, and

(b) it appears to the Director that the conditions specified in the next following subsection are fulfilled,

the Director may, if he thinks fit, bring those proceedings in an appropriate alternative court instead of bringing them before the Restrictive Practices Court; and, in relation to any proceedings brought by virtue of this section, the appropriate alternative court in which they are brought shall have the like jurisdiction as the Restrictive Practices Court would have had if they had been brought in that Court.

(2) The conditions referred to in the preceding subsection are—

(a) that neither the person against whom the proceedings are to be brought nor the person against whom any associated proceedings have been or are intended to be brought is a body corporate having a share capital, paid up or credited as paid up, of an amount exceeding £10,000, and

(b) that neither those proceedings nor any associated proceedings involve or are likely to involve the determination of a question (whether of law or of fact) of such general application as to justify its being reserved for determination by the Restrictive Practices Court.

(3) For the purposes of this section, the following shall be appropriate alternative courts in relation to proceedings in respect of a course of conduct maintained in the course of a business, that is to say, the county court for any district (or, in Northern Ireland, any division) in which, or, in Scotland, any sheriff court within whose jurisdiction, that business is carried on.

(4) In relation to any proceedings brought in an appropriate alternative court by virtue of this section, or to any order made in any such proceedings, any reference in section 37, in section 39 or section 40 of this Act to the Restrictive Practices Court shall be construed as a reference to the appropriate alternative court in which the proceedings are brought.

(5) In this section "associated proceedings"—

(a) in relation to proceedings under section 35 of this Act, means proceedings under section 38 of this Act against a person as being a person consenting to or conniving at the course of conduct in question, and

(b) in relation to proceedings under section 38 of this Act, means proceedings under section 35 of this Act against a person as being the person by whom the course of conduct in question has been maintained.

Appeals from decisions or orders of courts under Part III

42.—(1) Notwithstanding anything in any other enactment, an appeal, whether on a question of fact or on a question of law, shall tie from any decision or order of any court in proceedings under Part III of this Act.

(2) Any such appeal shall lie—

    (a) in the case of proceedings in England and Wales, to the Court of Appeal;

    (b) in the case of proceedings in Scotland, to the Court of Session;

    (c) in the case of proceedings in Northern Ireland, to the Court of Appeal in Northern Ireland.

*　　*　　*　　*　　*

PART XII

MISCELLANEOUS AND SUPPLEMENTARY PROVISIONS

Publication of information and advice

124.—(1) With respect to any matter in respect of which the Director has any duties under section 2(1) of this Act, he may arrange for the publication, in such form and in such manner as he may consider appropriate, of such information and advice as it may appear to him to be expedient to give to consumers in the United Kingdom.

(2) In arranging for the publication of any such information or advice, the Director shall have regard to the need for excluding, so far as that is practicable,—

    (a) any matter which relates to the private affairs of an individual, where the publication of that matter would or might, in the opinion of the Director, seriously and prejudicially affect the interests of that individual, and

    (b) any matter which relates specifically to the affairs of a particular body of persons, whether corporate or unincorporate, where publication of that matter would or might, in the opinion of the Director, seriously and prejudicially affect the interests of that body.

(3) Without prejudice to the exercise of his powers under subsection (1) of this section, it shall be the duty of the Director to encourage relevant associations to prepare, and to disseminate to their members, codes of practice for guidance in safeguarding and promoting the interests of consumers in the United Kingdom.

(4) In this section "relevant association" means any association (whether incorporated or not) whose membership consists wholly or mainly of persons engaged in the production or supply of goods or in the supply of services or of persons employed by or representing persons so engaged and whose objects or activities include the promotion of the interests of persons so engaged.

Annual and other reports of Director

125.—(1) The Director shall, as soon as practicable after the end of the year 1974 and of each subsequent calendar year, make to the Secretary of State a report on his activities, and the activities of the Advisory Committee and of the Commission, during that year.

(2) Every such report shall include a general survey of developments, during the year to which it relates, in respect of matters falling within the scope of the Director's duties under any enactment (including any enactment contained in this Act, other than this section) and shall set out any directions given to the Director under section 2(2) of the Consumer Credit Act 1974 during that year.

(3) The Secretary of State shall lay a copy of every report made by the Director under subsection (1) of this section before each House of Parliament, and shall arrange for every such report to be published in such manner as he may consider appropriate.

(4) The Director may also prepare such other reports as appear to him to be expedient with respect to such matters as are mentioned in subsection (2) of this section, and may arrange for any such report to be published in such manner as he may consider appropriate.

(5) In making any report under this Act the Director shall have regard to the need for excluding so far as that is practicable, any such matter as is specified in paragraph (a) or paragraph (b) of section 124(2) of this Act.

(6) For the purposes of this section any period between the commencement of this Act and the end of the year 1973 shall be treated as included in the year 1974.

* * * * *

Time-limit for prosecutions

129.—(1) No prosecution for an offence under this Act shall be commenced after the expiration of three years from the commission of the offence or one year from its discovery by the prosecutor, whichever is the earlier.

(2) Notwithstanding anything in section 104 of the Magistrates' Courts Act 1952, a magistrates' court may try an information for an offence under this Act if the information was laid within twelve months from the commission of the offence.

(3) Notwithstanding anything in section 23 of the Summary Jurisdiction (Scotland) Act 1954, summary proceedings in Scotland for an offence under this Act may be commenced within twelve months from the commission of the offence, and subsection (2) of the said section 23 shall apply for the purposes of this subsection as it applies for the purposes of that section.

(4) In the application of this section to Northern Ireland, for the references in subsection (2) to section 127(1) of the Magistrates' Courts Act 1980 and to the trial and laying of an information there shall be substituted respectively references to Article 19(1) of the Magistrates' Courts (Northern Ireland) Order 1981 and to the hearing and determination and making of a complaint and as if in that subsection for the words ''an offence under this Act'' there were substituted the words ''an offence under section 30(1) or 46(2) of this Act''.

* * * * *

Notification of convictions and judgments to Director

131.—(1) Where in any criminal proceedings a person is convicted of an offence by or before a court in the United Kingdom, or a judgment is given against a person in civil proceedings in any such court, and it appears to the court—

> (a) having regard to the functions of the Director under Part III of this Act or under the Estate Agents Act 1979, that it would be expedient for the conviction or judgment to be brought to his attention, and

(b) that it may not be brought to his attention unless arrangements for the purpose are made by the court,

the court may make arrangements for that purpose notwithstanding that the proceedings have been finally disposed of by the court.

(2) In this section "judgment" includes any order or decree, and any reference to the giving of a judgment shall be construed accordingly.

Offences by bodies corporate

132.—(1) Where an offence under section 23, section 46, section 85(6), section 93B or Part XI of this Act, which has been committed by a body corporate, is proved to have been committed with the consent or connivance of, or to be attributable to any neglect on the part of, any director, manager, secretary or other similar officer of the body corporate, or any person who was purporting to act in any such capacity, he as well as the body corporate, shall be guilty of that offence and be liable to be proceeded against and punished accordingly.

(2) Where the affairs of a body corporate are managed by its members, subsection (1) of this section shall apply in relation to the acts and defaults of a member in connection with his functions of management as if he were a director of the body corporate.

*   *   *   *   *

Provisions as to orders

134.—(1) Any statutory instrument whereby any order is made under any of the preceding provisions of this Act, other than a provision which requires a draft of the order to be laid before Parliament before making the order, or whereby any regulations are made under this Act, shall be subject to annulment in pursuance of a resolution of either House of Parliament.

(2) Any power conferred by any provision of this Act to make an order by statutory instrument shall include power to revoke or vary the order by a subsequent order made under that provision.

*   *   *   *   *

Powers of Criminal Courts Act 1973[1]

(c. 62)

*   *   *   *   *

Compensation orders against convicted persons

35.—(1) Subject to the provisions of this Part of this Act and to section 40 of the Magistrates' Courts Act 1980 (which imposes a monetary limit on the powers of a magistrates' court under this section, a court by or before which a person is convicted of an offence, instead of or in addition to dealing with him in any other way, may, on application or otherwise, make an order (in this Act referred to as "a compensation order") requiring him to pay compensation for any personal injury, loss or damage resulting from that offence or any other offence which is taken into consideration by the court in determining sentence or to make payments for funeral expenses or bereavement in respect of a death resulting from any such offence, other than a death due to an accident arising out of the presence of a motor vehicle on a road; and a court shall give reasons, on passing sentence, if it does not make such an order in a case where this section empowers it to do so.

(1A) Compensation under subsection (1) above shall be of such amount as the court considers appropriate, having regard to any evidence and to any representations that are made by or on behalf of the accused or the prosecutor.

(2) In the case of an offence under the Theft Act 1968, where the property in question is recovered, any damage to the property occurring while it was out of the owner's possession shall be treated for the purposes of subsection (1) above as having resulted from the offence, however and by whomsoever the damage was caused.

(3) A compensation order may only be made in respect of injury loss or damage (other than loss suffered by a person's dependants in consequence of his death) which was due to an accident arising out of the presence of a motor vehicle on a road, if—

    (a) it is in respect of damage which is treated by subsection (2) above as resulting from an offence under the Theft Act 1968; or

    (b) it is in respect of injury, loss or damage as respects which—

        (i) the offender is uninsured in relation to the use of the vehicle; and

        (ii) compensation is not payable under any arrangements to which the Secretary of State is a party;

and, where a compensation order is made in respect of injury, loss or damage due to such an accident, the amount to be paid may include an amount representing the whole or part of any loss of or reduction in preferential rates of insurance attributable to the accident.

(3A) A vehicle the use of which is exempted from insurance by section 144

---

[1] The original provisions of the Powers of Criminal Courts Act 1973, ss. 35–38 (which do not extend to Scotland) have been much amended by the Magistrates' Courts Act 1980, the Criminal Justice Act 1982, the Criminal Justice Act 1988 and the Armed Forces Act 1991. The amendments are incorporated herein.

of the Road Traffic Act 1972 is not uninsured for the purposes of subsection (3) above.

(3B) A compensation order in respect of funeral expenses may be made for the benefit of anyone who incurred the expenses.

(3C) A compensation order in respect of bereavement may only be made for the benefit of a person for whose benefit a claim for damages for bereavement could be made under section 1A of the Fatal Accidents Act 1976.

(3D) The amounts of compensation in respect of bereavement shall not exceed the amount for the time being specified in section 1A(3) of the Fatal Accidents Act 1976.

(4) In determining whether to make a compensation order against any person, and in determining the amount to be paid by any person under such an order, the court shall have regard to his means so far as they appear or are known to the court.

(4A) Where the court considers—
- (a) that it would be appropriate both to impose a fine and to make a compensation order; but
- (b) that the offender has insufficient means to pay both an appropriate fine and appropriate compensation, the court shall give preference to compensation (though it may impose a fine as well).

(5) [*Repealed*]

Enforcement and appeals

36.—(1) A person in whose favour a compensation order is made shall not be entitled to receive the amount due to him until (disregarding any power of a court to grant leave to appeal out of time) there is no further possibility of an appeal on which the order could be varied or set aside.

(2) Rules under section 144 of the Magistrates' Courts Act 1980 may make provision regarding the way in which the magistrates' court for the time being having functions (by virtue of section 41(1) of the Administration of Justice Act 1970) in relation to the enforcement of a compensation order is to deal with money paid in satisfaction of the order where the entitlement of the person in whose favour it was made is suspended.

(3) The Court of Appeal may by order annul or vary any compensation order made by the court of trial, although the conviction is not quashed; and the order, if annulled, shall not take effect and, if varied, shall take effect as varied.

(4) Where the House of Lords restores a conviction, it may make any compensation order which the court of trial could have made.

(5) Where a compensation order has been made against any person in respect of an offence taken into consideration in determining his sentence—
- (a) the order shall cease to have effect if he successfully appeals against his conviction of the offence or, if more than one, all the offences, of which he was convicted in the proceedings in which the order was made;
- (b) he may appeal against the order as if it were part of the sentence imposed in respect of the offence or, if more than one, any of the offences, of which he was so convicted.

Review of compensation orders

37. At any time before the person against whom a compensation order has been made has paid into court the whole of the compensation which the order requires him to pay, but at a time when (disregarding any power of a court to grant leave to appeal out of time) there is no further possibility of an appeal on which the order could be varied or set aside, the magistrates' court for the time being having functions in relation to the enforcement of the order may, on the application of the person against whom it was made, discharge the order, or reduce the amount which remains to be paid, if it appears to the court—

    (a) that the injury, loss or damage in respect of which the order was made has been held in civil proceedings to be less than it was taken to be for the purposes of the order; or

    (b) in the case of an order in respect of the loss of any property, that the property has been recovered by the person in whose favour the order was made; or

    (c) that the means of the person against whom the order was made are insufficient to satisfy in full both the order and a confiscation order under Part VI of the Criminal Justice Act 1988 made against him in the same proceedings; or

    (d) that the person against whom the order was made has suffered a substantial reduction in his means which was unexpected at the time when the compensation order was made, and that his means seem unlikely to increase for a considerable period;

but where the order was made by the Crown Court, a magistrates' court shall not exercise any power conferred by this section in a case where it is satisfied as mentioned in paragraph (c) or (d) above unless it has first obtained the consent of the Crown Court.

Effect of compensation order on subsequent award of damages in civil proceedings

38.—(1) This section shall have effect where a compensation order or a service compensation order or award has been made in favour of any person in respect of any injury, loss or damage and a claim by him in civil proceedings for damages in respect of the injury, loss or damage subsequently falls to be determined.

(2) The damages in the civil proceedings shall be assessed without regard to the order or award; but the plaintiff may only recover an amount equal to the aggregate of the following—

    (a) any amount by which they exceed the compensation; and

    (b) a sum equal to any portion of the compensation which he fails to recover,

and may not enforce the judgment, so far as it relates to a sum such as is mentioned in paragraph (b) above, without the leave of the court.

(3) In this section a "service compensation or award" means

    (a) an order requiring the payment of compensation under paragraph 11 of Schedule 5A to the Army Act 1955, of Schedule 5A to the Air Force Act 1955 or of Schedule 4A to the Naval Discipline Act 1957; or

    (b) an award of stoppages payable by way of compensation under any of those Acts.

Consumer Credit Act 1974

(c. 39)

An Act to establish for the protection of consumers a new system, administered by the Director General of Fair Trading, of licensing and other control of traders concerned with the provision of credit, or the supply of goods on hire or hire-purchase, and their transactions, in place of the present enactments regulating moneylenders, pawnbrokers and hire-purchase traders and their transactions; and for related matters.   [31st July 1974]

PART I

DIRECTOR GENERAL OF FAIR TRADING

General functions of Director

1.—(1) It is the duty of the Director General of Fair Trading ("the Director")—

(a) to administer the licensing system set up by this Act,

(b) to exercise the adjudicating functions conferred on him by this Act in relation to the issue, renewal, variation, suspension and revocation of licences, and other matters,

(c) generally to superintend the working and enforcement of this Act, and regulations made under it, and

(d) where necessary or expedient, himself to take steps to enforce this Act, and regulations so made.

(2) It is the duty of the Director, so far as appears to him to be practicable and having regard both to the national interest and the interests of persons carrying on businesses to which this Act applies and their customers, to keep under review and from time to time advise the Secretary of State about—

(a) social and commercial developments in the United Kingdom and elsewhere relating to the provision of credit or bailment or (in Scotland) hiring of goods to individuals, and related activities; and

(b) the working and enforcement of this Act and orders and regulations made under it.

Powers of Secretary of State

2.—(1) The Secretary of State may by order—

(a) confer on the Director additional functions concerning the provision of credit or bailment or (in Scotland) hiring of goods to individuals, and related activities, and

(b) regulate the carrying out by the Director of his functions under this Act.

(2) The Secretary of State may give general directions indicating considerations to which the Director should have particular regard in carrying out his functions under this Act, and may give specific directions on any matter connected with the carrying out by the Director of those functions.

(3) The Secretary of State, on giving any directions under subsection (2),

shall arrange for them to be published in such manner as he thinks most suitable for drawing them to the attention of interested persons.

(4) With the approval of the Secretary of State and the Treasury, the Director may charge, for any service or facility provided by him under this Act, a fee of an amount specified by general notice (the "specified fee").

(5) Provision may be made under subsection (4) for reduced fees, or no fees at all, to be paid for certain services or facilities by persons of a specified description, and references in this Act to the specified fee shall, in such cases, be construed accordingly.

(6) An order under subsection (1)(a) shall be made by statutory instrument and shall be of no effect unless a draft of the order has been laid before and approved by each House of Parliament.

(7) References in subsection (2) to the functions of the Director under this Act do not include the making of a determination to which section 41 or 150 (appeals from Director to Secretary of State) applies.

3. [*Repealed*]

Dissemination of information and advice

4. The Director shall arrange for the dissemination, in such form and manner as he considers appropriate, of such information and advice as it may appear to him expedient to give to the public in the United Kingdom about the operation of this Act, the credit facilities available to them, and other matters within the scope of his functions under this Act.

Annual and other reports

5. [*Amends the Fair Trading Act 1973 s. 125(2) and is incorporated therein.*]

Form etc. of applications

6.—(1) An application to the Director under this Act is of no effect unless the requirements of this section are satisfied.

(2) The application must be in writing, and in such form, and accompanied by such particulars, as the Director may specify by general notice, and must be accompanied by the specified fee.

(3) After giving preliminary consideration to an application, the Director may by notice require the applicant to furnish him with such further information relevant to the application as may be described in the notice, and may require any information furnished by the applicant (whether at the time of the application or subsequently) to be verified in such manner as the Director may stipulate.

(4) The Director may by notice require the applicant to publish details of his application at a time or times and in a manner specified in the notice.

Penalty for false information

7. A person who, in connection with any application or request to the Director under this Act, or in response to any invitation or requirement of the Director under this Act, knowingly or recklessly gives information to the Director which, in a material particular, is false or misleading, commits an offence.

PART II

CREDIT AGREEMENTS, HIRE AGREEMENTS AND LINKED TRANSACTIONS

Consumer credit agreements

8.—(1) A personal credit agreement is an agreement between an individual ("the debtor") and any other person ("the creditor") by which the creditor provides the debtor with credit of any amount.

(2) A consumer credit agreement is a personal credit agreement by which the creditor provides the debtor with credit not exceeding £15,000.

(3) A consumer credit agreement is a regulated agreement within the meaning of this Act if it is not an agreement (an "exempt agreement") specified in or under section 16.

Meaning of credit

9.—(1) In this Act "credit" includes a cash loan, and any other form of financial accommodation.

(2) Where credit is provided otherwise than in sterling it shall be treated for the purposes of this Act as provided in sterling of an equivalent amount.

(3) Without prejudice to the generality of subsection (1), the person by whom goods are bailed or (in Scotland) hired to an individual under a hire-purchase agreement shall be taken to provide him with fixed-sum credit to finance the transaction of an amount equal to the total price of the goods less the aggregate of the deposit (if any) and the total charge for credit.

(4) For the purposes of this Act, an item entering into the total charge for credit shall not be treated as credit even though time is allowed for its payment.

Running-account credit and fixed-sum credit

10.—(1) For the purposes of this Act—

  (a) running-account credit is a facility under a personal credit agreement whereby the debtor is enabled to receive from time to time (whether in his own person, or by another person) from the creditor or a third party cash, goods and services (or any of them) to an amount or value such that, taking into account payments made by or to the credit of the debtor, the credit limit (if any) is not at any time exceeded; and

  (b) fixed-sum credit is any other facility under a personal credit agreement whereby the debtor is enabled to receive credit (whether in one amount or by instalments).

(2) In relation to running-account credit, "credit limit" means, as respects any period, the maximum debit balance which, under the credit agreement, is allowed to stand on the account during that period, disregarding any term of the agreement allowing that maximum to be exceeded merely temporarily.

(3) For the purposes of section 8(2), running-account credit shall be taken not to exceed the amount specified in that subsection ("the specified amount") if—

  (a) the credit limit does not exceed the specified amount; or

  (b) whether or not there is a credit limit, and if there is, notwithstanding that it exceeds the specified amount,—

    (i) the debtor is not enabled to draw at any one time an amount which, so far as (having regard to section 9(4)) it represents credit, exceeds the specified amount, or

    (ii) the agreement provides that, if the debit balance rises above a given amount (not exceeding the specified amount), the rate of the total charge for credit increases or any other condition favouring the creditor or his associate comes into operation, or

(iii) at the time the agreement is made it is probable, having regard to the terms of the agreement and any other relevant considerations, that the debit balance will not at any time rise above the specified amount.

Restricted-use credit and unrestricted-use credit

11.—(1) A restricted-use credit agreement is a regulated consumer credit agreement—

(a) to finance a transaction between the debtor and the creditor, whether forming part of that agreement or not, or

(b) to finance a transaction between the debtor and a person (the "supplier") other than the creditor, or

(c) to refinance any existing indebtedness of the debtor's, whether to the creditor or another person, and "restricted-use credit" shall be construed accordingly.

(2) An unrestricted-use credit agreement is a regulated consumer credit agreement not falling within subsection (1), and "unrestricted-use credit" shall be construed accordingly.

(3) An agreement does not fall within subsection (1) if the credit is in fact provided in such a way as to leave the debtor free to use it as he chooses, even though certain uses would contravene that or any other agreement.

(4) An agreement may fall within subsection (1)(b) although the identity of the supplier is unknown at the time the agreement is made.

Debtor-creditor supplier agreements

12. A debtor-creditor-supplier agreement is a regulated consumer credit agreement being—

(a) a restricted-use credit agreement which falls within section 11(1)(a), or

(b) a restricted-use credit agreement which falls within section 11(1)(b) and is made by the creditor under pre-existing arrangements, or in contemplation of future arrangements, between himself and the supplier, or

(c) an unrestricted-use credit agreement which is made by the creditor under pre-existing arrangements between himself and a person (the "supplier") other than the debtor in the knowledge that the credit is to be used to finance a transaction between the debtor and the supplier.

Debtor-creditor agreements

13. A debtor-creditor agreement is a regulated consumer credit agreement being—

(a) a restricted-use credit agreement which falls within section 11(1)(b) but is not made by the creditor under pre-existing arrangements, or in contemplation of future arrangements, between himself and the supplier, or

(b) a restricted-use credit agreement which falls within section 11(1)(c), or

(c) an unrestricted-use credit agreement which is not made by the creditor under pre-existing arrangements between himself and a person (the "supplier") other than the debtor in the knowledge that the credit is to be used to finance a transaction between the debtor and the supplier.

Credit-token agreements

14.—(1) A credit-token is a card, check, voucher, coupon, stamp, form, book-let or other document or thing given to an individual by a person carrying on a consumer credit business, who undertakes—

    (a) that on the production of it (whether or not some other action is also required) he will supply cash, goods and services (or any of them) on credit, or

    (b) that where, on the production of it to a third party (whether or not any other action is also required), the third party supplies cash, goods and services (or any of them), he will pay the third party for them (whether or not deducting any discount or commission), in return for payment to him by the individual.

(2) A credit-token agreement is a regulated agreement for the provision of credit in connection with the use of a credit-token.

(3) Without prejudice to the generality of section 9(1), the person who gives to an individual an undertaking falling within subsection (1)(b) shall be taken to provide him with credit drawn on whenever a third party supplies him with cash, goods or services.

(4) For the purposes of subsection (1), use of an object to operate a machine provided by the person giving the object or a third party shall be treated as the production of the object to him.

Consumer hire agreements

15.—(1) A consumer hire agreement is an agreement made by a person with an individual (the "hirer") for the bailment or (in Scotland) the hiring of goods to the hirer, being an agreement which—

    (a) is not a hire-purchase agreement, and

    (b) is capable of subsisting for more than three months, and

    (c) does not require the hirer to make payments exceeding £15,000.

(2) A consumer hire agreement is a regulated agreement if it is not an exempt agreement.

Exempt agreements[1]

16.—(1) This Act does not regulate a consumer credit agreement where the creditor is a local authority [*repealed*], or a body specified, or of a description specified, in an order made by the Secretary of State, being—

    (a) an insurance company,

    (b) a friendly society,

    (c) an organisation of employers or organisation of workers,

    (d) a charity,

    (e) a land improvement company, or

    (f) a body corporate named or specifically referred to in any public general Act.

    (ff) a body corporate named or specifically referred to in an order made under—section 156(4), 444(1) or 447(2)(a) of the Housing Act 1985, section 223 or 229 of the Housing (Scotland) Act 1987, or Article 154(1)(a) or 156AA of the Housing (Northern Ireland) Order 1981 or Article 10(6A) of the Housing (Northern Ireland) Order 1983; or

---

[1] For the current order (as amended) made under the Consumer Credit Act 1974, s. 16(1), (4), see the Consumer Credit (Exempt Agreements) Order 1989 (S.I. 1989 No. 869) printed below at p. 304.

    (g) a building society, or

    (h) an authorised institution or wholly-owned subsidiary (within the meaning of the Companies Act 1985) of such an institution.

(2) Subsection (1) applies only where the agreement is—

    (a) a debtor-creditor-supplier agreement financing—

        (i) the purchase of land, or

        (ii) the provision of dwellings on any land, and secured by a land mortgage on that land; or

    (b) a debtor-creditor agreement secured by any land mortgage; or

    (c) a debtor-creditor-supplier agreement financing a transaction which is a linked transaction in relation to—

        (i) an agreement falling within paragraph (a), or

        (ii) an agreement failing within paragraph (b) financing—

         (aa) the purchase of any land, or

         (bb) the provision of dwellings on any land,

and secured by a land mortgage on the land referred to in paragraph (a) or, as the case may be, the land referred to in sub-paragraph (ii).

(3) The Secretary of State shall not make, vary or revoke an order—

    (a) under subsection (1)(a) without consulting the Minister of the Crown responsible for insurance companies,

    (b) under subsection (1)(b) [*repealed*] without consulting the Chief Registrar of Friendly Societies,

    c) under subsection (1)(d) without consulting the Charity Commissioners, or

    d) under subsection (1)(e), (f) or (ff) without consulting any Minister of the Crown with responsibilities concerning the body in question, or

    e) under subsection (1)(g) without consulting the Building Societies Commission and the Treasury, or

    f) under subsection (1)(h) without consulting the Treasury and the Bank of England.

(4) An order under subsection (1) relating to a body may be limited so as to apply only to agreements by that body of a description specified in the order.

(5) The Secretary of State may by order provide that this Act shall not regulate other consumer credit agreements where—

    (a) the number of payments to be made by the debtor does not exceed the number specified for that purpose in the order, or

    (b) the rate of the total charge for credit does not exceed the rate so specified, or

    (c) an agreement has a connection with a country outside the United Kingdom.

(6) The Secretary of State may by order provide that this Act shall not regulate consumer hire agreements of a description specified in the order where—

    (a) the owner is a body corporate authorised by or under any enactment to supply electricity, gas or water, and

    (b) the subject of the agreement is a meter or metering equipment,

or where the owner is a public telecommunications office specified in the order.

(6A) This Act does not regulate a consumer credit agreement where the creditor is a housing authority and the agreement is secured by a land mortgage of a dwelling.

(6B) In subsection (6A) "housing authority" means—

    (a) as regards England and Wales, the Housing Corporation, Housing for

Wales and an authority or body within section 80(1) of the Housing Act 1985 (the landlord condition for secure tenancies), other than a housing association or a housing trust which is a charity;

(b) as regards Scotland, a development corporation established under an order made, or having effect as if made under the New Towns (Scotland) Act 1968, the Scottish Special Housing Association or the Housing Corporation;

(c) as regards Northern Ireland, the Northern Ireland Housing Executive.

(7) Nothing in this section affects the application of sections 137 to 140 (extortionate credit bargains).

(8) In the application of this section to Scotland subsection (3)(c) shall not have effect.

(9) In the application of this section to Northern Ireland subsection (3) shall have effect as if any reference to a Minister of the Crown were a reference to a Northern Ireland department, any reference to the Chief Registrar of Friendly Societies were a reference to the Registrar of Friendly Societies for Northern Ireland, and any reference to the Charity Commissioners were a reference to the Department of Finance for Northern Ireland.

Small agreements

17.— (1) A small agreement is—

(a) a regulated consumer credit agreement for credit not exceeding £50, other than a hire-purchase or conditional sale agreement; or

(b) a regulated consumer hire agreement which does not require the hirer to make payments exceeding £50,

being an agreement which is either unsecured or secured by a guarantee or indemnity only (whether or not the guarantee or indemnity is itself secured).

(2) Section 10(3)(a) applies for the purposes of subsection (1) as it applies for the purposes of section 8(2).

(3) Where—

(a) two or more small agreements are made at or about the same time between the same parties, and

(b) it appears probable that they would instead have been made as a single agreement but for the desire to avoid the operation of provisions of this Act which would have applied to that single agreement but, apart from this subsection, are not applicable to the small agreements,

this Act applies to the small agreements as if they were regulated agreements other than small agreements.

(4) If, apart from this subsection, subsection (3) does not apply to any agreements but would apply if, for any party or parties to any of the agreements, there were substituted an associate of that party, or associates of each of those parties, as the case may be, then subsection (3) shall apply to the agreements.

Multiple agreements

18.—(1) This section applies to an agreement (a "multiple agreement") if its terms are such as—

(a) to place a part of it within one category of agreement mentioned in this Act, and another part of it within a different category of agreement so mentioned, or within a category of agreement not so mentioned, or

(b) to place it, or a part of it, within two or more categories of agreement so mentioned.

(2) Where a part of an agreement falls within subsection (1), that part shall be treated for the purposes of this Act as a separate agreement.

(3) Where an agreement falls within subsection (1)(b), it shall be treated as an agreement in each of the categories in question, and this Act shall apply to it accordingly.

(4) Where under subsection (2) a part of a multiple agreement is to be treated as a separate agreement, the multiple agreement shall (with any necessary modifications) be construed accordingly; and any sum payable under the multiple agreement, if not apportioned by the parties, shall for the purposes of proceedings in any court relating to the multiple agreement be apportioned by the court as may be requisite.

(5) In the case of an agreement for running-account credit, a term of the agreement allowing the credit limit to be exceeded merely temporarily shall not be treated as a separate agreement or as providing fixed-sum credit in respect of the excess.

(6) This Act does not apply to a multiple agreement so far as the agreement relates to goods if under the agreement payments are to be made in respect of the goods in the form of rent (other than a rentcharge) issuing out of land.

Linked transactions

19.—(1) A transaction entered into by the debtor or hirer, or a relative of his, with any other person ("the other party"), except one for the provision of security, is a linked transaction in relation to an actual or prospective regulated agreement (the "principal agreement") of which it does not form part if—

(a) the transaction is entered into in compliance with a term of the principal agreement; or

(b) the principal agreement is a debtor-creditor-supplier agreement and the transaction is financed, or to be financed, by the principal agreement; or

(c) the other party is a person mentioned in subsection (2), and a person so mentioned initiated the transaction by suggesting it to the debtor or hirer, or his relative, who enters into it—

(i) to induce the creditor or owner to enter into the principal agreement, or

(ii) for another purpose related to the principal agreement, or

(iii) where the principal agreement is a restricted-use credit agreement, for a purpose related to a transaction financed, or to be financed, by the principal agreement.

(2) The persons referred to in subsection (1)(c) are—

(a) the creditor or owner, or his associate;

(b) a person who, in the negotiation of the transaction, is represented by a credit-broker who is also a negotiator in antecedent negotiations for the principal agreement;

(c) a person who, at the time the transaction is initiated, knows that the principal agreement has been made or contemplates that it might be made.

(3) A linked transaction entered into before the making of the principal agreement has no effect until such time (if any) as that agreement is made.

(4) Regulations may exclude linked transactions of the prescribed description from the operation of subsection (3).

Total charge for credit

20.—(1) The Secretary of State shall make regulations containing such provisions as appear to him appropriate for determining the true cost to the debtor of the credit provided or to be provided under an actual or prospective consumer credit agreement (the "total charge for credit"), and regulations so made shall prescribe—

    (a) what items are to be treated as entering into the total charge for credit, and how their amount is to be ascertained;

    (b) the method of calculating the rate of the total charge for credit.

(2) Regulations under subsection (1) may provide for the whole or part of the amount payable by the debtor or his relative under any linked transaction to be included in the total charge for credit, whether or not the creditor is a party to the transaction or derives benefit from it.

PART III

LICENSING OF CREDIT AND HIRE BUSINESSES

Licensing principles

Businesses needing a licence

21.—(1) Subject to this section, a licence is required to carry on a consumer credit business or consumer hire business.

(2) A local authority does not need a licence to carry on a business.

(3) A body corporate empowered by a public general Act naming it to carry on a business does not need a licence to do so.

Standard and group licences

22.—(1) A licence may be—

    (a) a standard licence, that is a licence, issued by the Director to a person named in the licence on an application made by him, which, during the prescribed period, covers such activities as are described in the licence, or

    (b) a group licence, that is a licence, issued by the Director (whether on the application of any person or of his own motion), which, during such period as the Director thinks fit or, if he thinks fit, indefinitely, covers such persons and activities as are described in the licence.

(2) A licence is not assignable or, subject to section 37, transmissible on death or in any other way.

(3) Except in the case of a partnership or an unincorporated body of persons, a standard licence shall not be issued to more than one person.

(4) A standard licence issued to a partnership or an unincorporated body of persons shall be issued in the name of the partnership or body.

(5) The Director may issue a group licence only if it appears to him that the public interest is better served by doing so than by obliging the persons concerned to apply separately for standard licences.

(6) The persons covered by a group licence may be described by general words, whether or not coupled with the exclusion of named persons, or in any other way the Director thinks fit.

(7) The fact that a person is covered by a group licence in respect of certain activities does not prevent a standard licence being issued to him in respect of those activities or any of them.

(8) A group licence issued on the application of any person shall be issued to that person, and general notice shall be given of the issue of any group licence (whether on application or not).

Authorisation of specific activities

23.—(1) Subject to this section, a licence to carry on a business covers all lawful activities done in the course of that business, whether by the licensee or other persons on his behalf.

(2) A licence may limit the activities it covers, whether by authorising the licensee to enter into certain types of agreement only, or in any other way.

(3) A licence covers the canvassing off trade premises of debtor-creditor-supplier agreements or regulated consumer hire agreements only if, and to the extent that, the licence specifically so provides; and such provision shall not be included in a group licence.

(4) Regulations may be made specifying other activities which, if engaged in by or on behalf of the person carrying on a business, require to be covered by an express term in his licence.

Control of name of business

24. A standard licence authorises the licensee to carry on a business under the name or names specified in the licence, but not under any other name.

Licensee to be a fit person

25.—(1) A standard licence shall be granted on the application of any person if he satisfies the Director that—

(a) he is a fit person to engage in activities covered by the licence, and

(b) the name or names under which he applies to be licensed is or are not misleading or otherwise undesirable.

(2) In determining whether an applicant for a standard licence is a fit person to engage in any activities, the Director shall have regard to any circumstances appearing to him to be relevant, and in particular any evidence tending to show that the applicant, or any of the applicant's employees, agents or associates (whether past or present) or, where the applicant is a body corporate, any person appearing to the Director to be a controller of the body corporate or an associate of any such person, has—

(a) committed any offence involving fraud or other dishonesty, or violence,

(b) contravened any provision made by or under this Act, or by or under any other enactment regulating the provision of credit to individuals or other transactions with individuals,

(c) practised discrimination on grounds of sex, colour, race or ethnic or national origins in, or in connection with, the carrying on of any business, or

(d) engaged in business practices appearing to the Director to be deceitful or oppressive, or otherwise unfair or improper (whether unlawful or not).

(3) In subsection (2), "associate", in addition to the persons specified in section 184, includes a business associate.

Conduct of business

26.—Regulations may be made as to the conduct by a licensee of his business, and may in particular specify—

(a) the books and other records to be kept by him, and

(b) the information to be furnished by him to persons with whom he does business or seeks to do business, and the way it is to be furnished.

Issue of licences

Determination of applications

27.—(1) Unless the Director determines to issue a licence in accordance with an application he shall, before determining the application, by notice—

(a) inform the applicant, giving his reasons, that, as the case may be, he is minded to refuse the application, or to grant it in terms different from those applied for describing them, and

(b) invite the applicant to submit to the Director representations in support of his application in accordance with section 34.

(2) If the Director grants the application in terms different from those applied for then, whether or not the applicant appeals, the Director shall issue the licence in the terms approved by him unless the applicant by notice informs him that he does not desire a licence in those terms.

Exclusion from group licence

28. Where the Director is minded to issue a group licence (whether on the application of any person or not), and in doing so to exclude any person from the group by name, he shall, before determining the matter,—

(a) give notice of that fact to the person proposed to be excluded, giving his reasons, and

(b) invite that person to submit to the Director representations against his exclusion in accordance with section 34.

Renewal, variation, suspension and revocation of licences

Renewal

29.—(1) If the licensee under a standard licence, or the original applicant for, or any licensee under, a group licence of limited duration, wishes the Director to renew the licence, whether on the same terms (except as to expiry) or on varied terms, he must, during the period specified by the Director by general notice or such longer period as the Director may allow, make an application to the Director for its renewal.

(2) The Director may of his own motion renew any group licence.

(3) The preceding provisions of this Part apply to the renewal of a licence as they apply to the issue of a licence, except that section 28 does not apply to a person who was already excluded in the licence up for renewal.

(4) Until the determination of an application under subsection (1) and, where an appeal lies from the determination, until the end of the appeal period, the licence shall continue in force, notwithstanding that apart from this subsection it would expire earlier.

(5) On the refusal of an application under this section, the Director may give directions authorising a licensee to carry into effect agreements made by him before the expiry of the licence.

(6) General notice shall be given of the renewal of a group licence.

Variation by request

30.—(1) On an application made by the licensee, the Director may if he thinks fit by notice to the licensee vary a standard licence in accordance with the application.

(2) In the case of a group licence issued on the application of any person, the Director, on an application made by that person, may if he thinks fit by

notice to that person vary the terms of the licence in accordance with the application; but the Director shall not vary a group licence under this subsection by excluding a named person, other than the person making the request, unless that named person consents in writing to his exclusion.

(3) In the case of a group licence from which (whether by name or description) a person is excluded, the Director, on an application made by that person, may if he thinks fit, by notice to that person, vary the terms of the licence so as to remove the exclusion.

(4) Unless the Director determines to vary a licence in accordance with an application he shall, before determining the application, by notice—

    (a) inform the applicant, giving his reasons, that he is minded to refuse the application, and

    (b) invite the applicant to submit to the Director representations in support of his application in accordance with section 34.

(5) General notice shall be given that a variation of a group licence has been made under this section.

Compulsory variation

31.—(1) Where at a time during the currency of a licence the Director is of the opinion that, if the licence had expired at that time, he would on an application for its renewal or futher renewal on the same terms (except as to expiry), have been minded to grant the application but on different terms, and that therefore the licence should be varied, he shall proceed as follows.

(2) In the case of a standard licence the Director shall, by notice—

    (a) inform the licensee of the variations the Director is minded to make in the terms of the licence, stating his reasons, and

    (b) invite him to submit to the Director representations as to the proposed variations in accordance with section 34.

(3) In the case of a group licence the Director shall—

    (a) give general notice of the variations he is minded to make in the terms of the licence, stating his reasons, and

    (b) in the notice invite any licensee to submit to him representations as to the proposed variations in accordance with section 34.

(4) In the case of a group licence issued on application the Director shall also—

    (a) inform the original applicant of the variations the Director is minded to make in the terms of the licence, stating his reasons, and

    (b) invite him to submit to the Director representations as to the proposed variations in accordance with section 34.

(5) If the Director is minded to vary a group licence by excluding any person (other than the original applicant) from the group by name the Director shall, in addition, take the like steps under section 28 as are required in the case mentioned in that section.

(6) General notice shall be given that a variation of any group licence has been made under this section.

(7) A variation under this section shall not take effect before the end of the appeal period.

Suspension and revocation

32.—(1) Where at a time during the currency of a licence the Director is of the opinion that if the licence had expired at that time he would have been minded not to renew it, and that therefore it should be revoked or suspended, he shall proceed as follows.

(2) In the case of a standard licence the Director shall, by notice—

    (a) inform the licensee that, as the case may be, the Director is minded to revoke the licence, or suspend it until a specified date or indefinitely, stating his reasons, and

    (b) invite him to submit representations as to the proposed revocation or suspension in accordance with section 34.

(3) In the case of a group licence the Director shall—

    (a) give general notice that, as the case may be, he is minded to revoke the licence, or suspend it until a specified date or indefinitely, stating his reasons, and

    (b) in the notice invite any licensee to submit to him representations as to proposed revocation or suspension in accordance with section 34.

(4) In the case of a group licence issued on application the Director shall also—

    (a) inform the original applicant that, as the case may be, the Director is minded to revoke the licence, or suspend it until a specified date or indefinitely, stating his reasons, and

    (b) invite him to submit representations as to the proposed revocation or suspension in accordance with section 34.

(5) If he revokes or suspends the licence, the Director may give directions authorising a licensee to carry into effect agreements made by him before the revocation or suspension.

(6) General notice shall be given of the revocation or suspension of a group licence.

(7) A revocation or suspension under this section shall not take effect before the end of the appeal period.

(8) Except for the purposes of section 29, a licensee under a suspended licence shall be treated, in respect of the period of suspension, as if the licence had not been issued; and where the suspension is not expressed to end on a specified date it may, if the Director thinks fit, be ended by notice given by him to the licensee or, in the case of a group licence, by general notice.

Application to end suspension

33.—(1) On an application made by a licensee the Director may, if he thinks fit, by notice to the licensee end the suspension of a licence, whether the suspension was for a fixed or indefinite period.

(2) Unless the Director determines to end the suspension in accordance with the application he shall, before determining the application, by notice—

    (a) inform the applicant, giving his reasons, that he is minded to refuse the application, and

    (b) invite the applicant to submit to the Director representations in support of his application in accordance with section 34.

(3) General notice shall be given that a suspension of a group licence has been ended under this section.

(4) In the case of a group licence issued on application—

    (a) the references in subsection (1) to a licensee include the original applicant;

    (b) the Director shall inform the original applicant that a suspension of a group licence has been ended under this section.

Miscellaneous

Representations to Director

34.—(1) Where this section applies to an invitation by the Director to any person to submit representations, the Director shall invite that person, within 21 days after the notice containing the invitation is given to him or published, or such longer period as the Director may allow—

(a) to submit his representations in writing to the Director, and

(b) to give notice to the Director, if he thinks fit, that he wishes to make representations orally,

and where notice is given under paragraph (b) the Director shall arrange for the oral representations to be heard.

(2) In reaching his determination the Director shall take into account any representations submitted or made under this section.

(3) The Director shall give notice of his determination to the persons who were required to be invited to submit representations about it or, where the invitation to submit representations was required to be given by general notice, shall give general notice of the determination.

The register

35.—(1) The Director shall establish and maintain a register, in which he shall cause to be kept particulars of—

(a) applications not yet determined for the issue, variation or renewal of licences, or for ending the suspension of a licence;

(b) licences which are in force, or have at any time been suspended or revoked, with details of any variation of the terms of a licence;

(c) decisions given by him under this Act, and any appeal from those decisions; and

(d) such other matters (if any) as he thinks fit.

(2) The Director shall give general notice of the various matters required to be entered in the register, and of any change in them made under subsection (1)(d).

(3) Any person shall be entitled on payment of the specified fee—

(a) to inspect the register during ordinary office hours and take copies of any entry, or

(b) to obtain from the Director a copy, certified by the Director to be correct, of any entry in the register.

(4) The Director may, if he thinks fit, determine that the right conferred by subsection (3)(a) shall be exercisable in relation to a copy of the register instead of, or in addition to, the original.

(5) The Director shall give general notice of the place or places where, and times when, the register or a copy of it may be inspected.

Duty to notify changes

36.—(1) Within 21 working days after change takes place in any particulars entered in the register in respect of a standard licence or the licensee under section 35(1)(d) (not being a change resulting from action taken by the Director), the licensee shall give the Director notice of the change; and the Director shall cause any necessary amendment to be made in the register.

(2) Within 21 working days after—

(a) any change takes place in the officers of—

        (i) a body corporate, or an unincorporated body of persons, which is the licensee under a standard licence, or

        (ii) a body corporate which is a controller of a body corporate which is such a licensee, or

    (b) a body corporate which is such a licensee becomes aware that a person has become or ceased to be a controller of the body corporate, or

    (c) any change takes place in the members of a partnership which is such a licensee (including a change on the amalgamation of the partnership with another firm, or a change whereby the number of partners is reduced to one), the licensee shall give the Director notice of the change.

(3) Within 14 working days after any change takes place in the officers of a body corporate which is a controller of another body corporate which is a licensee under a standard licence, the controller shall give the licensee notice of the change.

(4) Within 14 working days after a person becomes or ceases to be a controller of a body corporate which is a licensee under a standard licence, that person shall give the licensee notice of the fact.

(5) Where a change in a partnership has the result that the business ceases to be carried on under the name, or any of the names, specified in a standard licence the licence shall cease to have effect.

(6) Where the Director is given notice under sub-section (1) or (2) of any change, and subsection (5) does not apply, the Director may by notice require the licensee to furnish him with such information, verified in such manner, as the Director may stipulate.

Death, bankruptcy etc. of licensee

    37.—(1) A licence held by one individual terminates if he—

    (a) dies, or

    (b) is adjudged bankrupt, or

    (c) becomes a patient within the meaning of Part VIII of the Mental Health Act 1959.

(2) In relation to a licence held by one individual, or a partnership or other unincorporated body of persons, or a body corporate, regulations may specify other events relating to the licensee on the occurrence of which the licence is to terminate.

(3) Regulations may—

    (a) provide for the termination of a licence by subsection (1), or under subsection (2), to be deferred for a period not exceeding 12 months, and

    (b) authorise the business of the licensee to be carried on under the licence by some other person during the period of deferment, subject to such conditions as may be prescribed.

(4) This section does not apply to group licences.

Application of s. 37 to Scotland and Northern Ireland

    38.—(1) In the application of section 37 to Scotland the following shall be substituted for paragraphs (b) and (c) of subsection (1)—

    "(b) has his estate sequestrated, or

    (c) becomes incapable of managing his own affairs."

(2) In the application of section 37 to Northern Ireland the following shall be substituted for subsection (1)—

"(1) A licence held by one individual terminates if—
- (a) he dies, or
- (b) he is adjudged bankrupt or his estate and effects vest in the official assignee under section 349 of the Irish Bankrupt and Insolvent Act 1857, or
- (c) a declaration is made under section 15 of the Lunacy Regulation (Ireland) Act 1871 that he is of unsound mind and incapable of managing his person or property, or an order is made under section 68 of that Act in consequence of its being found that he is of unsound mind and incapable of managing his affairs.".

Offences against Part III

39.—(1) A person who engages in any activities for which a licence is required when he is not a licensee under a licence covering those activities commits an offence.

(2) A licensee under a standard licence who carries on business under a name not specified in the licence commits an offence.

(3) A person who fails to give the Director or a licensee notice under section 36 within the period required commits an offence.

Enforcement of agreements made by unlicensed trader

40.—(1) A regulated agreement, other than a non-commercial agreement, if made when the creditor or owner was unlicensed, is enforceable against the debtor or hirer only where the Director has made an order under this section which applies to the agreement.

(2) Where during any period an unlicensed person (the "trader") was carrying on a consumer credit business or consumer hire business, he or his successor in title may apply to the Director for an order that regulated agreements made by the trader during that period are to be treated as if he had been licensed.

(3) Unless the Director determines to make an order under subsection (2) in accordance with the application, he shall, before determining the application, by notice—
- (a) inform the applicant, giving his reasons, that, as the case may be, he is minded to refuse the application, or to grant it in terms different from those applied for, describing them, and
- (b) invite the applicant to submit to the Director representations in support of his application in accordance with section 34.

(4) In determining whether or not to make an order under subsection (2) in respect of any period the Director shall consider, in addition to any other relevant factors—
- (a) how far, if at all, debtors or hirers under regulated agreements made by the trader during that period were prejudiced by the trader's conduct,
- (b) whether or not the Director would have been likely to grant a licence covering that period on an application by the trader, and
- (c) the degree of culpability for the failure to obtain a licence.

(5) If the Director thinks fit, he may in an order under subsection (2)—
- (a) limit the order to specified agreements, or agreements of a specified description or made at a specified time;
- (b) make the order conditional on the doing of specified acts by the applicant.

Appeals to Secretary of State under Part III

41.—(1) If, in the case of a determination by the Director such as is mentioned in column 1 of the table set out at the end of this section, a person mentioned in relation to that determination in column 2 of the table is aggrieved by the determination he may, within the prescribed period, and in the prescribed manner, appeal to the Secretary of State.

(2) Regulations may make provision as to the persons by whom (on behalf of the Secretary of State) appeals under this section are to be heard, the manner in which they are to be conducted, and any other matter connected with such appeals.

(3) On an appeal under this section, the Secretary of State may give such directions for disposing of the appeal as he thinks just, including a direction for the payment of costs by any party to the appeal.

(4) A direction under subsection (3) for payment of costs may be made a rule of the High Court on the application of the party in whose favour it is given.

(5) in Scotland a direction under subsection (3) for payment of expenses may be enforced in like manner as a recorded decree arbitral.

TABLE[2]

Determination	*Appellant*
Refusal to issue, renew or vary licence in accordance with terms of application.	The applicant.
Exclusion of person from group licence.	The person excluded.
Refusal to give directions in respect of a licensee under section 29(5) or 32(5).	The licensee.
Compulsory variation, or suspension or revocation, of standard licence.	The original applicant or any licensee.
Refusal to end suspension of licence in accordance with terms of application.	The applicant.
Refusal to make order under section 40(2) in accordance with terms of application.	The applicant.

42. [*Repealed*]

PART IV

SEEKING BUSINESS

Advertising

Advertisements to which Part IV applies

43.—(1) This Part applies to any advertisement, published for the purposes of a carried on by the advertiser, indicating that he is willing—

---

[2] For a further entry to the Table, cf. s. 150; and note that S.I. 1992 No. 3218 (not reproduced here) has effect as if the Table had two further entries, *viz.*:

Determination	*Appellant*
Imposition of a prohibition or restriction or the variation of a restriction.	The European institution concerned.
Refusal of an application for the revocation of a prohibition or restriction.	The European institution concerned.

(a) to provide credit, or

(b) to enter into an agreement for the bailment or (in Scotland) the hiring of goods by him.

(2) An advertisement does not fall within subsection (1) if the advertiser does not carry on—

(a) a consumer credit business or consumer hire business, or

(b) a business in the course of which he provides credit to individuals secured on land, or

(c) a business which comprises or relates to unregulated agreements where—

(i) the law applicable to the agreement is the law of a country outside the United Kingdom, and

(ii) if the law applicable to the agreement were the law of a part of the United Kingdom it would be a regulated agreement.

(3) An advertisement does not fall within subsection (1)(a) if it indicates—

(a) that the credit must exceed £15,000, and that no security is required, or the security is to consist of property other than land, or

(b) that the credit is available only to a body corporate.

(4) An advertisement does not fall within subsection (1)(b) if it indicates that the advertiser is not willing to enter into a consumer hire agreement.

(5) The Secretary of State may by order provide that this Part shall not apply to other advertisements of a description specified in the order.

Form and content of advertisements

44.—(1) The Secretary of State shall make regulations as to the form and content of advertisements to which this Part applies, and the regulations shall contain such provisions as appear to him appropriate with a view to ensuring that, having regard to its subject-matter and the amount of detail included in it, an advertisement conveys a fair and reasonably comprehensive indication of the nature of the credit or hire facilities offered by the advertiser and of their true cost to persons using them.

(2) Regulations under subsection (1) may in particular—

(a) require specified information to be included in the prescribed manner in advertisements, and other specified material to be excluded;

(b) contain requirements to ensure that specified information is clearly brought to the attention of persons to whom advertisements are directed, and that one part of an advertisement is not given insufficient or excessive prominence compared with another.

Prohibition of advertisement where goods etc. not sold for cash

45. If an advertisement to which this Part applies indicates that the advertiser is willing to provide credit under a restricted-use credit agreement relating to goods or services to be supplied by any person, but at the time when the advertisement is published that person is not holding himself out as prepared to sell the goods or provide the services (as the case may be) for cash, the advertiser commits an offence.

False or misleading advertisements

46.—(1) If an advertisement to which this Part applies conveys information which in a material respect is false or misleading the advertiser commits an offence.

(2) Information stating or implying an intention on the advertiser's part which he has not got is false.

Advertising infringements

47.—(1) Where an advertiser commits an offence against regulations made under section 44 or against section 45 or 46 or would be taken to commit such an offence but for the defence provided by section 168, a like offence is committed by—

    (a) the publisher of the advertisement, and

    (b) any person who, in the course of a business carried on by him, devised the advertisement, or a part of it relevant to the first-mentioned offence, and

    (c) where the advertiser did not procure the publication of the advertisement, the person who did procure it.

(2) In proceedings for an offence under subsection (1)(a) it is a defence for the person charged to prove that—

    (a) the advertisement was published in the course of a business carried on by him, and

    (b) he received the advertisement in the course of that business, and did not know and had no reason to suspect that its publication would be an offence under this Part.

Canvassing, etc.

Definition of canvassing off trade premises (regulated agreements)

48.—(1) An individual (the "canvasser") canvasses a regulated agreement off trade premises if he solicits the entry (as debtor or hirer) of another individual (the "consumer") into the agreement by making oral representations to the consumer, or any other individual, during a visit by the canvasser to any place (not excluded by subsection (2)) where the consumer, or that other individual, as the case may be, is, being a visit—

    (a) carried out for the purpose of making such oral representations to individuals who are at that place, but

    (b) not carried out in response to a request made on a previous occasion.

(2) A place is excluded from subsection (1) if it is a place where a business is carried on (whether on a permanent or temporary basis) by—

    (a) the creditor or owner, or

    (b) a supplier, or

    (c) the canvasser, or the person whose employee or agent the canvasser is, or

    (d) the consumer.

Prohibition of canvassing debtor-creditor agreements off trade premises

49.—(1) It is an offence to canvass debtor-creditor agreements off trade premises.

(2) It is also an offence to solicit the entry of an individual (as debtor) into a debtor-creditor agreement during a visit carried out in response to a request made on a previous occasion, where—

    (a) the request was not in writing signed by or on behalf of the person making it, and

    (b) if no request for the visit had been made, the soliciting would have constituted the canvassing of a debtor-creditor agreement off trade premises.

(3) Subsections (1) and (2) do not apply to any soliciting for an agreement enabling the debtor to overdraw on a current account of any description kept with the creditor, where—

(a) the Director has determined that current accounts of that description kept with the creditor are excluded from subsections (1) and (2), and

(b) the debtor already keeps an account with the creditor (whether a current account or not).

(4) A determination under subsection (3)(a)—

(a) may be made subject to such conditions as the Director thinks fit, and

(b) shall be made only where the Director is of opinion that it is not against the interests of debtors.

(5) If soliciting is done in breach of a condition imposed under subsection (4)(a), the determination under subsection (3)(a) does not apply to it.

Circulars to minors

50.—(1) A person commits an offence who, with a view to financial gain, sends to a minor any document inviting him to—

(a) borrow money, or

(b) obtain goods on credit or hire, or

(c) obtain services on credit, or

(d) apply for information or advice on borrowing money or otherwise obtaining credit, or hiring goods.

(2) In proceedings under subsection (1) in respect of the sending of a document to a minor, it is a defence for the person charged to prove that he did not know, and had no reasonable cause to suspect, that he was a minor.

(3) Where a document is received by a minor at any school or other educational establishment for minors, a person sending it to him at that establishment knowing or suspecting it to be such an establishment shall be taken to have reasonable cause to suspect that he is a minor.

Prohibition of unsolicited credit-tokens

51.—(1) It is an offence to give a person a credit-token if he has not asked for it.

(2) To comply with subsection (1) a request must be contained in a document signed by the person making the request, unless the credit-token agreement is a small debtor-creditor-supplier agreement.

(3) Subsection (1) does not apply to the giving of a credit-token to a person—

(a) for use under a credit-token agreement already made, or

(b) in renewal or replacement of a credit-token previously accepted by him under a credit-token agreement which continues in force, whether or not varied.

Miscellaneous

Quotations

52.—(1) Regulations may be made—

(a) as to the form and content of any document (a "quotation") by which a person who carries on a consumer credit business or consumer hire business, or a business in the course of which he provides credit to individuals secured on land, gives prospective customers information about the terms on which he is prepared to do business;

(b) requiring a person carrying on such a business to provide quotations to such persons and in such circumstances as are prescribed.

(2) Regulations under subsection (1)(a) may in particular contain provisions relating to quotations such as are set out in relation to advertisements in section 44.

Duty to display information

53. Regulations may require a person who carries on a consumer credit business or consumer hire business, or a business in the course of which he provides credit to individuals secured on land, to display in the prescribed manner, at any premises where the business is carried on to which the public have access, prescribed information about the business.

Conduct of business regulations

54. Without prejudice to the generality of section 26, regulations under that section may include provisions further regulating the seeking of business by a licensee who carries on a consumer credit business or a consumer hire business.

PART V

ENTRY INTO CREDIT OR HIRE AGREEMENTS

Preliminary matters

Disclosure of information

55.—(1) Regulations may require specified information to be disclosed in the prescribed manner to the debtor or hirer before a regulated agreement is made.

(2) A regulated agreement is not properly executed unless regulations under subsection (1) were complied with before the making of the agreement.

Antecedent negotiations

56.—(1) In this Act "antecedent negotiations" means any negotiations with the debtoror hirer—

(a) conducted by the creditor or owner in relation to the making of any regulated agreement, or

(b) conducted by a credit-broker in relation to goods sold or proposed to be sold by the credit-broker to the creditor before forming the subject-matter of a debtor-creditor-supplier agreement within section 12(a), or

(c) conducted by the supplier in relation to a transaction financed or proposed to be financed by a debtor-creditor-supplier agreement within section 12(b) or (c),

and "negotiator" means the person by whom negotiations are so conducted with the debtor or hirer.

(2) Negotiations with the debtor in a case falling within subsection (1)(b) or (c) shall be deemed to be conducted by the negotiator in the capacity of agent of the creditor as well as in his actual capacity.

(3) An agreement is void if, and to the extent that, it purports in relation to an actual or prospective regulated agreement—

(a) to provide that a person acting as, or on behalf of, a negotiator is to be treated as the agent of the debtor or hirer, or

(b) to relieve a person from liability for acts or omissions of any p
        acting as, or on behalf of, a negotiator.

(4) For the purposes of this Act, antecedent negotiations shall be taken to
begin when the negotiator and the debtor or hirer first enter into communication
(including communication by advertisement), and to include any representations
made by the negotiator to the debtor or hirer and any other dealings between
them.

Withdrawal from prospective agreement

57.—(1) The withdrawal of a party from a prospective regulated agreement
shall operate to apply this Part to the agreement, any linked transaction and any
other thing done in anticipation of the making of the agreement as it would
apply if the agreement were made and then cancelled under section 69.

(2) The giving to a party of a written or oral notice which, however expressed,
indicates the intention of the other party to withdraw from a prospective regulated agreement operates as a withdrawal from it.

(3) Each of the following shall be deemed to be the agent of the creditor or
owner for the purpose of receiving a notice under subsection (2)—
    (a) a credit-broker or supplier who is the negotiator in antecedent negoti-
        ations, and
    (b) any person who, in the course of a business carried on by him, acts
        on behalf of the debtor or hirer in any negotiations for the agreement.

(4) Where the agreement, if made, would not be a cancellable agreement,
subsection (1) shall nevertheless apply as if the contrary were the case.

Opportunity for withdrawal from prospective land mortgage

58.—(1) Before sending to the debtor or hirer, for his signature, an unexecuted
agreement in a case where the prospective regulated agreement is to be secured
on land (the "mortgaged land"), the creditor or owner shall give the debtor or
hirer a copy of the unexecuted agreement which contains a notice in the prescribed form indicating the right of the debtor or hirer to withdraw from the
prospective agreement, and how and when the right is exercisable, together with
a copy of any other document referred to in the unexecuted agreement.

(2) Subsection (1) does not apply to—
    (a) a restricted-use credit agreement to finance the purchase of the mort-
        gaged land, or
    (b) an agreement for a bridging loan in connection with the purchase of
        the mortgaged land or other land.

Agreement to enter future agreement void

59.—(1) An agreement is void if, and to the extent that, it purports to bind
a person to enter as debtor or hirer into a prospective regulated agreement.

(2) Regulations may exclude from the operation of subsection (1) agreements
such as are described in the regulations.

Making the agreement

Form and content of agreements

60.—(1) The Secretary of State shall make regulations as to the form and
content of documents embodying regulated agreements, and the regulations shall
contain such provisions as appear to him appropriate with a view to ensuring
that the debtor or hirer is made aware of—

>   (a) the rights and duties conferred or imposed on him by the agreement,
>   (b) the amount and rate of the total charge for credit (in the case of a consumer credit agreement),
>   (c) the protection and remedies available to him under this Act, and
>   (d) any other matters which, in the opinion of the Secretary of State, it is desirable for him to know about in connection with the agreement.

(2) Regulations under subsection (1) may in particular—

   (a) require specified information to be included in the prescribed manner in documents, and other specified material to be excluded;

   (b) contain requirements to ensure that specified information is clearly brought to the attention of the debtor or hirer, and that one part of a document is not given insufficient or excessive prominence compared with another.

(3) If, on an application made to the Director by a person carrying on a consumer credit business or a consumer hire business, it appears to the Director impracticable for the applicant to comply with any requirement of regulations under subsection (1) in a particular case, he may, by notice to the applicant direct that the requirement be waived or varied in relation to such agreements, and subject to such conditions (if any), as he may specify, and this Act and the regulations shall have effect accordingly.

(4) The Director shall give a notice under subsection (3) only if he is satisfied that to do so would not prejudice the interests of debtors or hirers.

Signing of agreement

   61.—(1) A regulated agreement is not properly executed unless—

   (a) a document in the prescribed form itself containing all the prescribed terms and conforming to regulations under section 60(1) is signed in the prescribed manner both by the debtor or hirer and by or on behalf of the creditor or owner, and

   (b) the document embodies all the terms of the agreement, other than implied terms, and

   (c) the document is, when presented or sent to the debtor or hirer for signature, in such a state that all its terms are readily legible.

(2) In addition, where the agreement is one to which section 58(1) applies, it is not properly executed unless—

   (a) the requirements of section 58(1) were complied with, and

   (b) the unexecuted agreement was sent, for his signature, to the debtor or hirer by post not less than seven days after a copy of it was given to him under section 58(1), and

   (c) during the consideration period, the creditor or owner refrained from approaching the debtor or hirer (whether in person, by telephone or letter, or in any other way) except in response to a specific request made by the debtor or hirer after the beginning of the consideration period, and

   (d) no notice of withdrawal by the debtor or hirer was received by the creditor or owner before the sending of the unexecuted agreement.

(3) In subsection (2)(c), "the consideration period" means the period beginning with the giving of the copy under section 58(1) and ending—

   (a) at the expiry of seven days after the day on which the unexecuted agreement is sent, for his signature, to the debtor or hirer, or

   (b) on its return by the debtor or hirer after signature by him,

whichever first occurs.

(4) Where the debtor or hirer is a partnership or an unincorporated body of persons, subsection (1)(a) shall apply with the substitution for "by the debtor or hirer" of "by or on behalf of the debtor or hirer"

Duty to supply copy of unexecuted agreement

62.—(1) If the unexecuted agreement is presented personally to the debtor or hirer for his signature, but on the occasion when he signs it the document does not become an executed agreement, a copy of it, and of any other document referred to in it, must be there and then delivered to him.

(2) If the unexecuted agreement is sent to the debtor or hirer for his signature, a copy of it, and of any other document referred to in it, must be sent to him at the same time.

(3) A regulated agreement is not properly executed if the requirements of this section are not observed.

Duty to supply copy of executed agreement

63.—(1) If the unexecuted agreement is presented personally to the debtor or hirer for his signature, and on the occasion when he signs it the document becomes an executed agreement, a copy of the executed agreement, and of any other document referred to in it, must be there and then delivered to him.

(2) A copy of the executed agreement, and of any other document referred to in it, must be given to the debtor or hirer within the seven days following the making of the agreement unless—

    (a) subsection (1) applies, or

    (b) the unexecuted agreement was sent to the debtor or hirer for his signature and, on the occasion of his signing it, the document became an executed agreement.

(3) In the case of a cancellable agreement, a copy under subsection (2) must be sent by post.

(4) In the case of a credit-token agreement, a copy under subsection (2) need not be given within the seven days following the making of the agreement if it is given before or at the time when the credit-token is given to the debtor.

(5) A regulated agreement is not properly executed if the requirements of this section are not observed.

Duty to give notice of cancellation rights

64.—(1) In the case of a cancellable agreement, a notice in the prescribed form indicating the right of the debtor or hirer to cancel the agreement, how and when that right is exercisable, and the name and address of a person to whom notice of cancellation may be given,—

    (a) must be included in every copy given to the debtor or hirer under section 62 or 63, and

    (b) except where section 63(2) applied, must also be sent by post to the debtor or hirer within the seven days following the making of the agreement.

(2) In the case of a credit-token agreement, a notice under subsection (1)(b) need not be sent by post within the seven days following the making of the agreement if either—

    (a) it is sent by post to the debtor or hirer before the credit-token is given to him, or

    (b) it is sent by post to him together with the credit-token.

(3) Regulations may provide that except where section 63(2) applied a notice

sent under subsection (1)(b) shall be accompanied by a further copy of the executed agreement, and of any other document referred to in it.

(4) Regulations may provide that subsection (1)(b) is not to apply in the case of agreements such as are described in the regulations, being agreements made by a particular person, if—

    (a) on an application by that person to the Director, the Director has determined that, having regard to—

        (i) the manner in which antecedent negotiations for agreements with the applicant of that description are conducted, and

        (ii) the information provided to debtors or hirers before such agreements are made,

      the requirement imposed by subsection (1)(b) can be dispensed with without prejudicing the interests of debtors or hirers; and

    (b) any conditions imposed by the Director in making the determination are complied with.

(5) A cancellable agreement is not properly executed if the requirements of this section are not observed.

Consequences of improper execution

65.—(1) An improperly-executed regulated agreement is enforceable against the debtor or hirer on an order of the court only.

(2) A retaking of goods or land to which a regulated agreement relates is an enforcement of the agreement.

Acceptance of credit-tokens

66.—(1) The debtor shall not be liable under a credit-token agreement for use made of the credit-token by any person unless the debtor had previously accepted the credit-token, or the use constituted an acceptance of it by him.

(2) The debtor accepts a credit-token when—

    (a) it is signed, or

    (b) a receipt for it is signed, or

    (c) it is first used,

either by the debtor himself or by a person who, pursuant to the agreement, is authorised by him to use it.

Cancellation of certain agreements within cooling-off period

Cancellable agreements

67. A regulated agreement may be cancelled by the debtor or hirer in accordance with this Part if the antecedent negotiations included oral representations made when in the presence of the debtor or hirer by an individual acting as, or on behalf of, the negotiator, unless—

    (a) the agreement is secured on land, or is a restricted-use credit agreement to finance the purchase of land or is an agreement for a bridging loan in connection with the purchase of land, or

    (b) the unexecuted agreement is signed by the debtor or hirer at premises at which any of the following is carrying on any business (whether on a permanent or temporary basis)—

      (i) the creditor or owner;

      (ii) any party to a linked transaction (other than the debtor or hirer or a relative of his);

      (iii) the negotiator in any antecedent negotiations.

Cooling-off period

68. The debtor or hirer may serve notice of cancellation of a cancellable agreement between his signing of the unexecuted agreement and—

    (a) the end of the fifth day following the day on which he received a copy under section 63(2) or a notice under section 64(1)(*b*), or

    (b) if (by virtue of regulations made under section 64(4), section 64(1)(b) does not apply, the end of the fourteenth day following the day on which he signed the unexecuted agreement.

Notice of cancellation

69.—(1) If within the period specified in section 68 the debtor or hirer under a cancellable agreement serves on—

    (a) the creditor or owner, or

    (b) the person specified in the notice under section 64(1), or

    (c) a person who (whether by virtue of subsection (6) or otherwise) is the agent of the creditor or owner,

a notice (a "notice of cancellation") which, however expressed and whether or not conforming to the notice given under section 64(1), indicates the intention of the debtor or hirer to withdraw from the agreement, the notice shall operate—

    (i) to cancel the agreement, and any linked transaction, and

    (ii) to withdraw any offer by the debtor or hirer, or his relative, to enter into a linked transaction.

(2) In the case of a debtor-creditor-supplier agreement for restricted-use credit financing—

    (a) the doing of work or supply of goods to meet an emergency, or

    (b) the supply of goods which, before service of the notice of cancellation, had by the act of the debtor or his relative become incorporated in any land or thing not comprised in the agreement or any linked transaction,

subsection (1) shall apply with the substitution of the following for paragraph (i)—

    "(i) to cancel only such provisions of the agreement and any linked transaction as—

        (aa) relate to the provision of credit, or

        (bb) require the debtor to pay an item in the total charge for credit, or

        (cc) subject the debtor to any obligation other than to pay for the doing of the said work, or the supply of the said goods".

(3) Except so far as is otherwise provided, references in this Act to the cancellation of an agreement or transaction do not include a case within subsection (2).

(4) Except as otherwise provided by or under this Act, an agreement or transaction cancelled under subsection (1) shall be treated as if it had never been entered into.

(5) Regulations may exclude linked transactions of the prescribed description from subsection (1)(i) or (ii).

(6) Each of the following shall be deemed to be the agent of the creditor or owner for the purpose of receiving a notice of cancellation—

    (a) a credit-broker or supplier who is the negotiator in antecedent negotiations, and

    (b) any person who, in the course of a business carried on by him, acts on behalf of the debtor or hirer in any negotiations for the agreement.

(7) Whether or not it is actually received by him, a notice of cancellation

sent by post to a person shall be deemed to be served on him at the time of posting.

Cancellation: recovery of money paid by debtor or hirer

70.—(1) On the cancellation of a regulated agreement, and of any linked transaction,—

(a) any sum paid by the debtor or hirer, or his relative, under or in contemplation of the agreement or transaction, including any item in the total charge for credit, shall become repayable, and

(b) any sum, including any item in the total charge for credit, which but for the cancellation is, or would or might become, payable by the debtor or hirer, or his relative, under the agreement or transaction shall cease to be, or shall not become, so payable, and

(c) in the case of a debtor-creditor-supplier agreement falling within section 12(b), any sum paid on the debtor's behalf by the creditor to the supplier shall become repayable to the creditor.

(2) If, under the terms of a cancelled agreement or transaction, the debtor or hirer, or his relative, is in possession of any goods, he shall have a lien on them for any sum repayable to him under subsection (1) in respect of that agreement or transaction, or any other linked transaction.

(3) A sum repayable under subsection (1) is repayable by the person to whom it was originally paid, but in the case of a debtor-creditor-supplier agreement falling within section 12(b) the creditor and the supplier shall be under a joint and several liability to repay sums paid by the debtor, or his relative, under the agreement or under a linked transaction falling within section 19(1)(b) and accordingly, in such a case, the creditor shall be entitled, in accordance with rules of court, to have the supplier made a party to any proceedings brought against the creditor to recover any such sums.

(4) Subject to any agreement between them, the creditor shall be entitled to be indemnified by the supplier for loss suffered by the creditor in satisfying his liability under subsection (3), including costs reasonably incurred by him in defending proceedings instituted by the debtor.

(5) Subsection (1) does not apply to any sum which, if not paid by a debtor, would be payable by virtue of section 71, and applies to a sum paid or payable by a debtor for the issue of a credit-token only where the credit-token has been returned to the creditor or surrendered to a supplier.

(6) If the total charge for credit includes an item in respect of a fee or commission charged by a credit-broker, the amount repayable under subsection (1) in respect of that item shall be the excess over £3 of the fee or commission.

(7) If the total charge for credit includes any sum payable or paid by the debtor to a credit-broker otherwise than in respect of a fee or commission charged by him, that sum shall for the purposes of subsection (6) be treated as if it were such a fee or commission.

(8) So far only as is necessary to give effect to section 69(2), this section applies to an agreement or transaction within that subsection as it applies to a cancelled agreement or transaction.

Cancellation: repayment of credit

71.—(1) Notwithstanding the cancellation of a regulated consumer credit agreement, other than a debtor-creditor-supplier agreement for restricted-use credit, the agreement shall continue in force so far as it relates to repayment of credit and payment of interest.

(2) If, following the cancellation of a regulated consumer credit agreement, the debtor repays the whole or a portion of the credit—

    (a) before the expiry of one month following service of the notice of cancellation, or

    (b) in the case of a credit repayable by instalments, before the date on which the first instalment is due,

no interest shall be payable on the amount repaid.

(3) If the whole of a credit repayable by instalments is not repaid on or before the date specified in subsection (2)(b), the debtor shall not be liable to repay any of the credit except on receipt of a request in writing in the prescribed form, signed by or on behalf of the creditor, stating the amounts of the remaining instalments (recalculated by the creditor as nearly as may be in accordance with the agreement and without extending the repayment period), but excluding any sum other than principal and interest.

(4) Repayment of a credit, or payment of interest, under a cancelled agreement shall be treated as duly made if it is made to any person on whom, under section 69, a notice of cancellation could have been served, other than a person referred to in section 69(6)(b).

Cancellation: return of goods

72.—(1) This section applies where any agreement or transaction relating to goods, being—

    (a) a restricted-use debtor-creditor-supplier agreement, a consumer hire agreement, or a linked transaction to which the debtor or hirer under any regulated agreement is a party, or

    (b) a linked transaction to which a relative of the debtor or hirer under any regulated agreement is a party,

is cancelled after the debtor or hirer (in a case within paragraph (a)) or the relative (in a case within paragraph (b)) has acquired possession of the goods by virtue of the agreement or transaction.

(2) In this section—

    (a) "the possessor" means the person who has acquired possession of the goods as mentioned in subsection (1),

    (b) "the other party" means the person from whom the possessor acquired possession, and

    (c) "the pre-cancellation period" means the period beginning when the possessor acquired possession and ending with the cancellation.

(3) The possessor shall be treated as having been under a duty throughout the pre-cancellation period—

    (a) to retain possession of the goods, and

    (b) to take reasonable care of them.

(4) On the cancellation, the possessor shall be under a duty, subject to any lien, to restore the goods to the other party in accordance with this section, and meanwhile to retain possession of the goods and take reasonable care of them.

(5) The possessor shall not be under any duty to deliver the goods except at his own premises and in pursuance of a request in writing signed by or on behalf of the other party and served on the possessor either before, or at the time when, the goods are collected from those premises.

(6) If the possessor—

    (a) delivers the goods (whether at his own premises or elsewhere) to any person on whom, under section 69, a notice of cancellation could have been served (other than a person referred to in section 69(6)(b)), or

(b) sends the goods at his own expense to such a person,
he shall be discharged from any duty to retain the goods or deliver them to any person.

(7) Where the possessor delivers the goods as mentioned in subsection (6)(a), his obligation to take care of the goods shall cease; and if he sends the goods as mentioned in subsection (6)(b), he shall be under a duty to take reasonable care to see that they are received by the other party and not damaged in transit, but in other respects his duty to take care of the goods shall cease.

(8) Where, at any time during the period of 21 days following the cancellation, the possessor receives such a request as is mentioned in subsection (5), and unreasonably refuses or unreasonably fails to comply with it, his duty to take reasonable care of the goods shall continue until he delivers or sends the goods as mentioned in subsection (6), but if within that period he does not receive such a request his duty to take reasonable care of the goods shall cease at the end of that period.

(9) The preceding provisions of this section do not apply to—
  (a) perishable goods, or
  (b) goods which by their nature are consumed by use and which, before the cancellation, were so consumed, or
  (c) goods supplied to meet an emergency, or
  (d) goods which, before the cancellation, had become incorporated in any land or thing not comprised in the cancelled agreement or a linked transaction.

(10) Where the address of the possessor is specified in the executed agreement, references in this section to his own premises are to that address and no other.

(11) Breach of a duty imposed by this section is actionable as a breach of statutory duty.

Cancellation: goods given in part-exchange

73.—(1) This section applies on the cancellation of a regulated agreement where, in antecedent negotiations, the negotiator agreed to take goods in part-exchange (the "part-exchange goods") and those goods have been delivered to him.

(2) Unless, before the end of the period of ten days beginning with the date of cancellation, the part-exchange goods are returned to the debtor or hirer in a condition substantially as good as when they were delivered to the negotiator, the debtor or hirer shall be entitled to recover from the negotiator a sum equal to the part-exchange allowance (as defined in subsection (7)(b)).

(3) In the case of a debtor-creditor-supplier agreement within section 12(b), the negotiator and the creditor shall be under a joint and several liability to pay to the debtor a sum recoverable under subsection (2).

(4) Subject to any agreement between them, the creditor shall be entitled to be indemnified by the negotiator for loss suffered by the creditor in satisfying his liability under subsection (3), including costs reasonably incurred by him in defending proceedings instituted by the debtor.

(5) During the period of ten days beginning with the date of cancellation, the debtor or hirer, if he is in possession of goods to which the cancelled agreement relates, shall have a lien on them for—
  (a) delivery of the part-exchange goods, in a condition substantially as good as when they were delivered to the negotiator, or

    (b) a sum equal to the part-exchange allowance;
and if the lien continues to the end of that period it shall thereafter subsist only as a lien for a sum equal to the part-exchange allowance.

    (6) Where the debtor or hirer recovers from the negotiator or creditor, or both of them jointly, a sum equal to the part-exchange allowance, then, if the title of the debtor or hirer to the part-exchange goods has not vested in the negotiator, it shall so vest on the recovery of that sum.

    (7) For the purposes of this section—

      (a) the negotiator shall be treated as having agreed to take goods in part-exchange if, in pursuance of the antecedent negotiations, he either purchased or agreed to purchase those goods or accepted or agreed to accept them as part of the consideration for the cancelled agreement, and

      (b) the part-exchange allowance shall be the sum agreed as such in the antecedent negotiations or, if no such agreement was arrived at, such sum as it would have been reasonable to allow in respect of the part-exchange goods if no notice of cancellation had been served.

    (8) In an action brought against the creditor for a sum recoverable under subsection (2), he shall be entitled, in accordance with rules of court, to have the negotiator made a party to the proceedings.

Exclusion of certain agreements from Part V

    74.—(1) This Part (except section 56) does not apply to—

      (a) a non-commercial agreement, or

      (b) a debtor-creditor agreement enabling the debtor to overdraw on a current account, or

      (c) a debtor-creditor agreement to finance the making of such payments arising on, or connected with, the death of a person as may be prescribed.

    (2) This Part (except sections 55 and 56) does not apply to a small debtor-creditor-supplier agreement for restricted-use credit.

    (2A) In the case of an agreement to which the Consumer Protection (Cancellation of Contracts Concluded Away from Business Premises) Regulations 1987 apply the reference in subsection (2) to a small agreement shall be construed as if in section 17(1)(a) and (b) "£35" were substituted for "£50".

    (3) Subsection (1)(b) or (c) applies only where the Director so determines, and such a determination—

      (a) may be made subject to such conditions as the Director thinks fit, and

      (b) shall be made only if the Director is of opinion that it is not against the interests of debtors.

    (3A) Notwithstanding anything in subsection (3)(b) above, in relation to a debtor-creditor agreement under which the creditor is the Bank of England or a bank within the meaning of the Bankers' Books Evidence Act 1879, the Director shall make a determination that subsection (1)(b) above applies unless he considers that it would be against the public interest to do so.

    (4) If any term of an agreement falling within subsection (1)(c) or (2) is expressed in writing, regulations under section 60(1) shall apply to that term (subject to section 60(3)) as if the agreement were a regulated agreement not falling within subsection (1)(c) or (2).

PART VI

MATTERS ARISING DURING CURRENCY OF CREDIT OR HIRE AGREEMENTS

Liability of creditor for breaches by supplier

75.—(1) If the debtor under a debtor-creditor-supplier agreement falling within section 12(b) or (c) has, in relation to a transaction financed by the agreement, any claim against the supplier in respect of a misrepresentation or breach of contract, he shall have a like claim against the creditor, who, with the supplier, shall accordingly be jointly and severally liable to the debtor.

(2) Subject to any agreement between them, the creditor shall be entitled to be indemnified by the supplier for loss suffered by the creditor in satisfying his liability under subsection (1), including costs reasonably incurred by him in defending proceedings instituted by the debtor.

(3) Subsection (1) does not apply to a claim—

    (a) under a non-commercial agreement, or

    (b) so far as the claim relates to any single item to which the supplier has attached a cash price not exceeding £100 or more than £30,000.

(4) This section applies notwithstanding that the debtor, in entering into the transaction, exceeded the credit limit or otherwise contravened any term of the agreement.

(5) In an action brought against the creditor under subsection (1) he shall be entitled, in accordance with rules of court, to have the supplier made a party to the proceedings.

Duty to give notice before taking certain action

76.—(1) The creditor or owner is not entitled to enforce a term of a regulated agreement by—

    (a) demanding earlier payment of any sum, or

    (b) recovering possession of any goods or land, or

    (c) treating any right conferred on the debtor or hirer by the agreement as terminated, restricted or deferred,

except by or after giving the debtor or hirer not less than seven days' notice of his intention to do so.

(2) Subsection (1) applies only where—

    (a) a period for the duration of the agreement is specified in the agreement, and

    (b) that period has not ended when the creditor or owner does an act mentioned in subsection (1),

but so applies notwithstanding that, under the agreement, any party is entitled to terminate it before the end of the period so specified.

(3) A notice under subsection (1) is ineffective if not in the prescribed form.

(4) Subsection (1) does not prevent a creditor from treating the right to draw on any credit as restricted or deferred and taking such steps as may be necessary to make the restriction or deferment effective.

(5) Regulations may provide that subsection (1) is not to apply to agreements described by the regulations.

(6) Subsection (1) does not apply to a right of enforcement arising by reason of any breach by the debtor or hirer of the regulated agreement.

Duty to give information to debtor under fixed-sum credit agreement

77.—(1) The creditor under a regulated agreement for fixed-sum credit, within the prescribed period after receiving a request in writing to that effect from the debtor and payment of a fee of 50p, shall give the debtor a copy of the executed agreement (if any) and of any other document referred to in it, together with a statement signed by or on behalf of the creditor showing, according to the information to which it is practicable for him to refer,—

(a) the total sum paid under the agreement by the debtor;

(b) the total sum which has become payable under the agreement by the debtor but remains unpaid, and the various amounts comprised in that total sum, with the date when each became due; and

(c) the total sum which is to become payable under the agreement by the debtor, and the various amounts comprised in that total sum, with the date, or mode of determining the date, when each becomes due.

(2) If the creditor possesses insufficient information to enable him to ascertain the amounts and dates mentioned in subsection (1)(c), he shall be taken to comply with that paragraph if his statement under subsection (1) gives the basis on which, under the regulated agreement, they would fall to be ascertained.

(3) Subsection (1) does not apply to—

(a) an agreement under which no sum is, or will or may become, payable by the debtor, or

(b) a request made less than one month after a previous request under that subsection relating to the same agreement was complied with.

(4) If the creditor under an agreement fails to comply with subsection (1)—

(a) he is not entitled, while the default continues, to enforce the agreement; and

(b) if the default continues for one month he commits an offence.

(5) This section does not apply to a non-commercial agreement.

Duty to give information to debtor under running-account credit agreement

78.—(1) The creditor under a regulated agreement for running-account credit, within the prescribed period after receiving a request in writing to that effect from the debtor and payment of a fee of 50p, shall give the debtor a copy of the executed agreement (if any) and of any other document referred to in it, together with a statement signed by or on behalf of the creditor showing, according to the information to which it is practicable for him to refer,—

(a) the state of the account, and

(b) the amount, if any, currently payable under the agreement by the debtor to the creditor, and

(c) the amounts and due dates of any payments which, if the debtor does not draw further on the account, will later become payable under the agreement by the debtor to the creditor.

(2) If the creditor possesses insufficient information to enable him to ascertain the amounts and dates mentioned in subsection (1)(c), he shall be taken to comply with that paragraph if his statement under subsection (1) gives the basis on which, under the regulated agreement, they would fall to be ascertained.

(3) Subsection (1) does not apply to—

(a) an agreement under which no sum is, or will or may become, payable by the debtor, or

(b) a request made less than one month after a previous request under that subsection relating to the same agreement was complied with.

(4) Where running-account credit is provided under a regulated agreement, the creditor shall give the debtor statements in the prescribed form, and with the prescribed contents—

    (a) showing according to the information to which it is practicable for him to refer, the state of the account at regular intervals of not more than twelve months, and

    (b) where the agreement provides, in relation to specified periods, for the making of payments by the debtor, or the charging against him of interest or any other sum, showing according to the information to which it is practicable for him to refer the state of the account at the end of each of those periods during which there is any movement in the account.

(5) A statement under subsection (4) shall be given within the prescribed period after the end of the period to which the statement relates.

(6) If the creditor under an agreement fails to comply with subsection (1)—

    (a) he is not entitled, while the default continues, to enforce the agreement; and

    (b) if the default continues for one month he commits an offence.

(7) This section does not apply to a non-commercial agreement, and subsections (4) and (5) do not apply to a small agreement.

Duty to give hirer information

79.—(1) The owner under a regulated consumer hire agreement, within the prescribed period after receiving a request in writing to that effect from the hirer and payment of a fee of 50p, shall give to the hirer a copy of the executed agreement and of any other document referred to in it, together with a statement signed by or on behalf of the owner showing, according to the information to which it is practicable for him to refer, the total sum which has become payable under the agreement by the hirer but remains unpaid and the various amounts comprised in that total sum, with the date when each became due.

(2) Subsection (1) does not apply to—

    (a) an agreement under which no sum is, or will or may become, payable by the hirer, or

    (b) a request made less than one month after a previous request under that subsection relating to the same agreement was complied with.

(3) If the owner under an agreement fails to comply with subsection (1)—

    (a) he is not entitled, while the default continues, to enforce the agreement; and

    (b) if the default continues for one month he commits an offence.

(4) This section does not apply to a non-commercial agreement.

Debtor or hirer to give information about goods

80.—(1) Where a regulated agreement, other than a non-commercial agreement, requires the debtor or hirer to keep goods to which the agreement relates in his possession or control, he shall, within seven working days after he has received a request in writing to that effect from the creditor or owner, tell the creditor or owner where the goods are.

(2) If the debtor or hirer fails to comply with subsection (1), and the default continues for 14 days, he commits an offence.

Appropriation of payments

81.—(1) Where a debtor or hirer is liable to make to the same person payments in respect of two or more regulated agreements, he shall be entitled, on making any payment in respect of the agreements which is not sufficient to discharge the total amount then due under all the agreements, to appropriate the sum so paid by him—

    (a) in or towards the satisfaction of the sum due under any one of the agreements, or

    (b) in or towards the satisfaction of the sums due under any two or more of the agreements in such proportions as he thinks fit.

(2) If the debtor or hirer fails to make any such appropriation where one or more of the agreements is—

    (a) a hire-purchase agreement or conditional sale agreement, or

    (b) a consumer hire agreement, or

    (c) an agreement in relation to which any security is provided,

the payment shall be appropriated towards the satisfaction of the sums due under the several agreements respectively in the proportions which those sums bear to one another.

Variation of agreements

82.—(1) Where, under a power contained in a regulated agreement, the creditor or owner varies the agreement, the variation shall not take effect before notice of it is given to the debtor or hirer in the prescribed manner.

(2) Where an agreement (a "modifying agreement") varies or supplements an earlier agreement, the modifying agreement shall for the purposes of this Act be treated as—

    (a) revoking the earlier agreement, and

    (b) containing provisions reproducing the combined effect of the two agreements, and obligations outstanding in relation to the earlier agreement shall accordingly be treated as outstanding instead in relation to the modifying agreement.

(3) If the earlier agreement is a regulated agreement but (apart from this subsection) the modifying agreement is not then, unless the modifying agreement is for running-account credit, it shall be treated as a regulated agreement.

(4) If the earlier agreement is a regulated agreement for running-account credit, and by the modifying agreement the creditor allows the credit limit to be exceeded but intends the excess to be merely temporary, Part V (except section 56) shall not apply to the modifying agreement.

(5) If—

    (a) the earlier agreement is a cancellable agreement, and

    (b) the modifying agreement is made within the period applicable under section 68 to the earlier agreement,

then, whether or not the modifying agreement would, apart from this subsection, be a cancellable agreement, it shall be treated as a cancellable agreement in respect of which a notice may be served under section 68 not later than the end of the period applicable under that section to the earlier agreement.

(6) Except under subsection (5), a modifying agreement shall not be treated as a cancellable agreement.

(7) This section does not apply to a non-commercial agreement.

Liability for misuse of credit facilities

83.—(1) The debtor under a regulated consumer credit agreement shall not be liable to the creditor for any loss arising from use of the credit facility by another person not acting, or to be treated as acting, as the debtor's agent.

(2) This section does not apply to a non-commercial agreement, or to any

loss in so far as it arises from misuse of an instrument to which section 4 of the Cheques Act 1957 applies.

Misuse of credit-tokens

84.—(1) Section 83 does not prevent the debtor under a credit-token agreement from being made liable to the extent of £50 (or the credit limit if lower) for loss to the creditor arising from use of the credit-token by other persons during a period beginning when the credit-token ceases to be in the possession of any authorised person and ending when the credit-token is once more in the possession of an authorised person.

(2) Section 83 does not prevent the debtor under a credit-token agreement from being made liable to any extent for loss to the creditor from use of the credit-token by a person who acquired possession of it with the debtor's consent.

(3) Subsection (1) and (2) shall not apply to any use of the credit-token after the creditor has been given oral or written notice that it is lost or stolen, or is for any other reason liable to misuse.

(4) Subsections (1) and (2) shall not apply unless there are contained in the credit-token agreement in the prescribed manner particulars of the name, address and telephone number of a person stated to be the person to whom notice is to be given under subsection (3).

(5) Notice under subsection (3) takes effect when received, but where it is given orally, and the agreement so requires, it shall be treated as not taking effect if not confirmed in writing within seven days.

(6) Any sum paid by the debtor for the issue of the credit- token to the extent (if any) that it has not been previously offset by use made of the credit-token, shall be treated as paid towards satisfaction of any liability under subsection (1) or (2).

(7) The debtor, the creditor, and any person authorised by the debtor to use the credit-token, shall be authorised persons for the purposes of subsection (1).

(8) Where two or more credit-tokens are given under one credit-token agreement, the preceding provisions of this section apply to each credit-token separately.

Duty on issue of new credit-tokens

85.—(1) Whenever, in connection with a credit-token agreement, a credit-token (other than the first) is given by the creditor to the debtor, the creditor shall give the debtor a copy of the executed agreement (if any) and of any other document referred to in it.

(2) If the creditor fails to comply with this section—
  (a) he is not entitled, while the default continues, to enforce the agreement, and
  (b) if the default continues for one month he commits an offence.

(3) This section does not apply to a small agreement.

Death of debtor or hirer

86.—(1) The creditor or owner under a regulated agreement is not entitled, by reason of the death of the debtor or hirer, to do an act specified in paragraphs (a) to (e) of section 87(1) if at the death the agreement is fully secured.

(2) If at the death of the debtor or hirer a regulated agreement is only partly secured or is unsecured, the creditor or owner is entitled, by reason of the death of the debtor or hirer, to do an act specified in paragraphs (a) to (e) of section 87(1) on an order of the court only.

(3) This section applies in relation to the termination of an agreement only where—

    (a) a period for its duration is specified in the agreement, and

    (b) that period has not ended when the creditor or owner purports to terminate the agreement,

but so applies notwithstanding that, under the agreement, any party is entitled to terminate it before the end of the period so specified.

(4) This section does not prevent the creditor from treating the right to draw on any credit as restricted or deferred, and taking such steps as may be necessary to make the restriction or deferment effective.

(5) This section does not affect the operation of any agreement providing for payment of sums—

    (a) due under the regulated agreement, or

    (b) becoming due under it on the death of the debtor or hirer, out of the proceeds of a policy of assurance on his life.

(6) For the purposes of this section an act is done by reason of the death of the debtor or hirer if it is done under a power conferred by the agreement which is—

    (a) exercisable on his death, or

    (b) exercisable at will and exercised at any time after his death.

PART VII

DEFAULT AND TERMINATION

Default notices

Need for default notice

87.—(1) Service of a notice on the debtor or hirer in accordance with section 88 (a "default notice") is necessary before the creditor or owner can become entitled, by reason of any breach by the debtor or hirer of a regulated agreement,—

    (a) to terminate the agreement, or

    (b) to demand earlier payment of any sum, or

    (c) to recover possession of any goods or land, or

    (d) to treat any right conferred on the debtor or hirer by the agreement as terminated, restricted or deferred, or

    (e) to enforce any security.

(2) Subsection (1) does not prevent the creditor from treating the right to draw upon any credit as restricted or deferred, and taking such steps as may be necessary to make the restriction or deferment effective.

(3) The doing of an act by which a floating charge becomes fixed is not enforcement of a security.

(4) Regulations may provide that section (1) is not to apply to agreements described by the regulations.

Contents and effect of default notice

88.—(1) The default notice must be in the prescribed form and specify—

    (a) the nature of the alleged breach;

    (b) if the breach is capable of remedy, what action is required to remedy it and the date before which that action is to be taken;

    (c) if the breach is not capable of remedy, the sum (if any) required to be

paid as compensation for the breach, and the date before which it is
to be paid.

(2) A date specified under subsection (1) must not be less than seven days
after the date of service of the default notice, and the creditor or owner shall
not take action such as is mentioned in section 87(1) before the date so specified
or (if no requirement is made under subsection (1)) before those seven days
have elapsed.

(3) The default notice must not treat as a breach failure to comply with a
provision of the agreement which becomes operative only on breach of some
other provision, but if the breach of that other provision is not duly remedied
or compensation demanded under subsection (1) is not duly paid, or (where no
requirement is made under subsection (1)) if the seven days mentioned in subsection (2) have elapsed, the creditor or owner may treat the failure as a breach
and section 87(1) shall not apply to it.

(4) The default notice must contain information in the prescribed terms about
the consequences of failure to comply with it.

(5) A default notice making a requirement under subsection (1) may include
a provision for the taking of action such as is mentioned in section 87(1) at any
time after the restriction imposed by subsection (2) will cease, together with a
statement that the provision will be ineffective if the breach is duly remedied
or the compensation duly paid.

Compliance with default notice

89.   If before the date specified for that purpose in the default notice the
debtor or hirer takes the action specified under section 88(1)(b) or (c) the breach
shall be treated as not having occurred.

Further restriction of remedies for default

Retaking of protected hire-purchase etc. goods

90.—(1) At any time when—
  (a) the debtor is in breach of a regulated hire-purchase or a regulated con-
      ditional sale agreement relating to goods, and
  (b) the debtor has paid to the creditor one-third or more of the total price
      of the goods and
  (c) the property in the goods remains in the creditor,
the creditor is not entitled to recover possession of the goods from the debtor
except on an order of the court.

(2) Where under a hire-purchase or conditional sale agreement the creditor
is required to carry out any installation and the agreement specifies, as part of
the total price, the amount to be paid in respect of the installation (the "installation charge") the reference in subsection (1)(b) to one-third of the total price
shall be construed as a reference to the aggregate of the installation charge and
one-third of the remainder of the total price.

(3) In a case where—
  (a) subsection (1)(a) is satisfied, but not subsection (1)(b), and
  (b) subsection (1)(b) was satisfied on a previous occasion in relation to an
      earlier agreement, being a regulated hire-purchase or regulated condi-
      tional sale agreement, between the same parties, and relating to any of
      the goods comprised in the later agreement (whether or not other goods
      were also included),

subsection (1) shall apply to the later agreement with the omission of paragraph (b).

(4) If the later agreement is a modifying agreement, subsection (3) shall apply with the substitution, for the second reference to the later agreement, of a reference to the modifying agreement.

(5) Subsection (1) shall not apply, or shall cease to apply, to an agreement if the debtor has terminated, or terminates, the agreement.

(6) Where subsection (1) applies to an agreement at the death of the debtor, it shall continue to apply (in relation to the possessor of the goods) until the grant of probate or administration, or (in Scotland) confirmation (on which the personal representative would fall to be treated as the debtor).

(7) Goods falling within this section are in this Act referred to as "protected goods".

Consequences of breach of s. 90

91.—If goods are recovered by the creditor in contravention of section 90—

    (a) the regulated agreement, if not previously terminated, shall terminate, and

    (b) the debtor shall be released from all liability under the agreement, and shall be entitled to recover from the creditor all sums paid by the debtor under the agreement.

Recovery of possession of goods or land

92.—(1) Except under an order of the court, the creditor or owner shall not be entitled to enter any premises to take possession of goods subject to a regulated hire-purchase agreement, regulated conditional sale agreement or regulated consumer hire agreement.

(2) At any time when the debtor is in breach of a regulated conditional sale agreement relating to land, the creditor is entitled to recover possession of the land from the debtor, or any person claiming under him, on an order of the court only.

(3) An entry in contravention of section (1) or (2) is actionable as a breach of statutory duty.

Interest not to be increased on default

93. The debtor under a regulated consumer credit agreement shall not be obliged to pay interest on sums which, in breach of the agreement, are unpaid by him at a rate—

    (a) where the total charge for credit includes an item in respect of interest, exceeding the rate of that interest, or

    (b) in any other case, exceeding what would be the rate of the total charge for credit if any items included in the total charge for credit by virtue of section 20(2) were disregarded.

Summary diligence not competent in Scotland

93A. Summary diligence shall not be competent in Scotland to enforce payment of a debt due under a regulated agreement or under any security related thereto.

Early payment by debtor

Right to complete payments ahead of time

94.—(1) The debtor under a regulated consumer credit agreement is entitled at any time, by notice to the creditor and the payment to the creditor of all amounts payable by the debtor to him under the agreement (less any rebate allowable under section 95), to discharge the debtor's indebtedness under the agreement.

(2) A notice under subsection (1) may embody the exercise by the debtor of any option to purchase goods conferred on him by the agreement, and deal with any other matter arising on, or in relation to, the termination of the agreement.

Rebate on early settlement

95.—(1) Regulations may provide for the allowance of a rebate of charges for credit to the debtor under a regulated consumer credit agreement where, under section 94, on refinancing, on breach of the agreement, or for any other reason, his indebtedness is discharged or becomes payable before the time fixed by the agreement, or any sum becomes payable by him before the time so fixed.

(2) Regulations under subsection (1) may provide for calculation of the rebate by reference to any sums paid or payable by the debtor or his relative under or in connection with the agreement (whether to the creditor or some other person), including sums under linked transactions and other items in the total charge for credit.

Effect on linked transactions

96.—(1) Where for any reason the indebtedness of the debtor under a regulated consumer credit agreement is discharged before the time fixed by the agreement, he, and any relative of his, shall at the same time be discharged from any liability under a linked transaction, other than a debt which has already become payable.

(2) Subsection (1) does not apply to a linked transaction which is itself an agreement providing the debtor or his relative with credit.

(3) Regulations may exclude linked transactions of the prescribed description from the operation of subsection (1).

Duty to give information

97.—(1) The creditor under a regulated consumer credit agreement, within the prescribed period after he has received a request in writing to that effect from the debtor, shall give the debtor a statement in the prescribed form indicating, according to the information to which it is practicable for him to refer, the amount of the payment required to discharge the debtor's indebtedness under the agreement, together with the prescribed particulars showing how the amount is arrived at.

(2) Subsection (1) does not apply to a request made less than one month after a previous request under that subsection relating to the same agreement was complied with.

(3) If the creditor fails to comply with subsection (1)—

(a) he is not entitled, while the default continues, to enforce the agreement; and

(b) if the default continues for one month he commits an offence.

Termination of agreements

Duty to give notice of termination (non-default cases)

98.—(1) The creditor or owner is not entitled to terminate a regulated agreement except by or after giving the debtor or hirer not less than seven days' notice of the termination.

(2) Subsection (1) applies only where—

(a) a period for the duration of the agreement is specified in the agreement, and

(b) that period has not ended when the creditor or owner does an act mentioned in subsection (1),

but so applies notwithstanding that, under the agreement, any party is entitled to terminate it before the end of the period so specified.

(3) A notice under subsection (1) is ineffective if not in the prescribed form.

(4) Subsection (1) does not prevent a creditor from treating the right to draw on any credit as restricted or deferred and taking such steps as may be necessary to make the restriction or deferment effective.

(5) Regulations may provide that subsection (1) is not to apply to agreements described by the regulations.

(6) Subsection (1) does not apply to the termination of a regulated agreement by reason of any breach by the debtor or hirer of the agreement.

Right to terminate hire-purchase etc. agreements

99.—(1) At any time before the final payment by the debtor under a regulated hire-purchase or regulated conditional sale agreement falls due, the debtor shall be entitled to terminate the agreement by giving notice to any person entitled or authorised to receive the sums payable under the agreement.

(2) Termination of an agreement under subsection (1) does not affect any liability under the agreement which has accrued before the termination.

(3) Subsection (1) does not apply to a conditional sale agreement relating to land after the title to the land has passed to the debtor.

(4) In the case of a conditional sale agreement relating to goods, where the property in the goods, having become vested in the debtor, is transferred to a person who does not become the debtor under the agreement, the debtor shall not thereafter be entitled to terminate the agreement under subsection (1).

(5) Subject to subsection (4), where a debtor under a conditional sale agreement relating to goods terminates the agreement under this section after the property in the goods has become vested in him, the property in the goods shall thereupon vest in the person (the "previous owner") in whom it was vested immediately before it became vested in the debtor:

Provided that if the previous owner has died, or any other event has occurred whereby that property, if vested in him immediately before that event, would thereupon have vested in some other person, the property shall be treated as having devolved as if it had been vested in the previous owner immediately before his death or immediately before that event, as the case may be.

Liability of debtor on termination of hire-purchase etc. agreement

100.—(1) Where a regulated hire-purchase or regulated conditional sale agreement is terminated under section 99 the debtor shall be liable, unless the agreement provides for a smaller payment, or does not provide for any payment, to pay to the creditor the amount (if any) by which one-half of the total price exceeds the aggregate of the sums paid and the sums due in respect of the total price immediately before the termination.

(2) Where under a hire-purchase or conditional sale agreement the creditor is required to carry out any installation and the agreement specifies, as part of the total price, the amount to be paid in respect of the installation (the "installation charge") the reference in subsection (1) to one-half of the total price shall be construed as a reference to the aggregate of the installation charge and one-half of the remainder of the total price.

(3) If in any action the court is satisfied that a sum less than the amount specified in subsection (1) would be equal to the loss sustained by the creditor in consequence of the termination of the agreement by the debtor, the court may make an order for the payment of that sum in lieu of the amount specified in subsection (1).

(4) If the debtor has contravened an obligation to take reasonable care of the goods or land, the amount arrived at under subsection (1) shall be increased by the sum required to recompense the creditor for that contravention, and subsection (2) shall have effect accordingly.

(5) Where the debtor, on the termination of the agreement, wrongfully retains possession of goods to which the agreement relates, then, in any action brought by the creditor to recover possession of the goods from the debtor, the court, unless it is satisfied that having regard to the circumstances it would not be just to do so, shall order the goods to be delivered to the creditor without giving the debtor an option to pay the value of the goods.

Right to termininate hire agreement

101.—(1) The hirer under a regulated consumer hire agreement is entitled to terminate the agreement by giving notice to any person entitled or authorised to receive the sums payable under the agreement.

(2) Termination of an agreement under subsection (1) does not affect any liability under the agreement which has accrued before the termination.

(3) A notice under subsection (1) shall not expire earlier than eighteen months after the making of the agreement, but apart from that the minimum period of notice to be given under subsection (1), unless the agreement provides for a shorter period, is as follows.

(4) If the agreement provides for the making of payments by the hirer to the owner at equal intervals, the minimum period of notice is the length of one interval or three months, whichever is less.

(5) If the agreement provides for the making of such payments at differing intervals, the minimum period of notice is the length of the shortest interval or three months, whichever is less.

(6) In any other case, the minimum period of notice is three months.

(7) This section does not apply to—

 (a) any agreement which provides for the making by the hirer of payments which in total (and without breach of the agreement) exceed £900 in any year, or

 (b) any agreement where—

  (i) goods are bailed or (in Scotland) hired to the hirer for the purposes of a business carried on by him, or the hirer holds himself out as requiring the goods for those purposes, and

  (ii) the goods are selected by the hirer, and acquired by the owner for the purposes of the agreement at the request of the hirer from any person other than the owner's associate, or

(c) any agreement where the hirer requires, or holds himself out as requiring, the goods for the purpose of bailing or hiring them to other persons in the course of a business carried on by him.

(8) If, on an application made to the Director by a person carrying on a consumer hire business, it appears to the Director that it would be in the interest of hirers to do so, he may by notice to the applicant direct that this section shall not apply to consumer hire agreements made by the applicant, and subject to such conditions (if any) as the Director may specify, this Act shall have effect accordingly.

(9) In the case of a modifying agreement, subsection (3) shall apply with the substitution for "the making of the agreement" of "the making of the original agreement".

Agency for receiving notice of rescission

102.—(1) Where the debtor or hirer under a regulated agreement claims to have a right to rescind the agreement, each of the following shall be deemed to be the agent of the creditor or owner for the purpose of receiving any notice rescinding the agreement which is served by the debtor or hirer—

(a) a credit-broker or supplier who was the negotiator in antecedent negotiations, and

(b) any person who, in the course of a business carried on by him, acted on behalf of the debtor or hirer in any negotiations for the agreement.

(2) In subsection (1) "rescind" does not include—

(a) service of a notice of cancellation, or

(b) termination of an agreement under section 99 or 101 or by the exercise of a right or power in that behalf expressly conferred by the agreement.

Termination statements

103.—(1) If an individual (the "customer") serves on any person (the "trader") a notice—

(a) stating that—

    (i) the customer was the debtor or hirer under a regulated agreement described in the notice, and the trader was the creditor or owner under the agreement, and

    (ii) the customer has discharged his indebtedness to the trader under the agreement, and

    (iii) the agreement has ceased to have any operation; and

(b) requiring the trader to give the customer a notice, signed by or on behalf of the trader, confirming that those statements are correct,

the trader shall, within the prescribed period after receiving the notice, either comply with it or serve on the customer a counter-notice stating that, as the case may be, he disputes the correctness of the notice or asserts that the customer is not indebted to him under the agreement.

(2) Where the trader disputes the correctness of the notice he shall give particulars of the way in which he alleges it to be wrong.

(3) Subsection (1) does not apply in relation to any agreement if the trader has previously complied with that subsection on the service of a notice under it with respect to that agreement.

(4) Subsection (1) does not apply to a non-commercial agreement

(5) If the trader fails to comply with subsection (1), and the default continues for one month, he commits an offence.

Goods not to be treated as subject to landlord's hypothec in Scotland

   104.   Goods comprised in a hire-purchase agreement or goods comprised in a conditional sale agreement which have not become vested in the debtor shall not be treated in Scotland as subject to the landlord's hypothec—

   (a) during the period between the service of a default notice in respect of the goods and the date on which the notice expires or is earlier complied with; or

   (b) if the agreement is enforceable on an order of the court only, during the period between the commencement and termination of an action by the creditor to enforce the agreement.

*   *   *   *   *

PART IX

JUDICIAL CONTROL

Enforcement of certain regulated agreements and securities

Enforcement orders in cases of infringement

   127.—(1) In the case of an application for an enforcement order under—

   (a) section 65(1) (improperly executed agreements), or

   (b) section 105(7)(a) or (b) (improperly executed security instruments), or

   (c) section 111(2) (failure to serve copy of notice on surety), or

   (d) section 124(1) or (2) (taking of negotiable instrument in contravention of section 123),

the court shall dismiss the application if, but (subject to subsections (3) and (4)) only if, it considers it just to do so having regard to—

   (i) prejudice caused to any person by the contravention in question, and the degree of culpability for it; and

   (ii) the powers conferred on the court by subsection (2) and sections 135 and 136.

   (2) If it appears to the court just to do so, it may in an enforcement order reduce or discharge any sum payable by the debtor or hirer, or any surety, so as to compensate him for prejudice suffered as a result of the contravention in question.

   (3) The court shall not make an enforcement order under section 65(1) if section 61(1)(a) (signing of agreements) was not complied with unless a document (whether or not in the prescribed form and complying with regulations under section 60(1)) itself containing an the prescribed terms of the agreement was signed by the debtor or hirer (whether or not in the prescribed manner).

   (4) The court shall not make an enforcement order under section 65(1) in the case of a cancellable agreement if—

   (a) a provision of section 62 or 63 was not complied with, and the creditor or owner did not give a copy of the executed agreement, and of any other document referred to in it, to the debtor or hirer before the commencement of the proceedings in which the order is sought, or

   (b) section 64(1) was not complied with.

   (5) Where an enforcement order is made in a case to which subsection (3) applies, the order may direct that the regulated agreement is to have effect as

if it did not include a term omitted from the document signed by the debtor or hirer.

Enforcement orders on death of debtor or hirer

128. The court shall make an order under section 86(2) if, but only if, the creditor or owner proves that he has been unable to satisfy himself that the present and future obligations of the debtor or hirer under the agreement are likely to be discharged.

Extension of time

Time orders

129.—(1) Subject to subsection (3) below if it appears to the court just to do so—

    (a) on an application for an enforcement order; or

    (b) on an application made by a debtor or hirer under this paragraph after service on him of—

        (i) a default notice, or

        (ii) a notice under section 76(1) or 98(1); or

    (c) in an action brought by a creditor or owner to enforce a regulated agreement or any security, or recover possession of any goods or land to which a regulated agreement relates,

the court may make an order under this section (a "time order").

(2) A time order shall provide for one or both of the following, as the court considers just—

    (a) the payment by the debtor or hirer or any surety of any sum owed under a regulated agreement or a security by such instalments, payable at such times, as the court having regard to the means of the debtor or hirer and any surety, considers reasonable;

    (b) the remedying by the debtor or hirer of any breach of a regulated agreement (other than non-payment of money) within such period as the court may specify.

(3) Where in Scotland a time to pay direction or a time to pay order has been made in relation to a debt, it shall not thereafter be competent to make a time order in relation to the same debt.

Supplemental provisions about time orders

130.—(1) Where in accordance with rules of court an offer to pay any sum by instalments is made by the debtor or hirer and accepted by the creditor or owner, the court may in accordance with rules of court make a time order under section 129(2)(a) giving effect to the offer without hearing evidence of means.

(2) In the case of a hire-purchase or conditional sale agreement only, a time order under section 129(2)(a) may deal with sums which, although not payable by the debtor at the time the order is made, would if the agreement continued in force become payable under it subsequently.

(3) A time order under section 129(2)(a) shall not be made where the regulated agreement is secured by a pledge if, by virtue of regulations made under section 76(5), 87(4) or 98(5), service of a notice is not necessary for enforcement of the pledge.

(4) Where, following the making of a time order in relation to a regulated hire-purchase or conditional sale agreement or a regulated consumer hire agreement, the debtor or hirer is in possession of the goods, he shall be treated (except

in the case of a debtor to whom the creditor's title has passed) as a bailee or (in Scotland) a custodier of the goods under the terms of the agreement, notwithstanding that the agreement has been terminated.

(5) Without prejudice to anything done by the creditor or owner before the commencement of the period specified in a time order made under section 129(2)(b) ("the relevant period"),—

    (a) he shall not while the relevant period subsists take in relation to the agreement any action such as is mentioned in section 87(1);

    (b) where—

        (i) a provision of the agreement ("the secondary provision") becomes operative only on breach of another provision of the agreement ("the primary provision"), and

        (ii) the time order provides for the remedying of such a breach of the primary provision within the relevant period,

    he shall not treat the secondary provision as operative before the end of that period;

    (c) if while the relevant period subsists the breach to which the order relates is remedied it shall be treated as not having occurred.

(6) On the application of any person affected by a time order, the court may vary or revoke the order.

Protection of property pending proceedings

Protection orders

131. The court, on application of the creditor or owner under a regulated agreement, may make such orders as it thinks just for protecting any property of the creditor or owner, or property subject to any security, from damage or depreciation pending the determination of any proceedings under this Act, including orders restricting or prohibiting use of the property or giving directions as to its custody.

Hire and hire-purchase etc. agreements

Financial relief for hirer

132.—(1) Where the owner under a regulated consumer hire agreement recovers possession of goods to which the agreement relates otherwise than by action, the hirer may apply to the court for an order that—

    (a) the whole or part of any sum paid by the hirer to the owner in respect of the goods shall be repaid, and

    (b) the obligation to pay the whole or part of any sum owed by the hirer to the owner in respect of the goods shall cease,

and if it appears to the court just to do so, having regard to the extent of the enjoyment of the goods by the hirer, the court shall grant the application in full or in part.

(2) Where in proceedings relating to a regulated consumer hire agreement the court makes an order for the delivery to the owner of goods to which the agreement relates the court may include in the order the like provision as may be made in an order under subsection (1).

Hire-purchase etc. agreements: special powers of court

133.—(1) If, in relation to a regulated hire-purchase or conditional sale agreement, it appears to the court just to do so—

(a) on an application for an enforcement order or time order; or

(b) in an action brought by the creditor to recover possession of goods to which the agreement relates,

the court may—

    (i) make an order (a "return order") for the return to the creditor of goods to which the agreement relates;

    (ii) make an order (a "transfer order") for the transfer to the debtor of the creditor's title to certain goods to which the agreement relates ("the transferred goods"), and the return to the creditor of the remainder of the goods.

(2) In determining for the purposes of this section how much of the total price has been paid ("the paid-up sum"), the court may—

(a) treat any sum paid by the debtor, or owed by the creditor, in relation to the goods as part of the paid-up sum;

(b) deduct any sum owed by the debtor in relation to the goods (otherwise than as part of the total price) from the paid-up sum,

and make corresponding reductions in amounts so owed.

(3) Where a transfer order is made, the transferred goods shall be such of the goods to which the agreement relates as the court thinks just; but a transfer order shall be made only where the paid-up sum exceeds the part of the total price referable to the transferred goods by an amount equal to at least one-third of the unpaid balance of the total price.

(4) Notwithstanding the making of a return order or transfer order, the debtor may at any time before the goods enter the possession of the creditor, on payment of the balance of the total price and the fulfilment of any other necessary conditions, claim the goods ordered to be returned to the creditor.

(5) When, in pursuance of a time order or under this section, the total price of goods under a regulated hire-purchase agreement or regulated conditional sale agreement is paid and any other necessary conditions are fulfilled, the creditor's title to the goods vests in the debtor.

(6) If, in contravention of a return order or transfer order, any goods to which the order relates are not returned to the creditor, the court, on the application ofthe creditor, may—

(a) revoke so much of the order as relates to those goods, and

(b) order the debtor to pay the creditor the unpaid portion of so much of the total price as is referable to those goods.

(7) For the purposes of this section, the part of the total price referable to any goods is the part assigned to those goods by the agreement or (if no such assignment is made) the part determined by the court to be reasonable.

Evidence of adverse detention in hire-purchase etc. cases

134.—(1) Where goods are comprised in a regulated hire-purchase agreement, regulated conditional sale agreement or regulated consumer hire agreement, and the creditor or owner—

(a) brings an action or makes an application to enforce a right to recover possession of the goods from the debtor or hirer, and

(b) proves that a demand for the delivery of the goods was included in the default notice under section 88(5), or that, after the right to recover possession of the goods accrued but before the action was begun or the application was made, he made a request in writing to the debtor or hirer to surrender the goods,

then, for the purposes of the claim of the creditor or owner to recover possession of the goods, the possession of them by the debtor or hirer shall be deemed to be adverse to the creditor or owner.

(2) In subsection (1) "the debtor or hirer" includes a person in possession of the goods at any time between the debtor's or hirer's death and the grant of probate or administration, or (in Scotland) confirmation.

(3) Nothing in this section affects a claim for damages for conversion or (in Scotland) for delict.

Supplemental provisions as to orders

Power to impose conditions, or suspend operation of order

135.—(1) If it considers it just to do so, the court may in an order made by it in relation to a regulated agreement include provisions—

(a) making the operation of any term of the order conditional on the doing of specified acts by any party to the proceedings;

(b) suspending the operation of any term of the order either—
(i) until such time as the court subsequently directs, or
(ii) until the occurrence of a specified act or omission.

(2) The court shall not suspend the operation of a term requiring the delivery up of goods by any person unless satisfied that the goods are in his possession or control.

(3) In the case of a consumer hire agreement, the court shall not so use its powers under subsection (1)(b) as to extend the period for which, under the terms of the agreement, the hirer is entitled to possession of the goods to which the agreement relates.

(4) On the application of any person affected by a provision included under subsection (1), the court may vary the provision.

Power to vary agreements and securities

136.—(1) The court may in an order made by it under this Act include such provision as it considers just for amending any agreement or security in consequence of a term of the order.

Extortionate credit bargains

Extortionate credit bargains

137.—(1) If the court finds a credit bargain extortionate it may reopen the credit agreement so as to do justice between the parties.

(2) In this section and sections 138 to 140,—

(a) "credit agreement" means any agreement between an individual (the "debtor") and any other person (the "creditor") by which the creditor provides the debtor with credit of any amount, and

(b) "credit bargain"—
(i) where no transaction other than the credit agreement is to be taken into account in computing the total charge for credit, means the credit agreement, or
(ii) where one or more other transactions are to be so taken into account, means the credit agreement and those other transactions, taken together.

When bargains are extortionate

138.—(1) A credit bargain is extortionate if it—

(a) requires the debtor or a relative of his to make payments (whether unconditionally, or on certain contingencies) which are grossly exorbitant, or

(b) otherwise grossly contravenes ordinary principles of fair dealing.

(2) In determining whether a credit bargain is extortionate, regard shall be had to such evidence as is adduced concerning—

(a) interest rates prevailing at the time it was made,

(b) the factors mentioned in subsection (3) to (5), and

(c) any other relevant considerations.

(3) Factors applicable under subsection (2) in relation to the debtor include—

(a) his age, experience, business capacity and state of health; and

(b) the degree to which, at the time of making the credit bargain, he was under financial pressure, and the nature of that pressure.

(4) Factors applicable under subsection (2) in relation to the creditor include—

(a) the degree of risk accepted by him, having regard to the value of any security provided;

(b) his relationship to the debtor; and

(c) whether or not a colourable cash price was quoted for any goods or services included in the credit bargain.

(5) Factors applicable under subsection (2) in relation to a linked transaction include the question how far the transaction was reasonably required for the protection of debtor or creditor, or was in the interest of the debtor.

Reopening of extortionate agreements

139.—(1) A credit agreement may, if the court thinks just, be reopened on the ground that the credit bargain is extortionate—

(a) on an application for the purpose made by the debtor or any surety to the High Court, county court or sheriff court; or

(b) at the instance of the debtor or a surety in any proceedings to which the debtor and creditor are parties, being proceedings to enforce the credit agreement, any security relating to it, or any linked transaction; or

(c) at the instance of the debtor or a surety in other proceedings in any court where the amount paid or payable under the credit agreement is relevant.

(2) In reopening the agreement, the court may, for the purpose of relieving the debtor or a surety from payment of any sum in excess of that fairly due and reasonable, by order—

(a) direct accounts to be taken, or (in Scotland) an accounting to be made, between any persons,

(b) set aside the whole or part of any obligation imposed on the debtor or a surety by the credit bargain or any related agreement,

(c) require the creditor to repay the whole or part of any sum paid under the credit bargain or any related agreement by the debtor or a surety, whether paid to the creditor or any other person,

(d) direct the return to the surety of any property provided for the purposes of the security, or

(e) alter the terms of the credit agreement or any security instrument.

(3) An order may be made under subsection (2) notwithstanding that its effect

is to place a burden on the creditor in respect of an advantage unfairly enjoyed by another person who is a party to a linked transaction.

(4) An order under subsection (2) shall not alter the effect of any judgment.

(5) In England and Wales an application under subsection (1)(a) shall be brought only in the county court in the case of—

    (a) a regulated agreement, or

    (b) an agreement (not being a regulated agreement) under which the creditor provides the debtor with fixed-sum credit or running-account credit.

(5A) [*Repealed*]

(6) In Scotland an application under subsection (1)(a) may be brought in the sheriff court for the district in which the debtor or surety resides or carries on business.

(7) In Northern Ireland an application under subsection (1)(a) may be brought in the county court in the case of—

    (a) a regulated agreement, or

    (b) an agreement (not being a regulated agreement) under which the creditor provides the debtor with fixed-sum credit not exceeding £10,000 or running-account credit on which the credit limit does not exceed £10,000.

Interpretation of sections 137 to 139

140. Where the credit agreement is not a regulated agreement, expressions used in sections 137 to 139 which, apart from this section, apply only to regulated agreements, shall be construed as nearly as may be as if the credit agreement were a regulated agreement.

Miscellaneous

Jurisdiction and parties

141.—(1) In England and Wales the county court shall have jurisdiction to hear and determine—

    (a) any action by the creditor or owner to enforce a regulated agreement or any security relating to it;

    (b) any action to enforce any linked transaction against the debtor or hirer or his relative,

and such an action shall not be brought in any other court.

(2) Where an action or application is brought in the High Court which, by virtue of this Act, ought to have been brought in the county court it shall not be treated as improperly brought, but shall be transferred to the county court.

(3) In Scotland the sheriff court shall have jurisdiction to hear and determine any action falling within subsection (1) and such an action shall not be brought in any other court.

(3A) Subject to subsection (3B) an action which is brought in the sheriff court by virtue of subsection (3) shall be brought only in one of the following courts, namely—

    (a) the court for the place where the debtor or hirer is domiciled (within the meaning of section 41 or 42 of the Civil Jurisdiction and Judgments Act 1982);

    (b) the court for the place where the debtor or hirer carries on business; and

    (c) where the purpose of the action is to assert, declare or determine propri-

etary or possessory rights, or rights of security, in or over movable
property, or to obtain authority to dispose of movable property, the
court for the place where the property is situated.

(3B) Subsection (3A) shall not apply—

(a) where Rule 3 of Schedule 8 to the said Act of 1982 applies; or

(b) where the jurisdiction of another court has been prorogated by an
agreement entered into after the dispute has arisen.

(4) In Northern Ireland the county court shall have jurisdiction to hear and
determine any action or application falling within subsection (1).

(5) Except as may be provided by rules of court, all the parties to a regulated
agreement, and any surety, shall be made parties to any proceedings relating to
the agreement.

Power to declare rights of parties

142.—(1) Where under any provision of this Act a thing can be done by a
creditor or owner on an enforcement order only, and either—

(a) the court dismisses (except on technical grounds only) an application
for an enforcement order, or

(b) where no such application has been made or such an application has
been dismissed on technical grounds only, an interested party applies
to the court for a declaration under this subsection,

the court may if it thinks just make a declaration that the creditor or owner is
not entitled to do that thing, and thereafter no application for an enforcement
order in respect of it shall be entertained.

(2) Where—

(a) a regulated agreement or linked transaction is cancelled under section
69(1), or becomes subject to section 69(2), or

(b) a regulated agreement is terminated under section 91,

and an interested party applies to the court for a declaration under this subsection, the court may make a declaration to that effect.

Northern Ireland

Jurisdiction of county court in Northern Ireland.

143. Without prejudice to any provision which may be made by rules of
court made in relation to county courts in Northern Ireland such rules may
provide—

(a) that any action or application such as is mentioned in section 141(4)
which is brought against the debtor or hirer in the county court may
be brought in the county court for the division in which the debtor or
hirer resided or carried on business at the date on which he last made
a payment under the regulated agreement;

(b) that an application by a debtor or hirer or any surety under section
129(1)(b), 132(1), 139(1)(a) or 142(1)(b) which is brought in the
county court may be brought in the county court for the division in
which the debtor, or, as the case may be, the hirer or surety resides or
carries on business;

(c) for service of process on persons outside Northern Ireland.

Appeal from county court in Northern Ireland.

144. Any person dissatisfied—

(a) with an order, whether adverse to him or in his favour, made by a county court in Northern Ireland in the exercise of any jurisdiction conferred by this Act, or

(b) with the dismissal or refusal by such a county court of any action or application instituted by him under the provisions of this Act,

shall be entitled to appeal from the order or from the dismissal or refusal as if the order, dismissal or refusal had been made in exercise of the jurisdiction conferred by Part III of the County Courts (Northern Ireland) Order 1980 and the appeal brought under Part VI of that Order and Articles 61 and 62 of that Order shall apply accordingly.

PART X

ANCILLARY CREDIT BUSINESSES

Definitions

Types of ancillary credit business

145.—(1) An ancillary credit business is any business so far as it comprises or relates to—

(a) credit brokerage,

(b) debt-adjusting,

(c) debt-counselling,

(d) debt-collecting, or

(e) the operation of a credit reference agency.

(2) Subject to section 146(5), credit brokerage is the effecting of introductions—

(a) of individuals desiring to obtain credit—

    (i) to persons carrying on businesses to which this sub-paragraph applies, or

    (ii) in the case of an individual desiring to obtain credit to finance the acquisition or provision of a dwelling occupied or to be occupied by himself or his relative, to any person carrying on a business in the course of which he provides credit secured on land, or

(b) of individuals desiring to obtain goods on hire to persons carrying on businesses to which this paragraph applies, or

(c) of individuals desiring to obtain credit, or to obtain goods on hire, to other credit-brokers.

(3) Subsection (2)(a)(i) applies to—

(a) a consumer credit business;

(b) a business which comprises or relates to consumer credit agreements being, otherwise than by virtue of section 16(5)(a), exempt agreements;

(c) a business which comprises or relates to unregulated agreements where—

    (i) the law applicable to the agreement is the law of a country outside the United Kingdom, and

    (ii) if the law applicable to the agreement were the law of a part of the United Kingdom it would be a regulated consumer credit agreement.

(4) Subsection (2)(b) applies to—

(a) a consumer hire business;

(b) a business which comprises or relates to unregulated agreements where—

(i) the law applicable to the agreement is the law of a country outside the United Kingdom, and

(ii) if the law applicable to the agreement were the law of a part of the United Kingdom it would be a regulated consumer hire agreement.

(5) Subject to section 146(6), debt-adjusting is, in relation to debts due under consumer credit agreements or consumer hire agreements,—

(a) negotiating with the creditor or owner, on behalf of the debtor or hirer, terms for the discharge of a debt, or

(b) taking over, in return for payments by the debtor or hirer, his obligation to discharge a debt, or

(c) any similiar activity concerned with the liquidation of a debt.

(6) Subject to section 146(6), debt-counselling is the giving of advice to debtors or hirers about the liquidation of debts due under consumer credit agreements or consumer hire agreements.

(7) Subject to section 146(6), debt-collecting is the taking of steps to procure payment of debts due under consumer credit agreements or consumer hire agreements.

(8) A credit reference agency is a person carrying on a business comprising the furnishing of persons with information relevant to the financial standing of individuals, being information collected by the agency for that purpose.

Exceptions from section 145

146.—(1) A barrister or advocate acting in that capacity is not be treated as doing so in the course of any ancillary credit business.

(2) A solicitor engaging in contentious business (as defined in section 86(1) of the Solicitors Act 1957) is not to be treated as doing so in the course of any ancillary credit business.

(3) A solicitor within the meaning of the Solicitors (Scotland) Act 1933 engaging in business done in or for the purposes of proceedings before a court or before an arbiter is not to be treated as doing so in the course of any ancillary credit business.

(4) A solicitor in Northern Ireland engaging in business done, whether as solicitor or advocate, in or for the purposes of proceedings begun before a court (including the Lands Tribunal for Northern Ireland) or before an arbitrator appointed under the Arbitration Act (Northern Ireland) 1937, not being business which falls within the definition of non-contentious probate business contained in Article 2(2) of the Administration of Estates (Northern Ireland) Order 1979, is not to be treated as doing so in the course of any ancillary credit business.

(5) For the purposes of section 145(2), introductions effected by an individual by canvassing off trade premises either debtor-creditor-supplier agreements falling within section 12(a) or regulated consumer hire agreements shall be disregarded if—

(a) the introductions are not effected by him in the capacity of an employee, and

(b) he does not by any other method effect introductions falling within section 145(2).

(6) It is not debt-adjusting, debt-counselling or debt-collecting for a person to do anything in relation to a debt arising under an agreement if—

(a) he is the creditor or owner under the agreement, otherwise than by virtue of an assignment, or

(b) he is the creditor or owner under the agreement by virtue of an assignment made in connection with the transfer to the assignee of any business other than a debt-collecting business, or

(c) he is the supplier in relation to the agreement, or

(d) he is a credit-broker who has acquired the business of the person who was the supplier in relation to the agreement, or

(e) he is a person prevented by subsection (5) from being treated as a credit-broker, and the agreement was made in consequence of an introduction (whether made by him or another person) which, under subsection (5), is to be disregarded.

Licensing

Application of Part III

147.—(1) The provisions of Part III (except section 40) apply to an ancillary credit business as they apply to a consumer credit business.

(2) Without prejudice to the generality of section 26, regulations under that section (as applied by subsection (1)) may include provisions regulating the collection and dissemination of information by credit reference agencies.

Agreement for services of unlicensed trader

148.—(1) An agreement for the services of a person carrying on ancillary credit business (the "trader"), if made when the trader was unlicensed, is enforceable against the other party (the "customer") only where the Director has made an order under subsection (2) which applies to the agreement.

(2) The trader or his successor in title may apply to the Director for an order that agreements within subsection (1) are to be treated as if made when the trader was licensed.

(3) Unless the Director determines to make an order under subsection (2) in accordance with the application, he shall, before determining the application, by notice—

(a) inform the trader, giving his reasons, that, as the case may be, he is minded to refuse the application, or to grant it in terms different from those applied for, describing them, and

(b) invite the trader to submit to the Director representations in support of his application in accordance with section 34.

(4) In determining whether or not to make an order under subsection (2) in respect of any period the Director shall consider, in addition to any other relevant factors,—

(a) how far, if at all, customers under agreements made by the trader during that period were prejudiced by the trader's conduct,

(b) whether or not the Director would have been likely to grant a licence covering that period on an application by the trader, and

(c) the degree of culpability for the failure to obtain a licence.

(5) If the Director thinks fit, he may in an order under subsection (2)—

(a) limit the order to specified agreements, or agreements of a specified description or made at a specified time;

(b) make the order conditional on the doing of specified acts by the trader.

Regulated agreements made on introductions by unlicensed credit-broker

149.—(1) A regulated agreement made by a debtor or hirer who, for the purpose of making that agreement, was introduced to the creditor or owner by an unlicensed credit-broker is enforceable against the debtor or hirer only where—

    (a) on the application of the credit-broker, the Director has made an order under section 148(2) in respect of a period including the time when the introduction was made, and the order does not (whether in general terms or specifically) exclude the application of this paragraph to the regulated agreement, or

    (b) the Director has made an order under subsection (2) which applies to the agreement.

(2) Where during any period individuals were introduced to a person carrying on a consumer credit business or consumer hire business by an unlicensed credit-broker for the purpose of making regulated agreements with the person carrying on that business, that person or his successor in title may apply to the Director for an order that regulated agreements so made are to be treated as if the credit-broker had been licensed at the time of the introduction.

(3) Unless the Director determines to make an order under subsection (2) in accordance with the application, he shall, before determining the application, by notice—

    (a) inform the applicant, giving his reasons, that, as the case may be, he is minded to refuse the application, or to grant it in terms different from those applied for, describing them, and

    (b) invite the applicant to submit to the Director representations in support of his application in accordance with section 34.

(4) In determining whether or not to make an order under subsection (2) the Director shall consider, in addition to any other relevant factors—

    (a) how far, if at all, debtors or hirers under regulated agreements to which the application relates were prejudiced by the credit-broker's conduct, and

    (b) the degree of culpability of the applicant in facilitating the carrying on by the credit-broker of his business when unlicensed.

(5) If the Director thinks fit, he may in an order under subsection (2)—

    (a) limit the order to specified agreements, or agreements of a specified description or made at a specified time;

    (b) make the order conditional on the doing of specified acts by the applicant.

Appeals to the Secretary of State against licensing decisions

150. Section 41 (as applied by section 147(1)) shall have effect as if the following entry were included in the table set out at the end—

Determination	Appellant
Refusal to make order under section 148(2) or 149(2) in accordance with terms of application.	The applicant.

Seeking business

Advertisements

151.—(1) Sections 44 to 47 apply to an advertisement published for the purposes of a business of credit brokerage carried on by any person, whether it advertises the services of that person or the services of persons to whom he effects introductions, as they apply to an advertisement to which Part IV applies.

(2) Sections 44, 46 and 47 apply to an advertisement, published for the purposes of a business carried on by the advertiser, indicating that he is willing to advise on debts, or engage in transactions concerned with the liquidation of debts, as they apply to an advertisement to which Part IV applies.

(3) The Secretary of State may by order provide that an advertisement published for the purposes of a business of credit brokerage, debt adjusting or debt counselling shall not fall within subsection (1) or (2) if it is of a description specified in the order.

(4) An advertisement does not fall within subsection (2) if it indicates that the advertiser is not willing to act in relation to consumer credit agreements and consumer hire agreements.

(5) In subsections (1) and (3) "credit brokerage" includes the effecting of introductions of individuals desiring to obtain credit to any person carrying on a business in the course of which he provides credit secured on land.

Application of sections 52 to 54 to credit brokerage etc.

152.—(1) Sections 52 to 54 apply to a business of credit brokerage, debt-adjusting or debt-counselling as they apply to a consumer credit business.

(2) In their application to a business of credit brokerage, sections 52 and 53 shall apply to the giving of quotations and information about the business of any person to whom the credit-broker effects introductions as well as to the giving of quotations and information about his own business.

Definition of canvassing off trade premises (agreements for ancillary credit services)

153.—(1) An individual (the "canvasser") canvasses off trade premises the services of a person carrying on an ancillary credit business if he solicits the entry of another individual (the "consumer") into an agreement for the provision to the consumer of those services by making oral representations to the consumer, or any other individual, during a visit by the canvasser to any place (not excluded by subsection (2)) where the consumer, or that other individual as the case may be, is, being a visit—

   (a) carried out for the purpose of making such oral representations to individuals who are at that place, but

   (b) not carried out in response to a request made on a previous occasion.

(2) A place is excluded from subsection (1) if it is a place where (whether on a permanent or temporary basis)—

   (a) the ancillary credit business is carried on, or

   (b) any business is carried on by the canvasser or the person whose employee or agent the canvasser is, or by the consumer.

Prohibition of canvassing certain ancillary credit services off trade premises

154.   It is an offence to canvass off trade premises the services of a person carrying on a business of credit-brokerage, debt-adjusting or debt counselling.

Right to recover brokerage fees

155.—(1) The excess over £3 of a fee or commission for his services charged by a credit-broker to an individual to whom this subsection applies shall cease to be payable or, as the case may be, shall be recoverable by the individual if the introduction does not result in his entering into a relevant agreement within the six months following the introduction (disregarding any agreement which is cancelled under section 69(1) or becomes subject to section 69(2)).

(2) Subsection (1) applies to an individual who sought an introduction for a purpose which would have been fulfilled by his entry into—

    (a) a regulated agreement, or

    (b) in the case of an individual such as is referred to in section 145(2)(a)(ii), an agreement for credit secured on land, or

    (c) an agreement such as is referred to in section 145(3)(b) or (c) or (4)(b).

(3) An agreement is a relevant agreement for the purposes of subsection (1) in relation to an individual if it is an agreement such as is referred to in subsection (2) in relation to that individual.

(4) In the case of an individual desiring to obtain credit under a consumer credit agreement, any sum payable or paid by him to a credit-broker otherwise than as a fee or commission for the credit-broker's services shall for the purposes of subsection (1) be treated as such a fee or commission if it enters, or would enter, into the total charge for credit.

Entry into agreements

Entry into agreements

156. Regulations may make provision, in relation to agreements entered into in the course of a business of credit brokerage, debt-adjusting or debt-counselling, corresponding, with such modifications as the Secretary of State thinks fit, to the provision which is or may be made by or under sections 55, 60, 61, 62, 63, 65, 127, 179 or 180 in relation to agreements to which those sections apply.

Credit reference agencies

Duty to disclose name etc. of agency

157. (1) A creditor, owner or negotiator, within the prescribed period after receiving a request in writing to that effect from the debtor or hirer, shall give him notice of the name and address of any credit reference agency from which the creditor, owner or negotiator has, during the antecedent negotiations, applied for information about his financial standing.

(2) Subsection (1) does not apply to a request received more than 28 days after the termination of the antecedent negotiations, whether on the making of the regulated agreement or otherwise.

(3) If the creditor, owner or negotiator fails to comply with subsection (1) he commits an offence.

Duty of agency to disclose filed information

158.—(1) A credit reference agency, within the prescribed period after receiving,—

    (a) a request in writing to that effect from any individual (the "consumer"), and

    (b) such particulars as the agency may reasonably require to enable them to identify the file, and

    (c) a fee of £1,

shall give the consumer a copy of the file relating to him kept by the agency.

(2) When giving a copy of the file under subsection (1), the agency shall also

give the consumer a statement in the prescribed form of his rights under section 159.

(3) If the agency does not keep a file relating to the consumer it shall give him notice of that fact, but need not return any money paid.

(4) If the agency contravenes any provision of this section it commits an offence.

(5) In this Act "file", in relation to an individual, means all the information about him kept by a credit reference agency, regardless of how the information is stored, and "copy of the file", as respects information not in plain English, means a transcript reduced into plain English.

Correction of wrong information

159.—(1) A consumer given information under section 158 who considers that an entry in his file is incorrect, and that if it is not corrected he is likely to be prejudiced, may give notice to the agency requiring it either to remove the entry from the file or amend it.

(2) Within 28 days after receiving a notice under subsection (1), the agency shall by notice inform the consumer that it has—

(a) removed the entry from the file, or

(b) amended the entry, or

(c) taken no action,

and if the notice states that the agency has amended the entry it shall include a copy of the file so far as it comprises the amended entry.

(3) Within 28 days after receiving a notice under subsection (2), or where no such notice was given, within 28 days after the expiry of the period mentioned in subsection (2), the consumer may, unless he has been informed by the agency that it has removed the entry from his file, serve a further notice on the agency requiring it to add to the file an accompanying notice of correction (not exceeding 200 words) drawn up by the consumer, and include a copy of it when furnishing information included in or based on that entry.

(4) Within 28 days after receiving a notice under subsection (3), the agency, unless it intends to apply to the Director under subsection (5), shall by notice inform the consumer that it has received the notice under subsection (3) and intends to comply with it.

(5) If—

(a) the consumer has not received a notice under subsection (4) within the time required, or

(b) it appears to the agency that it would be improper for it to publish a notice of correction because it is incorrect, or unjustly defames any person, or is frivolous or scandalous, or is for any other reason unsuitable,

the consumer or, as the case may be, the agency may, in the prescribed manner and on payment of the specified fee, apply to the Director, who may make such order on the application as he thinks fit.

(6) If a person to whom an order under this section is directed fails to comply with it within the period specified in the order he commits an offence.

Alternative procedure for business consumers

160.—(1) The Director, on an application made by a credit reference agency, may direct that this section shall apply to the agency if he is satisfied—

(a) that compliance with section 158 in the case of consumers who carry on a business would adversely affect the service provided to its customers by the agency, and

(b) that, having regard to the methods employed by the agency and to any other relevant facts, it is probable that consumers carrying on a business would not be prejudiced by the making of the direction.

(2) Where an agency to which this section applies receives a request, particulars and a fee under section 158(1) from a consumer who carries on a business and section 158(3) does not apply, the agency, instead of complying with section 158, may elect to deal with the matter under the following subsections.

(3) Instead of giving the consumer a copy of the file, the agency shall within the prescribed period give notice to the consumer that it is proceeding under this section, and by notice give the consumer such information included in or based on entries in the file as the Director may direct, together with a statement in the prescribed form of the consumer's rights under subsections (4) and (5).

(4) If within 28 days after receiving the information given him under subsection (3), or such longer period as the Director may allow, the consumer—

(a) gives notice to the Director that he is dissatisfied with the information, and

(b) satisfies the Director that he has taken such steps in relation to the agency as may be reasonable with a view to removing the cause of his dissatisfaction, and

(c) pays the Director the specified fee,

the Director may direct the agency to give the Director a copy of the file, and the Director may disclose to the consumer such of the information on the file as the Director thinks fit.

(5) Section 159 applies with any necessary modifications to information given to the consumer under this section as it applies to information given under section 158.

(6) If an agency making an election under subsection (2) fails to comply with subsection (3) or (4) it commits an offence.

PART XI

ENFORCEMENT OF ACT

Enforcement authorities

161.—(1) The following authorities ("enforcement authorities") have a duty to enforce this Act and regulations made under it—

(a) the Director,

(b) in Great Britain, the local weights and measures authority,

(c) in Northern Ireland, the Department of Commerce for Northern Ireland.

(2) Where a local weights and measures authority in England or Wales propose to institute proceedings for an offence under this Act (other than an offence under section 162(6), 165(1) or (2) or 174(5)) it shall, as between the authority and the Director, be the duty of the authority to give the Director notice of the intended proceedings, together with a summary of the facts on which the charges are to be founded, and postpone institution of the proceedings until either—

(a) 28 days have expired since that notice was given, or

(b) the Director has notified them of receipt of the notice and summary.

(3) Every local weights and measures authority shall, whenever the Director

requires, report to him in such form and with such particulars as he requires on
the exercise of their functions under this Act.

(4)–(6) [*Repealed*]

Powers of entry and inspection

162.—(1) A duly authorised officer of an enforcement authority, at all reasonable hours and on production, if required, of his credentials, may—

(a) in order to ascertain whether a breach of any provision of or under
this Act has been committed, inspect any goods and enter any premises
(other than premises used only as a dwelling);

(b) if he has reasonable cause to suspect that a breach of any provision of
or under this Act has been committed, in order to ascertain whether it
has been committed, require any person—

(i) carrying on, or employed in connection with, a business to produce
any books or documents relating to it; or

(ii) having control of any information relating to a business recorded
otherwise than in a legible form to provide a document containing
a legible reproduction of the whole or any part of the information,

and take copies of, or of any entry in, the books or documents;

(c) if he has reasonable cause to believe that a breach of any provision of
or under this Act has been committed, seize and detain any goods in
order to ascertain (by testing or otherwise) whether such a breach has
been committed;

(d) seize and detain any goods, books or documents which he has reason
to believe may be required as evidence in proceedings for an offence
under this Act;

(e) for the purpose of exercising his powers under this subsection to seize
goods, books or documents, but only if and to the extent that it is
reasonably necessary for securing that the provisions of this Act and
of any regulations made under it are duly observed, require any person
having authority to do so to break open any container and, if that person
does not comply, break it open himself.

(2) An officer seizing goods, books or documents in exercise of his powers
under this section shall not do so without informing the person he seizes them
from.

(3) If a justice of the peace, on sworn information in writing, or, in Scotland,
a sheriff or a magistrate or justice of the peace, on evidence on oath,—

(a) is satisfied that there is reasonable ground to believe either—

(i) that any goods, books or documents which a duly authorised officer
has power to inspect under this section are on any premises and
their inspection is likely to disclose evidence of a breach of any
provision of or under this Act; or

(ii) that a breach of any provision of or under this Act has been, is
being or is about to be committed on any premises; and

(b) is also satisfied either—

(i) that admission to the premises has been or is likely to be refused
and that notice of intention to apply for a warrant under this subsection has been given to the occupier; or

(ii) that an application for admission, or the giving of such a notice,
would defeat the object of the entry or that the premises are unoccu-

pied or that the occupier is temporarily absent and it might defeat
the object of the entry to wait for his return,

the justice or, as the case may be, the sheriff or magistrate may by warrant under
his hand, which shall continue in force for a period of one month, authorise an
officer of an enforcement authority to enter the premises (by force if need be).

(4) An officer entering premises by virtue of this section may take such other
persons and equipment with him as he thinks necessary ; and on leaving premises entered by virtue of a warrant under subsection (3) shall, if they are
unoccupied or the occupier is temporarily absent, leave them as effectively
secured against trespassers as he found them.

(5) Regulations may provide that, in cases described by the regulations, an
officer of a local weights and measures authority is not to be taken to be duly
authorised for the purposes of this section unless he is authorised by the
Director.

(6) A person who is not a duly authorised officer of an enforcement authority,
but purports to act as such under this section, commits an offence.

(7) Nothing in this section compels a barrister, advocate or solicitor to produce
a document containing a privileged communication made by or to him in that
capacity or authorises the seizing of any such document in his possession.

Compensation for loss

163.—(1) Where, in exercising his powers under section 162, an officer of
an enforcement authority seizes and detains goods and their owner suffers loss
by reason of—

    (a) that seizure, or

    (b) the loss, damage or deterioration of the goods during detention,

then, unless the owner is convicted of an offence under this Act committed in
relation to the goods, the authority shall compensate him for the loss so suffered.

(2) Any dispute as to the right to or amount of any compensation under
subsection (1) shall be determined by arbitration.

Power to make test purchases etc.

164.—(1) An enforcement authority may—

    (a) make, or authorise any of their officers to make on their behalf, such
        purchases of goods; and

    (b) authorise any of their officers to procure the provision of such services
        or facilities or to enter into such agreements or other transactions,

as may appear to them expedient for determining whether any provisions made
by or under this Act are being complied with.

(2) Any act done by an officer authorised to do it under subsection (1) shall
be treated for the purposes of this Act as done by him as an individual on his
own behalf.

(3) Any goods seized by an officer under this Act may be tested, and in the
event of such a test he shall inform the person mentioned in section 162(2) of
the test results.

(4) Where any test leads to proceedings under this Act, the enforcement
authority shall—

    (a) if the goods were purchased, inform the person they were purchased
        from of the test results, and

    (b) allow any person against whom the proceedings are taken to have the
        goods tested on his behalf if it is reasonably practicable to do so.

Obstruction of authorised officers

165.—(1) Any person who—

(a) wilfully obstructs an officer of an enforcement authority acting in pursuance of this Act; or

(b) wilfully fails to comply with any requirement properly made to him by such an officer under section 162; or

(c) without reasonable cause fails to give such an officer (so acting) other assistance or information he may reasonably require in performing his functions under this Act,

commits an offence.

(2) If any person, in giving such information as is mentioned in subsection (1)(c), makes any statement which he knows to be false, he commits an offence.

(3) Nothing in this section requires a person to answer any question or give any information if to do so might incriminate that person or (where that person is married) the husband or wife of that person.

Notification of convictions and judgments to Director

166.—Where a person is convicted of an offence or has a judgment given against him by or before any court in the United Kingdom and it appears to the court—

(a) having regard to the functions of the Director under this Act, that the conviction or judgment should be brought to the Director's attention, and

(b) that it may not be brought to his attention unless arrangements for that purpose are made by the court,

the court may make such arrangements notwithstanding that the proceedings have been finally disposed of.

Penalties

167.—(1) An offence under a provision of this Act specified in column 1 of Schedule 1 is triable in the mode or modes indicated in column 3, and on conviction is punishable as indicated in column 4 (where a period of time indicates the maximum term of imprisonment, and a monetary amount indicates the maximum fine, for the offence in question).

(2) A person who contravenes any regulations made under section 44, 52, 53, or 112, or made under section 26 by virtue of section 54, commits an offence.

Defences

168.—(1) In any proceedings for an offence under this Act it is a defence for the person charged to prove—

(a) that his act or omission was due to a mistake, or to reliance on information supplied to him, or to an act or omission by another person, or to an accident or some other cause beyond his control, and

(b) that he took all reasonable precautions and exercised all due diligence to avoid such an act or omission by himself or any person under his control.

(2) If in any case the defence provided by subsection (1) involves the allegation that the act or omission was due to an act or omission by another person or to reliance on information supplied by another person, the person charged shall not, without leave of the court, be entitled to rely on that defence unless, within a period ending seven clear days before the hearing, he has served on

the prosecutor a notice giving such information identifying or assisting in the identification of that other person as was then in his possession.

Offences by bodies corporate

169. Where at any time a body corporate commits an offence under this Act with the consent or connivance of, or because of neglect by, any individual, the individual commits the like offence if at that time—

(a) he is a director, manager, secretary or similar officer of the body corporate, or

(b) he is purporting to act as such an officer, or

(c) the body corporate is managed by its members of whom he is one.

No further sanctions for breach of Act

170.—(1) A breach of any requirement made (otherwise than by any court) by or under this Act shall incur no civil or criminal sanction as being such a breach, except to the extent (if any) expressly provided by or under this Act.

(2) In exercising his functions under this Act the Director may take account of any matter appearing to him to constitute a breach of a requirement made by or under this Act, whether or not any sanction for that breach is provided by or under this Act and, if it is so provided, whether or not proceedings have been brought in respect of the breach.

(3) Subsection (1) does not prevent the grant of an injunction, or the making of an order of certiorari, mandamus or prohibition or as respects Scotland the grant of an interdict or of an order under section 91 of the Court of Session Act 1868 (order for specific performance of statutory duty).

Onus of proof in various proceedings

171.—(1) If an agreement contains a term signifying that in the opinion of the parties section 10(3)(b)(iii) does not apply to the agreement, it shall be taken not to apply unless the contrary is proved.

(2) It shall be assumed in any proceedings, unless the contrary is proved, that when a person initiated a transaction as mentioned in section 19(1)(c) he knew the principal agreement had been made, or contemplated that it might be made.

(3) Regulations under section 44 or 52 may make provision as to the onus of proof in any proceedings to enforce the regulations.

(4) In proceedings brought by the creditor under a credit-token agreement—

(a) it is for the creditor to prove that the credit-token was lawfully supplied to the debtor, and was accepted by him, and

(b) if the debtor alleges that any use made of the credit-token was not authorised by him, it is for the creditor to prove either—

(i) that the use was so authorised, or

(ii) that the use occurred before the creditor had been given notice under section 84(3).

(5) In proceedings under section 50(1) in respect of a document received by a minor at any school or other educational establishment for minors, it is for the person sending it to him at that establishment to prove that he did not know or suspect it to be such an establishment.

(6) In proceedings under section 119(1) it is for the pawnee to prove that he had reasonable cause to refuse to allow the pawn to be redeemed.

(7) If, in proceedings referred to in section 139(1), the debtor or any surety alleges that the credit bargain is extortionate it is for the creditor to prove the contrary.

Statements by creditor or owner to be binding

172.—(1) A statement by a creditor or owner is binding on him if given under—

> section 77(1),
> section 78(1),
> section 79(1),
> section 97(1),
> section 107(1)(c),
> section 108(1)(c), or
> section 109(1)(c).

(2) Where a trader—

> (a) gives a customer a notice in compliance with section 103(1)(b), or
> (b) gives a customer a notice under section 103(1) asserting that the customer is not indebted to him under an agreement,

the notice is binding on the trader.

(3) Where in proceedings before any court—

> (a) it is sought to reply on a statement or notice given as mentioned in subsection (1) or (2), and
> (b) the statement or notice is shown to be incorrect,

the court may direct such relief (if any) to be given to the creditor or owner from the operation of subsection (1) or (2) as appears to the court to be just.

Contracting-out forbidden

173.—(1) A term contained in a regulated agreement or linked transaction, or in any other agreement relating to an actual or prospective regulated agreement or linked transaction, is void if, and to the extent that, it is inconsistent with a provision for the protection of the debtor or hirer or his relative or any surety contained in this Act or in any regulation made under this Act.

(2) Where a provision specifies the duty or liability of the debtor or hirer or his relative or any surety in certain circumstances, a term is inconsistent with that provision if it purports to impose, directly or indirectly, an additional duty or liability on him in those circumstances.

(3) Notwithstanding subsection (1), a provision of this Act under which a thing may be done in relation to any person on an order of the court or the Director only shall not be taken to prevent its being done at any time with that person's consent given at that time, but the refusal of such consent shall not give rise to any liability.

Part XII

Supplemental

Restrictions on disclosure of information

174.—(1) No information obtained under or by virtue of this Act about any individual shall be disclosed without his consent.

(2) No information obtained under or by virtue of this Act about any business shall be disclosed except, so long as the business continues to be carried on, with the consent of the person for the time being carrying it on.

(3) Subsections (1) and (2) do not apply to any disclosure of information made—

> (a) for the purpose of facilitating the performance of any functions, under this Act, the Trade Descriptions Act 1968 or Part II or III or section

125 (annual and other reports of Director) of the Fair Trading Act 1973 or the Estate Agents Act 1979 or the Competition Act 1980 or the Telecommunications Act 1984 or the Gas Act 1986 or the Airports Act 1986 or the Consumer Protection Act 1987 or Part II of the Consumer Protection (Northern Ireland) Order 1987 or the Control of Misleading Advertisements Regulations 1988 or the Courts and Legal Services Act 1990 or the Railways Act 1993 or the Coal Industry Act 1994 or the Water Act 1989 or the Water Industry Act 1991 or any of the other consolidation Acts (within the meaning of section 206 of that Act of 1991) or the Electricity Act 1989 or the Electricity (Northern Ireland) Order 1992 or Part IV of the Airports (Northern Ireland) Order 1994, of the Secretary of State, any other Minister, the Director General of Telecommunications, the Director General of Gas Supply, the Civil Aviation Authority the Director General of Water Services, the Director General of Electricity Supply or the Director General of Electricity Supply for Northern Ireland the Rail Regulator or the Authorised Conveyancing Practitioners Board the Coal Authority any enforcement authority or any Northern Ireland department, or

(b) in connection with the investigation of any criminal offence or for the purposes of any criminal proceedings, or

(c) for the purposes of any civil proceedings brought under or by virtue of this Act or under Part III of the Fair Trading Act 1973 or under the Control of Misleading Advertisements Regulations 1988.

(3A) Subsections (1) and (2) do not apply to any disclosure of information by the Director to the Bank of England for the purpose of enabling or assisting the Bank to discharge its functions under the Banking Act 1987 or the Director to discharge his functions under this Act.

(4) Nothing in subsection (1) and (2) shall be construed—

(a) as limiting the particulars which may be entered in the register; or

(b) as applying to any information which has been made public as part of the register.

(5) Any person who discloses information in contravention of this section commits an offence.

Duty of persons deemed to be agents

175. Where under this Act a person is deemed to receive a notice or payment as agent of the creditor or owner under regulated agreement, he shall be deemed to be under a contractual duty to the creditor or owner to transmit the notice, or remit the payment, to him forthwith.

Service of documents

176.—(1) A document to be served under this Act by one person ("the server") on another person ("the subject") is to be treated as properly served on the subject if dealt with as mentioned in the following subsections.

(2) The document may be delivered or sent by post to the subject, or addressed to him by name and left at his proper address.

(3) For the purposes of this Act, a document sent by post to, or left at, the address last known to the server as the address of a person shall be treated as sent by post to, or left at, his proper address.

(4) Where the document is to be served on the subject as being the person having any interest in land, and it is not practicable after reasonable inquiry to ascertain the subject's name or address, the document may be served by—

    (a) addressing it to the subject by the description of the person having that interest in the land (naming it), and

    (b) delivering the document to some responsible person on the land or affixing it, or a copy of it, in a conspicuous position on the land.

(5) Where a document to be served on the subject as being a debtor, hirer or surety, or as having any other capacity relevant for the purposes of this Act, is served at any time on another person who—

    (a) is the person last known to the server as having that capacity, but

    (b) before that time had ceased to have it, the document shall be treated as having been served at that time on the subject.

(6) Anything done to a document in relation to a person who (whether to the knowledge of the server or not) has died shall be treated for the purposes of subsection (5) as service of the document on that person if it would have been so treated had he not died.

(7) The following enactments shall be construed as authorising service on the Public Trustee (in England and Wales) or the Probate Judge (in Northern Ireland) of any document which is to be served under this Act—

    section 9 of the Administration of Estates Act 1925;

    section 3 of the Administration of Estates Act (Northern Ireland) 1955.

(8) References in the preceding subsections to the serving of a document on a person include the giving of the document to that person.

Saving for registered charges

    177.—(1) Nothing in this Act affects the rights of a proprietor of a registered charge (within the meaning of the Land Registration Act 1925), who—

    (a) became the proprietor under a transfer for valuable consideration without notice of any defect in the title arising (apart from this section) by virtue of this Act, or

    (b) derives title from such a proprietor.

(2) Nothing in this Act affects the operation of section 104 of the Law of Property Act 1925 (protection of purchaser where mortgagee exercises power of sale).

(3) Subsection (1) does not apply to a proprietor carrying on a business of debt-collecting.

(4) Where, by virtue of subsection (1), a land mortgage is enforced which apart from this section would be treated as never having effect, the original creditor or owner shall be liable to indemnify the debtor or hirer against any loss thereby suffered by him.

(5) In the application of this section to Scotland for subsections (1) to (3) there shall be substituted the following subsections—

"(1) Nothing in this Act affects the rights of a creditor in a heritable security who—

    (a) became the creditor under a transfer for value without notice of any defect in the title arising (apart from this section) by virtue of this Act; or

    (b) derives title from such a creditor.

(2) Nothing in this Act affects the operation of section 41 of the Conveyancing (Scotland) Act 1924 (protection of purchasers), or of that section as applied to standard securities by section 32 of the Conveyancing and Feudal Reform (Scotland) Act 1970.

(3) Subsection (1) does not apply to a creditor carrying on a business of debt-collecting.".

(6) In the application of this section to Northern Ireland—

(a) any reference to the proprietor of a registered charge (within the meaning of the Land Registration Act 1925) shall be construed as a reference to the registered owner of a charge under the Local Registration of Title (Ireland) Act 1891 or Part IV of the Land Registration Act (Northern Ireland) 1970, and

(b) for the reference to section 104 of the Law Property Act 1925 there shall be substituted a reference to section 21 of the Conveyancing and Law of Property Act 1881 and section 5 of the Conveyancing Act 1911.

Local Acts

178. The Secretary of State or the Department of Commerce for Northern Ireland may by order make such amendments or repeals of any provision of any local Act as appears to the Secretary of State or, as the case may be, the Department, necessary or expedient in consequence of the replacement by this Act of the enactments relating to pawnbrokers and moneylenders.

Regulations, orders, etc.

Power to prescribe form etc. of secondary documents

179.—(1) Regulations may be made as to the form and content of credit-cards, trading-checks, receipts, vouchers and other documents or things issued by creditors, owners or suppliers under or in connection with regulated agreements or by other persons in connection with linked transactions, and may in particular—

(a) require specified information to be included in the prescribed manner in documents, and other specified material to be excluded;

(b) contain requirements to ensure that specified information is clearly brought to the attention of the debtor or hirer, or his relative, and that one part of a document is not given insufficient or excessive prominence compared with another.

(2) If a person issues any document or thing in contravention of regulations under subsection (1) then, as from the time of the contravention but without prejudice to anything done before it, this Act shall apply as if the regulated agreement had been improperly executed by reason of a contravention of regulations under section 60(1).

Power to prescribe form etc. of copies

180.—(1) Regulations may be made as to the form and content of documents to be issued as copies of any executed agreement, security instrument or other document referred to in this Act, and may in particular—

(a) require specified information to be included in the prescribed manner in any copy, and contain requirements to ensure that such information is clearly brought to the attention of a reader of the copy;

(b) authorise the omission from a copy of certain material contained in the original, or the inclusion of such material in condensed form.

(2) A duty imposed by any provision of this Act (except section 35) to supply a copy of any document—

(a) is not satisfied unless the copy supplied is in the prescribed form and conforms to the prescribed requirements;

(b) is not infringed by the omission of any material, or its inclusion in condensed form, if that is authorised by regulations;

and references in this Act to copies shall be construed accordingly.

(3) Regulations may provide that a duty imposed by this Act to supply a copy of a document referred to in an unexecuted agreement or an executed agreement shall not apply to documents of a kind specified in the regulations.

Power to alter monetary limits etc

181.—(1) The Secretary of State may by order made by statutory instrument amend, or further amend, any of the following provisions of this Act so as to reduce or increase a sum mentioned in that provision, namely, sections 8(2), 15(1)(c), 17(1), 43(3)(a), 70(6), 75(3)(b), 77(1), 78(1), 79(1), 84(1), 101(7)(a), 107(1), 108(1), 109(1), 110(1), 118(1)(b), 120(1)(a), 139(5) and (7), 155(1) and 158(1).

(2) An order under subsection (1) amending section 8(2), 15(1)(c), 17(1), 43(3)(a), 75(3)(b) or 139(5) or (7) shall be of no effect unless a draft of the order has been laid before and approved by each House of Parliament.

Regulations and orders

182.—(1) Any power of the Secretary of State to make regulations or orders under this Act, except the power conferred by sections 2(1)(a), 181 and 192 shall be exercisable by statutory instrument subject to annulment in pursuance of a resolution of either House of Parliament.

(2) Where a power to make regulations or orders is exercisable by the Secretary of State by virtue of this Act, regulations or orders made in the exercise of that power may—

(a) make different provision in relation to different cases or classes of case, and

(b) exclude certain cases or classes of case, and

(c) contain such transitional provision as the Secretary of State thinks fit.

(3) Regulations may provide that specified expressions, when used as described by the regulations, are to be given the prescribed meaning, notwithstanding that another meaning is intended by the person using them.

(4) Any power conferred on the Secretary of State by this Act to make orders includes power to vary or revoke an order so made.

Determinations etc. by Director

183. The Director may vary or revoke any determination or direction made or given by him under this Act (other than Part III, or Part III as applied by section 147).

Interpretation

Associates

184.—(1) A person is an associate of an individual if that person is the individual's husband or wife, or is a relative, or the husband or wife of a relative, of the individual or of the individual's husband or wife.

(2) A person is an associate of any person with whom he is in partnership, and of the husband or wife or a relative of any individual with whom he is in partnership.

(3) A body corporate is an associate of another body corporate—

(a) if the same person is a controller of both, or a person is a controller of one and persons who are his associates, or he and persons who are his associates, are controllers of the other; or

(b) if a group of two or more persons is controller of each company, and the groups either consist of the same persons or could be regarded as consisting of the same persons by treating (in one or more cases) a member of either group as replaced by a person of whom he is an associate.

(4) A body corporate is an associate of another person if that person is a controller of it or if that person and persons who are his associates together are controllers of it.

(5) In this section "relative" means brother, sister, uncle, aunt, nephew, niece, lineal ancestor or lineal descendant, and references to a husband or wife include a former husband or wife and a reputed husband or wife; and for the purposes of this subsection a relationship shall be established as if any illegitimate child, step-child or adopted child of a person had been a child born to him in wedlock.

Agreement with more than one debtor or hirer

185.—(1) Where an actual or prospective regulated agreement has two or more debtors or hirers (not being a partnership or an unincorporated body of persons)—

(a) anything required by or under this Act to be done to or in relation to the debtor or hirer shall be done to or in relation to each of them; and

(b) anything done under this Act by or on behalf of one of them shall have effect as if done by or on behalf of all of them.

(2) Notwithstanding subsection (1)(a), where running-account credit is provided to two or more debtors jointly, any of them may by a notice signed by him (a "dispensing notice") authorise the creditor not to comply in his case with section 78(4) (giving of periodical statement of account); and the dispensing notice shall have effect accordingly until revoked by a further notice given by the debtor to the creditor;

Provided that:

(a) a dispensing notice shall not take effect if previous dispensing notices are operative in the case of the other debtor, or each of the other debtors, as the case may be;

(b) any dispensing notices operative in relation to an agreement shall cease to have effect if any of the debtors dies;

(c) a dispensing notice which is operative in relation to an agreement shall be operative also in relation to any subsequent agreement which, in relation to the earlier agreement, is a modifying agreement.

(3) Subsection (1)(b) does not apply for the purposes of section 61(1)(a) or 127(3).

(4) Where a regulated agreement has two or more debtors or hirers (not being a partnership or an unincorporated body of persons), section 86 applies to the death of any of them.

(5) An agreement for the provision of credit, or the bailment or (in Scotland) the hiring of goods, to two or more persons jointly where—

(a) one or more of those persons is an individual, and

(b) one or more of them is a body corporate,

is a consumer credit agreement or consumer hire agreement if it would have been one had they all been individuals; and the body corporate or bodies corporate shall accordingly be included among the debtors or hirers under the agreement.

(6) Where subsection (5) applies, references in this Act to the signing of any

document by the debtor or hirer shall be construed in relation to a body corporate as referring to a signing on behalf of the body corporate.

Agreement with more than one creditor or owner

186. Where an actual or prospective regulated agreement has two or more creditors or owners, anything required by or under this Act to be done to, or in relation to, or by, the creditor or owner shall be effective if done to, or in relation to, or by, any one of them.

Arrangements between creditor and supplier

187.—(1) A consumer credit agreement shall be treated as entered into under pre-existing arrangements between a creditor and a supplier if it is entered into in accordance with, or in furtherance of, arrangements previously made between persons mentioned in subsection (4)(a), (b) or (c).

(2) A consumer credit agreement shall be treated as entered into in contemplation of future arrangements between a creditor and a supplier if it is entered into in the expectation that arrangements will subsequently be made between persons mentioned in subsection (4)(a), (b) or (c) for the supply of cash, goods and services (or any of them) to be financed by the consumer credit agreement.

(3) Arrangements shall be disregarded for the purposes of subsection (1) or (2) if—

    (a) they are arrangements for the making, in specified circumstances, of payments to the supplier by the creditor, and

    (b) the creditor holds himself out as willing to make, in such circumstances, payments of the kind to suppliers generally.

(3A) Arrangements shall also be disregarded for the purposes of subsections (1) and (2) if they are arrangements for the electronic transfer of funds from a current account at a bank within the meaning of the Bankers' Book Evidence Act 1879.

(4) The persons referred to in subsections (1) and (2) are—

    (a) the creditor and the supplier;

    (b) one of them and an associate of the other's;

    (c) an associate of one and an associate of the other's.

(5) Where the creditor is an associate of the supplier's, the consumer credit agreement shall be treated, unless the contrary is proved, as entered into under pre-existing arrangements between the creditor and the supplier.

Examples of use of new terminology

188.—(1) Schedule 2 shall have effect for illustrating the use of terminology employed in this Act.

(2) The examples given in Schedule 2 are not exhaustive.

(3) In the case of conflict between Schedule 2 and any other provision of this Act, that other provision shall prevail.

(4) The Secretary of State may by order amend Schedule 2 by adding further examples or in any other way.

Definitions

189.—(1) In this Act, unless the context otherwise requires—

"advertisement" includes every form of advertising, whether in a publication, by television or radio, by display of notices, signs, labels, showcards or goods, by distribution of samples, circulars, catalogues, price lists or other material, by exhibition of pictures, models or films, or in any other way, and references to the publishing of advertisements shall be construed accordingly;

"advertiser" in relation to an advertisement, means any person indicated by the advertisement as willing to enter into transactions to which the advertisement relates;

"ancillary credit business" has the meaning given by section 145(1),

"antecedent negotiations" has the meaning given by section 56;

"appeal period" means the period beginning on the first day on which an appeal to the Secretary of State may be brought and ending on the last day on which it may be brought or, if it is brought, ending on its final determination, or abandonment;

"assignment", in relation to Scotland, means assignation;

"associate" shall be construed in accordance with section 184;

"authorised institution" means an institution authorised under the Banking Act 1987;

"bill of sale" has the meaning given by section 4 of the Bills of Sale Act 1878 or, for Northern Ireland, by section 4 of the Bills of Sale (Ireland) Act 1879;

"building society" means a building society within the meaning of the Building Societies Act 1986;

"business" includes profession or trade, and references to a business apply subject to subsection (2);

"cancellable agreement" means a regulated agreement which, by virtue of section 67, may be cancelled by the debtor or hirer;

"canvass" shall be construed in accordance with sections 48 and 153;

"cash" includes money in any form;

"charity" means as respects England and Wales a charity registered under the Charities Act 1993 or an exempt charity (within the meaning of that Act), and as respects Scotland and Northern Ireland an institution or other organisation established for charitable purposes only ("organisation" including any persons administering a trust and "charitable" being construed in the same way as if it were contained in the Income Tax Acts);

"conditional sale agreement" means an agreement for the sale of goods or land under which the purchase price or part of it is payable by instalments, and the property in the goods or land is to remain in the seller (notwithstanding that the buyer is to be in possession of the goods or land) until such conditions as to the payment of instalments or otherwise as may be specified in the agreement are fulfilled;

"consumer credit agreement" has the meaning given by section 8, and includes a consumer credit agreement which is cancelled under section 69(1), or becomes subject to section 69(2), so far as the agreement remains in force;

"consumer credit business" means any business so far as it comprises or relates to the provision of credit under regulated consumer credit agreements;

"consumer hire agreement" has the meaning given by section 15;

"consumer hire business" means any business so far as it comprises or relates to the bailment or (in Scotland) the hiring of goods under regulated consumer hire agreements;

"controller", in relation to a body corporate, means a person—

    (a) in accordance with whose directions or instructions the directors of the body corporate or of another body corporate which is its controller (or any of them) are accustomed to act, or

    (b) who, either alone or with any associate or associates, is entitled to exercise, or control the exercise of, one third or more of the voting power at any general meeting of the body corporate or of another body corporate which is its controller;

"copy" shall be construed in accordance with section 180;

"costs", in relation to Scotland, means expenses;

"court" means in relation to England and Wales the county court, in relation to Scotland the sheriff court and in relation to Northern Ireland the High Court or the county court;

"credit" shall be construed in accordance with section 9;

"credit-broker" means a person carrying on a business of credit-brokerage;

"credit-brokerage" has the meaning given by section 145(2);

"credit limit" has the meaning given by section 10(2);

"creditor" means the person providing credit under a consumer credit agreement or the person to whom his rights and duties under the agreement have passed by assignment or operation of law, and in relation to a prospective consumer agreement, includes the prospective creditor;

"credit reference agency" has the meaning given by section 145(8);

"credit-sale agreement" means an agreement for the sale of goods, under which the purchase price or part of it is payable by instalments, but which is not a conditional sale agreement;

"credit-token" has the meaning given by section 14(1);

"credit-token agreement" means a regulated agreement for the provision of credit in connection with the use of a credit-token;

"debt-adjusting" has the meaning given by section 145(5);

"debt-collecting" has the meaning given by section 145(7);

"debt-counselling" has the meaning given by section 145(6);

"debtor" means the individual receiving credit under a consumer credit agreement or the person to whom his rights and duties under the agreement have passed by assignment or operation of law, and in relation to a prospective consumer credit agreement includes the prospective debtor;

"debtor-creditor agreement" has the meaning given by section 13;

"debtor-creditor-supplier agreement" has the meaning given by section 12;

"default notice" has the meaning given by section 87(1);

"deposit" means any sum payable by a debtor or hirer by way of deposit or downpayment, or credited or to be credited to him on account of any deposit or downpayment, whether the sum is to be or has been paid to the creditor or owner or any other person, or is to be or has been discharged by a payment of money or a transfer or delivery of goods or by any other means;

"Director" means the Director General of Fair Trading;

"electric line" has the meaning given by the Electricity Act 1989 or, for Northern Ireland the Electricity Supply (Northern Ireland) Order 1972;

"embodies" and related words shall be construed in accordance with subsection (4);

"enforcement authority" has the meaning given by section 161(1);

"enforcement order" means an order under section 65(1), 105(7)(a) or (b), 111(2) or 124(1) or (2);

"executed agreement" means a document, signed by or on behalf of the parties, embodying the terms of a regulated agreement, or such of them as have been reduced to writing;

"exempt agreement" means an agreement specified in or under section 16;

"finance" means to finance wholly or partly, and "financed" and "refinanced" shall be construed accordingly;

"file" and "copy of the file" have the meanings given by section 158(5);

"fixed-sum credit" has the meaning given by section 10(1)(b);

"friendly society" means a society registered under the "Friendly Societies Acts 1896 to 1971;

"future arrangements" shall be construed in accordance with section 187;

"general notice" means a notice published by the Director at a time and in a manner appearing to him suitable for securing that the notice is seen within a reasonable time by persons likely to be affected by it;

"give" means deliver or send by post to;

"goods" has the meaning given by section 61(1) of the Sale of Goods Act 1979;

"group licence" has the meaning given by section 22(1)(b);

"High Court" means Her Majesty's High Court of Justice, or the Court of Session in Scotland or the High Court of Justice in Northern Ireland;

"hire-purchase agreement" means an agreement, other than a conditional sale agreement, under which—

    (a) goods are bailed or (in Scotland) hired in return for periodical payments by the person to whom they are bailed or hired, and

    (b) the property in the goods will pass to that person if the terms of the agreement are complied with and one or more of the following occurs—

        (i) the exercise of an option to purchase by that person,

        (ii) the doing of any other specified act by any party to the agreement,

        (iii) the happening of any other specified event;

"hirer" means the individual to whom goods are bailed or (in Scotland) hired under a consumer hire agreement, or the person to whom his rights and duties under the agreement have passed by assignment or operation of law, and in relation to a prospective consumer hire agreement includes the prospective hirer; "individual" includes a partnership or other unincorporated body of persons not consisting entirely of bodies corporate;

"installation" means—

    (a) the installing of any electric line or any gas or water pipe,

    (b) the fixing of goods to the premises where they are to be used, and the alteration of premises to enable goods to be used on them,

    (c) where it is reasonably necessary that goods should be constructed or erected on the premises where they are to be used, any work carried out for the purpose of constructing or erecting them on those premises;

"insurance company" has the meaning given by section 96(1) of the Insurance Companies Act 1982, but does not include a friendly society or an organisation of workers or organisation of employers;

"judgment" includes an order or decree made by any court;

"land" includes an interest in land, and in relation to Scotland includes heritable subjects of whatever description;

"land improvement company" means an improvement company as defined by section 7 of the improvement of Land Act 1899;

"land mortgage" includes any security charged on land;

"licence" means a licence under Part III (including that Part as applied to ancillary credit businesses by section 147);

"licensed", in relation to any act, means authorised by a licence to do the act or cause or permit another person to do it;

"licensee", in the case of a group licence, includes any person covered by the licence;

"linked transaction" has the meaning given by section 19(1);

"local authority", in relation to England and Wales, means a county council, a London borough council, a district council, the Common Council of the City of London, or the Council of the Isles of Scilly, and in relation to Scotland, means a regional, islands or district council, and, in relation to Northern Ireland, means a district council;

"modifying agreement" has the meaning given by section 82(2);

"mortgage", in relation to Scotland, includes any heritable security;

"multiple agreement" has the meaning given by section 18(1);

"negotiator" has the meaning given by section 56(1);

"non-commercial agreement" means a consumer credit agreement or a consumer hire agreement not made by the creditor or owner in the course of a business carried on by him;

"notice" means notice in writing;

"notice of cancellation" has the meaning given by section 69(1);

"owner" means a person who bails or (in Scotland) hires out goods under a consumer hire agreement or the person to whom his rights and duties under the agreement have passed by assignment or operation of law, and in relation to a prospective consumer hire agreement, includes the prospective bailor or person from whom the goods are to be hired;

"pawn" means any article subject to a pledge;

"pawn-receipt" has the meaning given by section 114;

"pawnee" and "pawnor" include any person to whom the rights and duties of the original pawnee or the original pawnor, as the case may be, have passed by assignment or operation of law;

"payment" includes tender;

"personal credit agreement" has the meaning given by section 8(1);

"pledge" means the pawnee's rights over an article taken in pawn;

"prescribed" means prescribed by regulations made by the Secretary of State;

"pre-existing arrangements" shall be construed in accordance with section 187;

"principal agreement" has the meaning given by section 19(1);

"protected goods" has the meaning given by section 90(7);

"quotation" has the meaning given by section 52(1)(a);

"redemption period" has the meaning given by section 116(3);

"register" means the register kept by the Director under section 35;

"regulated agreement" means a consumer credit agreement, or consumer hire agreement, other than an exempt agreement, and "regulated" and "unregulated" shall be construed accordingly;

"regulations" means regulations made by the Secretary of State;

"relative", except in section 184, means a person who is an associate by virtue of section 184(1);

"representation" includes any condition or warranty, and any other statement or undertaking, whether oral or in writing;

"restricted-use credit agreement" and "restricted-use credit" have the meanings given by section 11(1);

"rules of court", in relation to Northern Ireland means, in relation to the High Court, rules made under section 7 of the Northern Ireland Act 1962, and, in relation to any other court, rules made by the authority having for the time being power to make rules regulating the practice and procedure in that court;

"running-account credit", shall be construed in accordance with section 10;

"security", in relation to an actual or prospective consumer credit agreement or consumer hire agreement, or any linked transaction, means a mortgage, charge, pledge, bond, debenture, indemnity, guarantee, bill, note or other right provided by the debtor or hirer, or at his request (express or implied), to secure the carrying out of the obligations of the debtor or hirer under the agreement;

"security instrument" has the meaning given by section 105(2);

"serve on" means deliver or send by post to;

"signed" shall be construed in accordance with subsection (3);

"small agreement" has the meaning given by section 17(1), and "small" in relation to an agreement within any category shall be construed accordingly;

"specified fee" shall be construed in accordance with section 2(4) and (5);

"standard licence" has the meaning given by section 22(1)(a);

"supplier" has the meaning given by section 11(1)(b) or 12(c) or 13(c) or, in relation to an agreement failing within section 11(1)(a), means the creditor, and includes a person to whom the rights and duties of a supplier (as so defined) have passed by assignment or operation of law, or (in relation to a prospective agreement) the prospective supplier;

"surety" means the person by whom any security is provided, or the person to whom his rights and duties in relation to the security have passed by assignment or operation of law;

"technical grounds" shall be construed in accordance with subsection (5);

"time order" has the meaning given by section 129(1);

"total charge for credit" means a sum calculated in accordance with regulations under section 20(1);

"total price" means the total sum payable by the debtor under a hire-purchase agreement or a conditional sale agreement, including any sum payable on the exercise of an option to purchase, but excluding any sum payable as a penalty or as compensation or damages for a breach of the agreement;

"unexecuted agreement", means a document embodying the terms of a prospective regulated agreement, or such of them as it is intended to reduce to writing;

"unlicensed" means without a licence, but applies only in relation to acts for which a licence is required;

"unrestricted-use credit agreement" and "unrestricted-use credit" have the meanings given by section 11(2);

"working day" means any day other than—

    (a) Saturday or Sunday,

    (b) Christmas Day or Good Friday,

    (c) a bank holiday within the meaning given by section 1 of the Banking and Financial Dealings Act 1971.

(2) A person is not to be treated as carrying on a particular type of business merely because occasionally he enters into transactions belonging to a business of that type.

(3) Any provision of this Act requiring a document to be signed is complied with by a body corporate if the document is sealed by that body.

This subsection does not apply to Scotland.

(4) A document embodies a provision if the provision is set out either in the document itself or in another document referred to in it.

(5) An application dismissed by the court or the Director shall, if the court or the Director (as the case may be) so certifies, be taken to be dismissed on technical grounds only.

(6) Except in so far as the context otherwise requires, any reference in this

Act to an enactment shall be construed as a reference to that enactment as amended by or under any other enactment, including this Act.

(7) In this Act, except where otherwise indicated—

(a) a reference to a numbered Part, section or Schedule is a reference to the Part or section of, or the Schedule to, this Act so numbered, and

(b) a reference in a section to a numbered subsection is a reference to the subsection of that section so numbered, and

(c) a reference in a section, subsection or Schedule to a numbered paragraph is a reference to the paragraph of that section, subsection or Schedule so numbered.

Financial provisions

190.—(1) There shall be defrayed out of money provided by Parliament—

(a) all expenses incurred by the Secretary of State in consequence of the provisions of this Act;

(b) any expenses incurred in consequence of those provisions by any other Minister of the Crown or Government department;

(c) any increase attributable to this Act in the sums payable out of money so provided under the Superannuation Act 1972 or the Fair Trading Act 1973.

(2) Any fees received by the Director under this Act shall be paid into the Consolidated Fund.

Special provisions as to Northern Ireland

191.—(1) The Director may make arrangements with the Department of Commerce for Northern Ireland for the Department, on his behalf,—

(a) to receive applications, notices and fees;

(b) to maintain, and make available for inspection and copying, copies of entries in the register; and

(c) to provide certified copies of entries in the register,

to the extent that seems to him desirable for the convenience of persons in Northern Ireland.

(2) The Director shall give general notice of any arrangements made under subsection (1).

(3) Nothing in this Act shall authorise any Northern Ireland department to incur any expenses attributable to the provisions of this Act until provision has been made for those expenses to be defrayed out of money appropriated for the purpose.

(4) The power of the Department of Commerce for Northern Ireland to make an order under section 178 shall be exercisable by statutory rule for the purposes of the Statutory Rules (Northern Ireland) Order 1979, and any such order shall be subject to negative resolution within the meaning of the Interpretation Act (Northern Ireland) 1954 as if it were a statutory instrument within the meaning of that Act.

(5) In this Act "enactment" includes an enactment of the Parliament of Northern Ireland or the Northern Ireland Assembly, and "Act" shall be construed in a corresponding manner; and (without prejudice to section 189(6)) any reference in this Act to such an enactment shall include a reference to any enactment re-enacting it with or without modifications.

(6) Section 38 of the Interpretation Act 1889 (effect of repeals) shall have the same operation in relation to any repeal by this Act of an enactment of the

Section 191 is continued on p. 141

SCHEDULE 1

PROSECUTION AND PUNISHMENT OF OFFENCES

1 Section	2 Offence	3 Mode of prosecution	4 Imprisonment or fine
7	Knowingly or recklessly giving false information to Director	(a) Summarily. (b) On indictment.	The prescribed sum. 2 years or a fine or both.
39(1)	Engaging in activities requiring a licence when not a licensee.	(a) Summarily. (b) On indictment.	The prescribed sum. 2 years or a fine or both.
39(2)	Carrying on a business under a name not specified in licence.	(a) Summarily. (b) On indictment.	The prescribed sum. 2 years or a fine or both.
39(3)	Failure to notify changes in registered particulars.	(a) Summarily. (b) On indictment.	The prescribed sum. 2 years or a fine or both.
45	Advertising credit where goods etc. not available for cash.	(a) Summarily. (b) On indictment.	The prescribed sum. 2 years or a fine or both.
46(1)	False or misleading advertisements.	(a) Summarily. (b) On indictment.	The prescribed sum. 2 years or a fine or both.
47(1)	Advertising infringements.	(a) Summarily. (b) On indictment.	The prescribed sum. 2 years or a fine or both.
49(1)	Canvassing debtor–creditor agreements off trade premises.	(a) Summarily. (b) On indictment.	The prescribed sum. 1 year or a fine or both.
49(2)	Soliciting debtor–creditor agreements during visits made in response to previous oral requests	(a) Summarily. (b) On indictment.	The prescribed sum. 1 year or a fine or both.
50(1)	Sending circulars to minors	(a) Summarily. (b) On indictment.	The prescribed sum. 1 year or a fine or both.
51(1)	Supplying unsolicited credit-tokens	(a) Summarily. (b) On indictment.	The prescribed sum. 2 years or a fine or both.
77(4)	Failure of creditor under fixed-sum credit agreement to supply copies of documents etc.	Summarily.	Level 4 on the standard scale.
78(6)	Failure of creditor under running-account credit agreement to supply copies of documents etc.	Summarily.	Level 4 on the standard scale.

Section	Description	Mode of prosecution	Punishment
79(3)	Failure of owner under consumer hire agreement to supply copies of documents etc.	Summarily.	Level 4 on the standard scale.
80(2)	Failure to tell creditor or owner whereabouts of goods.	Summarily.	Level 3 on the standard scale.
85(2)	Failure of creditor to supply copy of credit-token agreement.	Summarily.	Level 4 on the standard scale.
97(3)	Failure to supply debtor with statement of amount required to discharge agreement.	Summarily.	Level 3 on the standard scale.
103(5)	Failure to deliver notice relating to discharge of agreements.	Summarily.	Level 3 on the standard scale.
107(4)	Failure of creditor to give information to surety under fixed-sum credit agreement	Summarily.	Level 4 on the standard scale.
108(4)	Failure of creditor to give information to surety under running-account credit agreement.	Summarily.	Level 4 on the standard scale.
109(3)	Failure of owner to give information to surety under consumer hire agreement.	Summarily.	Level 4 on the standard scale.
110(3)	Failure of creditor or owner to supply a copy of any security instrument to debtor or hirer.	Summarily.	Level 4 on the standard scale.
114(2)	Taking pledges from minors.	(a) Summarily. (b) On indictment.	The prescribed sum. / 1 year or a fine or both.
115	Failure to supply copies of a pledge agreement or pawn-receipt.	Summarily.	Level 4 on the standard scale.
119(1)	Unreasonable refusal to allow pawn to be redeemed.	Summarily.	Level 4 on the standard scale.
154	Canvassing ancillary credit services off trade premises.	(a) Summarily. (b) On indictment.	The prescribed sum. / 1 year or a fine or both.
157(3)	Refusal to give name etc. of credit reference agency.	Summarily.	Level 4 on the standard scale.
158(4)	Failure of credit reference agency to disclose filed information.	Summarily.	Level 4 on the standard scale.
159(6)	Failure of credit reference agency to correct information.	Summarily.	Level 4 on the standard scale.
160(6)	Failure of credit reference agency to comply with section 160(3) or (4).	Summarily.	Level 4 on the standard scale.
162(6)	Impersonation of enforcement authority officers.	(a) Summarily. (b) On indictment.	The prescribed sum. / 2 years or a fine or both.
165(1)	Obstruction of enforcement authority officers.	Summarily.	Level 4 on the standard scale.
165(2)	Giving false information to enforcement authority officers.	(a) Summarily. (b) On indictment.	The prescribed sum. / 2 years or a fine or both.
167(2)	Contravention of regulations under section 44, 52, 53, 54, or 112.	(a) Summarily. (b) On indictment.	The prescribed sum. / 2 years or a fine or both.
174(5)	Wrongful disclosure of information.	(a) Summarily. (b) On indictment.	The prescribed sum. / 2 years or a fine or both.

Parliament of Northern Ireland as it has in relation to the repeal of an Act of the Parliament of the United Kingdom, references in that section of the Act of 1889 to Acts and enactments being construed accordingly.

Transitional and commencement provisions, amendments and repeals
192.—(1) The provisions of Schedule 3 shall have effect for the purposes of this Act.

(2) The appointment of a day for the purposes of any provision of Schedule 3 shall be effected by an order of the Secretary of State made by statutory instrument; and any such order shall include a provision amending Schedule 3 so as to insert an express reference to the day appointed.

(3) Subject to subsection (4)—
   (a) the enactments specified in Schedule 4 shall have effect subject to the amendments specified in that Schedule (being minor amendments or amendments consequential on the preceding provisions of this Act), and
   (b) the enactments specified in Schedule 5 are hereby repealed to the extent shown in column 3 of that Schedule.

(4) The Secretary of State shall by order made by statutory instrument provide for the coming into operation of the amendments contained in Schedule 4 and the repeals contained in Schedule 5, and those amendments and repeals shall have effect only as provided by an order so made.

Short title and extent
193.—(1) This Act may be cited as the Consumer Credit Act 1974.

(2) This Act extends to Northern Ireland.

Section 188(1)

SCHEDULE 2

EXAMPLES OF USE OF NEW TERMINOLOGY
PART I
LIST OF TERMS

Term	Defined in section	Illustrated by example(s)
Advertisement	189(1)	2
Advertiser	189(1)	2
Antecedent negotiations	56	1, 2, 3, 4
Cancellable agreement	67	4
Consumer credit agreement	8	5, 6, 7, 15, 19, 21
Consumer hire agreement	15	20, 24
Credit	9	16, 19, 21
Credit-broker	189(1)	2
Credit limit	10(2)	6, 7, 19, 22, 23
Creditor	189(1)	1, 2, 3, 4
Credit-sale agreement	189(1)	5
Credit-token	14	3, 14, 16
Credit-token agreement	14	3, 14, 16, 22
Debtor-creditor agreement	13	8, 16, 17, 18
Debtor-creditor-supplier agreement	12	8, 16

Fixed-sum credit	10	9, 10, 17, 23
Hire-purchase agreement	189(1)	10
Individual	189(1)	19, 24
Linked transaction	19	11
Modifying agreement	82(2)	24
Multiple agreement	18	16, 18
Negotiator	56(1)	1, 2, 3, 4
Personal credit agreement	8(1)	19
Pre-existing arrangements	187	8, 21
Restricted-use credit	11	10, 12, 13, 14, 16
Running-account credit	10	15, 16, 18, 23
Small agreement	17	16, 17, 22
Supplier	189(1)	3, 14
Total charge for credit	20	5, 10
Total price	189(1)	10
Unrestricted-use credit	11	8, 12, 16, 17, 18

PART II
EXAMPLES

Example 1

Facts Correspondence passes between an employee of a money-lending company (writing on behalf of the company) and an individual about the terms on which the company would grant him a loan under a regulated agreement.

Analysis The correspondence constitutes antecedent negotiations falling within section 56(1)(a), the moneylending company being both creditor and negotiator.

Example 2

Facts Representations are made about goods in a poster displayed by a shopkeeper near the goods, the goods being selected by a customer who has read the poster and then sold by the shopkeeper to a finance company introduced by him (with whom he has a business relationship). The goods are disposed of by the finance company to the customer under a regulated hire-purchase agreement.

Analysis The representations in the poster constitute antecedent negotiations falling within section 56(1)(b), the shopkeeper being the credit-broker and negotiator and the finance company being the creditor. The poster is an advertisement and the shopkeeper is the advertiser.

Example 3

Facts Discussions take place between a shopkeeper and a customer about goods the customer wishes to buy using a credit-card issued by the D Bank under a regulated agreement.

Analysis The discussions constitute antecedent negotiations falling within section 56(1)(c), the shopkeeper being the supplier and negotiator and the D Bank the creditor. The credit-card is a credit-token as defined in section 14(1), and the regulated agreement under which it was issued is a credit-token agreement as defined in section 14(2).

Example 4

Facts Discussions take place and correspondence passes between a secondhand car dealer and a customer about a car, which is then sold by the dealer to the customer under a regulated conditional sale agreement. Subsequently, on a revocation of that agreement by consent, the car is resold by the dealer to a finance company introduced by him (with whom he has a business relationship), who in turn dispose of it to the same customer under a regulated hire-purchase agreement.

Analysis The discussions and correspondence constitute antecedent negotiations in relation both to the conditional sale agreement and the hire-purchase agreement. They fall under section 56(1)(a) in relation to the conditional sale agreement, the dealer being the creditor and the negotiator. In relation to the hire-purchase agreement they fall within section 56(1)(b), the dealer continuing to be treated as the negotiator but the finance company now being the creditor. Both agreements are cancellable if the discussions took place when the individual conducting the negotiations (whether the "negotiator" or his employee or agent) was in the presence of the debtor, unless the unexecuted agreement was signed by the debtor at trade premises (as defined in section 67(b)). If the discussions all took place by telephone however, or the unexecuted agreement was signed by the debtor on trade premises (as so defined) the agreements are not cancellable.

Example 5

Facts E agrees to sell to F (an individual) an item of furniture in return for 24 monthly instalments of £10 payable in arrear. The property in the goods passes to F immediately.

Analysis This is a credit-sale agreement (see definition of "credit-sale agreement" in section 189(1)). The credit provided amounts to £240 less the amount which, according to regulations made under section 20(1), constitutes the total charge for credit. (This amount is required to be deducted by section 9(4).) Accordingly the agreement falls within section 8(2) and is a consumer credit agreement.

Example 6

Facts The G Bank grants H (an individual) an unlimited over-draft, with an increased rate of interest on so much of any debit balance as exceeds £2,000.

Analysis Although the overdraft purports to be unlimited, the stipulation for increased interest above £2,000 brings the agreement within section 10(3)(b)(ii) and it is a consumer credit agreement.

Example 7

Facts J is an individual who owns a small shop which usually carries a stock worth about £1,000. K makes a stocking agreement under which he undertakes to provide on short-term credit the stock needed from time to time by J without any specified limit.

Analysis Although the agreement appears to provide unlimited credit, it is probable, having regard to the stock usually carried by J, that his indebtedness to K will not at any time rise above £5,000. Accordingly the agreement falls within section 10(3)(b)(iii) and is a consumer credit agreement.

Example 8

Facts   U, a moneylender, lends £500 to V (an individual) knowing he intends to use it to buy office equipment from W. W introduced V to U, it being his practice to introduce customers needing finance to him. Sometimes U gives W a commission for this and sometimes not. U pays the £500 direct to V.

Analysis   Although this appears to fall under section 11(1)(b), it is excluded by section 11(3) and is therefore (by section 11(2)) an unrestricted-use credit agreement. Whether it is a debtor-creditor agreement (by section 13(c)) or a debtor-creditor supplier agreement (by section 12(c)) depends on whether the previous dealings between U and W amount to "pre-existing arrangements", that is whether the agreement can be taken to have been entered into "in accordance with, or in furtherance of" arrangements previously made between U and W, as laid down in section 187(1).

Example 9

Facts   A agrees to lend B (an individual) £4,500 in nine monthly instalments of £500.

Analysis   This is a cash loan and is a form of credit (see section 9 and definition of "cash" in section 189(1)). Accordingly it falls within section 10(1)(b) and is fixed-sum credit amounting to £4,500.

Example 10

Facts   C (in England) agrees to bail goods to D (an individual) in return for periodical payments. The agreement provides for the property in the goods to pass to D on payment of a total of £7,500 and the exercise by D of an option to purchase. The sum of £7,500 includes a down-payment of £1,000. It also includes an amount which, according to regulations made under section 20(1), constitutes a total charge for credit of £1,500.

Analysis   This is a hire-purchase agreement with a deposit of £1,000 and a total price of £7,500 (see definitions of "hire-purchase agreement", "deposit" and "total price" in section 189(1)). By section 9(3), it is taken to provide credit amounting to £7,500—(£1,500 + £1,000), which equals £5,000. Under section 8(2), the agreement is therefore a consumer credit agreement, and under sections 9(3) and 11(1) it is a restricted-use credit agreement for fixed-sum credit. A similar result would follow if the agreement by C had been a hiring agreement in Scotland.

Example 11

Facts   X (an individual) borrows £500 from Y (Finance). As a condition of the granting of the loan X is required—

    (a) to execute a second mortgage on his house in favour of Y (Finance), and

    (b) to take out a policy of insurance on his life with Y (Insurances).

In accordance with the loan agreement, the policy is charged to Y (Finance) as collateral security for the loan. The two companies are associates within the meaning of section 184(3).

Analysis The second mortgage is a transaction for the provision of security and accordingly does not fall within section 19(1), but the taking out of the insurance policy is a linked transaction falling within section 19(1)(a). The charging of the policy is a separate transaction (made between different parties) for the provision of security and again is excluded from section 19(1). The only linked transaction is therefore the taking out of the insurance policy. If X had not been required by the loan agreement to take out the policy, but it had been done at the suggestion of Y (Finance) to induce them to enter into the loan agreement, it would have been a linked transaction under section 19(1)(c)(i) by virtue of section 19(2)(a).

Example 12

Facts The N Bank agrees to lend O (an individual) £2,000 to buy a car from P. To make sure the loan is used as intended, the N Bank stipulates that the money must be paid by it direct to P.

Analysis The agreement is a consumer credit agreement by virtue of section 8(2). Since it falls within section 11(1)(b), it is a restricted-use credit agreement, P being the supplier. If the N Bank had not stipulated for direct payment to the supplier, section 11(3) would have operated and made the agreement into one for unrestricted-use credit.

Example 13

Facts Q, a debt-adjuster, agrees to pay off debts owed by R (an individual) to various moneylenders. For this purpose the agreement provides for the making of a loan by Q to R in return for R's agreeing to repay the loan by instalments with interest. The loan money is not paid over to R but retained by Q and used to pay off the money lenders.

Analysis This is an agreement to refinance existing indebtedness of the debtor's, and if the loan by Q does not exceed £5,000 is a restricted-use credit agreement falling within section 11(1)(c).

Example 14

Facts On payment of £1, S issues to T (an individual) a trading check under which T can spend up to £20 at any shop which has agreed, or in future agrees, to accept S's trading checks.

Analysis The trading check is a credit-token falling within section 14(1)(b). The credit-token agreement is a restricted-use credit agreement within section 11(1)(b), any shop in which the credit-token is used being the "supplier". The fact that further shops may be added after the issue of the credit-token is irrelevant in view of section 11(4).

Example 15

Facts A retailer L agrees with M (an individual) to open an account in M's name and, in return for M's promise to pay a specified minimum sum into the account each month and to pay a monthly charge for credit, agrees to allow to be debited to the account, in respect of purchases made by M from L, such sums as will not increase the debit balance at any time beyond the credit limit, defined in the agreement as a given multiple of the specified minimum sum.

Analysis   This agreement provides credit falling within the definition of running-account credit in section 10(1)(a). Provided the credit limit is not over £5,000, the agreement falls within section 8(2) and is a consumer credit agreement for running-account credit.

Example 16

Facts   Under an unsecured agreement, A (Credit), an associate of the A Bank, issues to B (an individual) a credit-card for use in obtaining cash on credit from A (Credit), to be paid by branches of the A Bank (acting as agent of A (Credit)), or goods or cash from suppliers or banks who have agreed to honour credit-cards issued by A (Credit). The credit limit is £30.

Analysis   This is a credit-token agreement falling within section 14(1)(a) and (b). It is a regulated consumer credit agreement for running-account credit. Since the credit limit does not exceed £30, the agreement is a small agreement. So far as the agreement relates to goods it is a debtor-creditor-supplier agreement within section 12(b), since it provides restricted-use credit under section 11(1)(b). So far as it relates to cash it is a debtor-creditor agreement within section 13(c) and the credit it provides is unrestricted-use credit. This is therefore a multiple agreement. In that the whole agreement falls within several of the categories of agreement mentioned in this Act, it is, by section 18(3), to be treated as an agreement in each of those categories. So far as it is a debtor-creditor-supplier agreement providing restricted-use credit it is, by section 18(2), to be treated as a separate agreement; and similarly so far as it is a debtor-creditor agreement providing unrestricted-use credit. (See also Example 22.)

Example 17

Facts   The manager of the C Bank agrees orally with D (an individual) to open a current account in D's name. Nothing is said about overdraft facilities. After maintaining the account in credit for some weeks, D draws a cheque in favour of E for an amount exceeding D's credit balance by £20. E presents the cheque and the Bank pay it.

Analysis   In drawing the cheque D, by implication, requests the Bank to grant him an overdraft of £20 on its usual terms as to interest and other charges. In deciding to honour the cheque, the Bank by implication accept the offer. This constitutes a regulated small consumer credit agreement for unrestricted-use, fixed-sum credit. It is a debtor-creditor agreement, and falls within section 74(1)(b) if covered by a determination under section 74(3). (Compare Example 18.)

Example 18

Facts   F (an individual) has had a current account with the G Bank for many years. Although usually in credit, the account has been allowed by the Bank to become overdrawn from time to time. The maximum such overdraft has been is about £1,000. No explicit agreement has ever been made about overdraft facilities. Now, with a credit balance of £500, F draws a cheque for £1,300.

Analysis   It might well be held that the agreement with F (express or implied) under which the Bank operate his account includes an implied term giving him the right to overdraft facilities up to say £1,000. If so, the agreement is a regulated consumer credit agreement for unrestricted-use, running-account credit. It is a debtor-creditor agreement, and falls within section 74(1)(b) if covered by a direction under section 74(3). It is also a multiple agreement, part of which (i.e. the part not dealing with the overdraft), as referred to in section 18(1)(a), falls within a category of agreement not mentioned in this Act. (Compare Example 17.)

Example 19

Facts H (a finance house) agrees with J (a partnership of individuals) to open an unsecured loan account in J's name on which the debit balance is not to exceed £7,500 (having regard to payments into the account made from time to time by J). Interest is to be payable in advance on this sum, with provision for yearly adjustments. H is entitled to debit the account with interest, a "setting-up" charge, and other charges. Before J has an opportunity to draw on the account it is initially debited with £2,250 for advance interest and other charges.

Analysis This is a personal running-account credit agreement (see sections 8(1) and 10(1)(a), and definition of "individual" in section 189(1)). By section 10(2) the credit limit is £7,000. By section 9(4) however the initial debit of £2,250, and any other charges later debited to the account by H, are not to be treated as credit even though time is allowed for their payment. Effect is given to this by section 10(3). Although the credit limit of £7,000 exceeds the amount (£5,000) specified in section 8(2) as the maximum for a consumer credit agreement, so that the agreement is not within section 10(3)(a), it is caught by section 10(3)(b)(i). At the beginning J can effectively draw (as credit) no more than £4,750, so the agreement is a consumer credit agreement.

Example 20

Facts K (in England) agrees with L (an individual) to bail goods to L for a period of three years certain at £2,200 a year, payable quarterly. The agreement contains no provision for the passing of the property in the goods to L.

Analysis This is not a hire-purchase agreement (see paragraph (b) of the definition of that term in section 189(1)), and is capable of subsisting for more than three months. Paragraphs (a) and (b) of section 15(1) are therefore satisfied, but paragraph (c) is not. The payments by L must exceed £5,000 if he conforms to the agreement. It is true that under section 101 L has a right to terminate the agreement on giving K three month's notice expiring not earlier than eighteen months after the making of the agreement, but that section applies only where the agreement is a regulated consumer hire agreement apart from the section (see subsection (1)). So the agreement is not a consumer hire agreement, though it would be if the hire charge were say £1,500 a year, or there were a "break" clause in it operable by either party before the hire charges exceeded £5,000. A similar result would follow if the agreement by K had been a hiring agreement in Scotland.

Example 21

Facts The P Bank decides to issue cheque cards to its customers under a scheme whereby the bank undertakes to honour cheques of up to £30 in every case where the payee has taken the cheque in reliance on the cheque card, whether the customer has funds in his account or not. The P Bank writes to the major retailers advising them of this scheme and also publicises it by advertising. The Bank issues a cheque card to Q (an individual), who uses it to pay by cheque for goods costing £20 bought by Q from R, a major retailer. At the time, Q has £500 in his account at the P Bank.

Analysis The agreement under which the cheque card is issued to Q is a consumer credit agreement even though at all relevant times Q has more than £30 in his account. This is because Q is free to draw out his whole balance and then use the cheque card, in which case the Bank has bound itself to honour the cheque. In other words the cheque card agreement provides Q with credit, whether he avails himself of it or not. Since the amount of the credit is not subject to any express limit, the cheque card can be used any number of times. It may be presumed however that section 10(3)(b)(iii) will apply. The agreement is an unrestricted-use debtor-creditor agreement (by section 13(c)). Although the P Bank wrote to R informing R of the P Bank's willingness to honour any cheque taken by R in reliance on a cheque card, this does not constitute pre-existing arrangements as mentioned in section 13(c) because section 187(3) operates to prevent it. The agreement is not a credit-token agreement within section 14(1)(b) because payment by the P Bank to R, would be a payment of the cheque and not a payment for the goods.

Example 22

Facts The facts are as in Example 16. On one occasion B uses the credit-card in a way which increases his debit balance with A (Credit) to £40. A (Credit) writes to B agreeing to allow the excess on that occasion only, but stating that it must be paid off within one month.

Analysis In exceeding his credit limit B, by implication, requests A (Credit) to allow him a temporary excess (compare Example 17). A (Credit) is thus faced by B's action with the choice of treating it as a breach of contract or granting his implied request. He does the latter. If he had done the former, B would be treated as taking credit to which he was not entitled (see section 14(3)) and, subject to the terms of his contract with A (Credit), would be liable to damages for breach of contract. As it is, the agreement to allow the excess varies the original credit-token agreement by adding a new term. Under section 10(2), the new term is to be disregarded in arriving at the credit limit, so that the credit-token agreement at no time ceases to be a small agreement. By section 82(2) the later agreement is deemed to revoke the original agreement and contain provisions reproducing the combined effect of the two agreements. By section 82(4), this later agreement is exempted from Part V (except section 56).

Example 23

Facts Under an oral agreement made on 10th January, X (an individual) has an overdraft on his current account at the Y bank with a credit limit of £100. On 15th February, when his overdraft stands at £90, X draws a cheque for £25. It is the first time that X has exceeded his credit limit, and on 16th February the bank honours the cheque.

Analysis The agreement of 10th January is a consumer credit agreement for running-account credit. The agreement of 15th–16th February varies the earlier agreement by adding a term allowing the credit limit to be exceeded merely temporarily. By section 82(2) the later agreement is deemed to revoke the earlier agreement and reproduce the combined effect of the two agreements. By section 82(4), Part V of this Act (except section 56) does not apply to the later agreement. By section 18(5), a term allowing a merely temporary excess over the credit limit is not to be treated as a separate agreement, or as providing fixed-sum credit. The whole of the £115 owed to the bank by X on 16th February is therefore running-account credit.

Example 24

Facts On 1st March 1975 Z (in England) enters into an agreement with A (an unincorporated body of persons) to bail to A equipment consisting of two components (component P and component Q). The agreement is not a hire-purchase agreement and is for a fixed term of 3 years, so paragraphs (a) and (b) of section 15(1) are both satisfied. The rental is payable monthly at a rate of £2,400 a year, but the agreement provides that this is to be reduced to £1,200 a year for the remainder of the agreement if at any time during its currency A returns component Q to the owner Z. On 5th May 1976 A is incorporated as A Ltd., taking over A's assets and liabilities. On 1st March 1977, A Ltd. returns component Q. On 1st January 1978, Z and A Ltd. agree to extend the earlier agreement by one year, increasing the rental for the final year by £250 to £1,450.

Analysis When entered into on 1st March 1975, the agreement is a consumer hire agreement. A falls within the definition of "individual" in section 189(1) and if A returns component Q before 1st May 1976 the total rental will not exceed £5,000 (see section 15(1)(c)). When this date is passed without component Q having been returned it is obvious that the total rental must now exceed £5,000. Does this mean that the agreement then ceases to be a consumer hire agreement? The answer is no, because there has been no change in the terms of the agreement, and without such a change the agreement cannot move from one category to the other. Similarly, the fact that A's rights and duties under the agreement pass to a body corporate on 5th May 1976 does not cause the agreement to cease to be a consumer hire agreement (see definition of "hirer" in section 189(1)).

The effect of the modifying agreement of 1st January 1978 is governed by section 82(2), which requires it to be treated as containing provisions reproducing the combined effect of the two actual agreements, that is to say as providing that—

    (a) obligations outstanding on 1st January 1978 are to be treated as outstanding under the modifying agreement;

    (b) the modifying agreement applies at the old rate of hire for the months of January and February 1978, and

    (c) for the year beginning 1st March 1978 A Ltd. will be the bailee of component P at a rental of £1,450.

The total rental under the modifying agreement is £1,850. Accordingly the modifying agreement is a regulated agreement. Even if the total rental under the modifying agreement exceeded £5,000 it would still be regulated because of the provisions of section 82(3).

*   *   *   *   *

Unsolicited Goods and Services (Amendment) Act 1975[1]

(c. 13)

* * * * *

Provision for offence under section 3(2) of the Act of 1971 to be prosecuted on indictment

3.—(1) An offence under section 3(2) of the Act of 1971 may be prosecuted on indictment; and a person convicted on indictment of an offence under that section shall be liable to a fine.

(2) This section applies only to offences committed after the coming into operation of this section.

Short title, citation, commencement, transitional provisions and extent

4.—(1) This Act may be cited as the Unsolicited Goods and Services (Amendment) Act 1975 and the Unsolicited Goods and Services Act 1971 and this Act may be cited together as the Unsolicited Goods and Services Acts 1971 and 1975.

(2) Sections 1 and 3 of this Act and this section shall come into operation on the passing of this Act but any regulations made by virtue of the said section I shall not come into operation before the date appointed by order under subsection (3) below for the coming into operation of section 2 of this Act.

(3) Section 2 of this Act shall come into operation on such date as the Secretary of State may by order made by statutory instrument appoint; and different dates may be appointed by order under this subsection for different provisions of that section.

(4) The amendments made to sections 3(3) and 6(2) of the Act of 1971 by section 2 of this Act and any regulations made by virtue of section 1 of this Act shall not apply to any note of agreement signed, or invoice or similar document sent before the date appointed by order under subsection (3) above for the coming into operation of the said section 2.

(5) This Act shall not extend to Northern Ireland.

---

[1] Sections 1 and 2 amend (or prospectively amend) the Unsolicited Goods and Services Act 1971, and are incorporated therein.

Torts (Interference with Goods) Act 1977[1]

(c. 32)

*   *   *   *   *

Allowance for improvement of the goods

6.—(1) If in proceedings for wrongful interference against a person (the "improver") who has improved the goods, it is shown that the improver acted in the mistaken but honest belief that he had a good title to them, an allowance shall be made for the extent to which, at the time as at which the goods fall to be valued in assessing damages, the value of the goods is attributable to the improvement.

(2) If, in proceedings for wrongful interference against a person ("the purchaser") who has purported to purchase the goods—

    (a) from the improver, or

    (b) where after such a purported sale the goods passed by a further purported sale on one or more occasions, on any such occasion,

it is shown that the purchaser acted in good faith, an allowance shall be made on the principle set out in subsection (1).

For example, where a person in good faith buys a stolen car from the improver and is sued in conversion by the true owner the damages may be reduced to reflect the improvement, but if the person who bought the stolen car from the improver sues the improver for failure of consideration, and the improver acted in good faith, subsection (3) below will ordinarily make a comparable reduction in the damages he recovers from the improver.

(3) If in a case within subsection (2) the person purporting to sell the goods acted in good faith, then in proceedings by the purchaser for recovery of the purchase price because of failure of consideration, or in any other proceedings founded on that failure of consideration, an allowance shall, where appropriate, be made on the principle set out in subsection (1).

(4) This section applies, with the necessary modifications, to a purported bailment or other disposition of goods as it applies to a purported sale of goods.

*   *   *   *   *

[1] Section 12 and scheds. 1 and 2 to the Act (not reproduced here) empower bailees (*e.g.* traders) of unsolicited goods (*e.g.* goods accepted for repair) to impose an obligation on bailors (*e.g.* customers) to take delivery of the goods; if necessary the bailee may sell the goods after giving notice to the bailor in the prescribed manner of the intention to sell.

Unfair Contract Terms Act 1977

(c. 50)

An Act to impose further limits on the extent to which under the law of England and Wales and Northern Ireland civil liability for breach of contract, or for negligence or other breach of duty, can be avoided by means of contract terms and otherwise, and under the law of Scotland civil liability can be avoided by means of contract terms. [26th October 1977]

PART I

AMENDMENT OF LAW FOR ENGLAND AND WALES AND NORTHERN IRELAND

Introductory

Scope of Part I

1.—(1) For the purposes of this Part of this Act, "negligence" meas the breach—

(a) of any obligation, arising from the express or implied terms of a contract, to take reasonable care or exercise reasonable skill in the performance of the contract;

(b) of any common law duty to take reasonable care or exercise reasonable skill (but not any stricter duty);

(c) of the common duty of care imposed by the Occupiers' Liability Act 1957 or the Occupiers' Liability Act (Northern Ireland) 1957.

(2) This Part of this Act is subject to Part III; and in relation to contracts, the operation of sections 2 to 4 and 7 is subject to the exceptions made by Schedule 1.

(3) In the case of both contract and tort, sections 2 to 7 apply (except where the contrary is stated in section 6(4)) only to business liability, that is liability for breach of obligations or duties arising—

(a) from things done or to be done by a person in the course of a business (whether his own business or another's): or

(b) from the occupation of premises used for business purposes of the occupier;

and references to liability are to be read accordingly but liability of an occupier of premises for breach of an obligation or duty towards a person obtaining access to the premises for recreational or educational purposes, being liability for loss or damage suffered by reason of the dangerous state of the premises, is not a business liability of the occupier unless granting that person such access for the purposes concerned falls within the business purposes of the occupier.

(4) In relation to any breach of duty or obligation, it is immaterial for any purpose of this Part of this Act whether the breach was inadvertent or intentional, or whether liability for it arises directly or vicariously.

Avoidance of liability for negligence, breach of contract, etc

Negligence liability

2.—(1) A person cannot by reference to any contract term or to a notice given to persons generally or to particular persons exclude or restrict his liability for death or personal injury resulting from negligence.

(2) In the case of other loss or damage, a person cannot so exclude or restrict his liability for negligence except in so far as the term or notice satisfies the requirement of reasonableness.

(3) Where a contract term or notice purports to exclude or restrict liability for negligence a person's agreement to or awareness of it is not of itself to be taken as indicating his voluntary acceptance of any risk.

Liability arising in contract

3.—(1) This section applies as between contracting parties where one of them deals as consumer or on the other's written standard terms of business.

(2) As against that party, the other cannot by reference to any contract term—

> (a) when himself in breach of contract, exclude or restrict any liability of his in respect of the breach; or
>
> (b) claim to be entitled—
>
> > (i) to render a contractual performance substantially different from that which was reasonably expected of him, or
> >
> > (ii) in respect of the whole or any part of his contractual obligation, to render no performance at all.

except in so far as (in any of the cases mentioned above in this subsection) the contract term satisfies the requirement of reasonableness.

Unreasonable indemnity clauses

4.—(1) A person dealing as consumer cannot by reference to any contract term be made to indemnify another person (whether a party to the contract or not) in respect of liability that may be incurred by the other for negligence or breach of contract, except in so far as the contract term satisfies the requirement of reasonableness.

(2) This section applies whether the liability in question—

> (a) is directly that of the person to be indemnified or is incurred by him vicariously;
>
> (b) is to the person dealing as consumer or to someone else.

Liability arising from sale or supply of goods

"Guarantee" of consumer goods

5.—(1) In the case of goods of a type ordinarily supplied for private use or consumption, where loss or damage—

> (a) arises from the goods proving defective while in consumer use; and
>
> (b) results from the negligence of a person concerned in the manufacture or distribution of the goods,

liability for the loss or damage cannot be excluded or restricted by reference to any contract term or notice contained in or operating by reference to a guarantee of the goods.

(2) For these purposes—

> (a) goods are to be regarded as "in consumer use" when a person is using them, or has them in his possession for use, otherwise than exclusively for the purposes of a business; and
>
> (b) anything in writing is a guarantee if it contains or purports to contain some promise or assurance (however worded or presented) that defects will be made good by complete or partial replacement, or by repair, monetary compensation or otherwise.

(3) This section does not apply as between the parties to a contract under or in pursuance of which possession or ownership of the goods passed.

Sale and hire-purchase

6.—(1) Liability for breach of the obligations arising from—

    (a) section 12 of the Sale of Goods Act 1979 (seller's implied undertakings as to title, etc.);

    (b) section 8 of the Supply of Goods (Implied Terms) Act 1973 (the corresponding thing in relation to hire-purchase),

cannot be excluded or restricted by reference to any contract term.

(2) As against a person dealing as consumer, liability for breach of the obligations arising from—

    (a) section 13, 14 or 15 of the 1979 Act (seller's implied undertakings as to conformity of goods with description or sample, or as to their quality or fitness for a particular purpose);

    (b) section 9, 10 or 11 of the 1973 Act (the corresponding things in relation to hire-purchase),

cannot be excluded or restricted by reference to any contract term.

(3) As against a person dealing otherwise than as consumer, the liability specified in subsection (2) above can be excluded or restricted by reference to a contract term, but only in so far as the term satisfies the requirement of reasonableness.

(4) The liabilities referred to in this section are not only the business liabilities defined by section 1(3), but include those arising under any contract of sale of goods or hire-purchase agreement.

Miscellaneous contracts under which goods pass

7.—(1) Where the possession or ownership of goods passes under or in pursuance of a contract not governed by the law of sale of goods or hire-purchase, subsections (2) to (4) below apply as regards the effect (if any) to be given to contract terms excluding or restricting liability for breach of obligation arising by implication of law from the nature of the contract.

(2) As against a person dealing as consumer, liability in respect of the goods' correspondence with description or sample, or their quality or fitness for any particular purpose, cannot be excluded or restricted by reference to any such term.

(3) As against a person dealing otherwise than as consumer, that liability can be excluded or restricted by reference to such a term, but only in so far as the term satisfies the requirement of reasonableness.

(3A) Liability for breach of the obligations arising under section 2 of the Supply of Goods and Services Act 1982 (implied terms about title etc. in certain contracts for the transfer of the property in goods) cannot be excluded or restricted by references to any such term.

(4) Liability in respect of—

    (a) the right to transfer ownership of the goods, or give possession; or

    (b) the assurance of quiet possession to a person taking goods in pursuance of the contract,

cannot (in a case to which subsection (3A) above does not apply) be excluded or restricted by reference to any such term except in so far as the term satisfies the requirement of reasonableness.

(5) This section does not apply in the case of goods passing on a redemption

of trading stamps within the Trading Stamps Act 1964 or the Trading Stamps Act (Northern Ireland) 1965.

Other provisions about contracts

8. [*This section substituted a new provision for section 3 of the Misrepresentation Act 1967 and is incorporated therein.*]

Effect of breach
9.—(1) Where for reliance upon it a contract term has to satisfy the requirement of reasonableness, it may be found to do so and be given effect accordingly notwithstanding that the contract has been terminated either by breach or by a party electing to treat it as repudiated.

(2) Where on a breach the contract is nevertheless affirmed by a party entitled to treat it as repudiated, this does not of itself exclude the requirement of reasonableness in relation to any contract term.

Evasion by means of secondary contract
10. A person is not bound by any contract term prejudicing or taking away rights of his which arise under, or in connection with the performance of, another contract, so far as those rights extend to the enforcement of another's liability which this Part of this Act prevents that other from excluding or restricting.

Explanatory provisions

The "reasonableness" test
11.—(1) In relation to a contract term, the requirement of reasonableness for the purposes of this Part of this Act, section 3 of the Misrepresentation Act 1967 and section 3 of the Misrepresentation Act (Northern Ireland) 1967 is that the term shall have been a fair and reasonable one to be included having regard to the circumstances which were, or ought reasonably to have been, known to or in the contemplation of the parties when the contract was made.

(2) In determining for the purposes of section 6 or 7 above whether a contract term satisfies the requirement of reasonableness, regard shall be had in particular to the matters specified in Schedule 2 to this Act; but this subsection does not prevent the court or arbitrator from holding, in accordance with any rule of law, that a term which purports to exclude or restrict any relevant liability is not a term of the contract.

(3) In relation to a notice (not being a notice having contractual effect), the requirement of reasonableness under this Act is that it should be fair and reasonable to allow reliance on it, having regard to all the circumstances obtaining when the liability arose or (but for the notice) would have arisen.

(4) Where by reference to a contract term or notice a person seeks to restrict liability to a specified sum of money, and the question arises (under this or any other Act) whether the term or notice satisfies the requirement of reasonableness, regard shall be had in particular (but without prejudice to subsection (2) above in the case of contract terms) to—

    (a) the resources which he could expect to be available to him for the purpose of meeting the liability should it arise; and

    (b) how far it was open to him to cover himself by insurance.

(5) It is for those claiming that a contract term or notice satisfies the requirement of reasonableness to show that it does.

"Dealing as consumer"

12.—(1) A party to a contract "deals as consumer" in relation to another party if—

    (a) he neither makes the contract in the course of a business nor holds himself out as doing so; and

    (b) the other party does make the contract in the course of a business; and

    (c) in the case of a contract governed by the law of sale of goods or hire-purchase, or by section 7 of this Act, the goods passing under or in pursuance of the contract are of a type ordinarily supplied for private use or consumption.

(2) But on a sale by auction or by competitive tender the buyer is not in any circumstances to be regarded as dealing as consumer.

(3) Subject to this, it is for those claiming that a party does not deal as consumer to show that he does not.

Varieties of exemption clause

13.—(1) To the extent that this Part of this Act prevents the exclusion or restriction of any liability it also prevents—

    (a) making the liability or its enforcement subject to restrictive or onerous conditions;

    (b) excluding or restricting any right or remedy in respect of the liability, or subjecting a person to any prejudice in consequence of his pursuing any such right or remedy;

    (c) excluding or restricting rules of evidence or procedure;

and (to that extent) sections 2 and 5 to 7 also prevent excluding or restricting liability by reference to terms and notices which exclude or restrict the relevant obligation or duty.

(2) But an agreement in writing to submit present or future differences to arbitration is not to be treated under this Part of this Act as excluding or restricting any liability.

Interpretation of Part I

14. In this Part of this Act—

"business" includes a profession and the activities of any government department or local or public authority;

"goods" has the same meaning as in the Sale of Goods Act 1979;

"hire-purchase agreement" has the same meaning as in the Consumer Credit Act 1974;

"negligence" has the meaning given by section 1(1);

"notice" includes an announcement, whether or not in writing, and any other communication or pretended communication; and

"personal injury" includes any disease and any impairment of physical or mental condition.

PART II

AMENDMENT OF LAW FOR SCOTLAND

Scope of Part II

15.—(1) This Part of this Act applies only to contracts, is subject to Part III of this Act and does not affect the validity of any discharge or indemnity given by a person in consideration of the receipt by him of compensation in settlement of any claim which he has.

(2) Subject to subsection (3) below, sections 16 to 18 of this Act apply to any contract only to the extent that the contract—

    (a) relates to the transfer of the ownership or possession of goods from one person to another (with or without work having been done on them);

    (b) constitutes a contract of service or apprenticeship;

    (c) relates to services of whatever kind, including (without prejudice to the foregoing generality) carriage, deposit and pledge, care and custody, mandate, agency, loan and services relating to the use of land;

    (d) relates to the liability of an occupier of land to persons entering upon or using that land;

    (e) relates to a grant of any right or permission to enter upon or use land not amounting to an estate or interest in the land.

(3) Notwithstanding anything in subsection (2) above, sections 16 to 18—

    (a) do not apply to any contract to the extent that the contract—

        (i) is a contract of insurance (including a contract to pay an annuity on human life);

        (ii) relates to the formation, constitution or dissolution of any body corporate or unincorporated association or partnership;

    (b) apply to—

        a contract of marine salvage or towage;

        a charter party of a ship or hovercraft;

        a contract for the carriage of goods by ship or hovercraft; or,

        a contract to which subsection (4) below relates.

        only to the extent that—

        (i) both parties deal or hold themselves out as dealing in the course of a business (and then only in so far as the contract purports to exclude or restrict liability for breach of duty in respect of death or personal injury); or

        (ii) the contract is a consumer contract (and then only in favour of the consumer).

(4) This subsection relates to a contract in pursuance of which goods are carried by ship or hovercraft and which either—

    (a) specifies ship or hovercraft as the means of carriage over part of the journey to be covered; or

    (b) makes no provision as to the means of carriage and does not exclude ship or hovercraft as that means,

in so far as the contract operates for and in relation to the carriage of the goods by that means.

Liability for breach of duty

16.—(1) Subject to subsection (1A) below where a term of contract or a provision of a notice given to persons generally or to particular persons purports to exclude or restrict liability for breach of duty arising in the course of any business or from the occupation of any premises used for business purposes of the occupier, that term or provision—

    (a) shall be void in any case where such exclusion or restriction is in respect of death or personal injury;

    (b) shall, in any other case, have no effect if it was not fair and reasonable to incorporate the term in the contract or, as the case may be, if it is not fair and reasonable to allow reliance on the provision.

(1A) Nothing in paragraph (b) of subsection (1) above shall be taken as implying that a provision of a notice has effect in circumstances where, apart from that paragraph, it would not have effect.[1]

(2) Subsection (1)(a) above does not affect the validity of any discharge and indemnity given by a person, on or in connection with an award to him of compensation for pneumoconiosis attributable to employment in the coal industry, in respect of any further claim arising from his contracting that disease.

(3) Where under subsection (1) above a term of a contract or a provision of a notice is void or has no effect, the fact that a person has agreed to, or was aware of, the term or provision shall not of itself be sufficient evidence that he knowingly and voluntarily assumed any risk.

Control of unreasonable exemptions in consumer or standard from contracts

17.—(1) Any term of a contract which is a consumer contract or a standard form contract shall have no effect for the purpose of enabling a party to the contract—

    (a) who is in breach of a contractual relation, to exclude or restrict any liability of his to the consumer in respect of the breach;

    (b) in respect of a contractual relation, to render no performance, or to render a performance substantially different from that which the consumer or customer reasonably expected from the contract;

if it was not fair and reasonable to incorporate the term in the contract.

(2) In this section "customer" means a party to a standard form contract who deals on the basis of written standard terms of business of the other party to the contract who himself deals in the course of a business.

Unreasonable indemnity clauses in consumer contracts

18.—(1) Any term of a contract which is a consumer contract shall have no effect for the purpose of making the consumer indemnify another person (whether a party to the contract or not) in respect of liability which that other person may incur as a result of breach of duty or breach of contract, if it was not fair and reasonable to incorporate the term in the contract.

(2) In this section "liability" means liability arising in the course of any business or from the occupation of any premises used for business purposes of the occupier.

"Guarantee" of consumer goods

19.—(1) This section applies to a guarantee—

    (a) in relation to goods which are of a type ordinarily supplied for private use or consumption; and

    (b) which is not a guarantee given by one party to the other party to a contract under or in pursuance of which the ownership or possession of the goods to which the guarantee relates is transferred.

(2) A term of a guarantee to which this section applies shall be void in so far as it purports to exclude or restrict liability for loss or damage (including death or personal injury)—

---

[1] Subsection (1A) was added by the Law Reform (Miscellaneous Provisions) (Scotland) Act 1990, s. 68, but applies only to loss or damage suffered on or after April 1, 1991.

    (a) arising from the goods proving defective while—
       (i) in use otherwise than exclusively for the purposes of a business; or
       (ii) in the possession of a person for such use; and
    (b) resulting from the breach of duty of a person concerned in the manufacture or distribution of the goods.

(3) For the purposes of this section, any document is a guarantee if it contains or purports to contain some promise or assurance (however worded or presented) that defects will be made good by complete or partial replacement, or by repair, monetary compensation or otherwise.

Obligations implied by law in sale and hire-purchase contracts

20.—(1) Any term of a contract which purports to exclude or restrict liability for breach of the obligations arising from—
    (a) section 12 of the Sale of Goods Act 1979 (seller's implied undertakings as to title etc.);
    (b) section 8 of the Supply of Goods (Implied Terms) Act 1973 (implied terms as to title in hire-purchase agreements),
shall be void.

(2) Any term of a contract which purports to exclude or restrict liability for breach of the obligations arising from—
    (a) section 13, 14 or 15 of the said Act of 1979 (seller's implied undertakings as to conformity of goods with description or sample, or as to their quality or fitness for a particular purpose);
    (b) section 9, 10 or 11 of the said Act of 1973 (the corresponding provisions in relation to hire-purchase),
shall—
       (i) in the case of a consumer contract, be void against the consumer;
       (ii) in any other case, have no effect if it was not fair and reasonable to incorporate the term in the contract.

Obligations implied by law in other contracts for the supply of goods

21.—(1) Any term of a contract to which this section applies purporting to exclude or restrict liability for breach of an obligation—
    (a) such as is referred to in subsection (3)(*a*) below—
       (i) in the case of a consumer contract, shall be void against the consumer, and
       (ii) in any other case, shall have no effect if it was not fair and reasonable to incorporate the term in the contract;
    (b) such as is referred to in subsection (3)(*b*) below, shall have no effect if it was not fair and reasonable to incorporate the term in the contract.

(2) This section applies to any contract to the extent that it relates to any such matter as is referred to in section 15(2)(*a*) of this Act, but does not apply to—
    (a) a contract of sale of goods or a hire-purchase agreement; or
    (b) a charter party of a ship or hovercraft unless it is a consumer contract (and then only in favour of the consumer).

(3) An obligation referred to in this subsection is an obligation incurred under a contract in the course of a business and arising by implication of law from the nature of the contract which relates—
    (a) to the correspondence of goods with description or sample, or to the quality or fitness of the goods for any particular purpose; or

(b) to any right to transfer ownership or possession of goods, or to the enjoyment of quiet possession of goods.

(3A) Notwithstanding anything in the foregoing provisions of this section, any term of a contract which purports to exclude or restrict liability for breach of the obligations arising under section 11B of the Supply of Goods and Services Act 1982 (implied terms about title, freedom from encumbrances and quiet possession in certain contracts for the transfer of property in goods) shall be void.

(4) Nothing in this section applies to the supply of goods on a redemption of trading stamps within the Trading Stamps Act 1964.

Consequence of breach

22. For the avoidance of doubt, where any provision of this Part of this Act requires that the incorporation of a term in a contract must be fair and reasonable for that term to have effect—

(a) if that requirement is satisfied, the term may be given effect to notwithstanding that the contract has been terminated in consequence of breach of that contract;

(b) for the term to be given effect to, that requirement must be satisfied even where a party who is entitled to rescind the contract elects not to rescind it.

Evasion by means of secondary contract

23. Any term of any contract shall be void which purports to exclude or restrict, or has the effect of excluding or restricting—

(a) the exercise, by a party to any other contract, of any right or remedy which arises in respect of that other contract in consequence of breach of duty, or of obligation, liability for which could not by virtue of the provisions of this Part of this Act be excluded or restricted by a term of that other contract;

(b) the application of the provisions of this Part of this Act in respect of that or any other contract.

The "reasonableness" test

24.—(1) In determining for the purposes of this Part of this Act whether it was fair and reasonable to incorporate a term in a contract, regard shall be had only to the circumstances which were, or ought reasonably to have been, known to or in the contemplation of the parties to the contract at the time the contract was made.

(2) In determining for the purposes of section 20 or 21 of this Act whether it was fair and reasonable to incorporate a term in a contract, regard shall be had in particular to the matters specified in Schedule 2 to this Act; but this subsection shall not prevent a court or arbiter from holding, in accordance with any rule of law, that a term which purports to exclude or restrict any relevant liability is not a term of the contract.

(2A) In determining for the purposes of this Part of this Act whether it is fair and reasonable to allow reliance on a provision of a notice (not being a notice having contractual effect), regard shall be had to all the circumstances obtaining when the liability arose or (but for the provision) would have arisen.

(3) Where a term in a contract or a provision of a notice purports to restrict liability to a specified sum of money, and the question arises for the purposes of this Part of this Act whether it was fair and reasonable to incorporate the term in the contract or whether it is fair and reasonable to allow reliance on

the provision, then, without prejudice to subsection (2) above in the case of a term in a contract, regard shall be had in particular to—

(a) the resources which the party seeking to rely on that term or provision could expect to be available to him for the purposes of meeting the liability should it arise;

(b) how far it was open to that party to cover himself by insurance.

(4) The onus of proving that it was fair and reasonable to incorporate a term in a contract or that it is fair and reasonable to allow reliance on a provision of a notice shall lie on the party so contending.

Interpretation of Part II

25.—(1) In this part of this Act—

"breach of duty" means the breach—

(a) of any obligation, arising from the express or implied terms of a contract, to take reasonable care or exercise reasonable skill in the performance of the contract;

(b) of any common law duty to take reasonable care or exercise reasonable skill;

(c) of the duty of reasonable care imposed by section 2(1) of the Occupiers' Liability (Scotland) Act 1960;

"business" includes a profession and the activities of any government department or local or public authority;

"consumer" has the meaning assigned to that expression in the definition in this section of "consumer contract";

"consumer contract" means a contract (not being a contract of sale by auction or competitive tender) in which—

(a) one party to the contract deals, and the other party to the contract ("the consumer") does not deal or hold himself out as dealing, in the course of a business, and

(b) in the case of a contract such as is mentioned in section 15(2) (a) of this Act, the goods are of a type ordinarily supplied for private use or consumption;

and for the purposes of this Part of this Act the onus of proving that a contract is not to be regarded as a consumer contract shall lie on the party so contending;

"goods" has the same meaning as in the Sale of Goods Act 1979;

"hire-purchase agreement" has the same meaning as in section 189(1) of the Consumer Credit Act 1974;

"personal injury" includes any disease and any impairment of physical or mental condition.

(2) In relation to any breach of duty or obligation, it is immaterial for any purpose of this Part of this Act whether the act or omission giving rise to that breach was inadvertent or intentional, or whether liability for it arises directly or vicariously.

(3) In this Part of this Act, any reference to excluding or restricting any liability includes—

(a) making the liability or its enforcement subject to any restrictive or onerous conditions;

(b) excluding or restricting any right or remedy in respect of the liability, or subjecting a person to any prejudice in consequence of his pursuing any such right or remedy;

(c) excluding or restricting any rule of evidence or procedure;

(d) excluding or restricting any liability by reference to a notice having contractual effect,

but does not include an agreement to submit any question to arbitration.

(4) In subsection (3)(d) above "notice" includes an announcement, whether or not in writing, and any other communication or pretended communication.

(5) In sections 15 and 16 and 19 to 21 of this Act, any reference to excluding or restricting liability for breach of an obligation or duty shall include a reference to excluding or restricting the obligation or duty itself.

PART III

PROVISIONS APPLYING TO WHOLE OF UNITED KINGDOM

Miscellaneous

International supply contracts

26.—(1) The limits imposed by this Act on the extent to which a person may exclude or restrict liability by reference to a contract term do not apply to liability arising under such a contract as is described in subsection (3) below.

(2) The terms of such a contract are not subject to any requirement of reasonableness under section 3 or 4: and nothing in Part II of this Act shall require the incorporation of the terms of such a contract to be fair and reasonable for them to have effect.

(3) Subject to subsection (4), that description of contract is one whose characteristics are the following—

(a) either it is a contract of sale of goods or it is one under or in pursuance of which the possession or ownership of goods passes; and

(b) it is made by parties whose places of business (or, if they have none, habitual residences) are in the territories of different States (the Channel Islands and the Isle of Man being treated for this purpose as different States from the United Kingdom).

(4) A contract falls within subsection (3) above only if either—

(a) the goods in question are, at the time of the conclusion of the contract, in the course of carriage, or will be carried, from the territory of one State to the territory of another; or

(b) the acts constituting the offer and acceptance have been done in the territories of different States; or

(c) the contract provides for the goods to be delivered to the territory of a State other than that within whose territory those acts were done.

Choice of law clauses

27.—(1) Where the law applicable to a contract is the law of any part of the United Kingdom only by choice of the parties (and apart from that choice would be the law of some country outside the United Kingdom) sections 2 to 7 and 16 to 21 of this Act do not operate as part of the law applicable to the contract.

(2) This Act has effect notwithstanding any contract term which applies or purports to apply the law of some country outside the United Kingdom, where (either or both)—

(a) the term appears to the court, or arbitrator or arbiter to have been imposed wholly or mainly for the purpose of enabling the party imposing it to evade the operation of this Act; or

(b) in the making of the contract one of the parties dealt as consumer, and he was then habitually resident in the United Kingdom, and the essential steps necessary for the making of the contract were taken there, whether by him or by others on his behalf.

(3) In the application of subsection (2) above to Scotland, for paragraph (b) there shall be substituted—

"(b) the contract is a consumer contract as defined in Part II of this Act, and the consumer at the date when the contract was made was habitually resident in the United Kingdom, and the essential steps necessary for the making of the contract were taken there, whether by him or by others on his behalf.".

Temporary provision for sea carriage of passengers

28.—(1) This section applies to a contract for carriage by sea of a passenger or of a passenger and his luggage where the provisions of the Athens Convention (with or without modification) do not have, in relation to the contract, the force of law in the United Kingdom.

(2) In a case where—

(a) the contract is not made in the United Kingdom, and

(b) neither the place of departure nor the place of destination under it is in the United Kingdom,

a person is not precluded by this Act from excluding or restricting liability for loss or damage, being loss or damage for which the provisions of the Convention would, if they had the force of law in relation to the contract, impose liability on him.

(3) In any other case, a person is not precluded by this Act from excluding or restricting liability for that loss or damage—

(a) in so far as the exclusion or restriction would have been effective in that case had the provisions of the Convention had the force of law in relation to the contract; or

(b) in such circumstances and to such extent as may be prescribed, by reference to a prescribed term of the contract.

(4) For the purposes of subsection (3)(a), the values which shall be taken to be the official values in the United Kingdom of the amounts (expressed in gold francs) by reference to which liability under the provisions of the Convention is limited shall be such amounts in sterling as the Secretary of State may from time to time by order made by statutory instrument specify.

(5) In this section,—

(a) the references to excluding or restricting liability include doing any of those things in relation to the liability which are mentioned in section 13 or section 25(3) and (5); and

(b) "the Athens Convention" means the Athens Convention relating to the Carriage of Passengers and their Luggage by Sea, 1974; and

(c) "prescribed" means prescribed by the Secretary of State by regulations made by statutory instrument;

and a statutory instrument containing the regulations shall be subject to annulment in pursuance of a resolution of either House of Parliament.

Saving for other relevant legislation

29.—(1) Nothing in this Act removes or restricts the effect of, or prevents reliance upon, any contractual provision which—

(a) is authorised or required by the express terms or necessary implication of an enactment; or

    (b) being made with a view to compliance with an international agreement to which the United Kingdom is a party, does not operate more restrictively than is contemplated by the agreement.

(2) A contract term is to be taken—

    (a) for the purposes of Part I of this Act, as satisfying the requirement of reasonableness; and

    (b) for those of Part II, to have been fair and reasonable to incorporate,

if it is incorporated or approved by, or incorporated pursuant to a decision or ruling of, a competent authority acting in the exercise of any statutory jurisdiction or function and is not a term in a contract to which the competent authority is itself a party.

(3) In this section—

"competent authority" means any court, arbitrator or arbiter, government department or public authority;

"enactment" means any legislation (including subordinate legislation) of the United Kingdom or Northern Ireland and any instrument having effect by virtue of such legislation; and

"statutory" means conferred by an enactment.

30. [*Repealed*]

General

Commencement; amendments; repeals

31.—(1) This Act comes into force on 1st February 1978.

(2) Nothing in this Act applies to contracts made before the date on which it comes into force; but subject to this, it applies to liability for any loss or damage which is suffered on or after that date.

(3) The enactments specified in Schedule 3 to this Act are amended as there shown.

(4) The enactments specified in Schedule 4 to this Act are repealed to the extent specified in column 3 of that Schedule.

Citation and extent

32.—(1) This Act may be cited as the Unfair Contract Terms Act 1977.

(2) Part I of this Act extends to England and Wales and to Northern Ireland; but it does not extend to Scotland.

(3) Part II of this Act extends to Scotland only.

(4) This Part of this Act extends to the whole of the United Kingdom.

SCHEDULES

SCOPE OF SECTIONS 2 TO 4 AND 7

1. Sections 2 to 4 of this Act do not extend to—

    (a) any contract of insurance (including a contract to pay an annuity on human life);

    (b) any contract so far as it relates to the creation or transfer of an interest in land, or to the termination of such an interest, whether by extinction, merger, surrender, forfeiture or otherwise;

    (c) any contract so far as it relates to the creation or transfer of a right or interest in any patent, trade mark, copyright, or design right, registered

design, technical or commercial information or other intellectual property, or relates to the termination of any such right or interest;
  (d) any contract so far as it relates—
    (i) to the formation or dissolution of a company (which means any body corporate or unincorporated association and includes a partnership), or
    (ii) to its constitution or the rights or obligations of its corporators or members;
  (e) any contract so far as it relates to the creation or transfer of securities or of any right or interest in securities.
  2. Section 2(1) extends to—
  (a) any contract of marine salvage or towage;
  (b) any charterparty of a ship or hovercraft; and
  (c) any contract for the carriage of goods by ship or hovercraft;
but subject to this sections 2 to 4 and 7 do not extend to any such contract except in favour of a person dealing as consumer.
  3. Where goods are carried by ship or hovercraft in pursuance of a contract which either—
  (a) specifies that as the means of carriage over part of the journey to be covered, or
  (b) makes no provision as to the means of carriage and does not exclude that means,
then sections 2(2), 3 and 4 do not, except in favour of a person dealing as consumer, extend to the contract as it operates for and in relation to the carriage of the goods by that means.
  4. Section 2(1) and (2) do not extend to a contract of employment, except in favour of the employee.
  5. Section 2(1) does not affect the validity of any discharge and indemnity given by a person, on or in connection with an award to him of compensation for pneumoconiosis attributable to employment in the coal industry, in respect of any further claim arising from his contracting that disease.

SCHEDULE 2

"GUIDELINES" FOR APPLICATION OF REASONABLENESS TEST

The matters to which regard is to be had in particular for the purposes of sections 6(3), 7(3) and (4), 20 and 21 are any of the following which appear to be relevant—
  (a) the strength of the bargaining positions of the parties relative to each other, taking into account (among other things) alternative means by which the customer's requirements could have been met;
  (b) whether the customer received an inducement to agree to the term, or in accepting it had an opportunity of entering into a similar contract with other persons, but without having to accept a similar term;
  (c) whether the customer knew or ought reasonably to have known of the existence and extent of the term (having regard, among other things, to any custom of the trade and any previous course of dealing between the parties);
  (d) where the term excludes or restricts any relevant liability if some condition is not complied with, whether it was reasonable at the time of

the contract to expect that compliance with that condition would be practicable;

(e) whether the goods were manufactured, processed or adapted to the special order of the customer.

*   *   *   *   *

Estate Agents Act 1979[1]

(c. 38)

Application of Act

1.—(1) This Act applies, subject to subsections (2) to (4) below to things done by any person in the course of a business (including a business in which he is employed) pursuant to instructions received from another person (in this section referred to as "the client") who wishes to dispose of or acquire an interest in land—

    (a) for the purpose of, or with a view to, effecting the introduction to the client of a third person who wishes to acquire or, as the case may be, dispose of such an interest; and

    (b) after such an introduction has been effected in the course of that business, for the purpose of securing the disposal or, as the case may be, the acquisition of that interest;

and in this Act the expression "estate agency work" refers to things done as mentioned above to which this Act applies.

(2) This Act does not apply to things done—

    (a) in the course of his profession by a practising solicitor or a person employed by him or by an incorporated practice (within the meaning of the Solicitors (Scotland) Act 1980) or a person employed by it; or

    (b) in the course of credit brokerage, within the meaning of the Consumer Credit Act 1974; or

    (c) in the course of insurance brokerage by a person who is for the time being registered under section 2, or enrolled under section 4, of the Insurance Brokers (Registration) Act 1977; or

    (d) in the course of carrying out any survey or valuation pursuant to a contract which is distinct from that under which other things falling within subsection (1) above are done; or

    (e) in connection with applications and other matters arising under the Town and Country Planning Act 1990, the Planning (Listed Buildings and Conservation Areas) Act 1990 or the Town and Country Planning (Scotland) Act 1972 or the Planning (Northern Ireland) Order 1972.

(3) This Act does not apply to things done by any person—

    (a) pursuant to instructions received by him in the course of his employment in relation to an interest in land if his employer is the person who, on his own behalf, wishes to dispose of or acquire that interest; or

    (b) in relation to any interest in any property if the property is subject to a mortgage and he is the receiver of the income of it; or

    (c) in relation to a present, prospective or former employee of his or of any person by whom he also is employed if the things are done by reason of the employment (whether past, present or future).

(4) This Act does not apply to the publication of advertisements or the dissem-

---

[1] The following extract contains only those sections of the Estate Agents Act 1979 dealing (principally) with the power of the Director General of Fair Trading to make Orders prohibiting persons from carrying on estate agency work. The Act extends to Northern Ireland (s. 36(3)) and Scotland.

ination of information by a person who does no other acts which fall within subsection (1) above.

(5) In this section—

    (a) "practising solicitor" means, except in Scotland, a solicitor who is qualified to act as such under section 1 of the Solicitors Act 1974 or Article 4 of the Solicitors (Northern Ireland) Order 1976, and in Scotland includes a firm of practising solicitors;

    (b) "mortgage" includes a debenture and any other charge on property for securing money or money's worth; and

    (c) any reference to employment is a reference to employment under a contract of employment.

Interests in land

2.—(1) Subject to subsection (3) below, any reference in this Act to disposing of an interest in land is a reference to—

    (a) transferring a legal estate in fee simple absolute in possession; or

    (b) transferring or creating, elsewhere than in Scotland, a lease which, by reason of the level of the rent, the length of the term or both, has a capital value which may be lawfully realised on the open market; or

    (c) transferring or creating in Scotland any estate or interest in land which is capable of being owned or held as a separate interest and to which a title may be recorded in the Register of Sasines;

and any reference to acquiring an interest in land shall be construed accordingly.

(2) In subsection (1)(b) above the expression "lease" includes the rights and obligations arising under an agreement to grant a lease.

(3) Notwithstanding anything in subsections (1) and (2) above, references in this Act to disposing of an interest in land do not extend to disposing of—

    (a) the interest of a creditor whose debt is secured by way of a mortgage or charge of any kind over land or an agreement for any such mortgage or charge; or

    (b) in Scotland, the interest of a creditor in a heritable security as defined in section 9(8) of the Conveyancing and Feudal Reform (Scotland) Act 1970.

Orders by Director General of Fair Trading

Orders prohibiting unfit persons from doing estate agency work

3.—(1) The power of the Director General of Fair Trading (in this Act referred to as "the Director") to make an order under this section with respect to any person shall not be exercisable unless the Director is satisfied that that person—

    (a) has been convicted of—

        (i) an offence involving fraud or other dishonesty or violence, or

        (ii) an offence under any provision of this Act, other than section 10(6), section 22(3) or section 23(4), or

        (iii) any other offence which, at the time it was committed, was specified for the purposes of this section by an order made by the Secretary of State; or

    (b) has committed discrimination in the course of estate agency work; or

    (c) has failed to comply with any obligation imposed on him under any of sections 15 and 18 to 21 below; or

    (d) has engaged in a practice which, in relation to estate agency work, has been declared undesirable by an order made by the Secretary of State; and the provisions of Schedule 1 to the Act shall have effect for supplementing paragraphs (a) and (b) above.

(2) Subject to subsection (1) above, if the Director is satisfied that any person is unfit to carry on estate agency work generally or of a particular description he may make an order prohibiting that person—

    (a) from doing any estate agency work at all; or

    (b) from doing estate agency work of a description specified in the order;

and in determining whether a person is so unfit the Director may, in addition to taking account of any matters falling within subsection (1) above, also take account of whether, in the course of estate agency work or any other business activity, that person has engaged in any practice which involves breaches of a duty owed by virtue of any enactment, contract or rule of law and which is material to his fitness to carry on estate agency work.

(3) For the purposes of paragraphs (c) and (d) of subsection (1) above,—

    (a) anything done by a person in the course of his employment shall be treated as done by his employer as well as by him, whether or not it was done with the employer's knowledge or approval, unless the employer shows that he took such steps as were reasonably practicable to prevent the employee from doing that act, or from doing in the course of his employment acts of that description; and

    (b) anything done by a person as agent for another person with the authority (whether express or implied, and whether precedent or subsequent) of that person shall be treated as done by that other person as well as by him; and

    (c) anything done by a business associate of a person shall be treated as done by that person as well, unless he can show that the act was done without his connivance or consent.

(4) In an order under this section the Director shall specify as the grounds for the order those matters falling within paragraphs (a) to (d) of subsection (1) above as to which he is satisfied and on which, accordingly, he relies to give him power to make the order.

(5) If the Director considers it appropriate, he may in an order under this section limit the scope of the prohibition imposed by the order to a particular part of or area within the United Kingdom.

(6) An order under paragraph (a)(iii) or paragraph (d) of subsection (1) above—

    (a) shall be made by statutory instrument;

    (b) shall be laid before Parliament after being made; and

    (c) shall cease to have effect (without prejudice to anything previously done in reliance on the order) after the expiry of the period of twenty-eight days beginning with the date on which it was made unless within that period it has been approved by a resolution of each House of Parliament.

(7) In reckoning for the purposes of subsection (6)(c) above any period of twenty-eight days, no account shall be taken of any period during which Parliament is dissolved or prorogued or during which both Houses are adjourned for more than four days.

(8) A person who fails without reasonable excuse to comply with an order of the Director under this section shall be liable on conviction on indictment or on summary conviction to a fine which on summary conviction shall not exceed the statutory maximum.

Warning orders
   4.—(1) If the Director is satisfied that—
   (a) in the course of estate agency work any person has failed to comply
       with any such obligation as is referred to in section 3(1)(*c*) above (in
       this section referred to as a "relevant statutory obligation") or has
       engaged in such a practice as is referred to in section 3(1)(*d*) bove,
       and
   (b) if that person were again to fail to comply with a relevant statutory
       obligation or, as the case may be, were to continue to engage in that
       practice, the Director would consider him unfit as mentioned in subsec-
       tion (2) of section 3 above and would proceed to make an order under
       that section,
the Director may by order notify that person that he is so satisfied.
   (2) An order under this section shall state whether, in the opinion of the
Director, a further failure to comply with a relevant statutory obligation or, as
the case may be, continuation of the practice specified in the order would render
the person to whom the order is addressed unfit to carry on estate agency work
generally or estate agency work of a description specified in the order.
   (3) If, after an order has been made under this section, the person to whom
it is addressed fails to comply with a relevant statutory obligation or, as the
case may be, engages in the practice specified in the order then, for the purposes
of this Act, that fact shall be treated as conclusive evidence that he is unfit to
carry on estate agency work as stated in the order in accordance with subsection
(2) above; and the Director may proceed to make an order under section 3 above
accordingly.

Supplementary provisions as to orders under sections 3 and 4
   5.—(1) The provisions of Part I of Schedule 2 to this Act shall have effect—
   (a) with respect to the procedure to be followed before an order is made
       by the Director under section 3 or section 4 above; and
   (b) in connection with the making and coming into operation of any such
       order.
   (2) Where an order is made by the Director under section 3 or section 4
above against a partnership, it may, if the Director thinks it appropriate, have
effect also as an order against some or all of the partners individually, and in
such a case the order shall so provide and shall specify the names of the partners
affected by the order.
   (3) Nothing in section 62 of the Sex Discrimination Act 1975, section 53 of
the Race Relations Act 1976 or Article 62 of the Sex Discrimination (Northern
Ireland) Order 1976 (restriction of sanctions for breaches of those Acts and that
Order) shall be construed as applying to the making of an order by the Director
under section 3 above.
   (4) In any case where—
   (a) an order of the Director under section 3 above specifies a conviction
       as a ground for the order, and
   (b) the conviction becomes spent for the purposes of the Rehabilitation of
       Offenders Act 1974 or any corresponding enactment for the time being
       in force in Northern Ireland.
then, unless the order also specified other grounds which remain valid, the order
shall cease to have effect on the day on which the conviction becomes so spent.
   (5) In any case where—
   (a) an order of the Director under section 3 above specifies as grounds for

the order the fact that the person concerned committed discrimination by reason of the existence of any such finding or notice as is referred to in paragraph 2 of Schedule 1 to this Act, and

(b) the period expires at the end of which, by virtue of paragraph 3 of that Schedule, the person concerned would no longer be treated for the purposes of section 3(1)(b) above as having committed discrimination by reason only of that finding or notice,

then, unless the order also specifies other grounds which remain valid, the order shall cease to have effect at the end of that period.

Revocation and variation of orders under sections 3 and 4

6.—(1) On an application made to him by the person in respect of whom the Director has made an order under section 3 or section 4 above, the Director may revoke or vary the order.

(2) An application under subsection (1) above—

(a) shall state the reasons why the applicant considers that the order should be revoked or varied;

(b) in the case of an application for a variation, shall indicate the variation which the applicant seeks; and

(c) shall be accompanied by the prescribed fee.

(3) If the Director decides to accede to an application under subsection (1) above, he shall give notice in writing of his decision to the applicant and, upon the giving of that notice, the revocation or, as the case may be, the variation specified in the application shall take effect.

(4) The Director may decide to refuse an application under subsection (1) above—

(a) where it relates to an order under section 3 above, if he considers that the applicant remains unfit to carry on any estate agency work at all or, as the case may be, estate agency work of the description which is prohibited by the order; and

(b) where it relates to an order under section 4 above, if he considers that the applicant may again fail to comply with a relevant statutory obligation or, as the case may be, again engage in the practice specified in the order.

(5) If, on an application under subsection (1) above, the Director decides that—

(a) he cannot accede to the application because he considers that the applicant remains unfit to carry on any estate agency work at all in a particular part of or area within the United Kingdom or remains unfit to carry on estate agency work of a particular description (either throughout the United Kingdom or in a particular part of or area within it) or, as the case may be, remains likely to fail to comply with a relevant statutory obligation or to engage in a particular practice, but

(b) the order to which the application relates could, without detriment to the public, be varied in favour of the applicant,

the Director may make such a variation accordingly.

(6) The provisions of Part II of Schedule 2 to this Act shall have effect in relation to any application to the Director under subsection (1) above and the provisions of Part I of that Schedule shall have effect—

(a) with respect to the procedure to be followed before the Director comes to a decision under subsection (4) or subsection (5) above; and

(b) in connection with the making and coming into operation of such a
    decision.

(7) In this section "relevant statutory obligation" has the meaning assigned
to it by section 4(1)(a) above.

Appeals

7.—(1) A person who receives notice under paragraph 9 of Schedule 2 to
this Act of—

    (a) a decision of the Director to make an order in respect of him under
        section 3 or section 4 above, or

    (b) a decision of the Director under subsection (4) or subsection (5) of
        section 6 above on an application made by him,

may appeal against the decision to the Secretary of State.

(2) On an appeal under subsection (1) above the Secretary of State may give
such directions for disposing of the appeal as he thinks just, including a direction
for the payment of costs or expenses by any party to the appeal.

(3) The Secretary of State shall make provision by regulations with respect
to appeals under subsection (1) above—

    (a) as to the period within which and the manner in which such appeals
        are to be brought;

    (b) as to the persons by whom such appeals are to be heard on behalf of
        the Secretary of State;

    (c) as to the manner in which such appeals are to be conducted;

    (d) for taxing or otherwise settling any costs or expenses directed to be
        paid under subsection (2) above and for the enforcement of any such
        direction; and

    (e) as to any other matter connected with such appeals;

and such regulations shall be made by statutory instrument which shall be subject to annulment in pursuance of a resolution of either House of Parliament.

(4) If the appellant is dissatisfied in point of law with a decision of the Secretary of State under this section he may appeal against that decision to the High
Court, the Court of Session or a judge of the High Court in Northern Ireland.

(5) No appeal to the Court of Appeal or to the Court of Appeal in Northern
Ireland shall be brought from a decision under subsection (4) above except with
the leave of that Court or of the court or judge from whose decision the appeal
is brought.

(6) An appeal shall lie, with the leave of the Court of Session or the House
of Lords, from any decision of the Court of Session under this section, and such
leave may be given on such terms as to costs or otherwise as the Court of
Session or the House of Lords may determine.

Register of orders etc.

8.—(1) The Director shall establish and maintain a register on which there
shall be entered particulars of every order made by him under section 3 or
section 4 above and of his decision on any application for revocation or variation
of such an order.

(2) The particulars referred to in subsection (1) above shall include—

    (a) the terms of the order and of any variation of it; and

    (b) the date on which the order or variation came into operation or is
        expected to come into operation or if an appeal against the decision is
        pending and the order or variation has in consequence not come into
        operation, a statement to that effect.

(3) The Director may, of his own motion or on the application of any person aggrieved, rectify the register by the addition, variation or removal of any particulars; and the provisions of Part II of Schedule 2 to this Act shall have effect in relation to an application under this subsection.

(4) If it comes to the attention of the Director that any order of which particulars appear in the register is no longer in operation, he shall remove those particulars from the register.

(5) Any person shall be entitled on payment of the prescribed fee—

(a) to inspect the register during such office hours as may be specified by a general notice made by the Director and to take copies of any entry, or

(b) to obtain from the Director a copy, certified by him to be correct, of any entry in the register.

(6) A certificate given by the Director under subsection (5)(b) above shall be conclusive evidence of the fact that, on the date on which the certificate was given, the particulars contained in the copy to which the certificate relates were entered on the register; and particulars of any matters required to be entered on the register which are so entered shall be evidence and, in Scotland, sufficient evidence of those matters and shall be presumed, unless the contrary is proved, to be correct.

*   *   *   *   *

Sale of Goods Act 1979

(c. 54)

An Act to consolidate the law relating to the sale of goods.

[6th December 1979]

PART I

CONTRACTS TO WHICH ACT APPLIES

Contracts to which Act applies

1.—(1) This Act applies to contracts of sale of goods made on or after (but not to those made before) 1 January 1894.

(2) In relation to contracts made on certain dates, this Act applies subject to the modification of certain of its sections as mentioned in Schedule 1 below.

(3) Any such modification is indicated in the section concerned by a reference to Schedule 1 below.

(4) Accordingly, where a section does not contain such a reference, this Act applies in relation to the contract concerned without such modification of the section.

PART II

FORMATION OF THE CONTRACT

Contract of sale

Contract of sale

2.—(1) A contract of sale of goods is a contract by which the seller transfers or agrees to transfer the property in goods to the buyer for a money consideration, called the price.

(2) There may be a contract of sale between one part owner and another.

(3) A contract of sale may be absolute or conditional.

(4) Where under a contract of sale the property in the goods is transferred from the seller to the buyer the contract is called a sale.

(5) Where under a contract of sale the transfer of the property in the goods is to take place at a future time or subject to some condition later to be fulfilled the contract is called an agreement to sell.

(6) An agreement to sell becomes a sale when the time elapses or the conditions are fulfilled subject to which the property in the goods is to be transferred.

Capacity to buy and sell

3.—(1) Capacity to buy and sell is regulated by the general law concerning capacity to contract and to transfer and acquire property.

(2) Where necessaries are sold and delivered to a person who by reason of mental incapacity or drunkenness is incompetent to contract, he must pay a reasonable price for them.

(3) In subsection (2) above "necessaries" means goods suitable to the condi-

tion in life of the person concerned and to his actual requirements at the time of the sale and delivery.

Formalities of contract

How contract of sale is made
   4.—(1) Subject to this and any other Act, a contract of sale may be made in writing (either with or without seal), or by word of mouth, or partly in writing and partly by word of mouth, or may be implied from the conduct of the parties.
   (2) Nothing in this section affects the law relating to corporations.

Subject matter of contract

Existing or future goods
   5.—(1) The goods which form the subject of a contract of sale may be either existing goods, owned or possessed by the seller, or goods to be manufactured or acquired by him after the making of the contract of sale, in this Act called future goods.
   (2) There may be a contract for the sale of goods the acquisition of which by the seller depends on a contingency which may or may not happen.
   (3) Where by a contract of sale the seller purports to effect a present sale of future goods, the contract operates as an agreement to sell the goods.

Goods which have perished
   6. Where there is a contract for the sale of specific goods, and the goods without the knowledge of the seller have perished at the time when the contract is made, the contract is void.

Goods perishing before sale but after agreement to sell
   7. Where there is an agreement to sell specific goods and subsequently the goods, without any fault on the part of the seller or buyer, perish before the risk passes to the buyer, the agreement is avoided.

The price

Ascertainment of price
   8.—(1) The price in a contract of sale may be fixed by the contract, or may be left to be fixed in a manner agreed by the contract, or may be determined by the course of dealing between the parties.
   (2) Where the price is not determined as mentioned in subsection (1) above the buyer must pay a reasonable price.
   (3) What is a reasonable price is a question of fact dependent on the circumstances of each particular case.

Agreement to sell at valuation
   9.—(1) Where there is an agreement to sell goods on the terms that the price is to be fixed by the valuation of a third party, and he cannot or does not make the valuation, the agreement is avoided; but if the goods or any part of them have been delivered to and appropriated by the buyer he must pay a reasonable price for them.
   (2) Where the third party is prevented from making the valuation by the fault

of the seller or buyer, the party not at fault may maintain an action for damages against the party at fault.

Implied terms etc.

Stipulations about time

10.—(1) Unless a different intention appears from the terms of the contract, stipulations as to time of payment are not of the essence of a contract of sale.

(2) Whether any other stipulation as to time is or is not of the essence of the contract depends on the terms of the contract.

(3) In a contract of sale "month" prima facie means calendar month.

When condition to be treated as warranty

11.—(1) This section does not apply to Scotland.

(2) Where a contract of sale is subject to a condition to be fulfilled by the seller, the buyer may waive the condition, or may elect to treat the breach of the condition as a breach of warranty and not as a ground for treating the contract as repudiated.

(3) Whether a stipulation in a contract of sale is a condition, the breach of which may give rise to a right to treat the contract as repudiated, or a warranty, the breach of which may give rise to a claim for damages but not to a right to reject the goods and treat the contract as repudiated, depends in each case on the construction of the contract; and a stipulation may be a condition, though called a warranty in the contract.

(4) Subject to section 35A below where a contract of sale is not severable and the buyer has accepted the goods or part of them, the breach of a condition to be fulfilled by the seller can only be treated as a breach of warranty, and not as a ground for rejecting the goods and treating the contract as repudiated, unless there is an express or implied term of the contract to that effect.

(5) [*Repealed*]

(6) Nothing in this section affects a condition or warranty whose fulfilment is excused by law by reason of impossibility or otherwise.

(7) Paragraph 2 of Schedule 1 below applies in relation to a contract made before 22 April 1967 or (in the application of this Act to Northern Ireland) 28 July 1967.

Implied terms about title, etc.

12.—(1) In a contract of sale, other than one to which subsection (3) below applies, there is an implied term on the part of the seller that in the case of a sale he has a right to sell the goods, and in the case of an agreement to sell he will have such a right at the time when the property is to pass.

(2) In a contract of sale, other than one to which subsection (3) below applies, there is also an implied term that—

    (a) the goods are free, and will remain free until the time when the property is to pass, from any charge or encumbrance not disclosed or known to the buyer before the contract is made, and

    (b) the buyer will enjoy quiet possession of the goods except so far as it may be disturbed by the owner or other person entitled to the benefit of any charge or encumbrance so disclosed or known.

(3) This subsection applies to a contract of sale in the case of which there appears from the contract or is to be inferred from its circumstances an intention that the seller should transfer only such title as he or a third person may have.

(4) In a contract to which subsection (3) above applies there is an implied term that all charges or encumbrances known to the seller and not known to the buyer have been disclosed to the buyer before the contract is made.

(5) In a contract to which subsection (3) above applies there is also an implied term that none of the following will disturb the buyer's quiet possession of the goods, namely—

    (a) the seller;

    (b) in a case where the parties to the contract intend that the seller should transfer only such title as a third person may have, that person;

    (c) anyone claiming through or under the seller or that third person otherwise than under a charge or encumbrance disclosed or known to the buyer before the contract is made.

(5A) As regards England and Wales and Northern Ireland, the term implied by subsection (1) above is a condition and the terms implied by subsections (2), (4) and (5) above are warranties.

(6) Paragraph 3 of Schedule 1 below applies in relation to a contract made before 18 May 1973.

Sale by description

13.—(1) Where there is a contract for the sale of goods by description, there is an implied term that the goods will correspond with the description.

(1A) As regards England and Wales and Northern Ireland, the term applied by subsection (1) above is a condition.

(2) If the sale is by sample as well as by description it is not sufficient that the bulk of the goods corresponds with the sample if the goods do not also correspond with the description.

(3) A sale of goods is not prevented from being a sale by description by reason only that, being exposed for sale or hire, they are selected by the buyer.

(4) Paragraph 4 of Schedule 1 below applies in relation to a contract made before 18 May 1973.

Implied terms about quality or fitness

14.—(1) Except as provided by this section and section 15 below and subject to any other enactment, there is no implied term about the quality or fitness for any particular purpose of goods supplied under a contract of sale.

(2) Where the seller sells goods in the course of a business, there is an implied term that the goods supplied under the contract are of satisfactory quality.[1]

(2A) For the purposes of this Act, goods are of satisfactory quality if they meet the standard that a reasonable person would regard as satisfactory, taking account of any description of the goods, the price (if relevant) and all the other relevant circumstances.

(2B) For the purposes of this Act, the quality of goods includes their state and condition and the following (among others) are in appropriate cases aspects of the quality of goods—

    (a) fitness for all the purposes for which goods of the kind in question are commonly supplied,

    (b) appearance and finish,

---

[1] Subsections (2), (2A), (2B) and (2C) were substituted for the former subsection (2) [implied term about merchantable quality] by the Sale and Supply of Goods Act 1994, s. 1(1), which by s. 8 thereof applies to contracts made on or after January 3, 1995; the 1994 Act extends to Northern Ireland (s. 8(4)).

(c) freedom from minor defects,

(d) safety, and

(e) durability.

(2C) The term implied by subsection (2) above does not extend to any matter making the quality of goods unsatisfactory—

(a) which is specifically drawn to the buyer's attention before the contract is made,

(b) where the buyer examines the goods before the contract is made, which that examination ought to reveal, or

(c) in the case of a contract for sale by sample, which would have been apparent on a reasonable examination of the sample.

(3) Where the seller sells goods in the course of a business and the buyer, expressly or by implication, makes known—

(a) to the seller, or

(b) where the purchase price or part of it is payable by instalments and the goods were previously sold by a credit-broker to the seller, to that credit-broker,

any particular purpose for which the goods are being bought, there is an implied term that the goods supplied under the contract are reasonably fit for that purpose, whether or not that is a purpose for which such goods are commonly supplied, except where the circumstances show that the buyer does not rely, or that it is unreasonable for him to rely, on the skill or judgment of the seller or credit-broker.

(4) An implied term about quality or fitness for a particular purpose may be annexed to a contract of sale by usage.

(5) The preceding provisions of this section apply to a sale by a person who in the course of a business is acting as agent for another as they apply to a sale by a principal in the course of a business, except where that other is not selling in the course of a business and either the buyer knows that fact or reasonable steps are taken to bring it to the notice of the buyer before the contract is made.

(6) As regards England and Wales and Northern Ireland, the terms implied by subsections (2) and (3) above are conditions.

(7) Paragraph 5 of Schedule 1 below applies in relation to a contract made on or after 18 May 1973 and before the appointed day, and paragraph 6 in relation to one made before 18 May 1973.

(8) In subsection (7) above and paragraph 5 of Schedule 1 below references to the appointed day are to the day appointed for the purposes of those provisions by an order of the Secretary of State made by statutory instrument.

Sale by sample

Sale by sample

15.—(1) A contract of sale is a contract for sale by sample where there is an express or implied term to that effect in the contract.

(2) In the case of a contract for sale by sample there is an implied term—

(a) that the bulk will correspond with the sample in quality;

(b) [*Repealed*]

(c) that the goods will be free from any defect, making their quality unsatisfactory, which would not be apparent on reasonable examination of the sample.

(3) As regards England and Wales and Northern Ireland, the term implied by subsection (2) above is a condition.

(4) Paragraph 7 of Schedule 1 below applies in relation to a contract made before 18 May 1973.

Miscellaneous

Modification of remedies for breach of condition in non-consumer cases[2]

15A.—(1) Where in the case of a contract of sale—
- (a) the buyer would, apart from this subsection, have the right to reject goods by reason of a breach on the part of the seller of a term implied by section 13, 14 or 15 above, but
- (b) the breach is so slight that it would be unreasonable for him to reject them,

then, if the buyer does not deal as consumer, the breach is not to be treated as a breach of condition but may be treated as a breach of warranty.

(2) This section applies unless a contrary intention appears in, or is to be implied from, the contract.

(3) It is for the seller to show that a breach fell within subsection (1)(b) above.

(4) This section does not apply to Scotland.

Remedies for breach of contract as respects Scotland[3]

15B.—(1) Where in a contract of sale the seller is in breach of any term of the contract (express or implied), the buyer shall be entitled—
- (a) to claim damages, and
- (b) if the breach is material, to reject any goods delivered under the contract and treat it as repudiated.

(2) Where a contract of sale is a consumer contract, then, for the purposes of subsection (1)(b) above, breach by the seller of any term (express or implied)—
- (a) as to the quality of the goods or their fitness for a purpose,
- (b) if the goods are, or are to be, sold by description, that the goods will correspond with the description,
- (c) if the goods are, or are to be, sold by reference to a sample, that the bulk will correspond with the sample in quality,

shall be deemed to be a material breach.

(3) This section applies to Scotland only.

PART III

EFFECTS OF THE CONTRACT

Transfer of property as between seller and buyer

Goods must be ascertained

16. Subject to section 20A below where there is a contract for the sale of unascertained goods no property in the goods is transferred to the buyer unless and until the goods are ascertained.

---

[2] Section 15A was inserted by the Sale and Supply of Goods Act 1994, s. 4(1).
[3] Section 15B was inserted by the Sale and Supply of Goods Act 1994, s. 5(1).

Property passes when intended to pass

17.—(1) Where there is a contract for the sale of specific or ascertained goods the property in them is transferred to the buyer at such time as the parties to the contract intend it to be transferred.

(2) For the purpose of ascertaining the intention of the parties regard shall be had to the terms of the contract, the conduct of the parties and the circumstances of the case.

Rules for ascertaining intention

18.   Unless a different intention appears, the following are rules for ascertaining the intention of the parties as to the time at which the property in the goods is to pass to the buyer.

> *Rule 1.*—Where there is an unconditional contract for the sale of specific goods in a deliverable state the property in the goods passes to the buyer when the contract is made, and it is immaterial whether the time of payment or the time of delivery, or both, be postponed.
>
> *Rule 2.*—Where there is a contract for the sale of specific goods and the seller is bound to do something to the goods for the purpose of putting them into a deliverable state, the property does not pass until the thing is done and the buyer has notice that it has been done.
>
> *Rule 3.*—(1) Where there is a contract for the sale of specific goods in a deliverable state but the seller is bound to weigh, measure, test, or do some other act or thing with reference to the goods for the purpose of ascertaining the price, the property does not pass until the act or thing is done and the buyer has notice that it has been done.
>
> *Rule 4.*—(1) When goods are delivered to the buyer on approval or on sale or return or other similar terms the property in the goods passes to the buyer:—
>
> (a) when he signifies his approval or acceptance to the seller or does any other act adopting the transaction;
>
> (b) if he does not signify his approval or acceptance to the seller but retains the goods without giving notice of rejection, then, if a time has been fixed for the return of the goods, on the expiration of that time, and, if no time has been fixed, on the expiration of a reasonable time.
>
> *Rule 5.*—(1) Where there is a contract for the sale of unascertained or future goods by description, and goods of that description and in a deliverable state are unconditionally appropriated to the contract, either by the seller with the assent of the buyer or by the buyer with the assent of the seller, the property in the goods then passes to the buyer; and the assent may be express or implied, and may be given either before or after the appropriation is made.
>
> (2) Where, in pursuance of the contract, the seller delivers the goods to the buyer or to a carrier or other bailee or custodier (whether named by the buyer or not) for the purpose of transmission to the buyer, and does not reserve the right of disposal, he is to be taken to have unconditionally appropriated the goods to the contract.
>
> (3) Where there is a contract for the sale of a specified quantity of unascertained goods in a deliverable state forming part of a bulk which is identified either in the contract or by subsequent agreement between the parties and the bulk is reduced to (or to less than) that quantity, then,

if the buyer under that contract is the only buyer to whom goods are then due out of the bulk—

    (a) the remaining goods are to be taken as appropriated to that contract at the time when the bulk is so reduced; and

    (b) the property in those goods then passes to that buyer.

    (4) Paragraph (3) above applies also (with the necessary modifications) where a bulk is reduced to (or to less than) the aggregate of the quantities due to a single buyer under separate contracts relating to that bulk and he is the only buyer to whom goods are then due out of that bulk.[4]

Reservation of right of disposal

    19.—(1) Where there is a contract for the sale of specific goods or where goods are subsequently appropriated to the contract, the seller may, by the terms of the contract or appropriation, reserve the right of disposal of the goods until certain conditions are fulfilled; and in such a case, notwithstanding the delivery of the goods to the buyer, or to a carrier or other bailee or custodier for the purpose of transmission to the buyer, the property in the goods does not pass to the buyer until the conditions imposed by the seller are fulfilled.

    (2) Where goods are shipped, and by the bill of lading the goods are deliverable to the order of the seller or his agent, the seller is prima facie to be taken to reserve the right of disposal.

    (3) Where the seller of goods draws on the buyer for the price, and transmits the bill of exchange and bill of lading to the buyer together to secure acceptance or payment of the bill of exchange, the buyer is bound to return the bill of lading if he does not honour the bill of exchange, and if he wrongfully retains the bill of lading the property in the goods does not pass to him.

Risk prima facie passes with property

    20.—(1) Unless otherwise agreed, the goods remain at the seller's risk until the property in them is transferred to the buyer, but when the property in them is transferred to the buyer the goods are at the buyer's risk whether delivery has been made or not.

    (2) But where delivery has been delayed through the fault of either buyer or seller the goods are at the risk of the party at fault as regards any loss which might not have occurred but for such fault.

    (3) Nothing in this section affects the duties or liabilities of either seller or buyer as a bailee or custodier of the goods of the other party.

Undivided shares in goods forming part of a bulk[5]

    20A.—(1) This section applies to a contract for the sale of a specified quantity of unascertained goods if the following conditions are met—

    (a) the goods or some of them form part of a bulk which is identified either in the contract or by subsequent agreement between the parties; and

    (b) the buyer has paid the price for some or all of the goods which are the subject of the contract and which form part of the bulk.

    (2) Where this section applies, then (unless the parties agree otherwise), as

---

[4] Paragraphs (3) and (4) of Rule 5 were added by the Sale of Goods (Amendment) Act 1995, s. 1(2), which extends to Northern Ireland.

[5] Sections 20A and 20B were inserted by the Sale of Goods (Amendment) Act 1995, s. 3(3) which extends to Northern Ireland.

soon as the conditions specified in paragraphs (a) and (b) of subsection (1) above are met or at such later time as the parties may agree—

    (a) property in an undivided share in the bulk is transferred to the buyer, and

    (b) the buyer becomes an owner in common of the bulk.

(3) Subject to subsection (4) below, for the purposes of this section, the undivided share of a buyer in a bulk at any time shall be such share as the quantity of goods paid for and due to the buyer out of the bulk bears to the quantity of goods in the bulk at that time.

(4) Where the aggregate of the undivided shares of buyers in a bulk determined under subsection (3) above would at any time exceed the whole of the bulk at that time, the undivided share in the bulk of each buyer shall be reduced proportionately so that the aggregate of the undivided shares is equal to the whole bulk.

(5) Where a buyer has paid the price for only some of the goods due to him out of a bulk, any delivery to the buyer out of the bulk shall, for the purposes of this section, be ascribed in the first place to the goods in respect of which payment has been made.

(6) For the purpose of this section payment of part of the price for any goods shall be treated as payment for a corresponding part of the goods.

Deemed consent by co-owner to dealings in bulk goods[5]

20B.—(1) A person who has become an owner in common of a bulk by virtue of section 20A above shall be deemed to have consented to—

    (a) any delivery of goods out of the bulk to any other owner in common of the bulk, being goods which are due to him under his contract;

    (b) any dealing with or removal, delivery or disposal of goods in the bulk by any other person who is an owner in common of the bulk in so far as the goods fall within that co-owner's undivided share in the bulk at the time of the dealing, removal, delivery or disposal.

(2) No cause of action shall accrue to anyone against a person by reason of that person having acted in accordance with paragraph (a) or (b) of subsection (1) above in reliance on any consent deemed to have been given under that subsection.

(3) Nothing in this section or section 20A above shall—

    (a) impose an obligation on a buyer of goods out of a bulk to compensate any other buyer of goods out of that bulk for any shortfall in the goods received by that other buyer;

    (b) affect any contractual arrangement between buyers of goods out of a bulk for adjustments between themselves; or

    (c) affect the rights of any buyer under his contract.

Transfer of title

Sale by person not the owner

21.—(1) Subject to this Act, where goods are sold by a person who is not their owner, and who does not sell them under the authority or with the consent of the owner, the buyer acquires no better title to the goods than the seller had,

---

[5] Sections 20A and 20B were inserted by the Sale of Goods (Amendment) Act 1995, s. 3(3) which extends to Northern Ireland.

unless the owner of the goods is by his conduct precluded from denying the seller's authority to sell.

(2) Nothing in this Act affects—

(a) the provisions of the Factors Acts or any enactment enabling the apparent owner of goods to dispose of them as if he were their true owner;

(b) the validity of any contract of sale under any special common law or statutory power of sale or under the order of a court of competent jurisdiction.

22.—(1) [*Subsection (1), which relates to the sale of goods in market overt, has been repealed by the Sale of Goods (Amendment) Act 1994 (s.1), which extends to Northern Ireland and applies to any contract for the sale of goods which is made on or after January 3 1995.*]

(2) This section does not apply to Scotland.

(3) Paragraph 8 of Schedule 1 applies in relation to a contract under which goods were sold before 1 January 1968 or (in the application of this Act to Northern Ireland) 29 August 1967.

Sale under voidable title

23. When the seller of goods has a voidable title to them, but his title has not been avoided at the time of the sale, the buyer acquires a good title to the goods, provided he buys them in good faith and without notice of the seller's defect of title.

Seller in possession after sale

24. Where a person having sold goods continues or is in possession of the goods, or of the documents of title to the goods, the delivery or transfer by that person, or by a mercantile agent acting for him, of the goods or documents of title under any sale, pledge, or other disposition thereof, to any person receiving the same in good faith and without notice of the previous sale, has the same effect as if the person making the delivery or transfer were expressly authorised by the owner of the goods to make the same.

Buyer in possession after sale

25.—(1) Where a person having bought or agreed to buy goods obtains, with the consent of the seller, possession of the goods or the documents of title to the goods, the delivery or transfer by that person, or by a mercantile agent acting for him, of the goods or documents of title, under any sale, pledge, or other disposition thereof, to any person receiving the same in good faith and without notice of any lien or other right of the original seller in respect of the goods, has the same effect as if the person making the delivery or transfer were a mercantile agent in possession of the goods or documents of title with the consent of the owner.

(2) For the purposes of subsection (1) above—

(a) the buyer under a conditional sale agreement is to be taken not to be a person who has bought or agreed to buy goods, and

(b) "conditional sale agreement" means an agreement for the sale of goods which is a consumer credit agreement within the meaning of the Consumer Credit Act 1974 under which the purchase price or part of it is payable by instalments, and the property in the goods is to remain in the seller (notwithstanding that the buyer is to be in possession of the goods) until such conditions as to the payment of instalments or otherwise as may be specified in the agreement are fulfilled.

(3) Paragraph 9 of Schedule 1 below applies in relation to a contract under which a person buys or agrees to buy goods and which is made before the appointed day.

(4) In subsection (3) above and paragraph 9 of Schedule 1 below references to the appointed day are to the day appointed for the purposes of those provisions by an order of the Secretary of State made by statutory instrument.

Supplementary to sections 24 and 25

26.   In sections 24 and 25 above "mercantile agent" means a mercantile agent having in the customary course of his business as such agent authority either—

    (a) to sell goods, or

    (b) to consign goods for the purpose of sale, or

    (c) to buy goods, or

    (d) to raise money on the security of goods.

PART IV

PERFORMANCE OF THE CONTRACT

Duties of seller and buyer

27.   It is the duty of the seller to deliver the goods, and of the buyer to accept and pay for them, in accordance with the terms of the contract of sale.

Payment and delivery are concurrent conditions

28.   Unless otherwise agreed, delivery of the goods and payment of the price are concurrent conditions, that is to say, the seller must be ready and willing to give possession of the goods to the buyer in exchange for the price and the buyer must be ready and willing to pay the price in exchange for possession of the goods.

Rules about delivery

29.—(1) Whether it is for the buyer to take possession of the goods or for the seller to send them to the buyer is a question depending in each case on the contract, express or implied, between the parties.

(2) Apart from any such contract, express or implied, the place of delivery is the seller's place of business if he has one, and if not, his residence; except that, if the contract is for the sale of specific goods, which to the knowledge of the parties when the contract is made are in some other place, then that place is the place of delivery.

(3) Where under the contract of sale the seller is bound to send the goods to the buyer, but no time for sending them is fixed, the seller is bound to send them within a reasonable time.

(4) Where the goods at the time of sale are in the possession of a third person, there is no delivery by seller to buyer unless and until the third person acknowledges to the buyer that he holds the goods on his behalf; but nothing in this section affects the operation of the issue or transfer of any document of title to goods.

(5) Demand or tender of delivery may be treated as ineffectual unless made at a reasonable hour; and what is a reasonable hour is a question of fact.

(6) Unless otherwise agreed, the expenses of and incidental to putting the goods into a deliverable state must be borne by the seller.

Delivery of wrong quantity

30.—(1) Where the seller delivers to the buyer a quantity of goods less than he contracted to sell, the buyer may reject them, but if the buyer accepts the goods so delivered he must pay for them at the contract rate.

(2) Where the seller delivers to the buyer a quantity of goods larger than he contracted to sell, the buyer may accept the goods included in the contract and reject the rest, or he may reject the whole.

(2A) A buyer who does not deal as consumer may not—

(a) where the seller delivers a quantity of goods less than he contracted to sell, reject the goods under subsection (1) above, or

(b) where the seller delivers a quantity of goods larger than he contracted to sell, reject the whole under subsection (2) above,

if the shortfall or, as the case may be, excess is so slight that it would be unreasonable for him to do so.

(2B) It is for the seller to show that a shortfall or excess fell within subsection (2A) above.

(2C) Subsections (2A) and (2B) above do not apply to Scotland.

(2D) Where the seller delivers a quantity of goods—

(a) less than he contracted to sell, the buyer shall not be entitled to reject the goods under subsection (1) above,

(b) larger than he contracted to sell, the buyer shall not be entitled to reject the whole under subsection (2) above,

unless the shortfall or excess is material.

(2E) Subsection (2D) above applies to Scotland only.[6]

(3) Where the seller delivers to the buyer a quantity of goods larger than he contracted to sell and the buyer accepts the whole of the goods so delivered he must pay for them at the contract rate.

(4) [*Repealed*]

(5) This section is subject to any usage of trade, special agreement, or course of dealing between the parties.

Instalment deliveries

31.—(1) Unless otherwise agreed, the buyer of goods is not bound to accept delivery of them by instalments.

(2) Where there is a contract for the sale of goods to be delivered by stated instalments, which are to be separately paid for, and the seller makes defective deliveries in respect of one or more instalments, or the buyer neglects or refuses to take delivery of or pay for one or more instalments, it is a question in each case depending on the terms of the contract and the circumstances of the case whether the breach of contract is a repudiation of the whole contract or whether it is a severable breach giving rise to a claim for compensation but not to a right to treat the whole contract as repudiated.

Delivery to carrier

32.—(1) Where, in pursuance of a contract of sale, the seller is authorised or required to send the goods to the buyer, delivery of the goods to a carrier (whether named by the buyer or not) for the purpose of transmission to the buyer is prima facie deemed to be a delivery of the goods to the buyer.

(2) Unless otherwise authorised by the buyer, the seller must make such con-

---

[6] Subsections (2A), (2B) and (2C) were inserted by the Sale and Supply of Goods Act 1994, s. 4(2); and subsections (2D) and (2E) by s. 5(2) of the 1994 Act.

tract with the carrier on behalf of the buyer as may be reasonable having regard to the nature of the goods and the other circumstances of the case; and if the seller omits to do so, and the goods are lost or damaged in course of transit, the buyer may decline to treat the delivery to the carrier as a delivery to himself or may hold the seller responsible in damages.

(3) Unless otherwise agreed, where goods are sent by the seller to the buyer by a route involving sea transit, under circumstances in which it is usual to insure, the seller must give such notice to the buyer as may enable him to insure them during their sea transit; and if the seller fails to do so, the goods are at his risk during such sea transit.

Risk where goods are delivered at distant place

33. Where the seller of goods agrees to deliver them at his own risk at a place other than that where they are when sold, the buyer must nevertheless (unless otherwise agreed) take any risk of deterioration in the goods necesarily incident to the course of transit.

Buyer's right of examining the goods

34. Unless otherwise agreed, when the seller tenders delivery of goods to the buyer, he is bound on request to afford the buyer a reasonable opportunity of examining the goods for the purpose of ascertaining whether they are in conformity with the contract and in the case of a contract for sale by sample, of comparing the bulk with the sample.

Acceptance[7]

35.—(1) The buyer is deemed to have accepted the goods subject to subsection (2) below—

    (a) when he intimates to the seller that he has accepted them, or

    (b) when the goods have been delivered to him and he does any act in relation to them which is inconsistent with the ownership of the seller.

(2) Where goods are delivered to the buyer, and he has not previously examined them, he is not deemed to have accepted them under subsection (1) above until he has had a reasonable opportunity of examining them for the purpose—

    (a) of ascertaining whether they are in conformity with the contract, and

    (b) in the case of a contract for sale by sample, of comparing the bulk with the sample.

(3) Where the buyer deals as consumer or (in Scotland) the contract of sale is a consumer contract, the buyer cannot lose his right to rely on subsection (2) above by agreement, waiver or otherwise.

(4) The buyer is also deemed to have accepted the goods when after the lapse of a reasonable time he retains the goods without intimating to the seller that he has rejected them.

(5) The questions that are material in determining for the purposes of subsection (4) above whether a reasonable time has elapsed include whether the buyer has had a reasonable opportunity of examining the goods for the purpose mentioned in subsection (2) above.

(6) The buyer is not by virtue of this section deemed to have accepted the goods merely because—

---

[7] Section 35 incorporates amendments made by the Sale and Supply of Goods Act 1994, s. 2(1); s. 2(2) of the 1994 Act made consequential amendments to s. 34 above, which is printed as thus amended.

(a) he asks for, or agrees to, their repair by or under an arrangement with the seller, or

(b) the goods are delivered to another under a sub-sale or other disposition.

(7) Where the contract is for the sale of goods making one or more commercial units, a buyer accepting any goods included in a unit is deemed to have accepted all the goods making the unit; and in this subsection "commercial unit" means a unit division of which would materially impair the value of the goods or the character of the unit.

(8) Paragraph 10 of Schedule below applies in relation to a contract made before 22 April 1967 or (in the application of this Act to Northern Ireland) 28 July 1967.

Right of partial rejection[8]

35A.—(1) If the buyer—

(a) has the right to reject the goods by reason of a breach on the part of the seller that affects some or all of them, but

(b) accepts some of the goods, including, where there are any goods unaffected by the breach, all such goods,

he does not by accepting them lose his right to reject the rest.

(2) In the case of a buyer having the right to reject an instalment of goods, subsection (1) above applies as if references to the goods were references to the goods comprised in the instalment.

(3) For the purposes of subsection (1) above, goods are affected by a breach if by reason of the breach they are not in conformity with the contract.

(4) This section applies unless a contrary intention appears in, or is to be implied from, the contract.

Buyer not bound to return rejected goods

36. Unless otherwise agreed, where goods are delivered to the buyer, and he refuses to accept them, having the right to do so, he is not bound to return them to the seller, but it is sufficient if he intimates to the seller that he refuses to accept them.

Buyer's liability for not taking delivery of goods

37.—(1) When the seller is ready and willing to deliver the goods, and requests the buyer to take delivery, and the buyer does not within a reasonable time after such request take delivery of the goods, he is liable to the seller for any loss occasioned by his neglect or refusal to take delivery, and also for a reasonable charge for the care and custody of the goods.

(2) Nothing in this section affects the rights of the seller where the neglect or refusal of the buyer to take delivery amounts to a repudiation of the contract.

PART V

RIGHTS OF UNPAID SELLER AGAINST THE GOODS

Preliminary

Unpaid seller defined

38.—(1) The seller of goods is an unpaid seller within the meaning of this Act—

[8] Section 35A was inserted by the Sale and Supply of Goods Act 1994, s. 3(1).

    (a) when the whole of the price has not been paid or tendered;

    (b) when a bill of exchange or other negotiable instrument has been received as conditional payment, and the condition on which it was received has not been fulfilled by reason of the dishonour of the instrument or otherwise.

(2) In this Part of this Act "seller" includes any person who is in the position of a seller, as, for instance, an agent of the seller to whom the bill of lading has been indorsed, or a consignor or agent who has himself paid (or is directly responsible for) the price.

Unpaid seller's rights

39.—(1) Subject to this and any other Act, notwithstanding that the property in the goods may have passed to the buyer, the unpaid seller of goods, as such, has by implication of law—

    (a) a lien on the goods or right to retain them for the price while he is in possession of them;

    (b) in case of the insolvency of the buyer, a right of stopping the goods in transit after he has parted with the possession of them;

    (c) a right of re-sale as limited by this Act.

(2) Where the property in goods has not passed to the buyer, the unpaid seller has (in addition to his other remedies) a right of withholding delivery similar to and co-extensive with his rights of lien or retention and stoppage in transit where the property has passed to the buyer.

Attachment by seller in Scotland

40. In Scotland a seller of goods may attach them while in his own hands or possession by arrestment or poinding; and such arrestment or poinding shall have the same operation and effect in a competition or otherwise as an arrestment or poinding by a third party.

Unpaid seller's lien

Seller's lien

41.—(1) Subject to this Act, the unpaid seller of goods who is in possession of them is entitled to retain possession of them until payment or tender of the price in the following cases:—

    (a) where the goods have been sold without any stipulation as to credit;

    (b) where the goods have been sold on credit but the term of credit has expired;

    (c) where the buyer becomes insolvent.

(2) The seller may exercise his lien or right of retention notwithstanding that he is in possession of the goods as agent or bailee or custodier for the buyer.

Part delivery

42. Where an unpaid seller has made part delivery of the goods, he may exercise his lien or right of retention on the remainder, unless such part delivery has been made under such circumstances as to show an agreement to waive the lien or right of retention.

Termination of lien

43.—(1) The unpaid seller of goods loses his lien or right of retention in respect of them—

   (a) when he delivers the goods to a carrier or other bailee or custodier for the purpose of transmission to the buyer without reserving the right of disposal of the goods;

   (b) when the buyer or his agent lawfully obtains possession of the goods;

   (c) by waiver of the lien or right of retention.

(2) An unpaid seller of goods who has a lien or right of retention in respect of them does not lose his lien or right of retention by reason only that he has obtained judgment or decree for the price of the goods.

Stoppage in transit

Right of stoppage in transit

44. Subject to this Act, when the buyer of goods becomes insolvent the unpaid seller who has parted with the possession of the goods has the right of stopping them in transit, that is to say, he may resume possession of the goods as long as they are in course of transit, and may retain them until payment or tender of the price.

Duration of transit

45.—(1) Goods are deemed to be in course of transit from the time when they are delivered to a carrier or other bailee or custodier for the purpose of transmission to the buyer, until the buyer or his agent in that behalf takes delivery of them from the carrier or other bailee or custodier.

(2) If the buyer or his agent in that behalf obtains delivery of the goods before their arrival at the appointed destination, the transit is at an end.

(3) If, after the arrival of the goods at the appointed destination, the carrier or other bailee or custodier acknowledges to the buyer or his agent that he holds the goods on his behalf and continues in possession of them as bailee or custodier for the buyer or his agent, the transit is at an end, and it is immaterial that a further destination for the goods may have been indicated by the buyer.

(4) If the goods are rejected by the buyer, and the carrier or other bailee or custodier continues in possession of them, the transit is not deemed to be at an end, even if the seller has refused to receive them back.

(5) When goods are delivered to a ship chartered by the buyer it is a question depending on the circumstances of the particular case whether they are in the possession of the master as a carrier or as agent to the buyer.

(6) Where the carrier or other bailee or custodier wrongfully refuses to deliver the goods to the buyer or his agent in that behalf, the transit is deemed to be at an end.

(7) Where part delivery of the goods has been made to the buyer or his agent in that behalf, the remainder of the goods may be stopped in transit, unless such part delivery has been made under such circumstances as to show an agreement to give up possession of the whole of the goods.

How stoppage in transit is effected

46.—(1) The unpaid seller may exercise his right of stoppage in transit either by taking actual possession of the goods or by giving notice of his claim to the carrier or other bailee or custodier in whose possession the goods are.

(2) The notice may be given either to the person in actual possession of the goods or to his principal.

(3) If given to the principal, the notice is ineffective unless given at such time and under such circumstances that the principal, by the exercise of reason-

able diligence, may communicate it to his servant or agent in time to prevent a delivery to the buyer.

(4) When notice of stoppage in transit is given by the seller to the carrier or other bailee or custodier in possession of the goods, he must re-deliver the goods to, or according to the directions of, the seller; and the expenses of the re-delivery must be borne by the seller.

Re-sale etc. by buyer

Effect of sub-sale etc. by buyer

47.—(1) Subject to this Act, the unpaid seller's right of lien or retention or stoppage in transit is not affected by any sale or other disposition of the goods which the buyer may have made, unless the seller has assented to it.

(2) Where a document of title to goods has been lawfully transferred to any person as buyer or owner of the goods, and that person transfers the document to a person who takes it in good faith and for valuable consideration, then—

(a) if the last-mentioned transfer was by way of sale the unpaid seller's right of lien or retention or stoppage in transit is defeated; and

(b) if the last-mentioned transfer was made by way of pledge or other disposition for value, the unpaid seller's right of lien or retention or stoppage in transit can only be exercised subject to the rights of the transferee.

Rescission: and re-sale by seller

Rescission: and re-sale by seller

48.—(1) Subject to this section, a contract of sale is not rescinded by the mere exercise by an unpaid seller of his right of lien or retention or stoppage in transit.

(2) Where an unpaid seller who has exercised his right of lien or retention or stoppage in transit re-sells the goods, the buyer acquires a good title to them as against the original buyer.

(3) Where the goods are of a perishable nature, or where the unpaid seller gives notice to the buyer of his intention to re-sell, and the buyer does not within a reasonable time pay or tender the price, the unpaid seller may re-sell the goods and recover from the original buyer damages for any loss occasioned by his breach of contract.

(4) Where the seller expressly reserves the right of re-sale in case the buyer should make default, and on the buyer making default re-sells the goods, the original contract of sale is rescinded but without prejudice to any claim the seller may have for damages.

Part VI

Actions for Breach of the Contract

Seller's remedies

49.—(1) Where, under a contract of sale, the property in the goods has passed to the buyer and he wrongfully neglects or refuses to pay for the goods according to the terms of the contract, the seller may maintain an action against him for the price of the goods.

(2) Where, under a contract of sale, the price is payable on a day certain irrespective of delivery and the buyer wrongfully neglects or refuses to pay such price, the seller may maintain an action for the price, although the property in the goods has not passed and the goods have not been appropriated to the contract.

(3) Nothing in this section prejudices the right of the seller in Scotland to recover interest on the price from the date of tender of the goods, or from the date on which the price was payable, as the case may be.

Damages for non-acceptance

50.—(1) Where the buyer wrongfully neglects or refuses to accept and pay for the goods, the seller may maintain an action against him for damages for non-acceptance.

(2) The measure of damages is the estimated loss directly and naturally resulting, in the ordinary course of events, from the buyer's breach of contract.

(3) Where there is an available market for the goods in question the measure of damages is prima facie to be ascertained by the difference between the contract price and the market or current price at the time or times when the goods ought to have been accepted or (if no time was fixed for acceptance) at the time of the refusal to accept.

Buyer's remedies

Damages for non-delivery

51.—(1) Where the seller wrongfully neglects or refuses to deliver the goods to the buyer, the buyer may maintain an action against the seller for damages for non-delivery.

(2) The measure of damages is the estimated loss directly and naturally resulting, in the ordinary course of events, from the seller's breach of contract.

(3) Where there is an available market for the goods in question the measure of damages is prima facie to be ascertained by the difference between the contract price and the market or current price of the goods at the time or times when they ought to have been delivered or (if no time was fixed) at the time of the refusal to deliver.

Specific performance

52.—(1) In any action for breach of contract to deliver specific or ascertained goods the court may, if it thinks fit, on the plaintiff's application, by its judgment or decree direct that the contract shall be performed specifically, without giving the defendant the option of retaining the goods on payment of damages.

(2) The plaintiff's application may be made at any time before judgment or decree.

(3) The judgment or decree may be unconditional, or on such terms and conditions as to damages, payment of the price and otherwise as seem just to the court.

(4) The provisions of this section shall be deemed to be supplementary to, and not in derogation of, the right of specific implement in Scotland.

Remedy for breach of warranty

53.—(1) Where there is a breach of warranty by the seller, or where the buyer elects (or is compelled) to treat any breach of a condition on the part of the seller as a breach of warranty, the buyer is not by reason only of such breach of warranty entitled to reject the goods; but he may—

    (a) set up against the seller the breach of warranty in diminution or extinction of the price, or

    (b) maintain an action against the seller for damages for the breach of warranty.

(2) The measure of damages for breach of warranty is the estimated loss directly and naturally resulting, in the ordinary course of events, from the breach of warranty.

(3) In the case of breach of warranty of quality such loss is prima facie the difference between the value of the goods at the time of delivery to the buyer and the value they would have had if they had fulfilled the warranty.

(4) The fact that the buyer has set up the breach of warranty in diminution or extinction of the price does not prevent him from maintaining an action for the same breach of warranty if he has suffered further damage.

(5) This section does not apply to Scotland.

Measure of damages as respects Scotland[9]

53A.—(1) The measure of damages for the seller's breach of contract is the estimated loss directly and naturally resulting, in the ordinary course of events, from the breach.

(2) Where the seller's breach consists of the delivery of goods which are not of the quality required by the contract and the buyer retains the goods, such loss as aforesaid is prima facie the difference between the value of the goods at the time of delivery to the buyer and the value they would have had if they had fulfilled the contract.

(3) This section applies to Scotland only.

Interest, etc.

Interest, etc.

54.   Nothing in this Act affects the right of the buyer or the seller to recover interest or special damages in any case where by law interest or special damages may be recoverable, or to recover money paid where the consideration for the payment of it has failed.

PART VII

SUPPLEMENTARY

Exclusion of implied terms

55.—(1) Where a right, duty or liability would arise under a contract of sale of goods by implication of law, it may (subject to the Unfair Contract Terms Act 1977) be negatived or varied by express agreement, or by the course of dealing between the parties, or by such usage as binds both parties to the contract.

(2) An express term does not negative a term implied by this Act unless inconsistent with it.

(3) Paragraph 11 of Schedule 1 below applies in relation to a contract made

---

[9] Section 53A was inserted by the Sale and Supply of Goods Act 1994, s. 5(3).

on or after 18 May 1973 and before 1 February 1978, and paragraph 12 in relation to one made before 18 May 1973.

Conflict of laws

56. Paragraph 13 of Schedule 1 below applies in relation to a contract made on or after 18 May 1973 and before 1 February 1978, so as to make provision about conflict of laws in relation to such a contract.

Auction sales

57.—(1) Where goods are put up for sale by auction in lots, each lot is prima facie deemed to be the subject of a separate contract of sale.

(2) A sale by auction is complete when the auctioneer announces its completion by the fall of the hammer, or in other customary manner; and until the announcement is made any bidder may retract his bid.

(3) A sale by auction may be notified to be subject to a reserve or upset price, and a right to bid may also be reserved expressly by or on behalf of the seller.

(4) Where a sale by auction is not notified to be subject to a right to bid by or on behalf of the seller, it is not lawful for the seller to bid himself or to employ any person to bid at the sale, or for the auctioneer knowingly to take any bid from the seller or any such person.

(5) A sale contravening subsection (4) above may be treated as fraudulent by the buyer.

(6) Where, in respect of a sale by auction, a right to bid is expressly reserved (but not otherwise) the seller or any one person on his behalf may bid at the auction.

Payment into court in Scotland

58. In Scotland where a buyer has elected to accept goods which he might have rejected, and to treat a breach of contract as only giving rise to a claim for damages, he may, in an action by the seller for the price, be required, in the discretion of the court before which the action depends, to consign or pay into court the price of the goods, or part of the price, or to give other reasonable security for its due payment.

Reasonable time a question of fact

59. Where a reference is made in this Act to a reasonable time the question what is a reasonable time is a question of fact.

Rights etc. enforceable by action

60. Where a right, duty or liability is declared by this Act, it may (unless otherwise provided by this Act) be enforced by action.

Interpretation

61.—(1) In this Act, unless the context or subject matter otherwise requires,—
"action" includes counterclaim and set-off, and in Scotland condescendence and claim and compensation;
"bulk" means a mass or collection of goods of the same kind which—
   (a) is contained in a defined space or area; and
   (b) is such that any goods in the bulk are interchangeable with any other goods therein of the same number or quantity;
"business" includes a profession and the activities of any government department (including a Northern Ireland department) or local or public authority;

"buyer" means a person who buys or agrees to buy goods;

"consumer contract" has the same meaning as in section 25(1) of the Unfair Contract Terms Act 1977; and for the purposes of this Act the onus of proving that a contract is not to be regarded as a consumer contract shall lie on the seller;

"contract of sale" includes an agreement to sell as well as a sale;

"credit-broker" means a person acting in the course of a business of credit brokerage carried on by him, that is a business of effecting introductions of individuals desiring to obtain credit—

(a) to persons carrying on any business so far as it relates to the provision of credit, or

(b) to other persons engaged in credit brokerage;

"defendant" includes in Scotland defender, respondent, and claimant in a multiplepoinding;

"delivery" means voluntary transfer of possession from one person to another except that in relation to sections 20A and 20B above it includes such appropriation of goods to the contract as results in property in the goods being transferred to the buyer;

"document of title to goods" has the same meaning as it has in the Factors Acts;

"Factors Acts" means the Factors Act 1889, the Factors (Scotland) Act 1890, and any enactment amending or substituted for the same;

"fault" means wrongful act or default;

"future goods" means goods to be manufactured or acquired by the seller after the making of the contract of sale;

"goods" includes all personal chattels other than things in action and money, and in Scotland all corporeal moveables except money; and in particular "goods" includes emblements, industrial growing crops, and things attached to or forming part of the land which are agreed to be severed before sale or under the contract of sale and includes an undivided share in goods;

"plaintiff" includes pursuer, complainer, claimant in a multiplepoinding and defendant or defender counter-claiming;

"property" means the general property in goods, and not merely a special property;

"sale" includes a bargain and sale as well as a sale and delivery;

"seller" means a person who sells or agrees to sell goods;

"specific goods" means goods identified and agreed on at the time a contract of sale is made and includes an undivided share, specified as a fraction or percentage, of goods identified and agreed on as aforesaid;

"warranty" (as regards England and Wales and Northern Ireland) means an agreeement with reference to goods which are the subject of a contract of sale, but collateral to the main purpose of such contract, the breach of which gives rise to a claim for damages, but not to a right to reject the goods and treat the contract as repudiated.

(2) [*Repealed*]

(3) A thing is deemed to be done in good faith within the meaning of this Act when it is in fact done honestly, whether it is done negligently or not.

(4) A person is deemed to be insolvent within the meaning of this Act if he has either ceased to pay his debts in the ordinary course of business or he cannot pay his debts as they become due.

(5) Goods are in a deliverable state within the meaning of this Act when they

are in such a state that the buyer would under the contract be bound to take delivery of them.

(5A) References in this Act to dealing as consumer are to be construed in accordance with Part I of the Unfair Contract Terms Act 1977; and, for the purposes of this Act, it is for a seller claiming that the buyer does not deal as consumer to show that he does not.

(6) As regards the definition of "business" in subsection (1) above, paragraph 14 of Schedule 1 below applies in relation to a contract made on or after 18 May 1973 and before 1 February 1978, and paragraph 15 in relation to one made before 18 May 1973.

Savings: rules of law etc.

62.—(1) The rules in bankruptcy relating to contracts of sale apply to those contracts, notwithstanding anything in this Act.

(2) The rules of the common law, including the law merchant, except in so far as they are inconsistent with the provisions of this Act, and in particular the rules relating to the law of principal and agent and the effect of fraud, misrepresentation, duress or coercion, mistake, or other invalidating cause, apply to contracts for the sale of goods.

(3) Nothing in this Act or the Sale of Goods Act 1893 affects the enactments relating to bills of sale, or any enactment relating to the sale of goods which is not expressly repealed or amended by this Act or that.

(4) The provisions of this Act about contracts of sale do not apply to a transaction in the form of a contract of sale which is intended to operate by way of mortgage, pledge, charge, or other security.

(5) Nothing in this Act prejudices or affects the landlord's right of hypothec or sequestration for rent in Scotland.

Consequential amendments, repeals and savings

63.—(1) Without prejudice to section 17 of the Interpretation Act 1978 (repeal and re-enactment), the enactments mentioned in Schedule 2 below have effect subject to the amendments there specified (being amendments consequential on this Act).

(2) The enactments mentioned in Schedule 3 below are repealed to the extent specified in column 3, but subject to the savings in Schedule 4 below.

(3) The savings in Schedule 4 below have effect.

Short title and commencement

64.—(1) This Act may be cited as the Sale of Goods Act 1979.

(2) This Act comes into force on 1 January 1980.

SCHEDULE 1

MODIFICATION OF ACT FOR CERTAIN CONTRACTS

This Schedule modifies the Act as it applies to contracts of sale of goods made on certain specified dates before 1 January 1980.

* * * * *

Magistrates' Courts Act 1980

(c. 43)

Restriction on amount payable under compensation order of magistrates' court

40.—(1) The compensation to be paid under a compensation order by a magistrates' court in respect of any offence of which the court has convicted the offender shall not exceed £5,000, and the compensation or total compensation to be paid under a compensation order or compensation orders made by a magistrates' court in respect of any offence or offences taken into consideration in determining the sentence shall not exceed the difference (if any) between the amount or total amount which under the preceding provisions of this subsection is the maximum for the offence or offences of which the offender has been convicted and the amount or total amounts (if any) which are in fact ordered to be paid in respect of that offence or those offences.

(2) In subsection (1) above "compensation order" has the meaning assigned to it by section 35 (1) of the Powers of Criminal Courts Act 1973.

*　　*　　*　　*　　*

Supply of Goods and Services Act 1982

(c. 29)

An Act to amend the law with respect to the terms to be implied in certain contracts for the transfer of the property in goods, in certain contracts for the hire of goods and in certain contracts for the supply of a service; and for connected purposes. [13th July 1982]

PART I

SUPPLY OF GOODS

Contracts for the transfer of property in goods

The contracts concerned

1.—(1) In this Act in its application to England and Wales and Northern Ireland a "contract for the transfer of goods" means a contract under which one person transfers or agrees to transfer to another the property in goods, other than an excepted contract.

(2) For the purposes of this section an excepted contract means any of the following:—

(a) a contract of sale of goods;

(b) a hire-purchase agreement;

(c) a contract under which the property in goods is (or is to be) transferred in exchange for trading stamps on their redemption;

(d) a transfer or agreement to transfer which is made by deed and for which there is no consideration other than the presumed consideration imported by the deed;

(e) a contract intended to operate by way of mortgage, pledge, charge or other security.

(3) For the purposes of this Act in its application to England and Wales and Northern Ireland a contract is a contract for the transfer of goods whether or not services are also provided or to be provided under the contract, and (subject to subsection (2) above) whatever is the nature of the consideration for the transfer or agreement to transfer.

Implied terms about title, etc.

2.—(1) In a contract for the transfer of goods, other than one to which subsection (3) below applies, there is an implied condition on the part of the transferor that in the case of a transfer of the property in the goods he has a right to transfer the property and in the case of an agreement to transfer the property in the goods he will have such a right at the time when the property is to be transferred.

(2) In a contract for the transfer of goods, other than one to which subsection (3) below applies, there is also an implied warranty that—

(a) the goods are free, and will remain free until the time when the property

197

is to be transferred, from any charge or encumbrance not disclosed or known to the transferee before the contract is made, and

(b) the transferee will enjoy quiet possession of the goods except so far as it may be disturbed by the owner or other person entitled to the benefit of any charge or encumbrance so disclosed or known.

(3) This subsection applies to a contract for the transfer of goods in the case of which there appears from the contract or is to be inferred from its circumstances an intention that the transferor should transfer only such title as he or a third person may have.

(4) In a contract to which subsection (3) above applies there is an implied warranty that all charges or encumbrances known to the transferor and not known to the transferee have been disclosed to the transferee before the contract is made.

(5) In a contract to which subsection (3) above applies there is also an implied warranty that none of the following will disturb the transferee's quiet possession of the goods, namely—

(a) the transferor;

(b) in a case where the parties to the contract intend that the transferor should transfer only such title as a third person may have, that person;

(c) anyone claiming through or under the transferor or that third person otherwise than under a charge or encumbrance disclosed or known to the transferee before the contract is made.

Implied terms where transfer is by description

3.—(1) This section applies where, under a contract for the transfer of goods, the transferor transfers or agrees to transfer the property in the goods by description.

(2) In such a case there is an implied condition that the goods will correspond with the description.

(3) If the transferor transfers or agrees to transfer the property in the goods by sample as well as by description it is not sufficient that the bulk of the goods corresponds with the sample if the goods do not also correspond with the description.

(4) A contract is not prevented from falling within subsection (1) above by reason only that, being exposed for supply, the goods are selected by the transferee.

Implied terms about quality or fitness

4.—(1) Except as provided by this section and section 5 below and subject to the provisions of any other enactment, there is no implied condition or warranty about the quality or fitness for any particular purpose of goods supplied under a contract for the transfer of goods.

(2) Where, under such a contract, the transferor transfers the property in goods in the course of a business, there is an implied condition that the goods supplied under the contract are of satisfactory quality.[1]

(2A) For the purposes of this section and section 5 below, goods are of satisfactory quality if they meet the standard that a reasonable person would regard

---

[1] Subsections (2) and (3) were substituted, and subsection (2A) inserted, by the Sale and Supply of Goods Act 1994, s. 7 and Sched. 2.

as satisfactory, taking account of any description of the goods, the price (if relevant) and all the other relevant circumstances.

(3) The condition implied by subsection (2) above does not extend to any matter making the quality of goods unsatisfactory—

    (a) which is specifically drawn to the transferee's attention before the contract is made,

    (b) where the transferee examines the goods before the contract is made, which that examination ought to reveal, or

    (c) where the property in the goods is transferred by reference to a sample, which would have been apparent on a reasonable examination of the sample.

(4) Subsection (5) below applies where, under a contract for the transfer of goods, the transferor transfers the property in goods in the course of a business and the transferee, expressly or by implication, makes known—

    (a) to the transferor, or

    (b) where the consideration or part of the consideration for the transfer is a sum payable by instalments and the goods were previously sold by a credit-broker to the transferor, to that credit-broker,

any particular purpose for which the goods are being acquired.

(5) In that case there is (subject to subsection (6) below) an implied condition that the goods supplied under the contract are reasonably fit for that purpose, whether or not that is a purpose for which such goods are commonly supplied.

(6) Subsection (5) above does not apply where the circumstances show that the transferee does not rely, or that it is unreasonable for him to rely, on the skill or judgment of the transferor or credit-broker.

(7) An implied condition or warranty about quality or fitness for a particular purpose may be annexed by usage to a contract for the transfer of goods.

(8) The preceding provisions of this section apply to a transfer by a person who in the course of a business is acting as agent for another as they apply to a transfer by a principal in the course of a business, except where that other is not transferring in the course of a business and either the transferee knows that fact or reasonable steps are taken to bring it to the transferee's notice before the contract concerned is made.

(9) [*Repealed*]

Implied terms where transfer is by sample

5.—(1) This section applies where, under a contract for the transfer of goods, the transferor transfers or agrees to transfer the property in the goods by reference to a sample.

(2) In such a case there is an implied condition—

    (a) that the bulk will correspond with the sample in quality; and

    (b) that the transferee will have a reasonable opportunity of comparing the bulk with the sample; and

    (c) that the goods will be free from any defect, making their quality unsatisfactory, which would not be apparent on reasonable examination of the sample.

(3) [*Repealed*]

(4) For the purposes of this section a transferor transfers or agrees to transfer the property in goods by reference to a sample where there is an express or implied term to that effect in the contract concerned.

Modification of remedies for breach of statutory condition in non-consumer cases[2]

5A.—(1) Where in the case of a contract for the transfer of goods—

(a) the transferee would, apart from this subsection, have the right to treat the contract as repudiated by reason of a breach on the part of the transferor of a term implied by section 3, 4 or 5(2)(a) or (c) above, but

(b) the breach is so slight that it would be unreasonable for him to do so,

then, if the transferee does not deal as consumer, the breach is not to be treated as a breach of condition but may be treated as a breach of warranty.

(2) This section applies unless a contrary intention appears in, or is to be implied from, the contract.

(3) It is for the transferor to show that a breach fell within subsection (1)(b) above.

Contracts for the hire of goods

The contracts concerned

6.—(1) In this Act in its application to England and Wales and Northern Ireland a "contract for the hire of goods" means a contract under which one person bails or agrees to bail goods to another by way of hire, other than an excepted contract.

(2) For the purposes of this section an excepted contract means any of the following:—

(a) a hire-purchase agreement;

(b) a contract under which goods are (or are to be) bailed in exchange for trading stamps on their redemption.

(3) For the purposes of this Act in its application to England and Wales and Northern Ireland a contract is a contract for the hire of goods whether or not services are also provided or to be provided under the contract, and (subject to subsection (2) above) whatever is the nature of the consideration for the bailment or agreement to bail by way of hire.

Implied terms about right to transfer possession, etc.

7.—(1) In a contract for the hire of goods there is an implied condition on the part of the bailor that in the case of a bailment he has a right to transfer possession of the goods by way of hire for the period of the bailment and in the case of an agreement to bail he will have such a right at the time of the bailment.

(2) In a contract for the hire of goods there is also an implied warranty that the bailee will enjoy quiet possession of the goods for the period of the bailment except so far as the possession may be disturbed by the owner or other person entitled to the benefit of any charge or encumbrance disclosed or known to the bailee before the contract is made.

(3) The preceding provisions of this section do not affect the right of the bailor to repossess the goods under an express or implied term of the contract.

Implied terms where hire is by description

8.—(1) This section applies where, under a contract for the hire of goods, the bailor bails or agrees to bail the goods by description.

---

[2] Section 5A was inserted by the Sale and Supply of Goods Act 1994, s. 7 and Sched. 2.

(2) In such a case there is an implied condition that the goods will correspond with the description.

(3) If under the contract the bailor bails or agrees to bail the goods by reference to a sample as well as a description it is not sufficient that the bulk of the goods corresponds with the sample if the goods do not also correspond with the description.

(4) A contract is not prevented from falling within subsection (1) above by reason only that, being exposed for supply, the goods are selected by the bailee.

Implied terms about quality or fitness

9.—(1) Except as provided by this section and section 10 below and subject to the provisions of any other enactment, there is no implied condition or warranty about the quality or fitness for any particular purpose of goods bailed under a contract for the hire of goods.

(2) Where, under such a contract, the bailor bails goods in the course of a business, there is an implied condition that the goods supplied under the contract are of satisfactory quality.[3]

(2A) For the purposes of this section and section 10 below, goods are of satisfactory quality if they meet the standard that a reasonable person would regard as satisfactory, taking account of any description of the goods, the consideration for the bailment (if relevant) and all the other relevant circumstances.

(3) The condition implied by subsection (2) above does not extend to any matter making the quality of goods unsatisfactory—

(a) which is specifically drawn to the bailee's attention before the contract is made,

(b) where the bailee examines the goods before the contract is made, which that examination ought to reveal, or

(c) where the goods are bailed by reference to a sample, which would have been apparent on a reasonable examination of the sample.

(4) Subsection (5) below applies where, under a contract for the hire of goods, the bailor bails goods in the course of a business and the bailee, expressly or by implication, makes known—

(a) to the bailor in the course of negotiations conducted by him in relation to the making of the contract, or

(b) to a credit-broker in the course of negotiations conducted by that broker in relation to goods sold by him to the bailor before forming the subject matter of the contract,

any particular purpose for which the goods are being bailed.

(5) In that case there is (subject to subsection (6) below) an implied condition that the goods supplied under the contract are reasonably fit for that purpose, whether or not that is a purpose for which such goods are commonly supplied.

(6) Subsection (5) above does not apply where the circumstances show that the bailee does not rely, or that it is unreasonable for him to rely, on the skill or judgment of the bailor or credit-broker.

(7) An implied condition or warranty about quality or fitness for a particular purpose may be annexed by usage to a contract for the hire of goods.

(8) The preceding provisions of this section apply to a bailment by a person who in the course of a business is acting as agent for another as they apply to a bailment by a principal in the course of a business, except where that other

---

[3] Subsections (2) and (3) were substituted, and subsection (2A) inserted, by the Sale and Supply of Goods Act 1994, s. 7 and Sched. 2.

is not bailing in the course of a business and either the bailee knows that fact or reasonable steps are taken to bring it to the bailee's notice before the contract concerned is made.

(9) [*Repealed*]

Implied terms where hire is by sample

10.—(1) This section applies where, under a contract for the hire of goods, the bailor bails or agrees to bail the goods by reference to a sample.

(2) In such a case there is an implied condition—

    (a) that the bulk will correspond with the sample in quality; and;

    (b) that the bailee will have a reasonable opportunity of comparing the bulk with the sample; and

    (c) that the goods will be free from any defect, making their quality unsatisfactory, which would not be apparent on reasonable examination of the sample.

(3) [*Repealed*]

(4) For the purposes of this section a bailor bails or agrees to bail goods by reference to a sample where there is an express or implied term to that effect in the contract concerned.

Modification of remedies for breach of statutory condition in non-consumer cases[4]

10A.—(1) Where in the case of a contract for the hire of goods—

    (a) the bailee would, apart from this subsection, have the right to treat the contract as repudiated by reason of a breach on the part of the bailor of a term implied by section 8, 9 or 10(2)(a) or (c) above, but

    (b) the breach is so slight that it would be unreasonable for him to do so,

then, if the bailee does not deal as consumer, the breach is not to be treated as a breach of condition but may be treated as a breach of warranty.

(2) This section applies unless a contrary intention appears in, or is to be implied from, the contract.

(3) It is for the bailor to show that a breach fell within subsection (1)(b) above.

Exclusion of implied terms, etc.

Exclusion of implied terms, etc.

11.—(1) Where a right, duty or liability would arise under a contract for the transfer of goods or a contract for the hire of goods by implication of law, it may (subject to subsection (2) below and the 1977 Act) be negatived or varied by express agreement, or by the course of dealing between the parties, or by such usage as binds both parties to the contract.

(2) An express condition or warranty does not negative a condition or warranty implied by the preceding provisions of this Act unless inconsistent with it.

(3) Nothing in the preceding provisions of this Act prejudices the operation of any other enactment or any rule of law whereby any condition or warranty (other than one relating to quality or fitness) is to be implied in a contract for the transfer of goods or a contract for the hire of goods.

---

[4] Section 10A was inserted by the Sale and Supply of Goods Act 1994, s. 7 and Sched. 2.

PART IA[5]

SUPPLY OF GOODS AS RESPECTS SCOTLAND

Contracts for the transfer of property in goods

The contracts concerned

11A.—(1) In this Act in its application to Scotland a "contract for the transfer of goods" means a contract under which one person transfers or agrees to transfer to another the property in goods, other than an excepted contract.

(2) For the purposes of this section an excepted contract means any of the following—

    (a) a contract of sale of goods;

    (b) a hire-purchase agreement;

    (c) a contract under which the property in goods is (or is to be) transferred in exchange for trading stamps on their redemption;

    (d) a transfer or agreement to transfer for which there is no consideration;

    (e) a contract intended to operate by way of mortgage, pledge, charge or other security.

(3) For the purposes of this Act in its application to Scotland a contract is a contract for the transfer of goods whether or not services are also provided or to be provided under the contract, and (subject to subsection (2) above) whatever is the nature of the consideration for the transfer or agreement to transfer.

Implied terms about title, etc.

11B.—(1) In a contract for the transfer of goods, other than one to which subsection (3) below applies, there is an implied term on the part of the transferor that in the case of a transfer of the property in the goods he has a right to transfer the property and in the case of an agreement to transfer the property in the goods he will have such a right at the time when the property is to be transferred.

(2) In a contract for the transfer of goods, other than one to which subsection (3) below applies, there is also an implied term that—

    (a) the goods are free, and will remain free until the time when the property is to be transferred, from any charge or encumbrance not disclosed or known to the transferee before the contract is made, and

    (b) the transferee will enjoy quiet possession of the goods except so far as it may be disturbed by the owner or other person entitled to the benefit of any charge or encumbrance so disclosed or known.

(3) This subsection applies to a contract for the transfer of goods in the case of which there appears from the contract or is to be inferred from its circumstances an intention that the transferor should transfer only such title as he or a third person may have.

(4) In a contract to which subsection (3) above applies there is an implied term that all charges or encumbrances known to the transferor and not known to the transferee have been disclosed to the transferee before the contract is made.

(5) In a contract to which subsection (3) above applies there is also an implied

---

[5] Part IA was inserted by the Sale and Supply of Goods Act 1994, s. 6 and Sched. 1.

term that none of the following will disturb the transferee's quiet possession of the goods, namely—
(a) the transferor;
(b) in a case where the parties to the contract intend that the transferor should transfer only such title as a third person may have, that person;
(c) anyone claiming through or under the transferor or that third person otherwise than under a charge or encumbrance disclosed or known to the transferee before the contract is made.

(6) [*Inserts new subsection into the Unfair Contract Terms Act 1977, s. 21 and is incorporated therein.*]

Implied terms where transfer is by description

11C.—(1) This section applies where, under a contract for the transfer of goods, the transferor transfers or agrees to transfer the property in the goods by description.

(2) In such a case there is an implied term that the goods will correspond with the description.

(3) If the transferor transfers or agrees to transfer the property in the goods by reference to a sample as well as by description it is not sufficient that the bulk of the goods corresponds with the sample if the goods do not also correspond with the description.

(4) A contract is not prevented from falling within subsection (1) above by reason only that, being exposed for supply, the goods are selected by the transferee.

Implied terms about quality or fitness

11D.—(1) Except as provided by this section and section 11E below and subject to the provisions of any other enactment, there is no implied term about the quality or fitness for any particular purpose of goods supplied under a contract for the transfer of goods.

(2) Where, under such a contract, the transferor transfers the property in goods in the course of a business, there is an implied term that the goods supplied under the contract are of satisfactory quality.

(3) For the purposes of this section and section 11E below, goods are of satisfactory quality if they meet the standard that a reasonable person would regard as satisfactory, taking account of any description of the goods, the price (if relevant) and all the other relevant circumstances.

(4) The term implied by subsection (2) above does not extend to any matter making the quality of goods unsatisfactory—
(a) which is specifically drawn to the transferee's attention before the contract is made,
(b) where the transferee examines the goods before the contract is made, which that examination ought to reveal, or
(c) where the property in the goods is, or is to be, transferred by reference to a sample, which would have been apparent on a reasonable examination of the sample.

(5) Subsection (6) below applies where, under a contract for the transfer of goods, the transferor transfers the property in goods in the course of a business and the transferee, expressly or by implication, makes known—
(a) to the transferor, or
(b) where the consideration or part of the consideration for the transfer is

a sum payable by instalments and the goods were previously sold by a credit-broker to the transferor, to that credit-broker,

any particular purpose for which the goods are being acquired.

(6) In that case there is (subject to subsection (7) below) an implied term that the goods supplied under the contract are reasonably fit for the purpose, whether or not that is a purpose for which such goods are commonly supplied.

(7) Subsection (6) above does not apply where the circumstances show that the transferee does not rely, or that it is unreasonable for him to rely, on the skill or judgment of the transferor or credit-broker.

(8) An implied term about quality or fitness for a particular purpose may be annexed by usage to a contract for the transfer of goods.

(9) The preceding provisions of this section apply to a transfer by a person who in the course of a business is acting as agent for another as they apply to a transfer by a principal in the course of a business, except where that other is not transferring in the course of a business and either the transferee knows that fact or reasonable steps are taken to bring it to the transferee's notice before the contract concerned is made.

Implied terms where transfer is by sample

11E.—(1) This section applies where, under a contract for the transfer of goods, the transferor transfers or agrees to transfer the property in the goods by reference to a sample.

(2) In such a case there is an implied term—

    (a) that the bulk will correspond with the sample in quality;

    (b) that the transferee will have a reasonable opportunity of comparing the bulk with the sample; and

    (c) that the goods will be free from any defect, making their quality unsatisfactory, which would not be apparent on reasonable examination of the sample.

(3) For the purposes of this section a transferor transfers or agrees to transfer the property in goods by reference to a sample where there is an express or implied term to that effect in the contract concerned.

Remedies for breach of contract

11F.—(1) Where in a contract for the transfer of goods a transferor is in breach of any term of the contract (express or implied), the other party to the contract (in this section referred to as "the transferee") shall be entitled—

    (a) to claim damages; and

    (b) if the breach is material, to reject any goods delivered under the contract and treat it as repudiated.

(2) Where a contract for the transfer of goods is a consumer contract and the transferee is the consumer, then, for the purposes of subsection (1)(b) above, breach by the transferor of any term (express or implied)—

    (a) as to the quality of the goods or their fitness for a purpose;

    (b) if the goods are, or are to be, transferred by description, that the goods will correspond with the description;

    (c) if the goods are, or are to be, transferred by reference to a sample, that the bulk will correspond with the sample in quality,

shall be deemed to be a material breach.

(3) In subsection (2) above, "consumer contract" has the same meaning as in section 25(1) of the 1977 Act; and for the purposes of that subsection the

onus of proving that a contract is not to be regarded as a consumer contract shall lie on the transferor.

Contracts for the hire of goods

The contracts concerned

11G.—(1) In this Act in its application to Scotland a "contract for the hire of goods" means a contract under which one person ("the supplier") hires or agrees to hire goods to another, other than an excepted contract.

(2) For the purposes of this section, an excepted contract means any of the following—

    (a) a hire-purchase agreement;

    (b) a contract under which goods are (or are to be) hired in exchange for trading stamps on their redemption.

(3) For the purposes of this Act in its application to Scotland a contract is a contract for the hire of goods whether or not services are also provided or to be provided under the contract, and (subject to subsection (2) above) whatever is the nature of the consideration for the hire or agreement to hire.

Implied terms about right to transfer possession etc

11H.—(1) In a contract for the hire of goods there is an implied term on the part of the supplier that—

    (a) in the case of a hire, he has a right to transfer possession of the goods by way of hire for the period of the hire; and

    (b) in the case of an agreement to hire, he will have such a right at the time of commencement of the period of the hire.

(2) In a contract for the hire of goods there is also an implied term that the person to whom the goods are hired will enjoy quiet possession of the goods for the period of the hire except so far as the possession may be disturbed by the owner or other person entitled to the benefit of any charge or encumbrance disclosed or known to the person to whom the goods are hired before the contract is made.

(3) The preceding provisions of this section do not affect the right of the supplier to repossess the goods under an express or implied term of the contract.

Implied terms where hire is by description

11I.—(1) This section applies where, under a contract for the hire of goods, the supplier hires or agrees to hire the goods by description.

(2) In such a case there is an implied term that the goods will correspond with the description.

(3) If under the contract the supplier hires or agrees to hire the goods by reference to a sample as well as by description it is not sufficient that the bulk of the goods corresponds with the sample if the goods do not also correspond with the description.

(4) A contract is not prevented from falling within subsection (1) above by reason only that, being exposed for supply, the goods are selected by the person to whom the goods are hired.

Implied terms about quality or fitness

11J.—(1) Except as provided by this section and section 11K below and subject to the provisions of any other enactment, there is no implied term about the quality or fitness for any particular purpose of goods hired under a contract for the hire of goods.

(2) Where, under such a contract, the supplier hires goods in the course of a business, there is an implied term that the goods supplied under the contract are of satisfactory quality.

(3) For the purposes of this section and section 11K below, goods are of satisfactory quality if they meet the standard that a reasonable person would regard as satisfactory, taking account of any description of the goods, the consideration for the hire (if relevant) and all the other relevant circumstances.

(4) The term implied by subsection (2) above does not extend to any matter making the quality of goods unsatisfactory—

    (a) which is specifically drawn to the attention of the person to whom the goods are hired before the contract is made, or

    (b) where that person examines the goods before the contract is made, which that examination ought to reveal; or

    (c) where the goods are hired by reference to a sample, which would have been apparent on reasonable examination of the sample.

(5) Subsection (6) below applies where, under a contract for the hire of goods, the supplier hires goods in the course of a business and the person to whom the goods are hired, expressly or by implication, makes known—

    (a) to the supplier in the course of negotiations conducted by him in relation to the making of the contract; or

    (b) to a credit-broker in the course of negotiations conducted by that broker in relation to goods sold by him to the supplier before forming the subject matter of the contract,

any particular purpose for which the goods are being hired.

(6) In that case there is (subject to subsection (7) below) an implied term that the goods supplied under the contract are reasonably fit for that purpose, whether or not that is a purpose for which such goods are commonly supplied.

(7) Subsection (6) above does not apply where the circumstances show that the person to whom the goods are hired does not rely, or that it is unreasonable for him to rely, on the skill or judgment of the hirer or credit-broker.

(8) An implied term about quality or fitness for a particular purpose may be annexed by usage to a contract for the hire of goods.

(9) The preceding provisions of this section apply to a hire by a person who in the course of a business is acting as agent for another as they apply to a hire by a principal in the course of a business, except where that other is not hiring in the course of a business and either the person to whom the goods are hired knows that fact or reasonable steps are taken to bring it to that person's notice before the contract concerned is made.

Implied terms where hire is by sample

11K.—(1) This section applies where, under a contract for the hire of goods, the supplier hires or agrees to hire the goods by reference to a sample.

(2) In such a case there is an implied term—

    (a) that the bulk will correspond with the sample in quality; and

    (b) that the person to whom the goods are hired will have a reasonable opportunity of comparing the bulk with the sample; and

    (c) that the goods will be free from any defect, making their quality unsatisfactory, which would not be apparent on reasonable examination of the sample.

(3) For the purposes of this section a supplier hires or agrees to hire goods

by reference to a sample where there is an express or implied term to that effect in the contract concerned.

Exclusion of implied terms, etc.

Exclusion of implied terms, etc.
    11L.—(1) Where a right, duty or liability would arise under a contract for the transfer of goods or a contract for the hire of goods by implication of law, it may (subject to subsection (2) below and the 1977 Act) be negatived or varied by express agreement, or by the course of dealing between the parties, or by such usage as binds both parties to the contract.
    (2) An express term does not negative a term implied by the preceding provisions of this Part of this Act unless inconsistent with it.
    (3) Nothing in the preceding provisions of this Part of this Act prejudices the operation of any other enactment or any rule of law whereby any term (other than one relating to quality or fitness) is to be implied in a contract for the transfer of goods or a contract for the hire of goods.

PART II

SUPPLY OF SERVICES

The contracts concerned
    12.—(1) In this Act a "contract for the supply of a service" means, subject to subsection (2) below, a contract under which a person ("the supplier") agrees to carry out a service.
    (2) For the purposes of this Act, a contract of service or apprenticeship is not a contract for the supply of a service.
    (3) Subject to subsection (2) above, a contract is a contract for the supply of a service for the purposes of this Act whether or not goods are also—
        (a) transferred or to be transferred, or
        (b) bailed or to be bailed by way of hire,
under the contract, and whatever is the nature of the consideration for which the service is to be carried out.
    (4) The Secretary of State may by order provide that one or more of sections 13 to 15 below shall not apply to services of a description specified in the order, and such an order may make different provision for different circumstances.[6]
    (5) The power to make an order under subsection (4) above shall be exercisable by statutory instrument subject to annulment in pursuance of a resolution of either House of Parliament.

Implied term about care and skill
    13. In a contract for the supply of a service where the supplier is acting in the course of a business, there is an implied term that the supplier will carry out the service with reasonable care and skill.

<hr>

[6] The Orders (not printed in this work) made under this subsection (S.I. 1982 No. 1771, S.I. 1983 No. 902, S.I. 1985 No. 1) exclude from s. 13 of the Act the services of an advocate; of a company director; of a director of a building society or a member of a committee of management of an industrial or provident society; and of an arbitrator (or umpire) in their respective capacities as such.

Implied term about time for performance

14.—(1) Where, under a contract for the supply of a service by a supplier acting in the course of a business, the time for the service to be carried out is not fixed by the contract, left to be fixed in a manner agreed by the contract or determined by the course of dealing between the parties, there is an implied term that the supplier will carry out the service within a reasonable time.

(2) What is a reasonable time is a question of fact.

Implied term about consideration

15.—(1) Where, under a contract for the supply of a service, the consideration for the service is not determined by the contract, left to be determined in a manner agreed by the contract or determined by the course of dealing between the parties, there is an implied term that the party contracting with the supplier will pay a reasonable charge.

(2) What is a reasonable charge is a question of fact.

Exclusion of implied terms, etc.

16.—(1) Where a right, duty or liability would arise under a contract for the supply of a service by virtue of this Part of this Act, it may (subject to subsection (2) below and the 1977 Act) be negatived or varied by express agreement, or by the course of dealing between the parties, or by such usage as binds both parties to the contract.

(2) An express term does not negative a term implied by this Part of this Act unless inconsistent with it.

(3) Nothing in this Part of this Act prejudices—

    (a) any rule of law which imposes on the supplier a duty stricter than that imposed by section 13 or 14 above; or

    (b) subject to paragraph (a) above, any rule of law whereby any term not inconsistent with this Part of this Act is to be implied in a contract for the supply of a service.

(4) This Part of this Act has effect subject to any other enactment which defines or restricts the rights, duties or liabilities arising in connection with a service of any description.

PART III

SUPPLEMENTARY

*   *   *   *   *

Interpretation: general

18.—(1) In the preceding provisions of this Act and this section—

"bailee", in relation to a contract for the hire of goods means (depending on the context) a person to whom the goods are bailed under the contract, or a person to whom they are to be so bailed, or a person to whom the rights under the contract of either of those persons have passed;

"bailor", in relation to a contract for the hire of goods, means (depending on the context) a person who bails the goods under the contract, or a person who agrees to do so, or a person to whom the duties under the contract of either of those persons have passed;

"business" includes a profession and the activities of any government department or local or public authority;

"credit-broker" means a person acting in the course of a business of credit brokerage carried on by him;

"credit brokerage" means the effecting of introductions—

(a) of individuals desiring to obtain credit to persons carrying on any business so far as it relates to the provision of credit; or

(b) of individuals desiring to obtain goods on hire to persons carrying on a business which comprises or relates to the bailment or as regards Scotland the hire of goods under a contract for the hire of goods; or

(c) of individuals desiring to obtain credit, or to obtain goods on hire, to other credit-brokers;

"enactment" means any legislation (including subordinate legislation) of the United Kingdom or Northern Ireland;

"goods" includes all personal chattels, other than things in action and money, and as regards Scotland all corporeal moveables; and in particular "goods" includes emblements, industrial growing crops, and things attached to or forming part of the land which are agreed to be severed before the transfer bailment or hire concerned or under the contract concerned;

"hire-purchase agreement" has the same meaning as in the 1974 Act;

"property", in relation to goods, means the general property in them and not merely a special property;

"redemption", in relation to trading stamps, has the same meaning as in the Trading Stamps Act 1964 or, as respects Northern Ireland, the Trading Stamps Act (Northern Ireland) 1965;

"trading stamps" has the same meaning as in the said Act of 1964 or, as respects Northern Ireland, the said Act of 1965;

"transferee", in relation to a contract for the transfer of goods, means (depending on the context) a person to whom the property in the goods is transferred under the contract, or a person to whom the property is to be so transferred, or a person to whom the rights under the contract of either of those persons have passed;

"transferor", in relation to a contract for the transfer of goods, means (depending on the context) a person who transfers the property in the goods under the contract, or a person who agrees to do so, or a person to whom the duties under the contract of either of those persons have passed.

(2) In subsection (1) above, in the definitions of bailee, bailor, transferee and transferor, a reference to rights or duties passing is to their passing by assignment assignation, operation of law or otherwise.

(3) For the purposes of this Act, the quality of goods includes their state and condition and the following (among others) are in appropriate cases aspects of the quality of goods—

(a) fitness for all the purposes for which goods of the kind in question are commonly supplied,

(b) appearance and finish,

(c) freedom from minor defects,

(d) safety, and

(e) durability.

(4) References in this Act to dealing as consumer are to be construed in accordance with Part I of the Unfair Contract Terms Act 1977; and, for the purposes of this Act, it is for the transferor or bailor claiming that the transferee or bailee does not deal as consumer to show that he does not.

Interpretation: references to Acts

19. In this Act—

"the 1973 Act" means the Supply of Goods (Implied Terms) Act 1973;

"the 1974 Act" means the Consumer Credit Act 1974;

"the 1977 Act" means the Unfair Contract Terms Act 1977; and

"the 1979 Act" means the Sale of Goods Act 1979.

Citation, transitional provisions, commencement and extent

20.—(1) This Act may be cited as the Supply of Goods and Services Act 1982.

(2) The transitional provisions in the Schedule to this Act shall have effect.

(3) Part I of this Act together with section 17 and so much of sections 18 and 19 above as relates to that Part shall not come into operation until 4th January 1983; and Part II of this Act together with so much of sections 18 and 19 above as relates to that Part shall not come into operation until such day as may be appointed by an order made by the Secretary of State.

(4) The power to make an order under subsection (3) above shall be exercisable by statutory instrument.

(5) No provision of this Act applies to a contract made before the provision comes into operation.

(6) This Act except Part IA, which extends only to Scotland extends to Northern Ireland and Parts I and II do not extend to Scotland.

*   *   *   *   *

Consumer Protection Act 1987[1]

(c. 43)

An Act to make provision with respect to the liability of persons for damage caused by defective products; to consolidate with amendments the Consumer Safety Act 1978 and the Consumer Safety (Amendment) Act 1986; to make provision with respect to the giving of price indications; to amend Part I of the Health and Safety at Work etc. Act 1974 and sections 31 and 80 of the Explosives Act 1875; to repeal the Trade Descriptions Act 1972 and the Fabrics (Misdescription) Act 1913; and for connected purposes.   [15th May 1987]

PART I

PRODUCT LIABILITY

Purpose and construction of Part I

1.—(1) This Part shall have effect for the purpose of making such provision as is necessary in order to comply with the product liability Directive and shall be construed accordingly.

(2) In this Part, except in so far as the context otherwise requires—

"agricultural produce" means any produce of the soil, of stock-farming or of fisheries;

"dependant" and "relative" have the same meaning as they have in, respectively, the Fatal Accidents Act 1976 and the Damages (Scotland) Act 1976;

"producer", in relation to a product, means—

    (a) the person who manufactured it;

    (b) in the case of a substance which has not been manufactured but has been won or abstracted, the person who won or abstracted it;

    (c) in the case of a product which has not been manufactured, won or abstracted but essential characteristics of which are attributable to an industrial or other process having been carried out (for example, in relation to agricultural produce), the person who carried out that process;

"product" means any goods or electricity and (subject to subsection (3) below) includes a product which is comprised in another product, whether by virtue of being a component part or raw material or otherwise; and

"the product liability Directive" means the Directive of the Council of the European Communities, dated 25th July 1985, (No. 85/374/EEC) on the approximation of the laws, regulations and administrative provisions of the member States concerning liability for defective products.

(3) For the purposes of this Part a person who supplies any product in which products are comprised, whether by virtue of being component parts or raw materials or otherwise, shall not be treated by reason only of his supply of that product as supplying any of the products so comprised.

---

[1] Part I of this Act implements Council Directive 85/374/EEC, printed below at p. 345.

Liability for defective products

2.—(1) Subject to the following provisions of this Part, where any damage is caused wholly or partly by a defect in a product, every person to whom subsection (2) below applies shall be liable for the damage.

(2) This subsection applies to—

    (a) the producer of the product;

    (b) any person who, by putting his name on the product or using a trade mark or other distinguishing mark in relation to the product, has held himself out to be the producer of the product;

    (c) any person who has imported the product into a member State from a place outside the member States in order, in the course of any business of his, to supply it to another.

(3) Subject as aforesaid, where any damage is caused wholly or partly by a defect in a product, any person who supplied the product (whether to the person who suffered the damage, to the producer of any product in which the product in question is comprised or to any other person) shall be liable for the damage if—

    (a) the person who suffered the damage requests the supplier to identify one or more of the persons (whether still in existence or not) to whom subsection (2) above applies in relation to the product;

    (b) that request is made within a reasonable period after the damage occurs and at a time when it is not reasonably practicable for the person making the request to identify all those persons; and

    (c) the supplier fails, within a reasonable period after receiving the request, either to comply with the request or to identify the person who supplied the product to him.

(4) Neither subsection (2) nor subsection (3) above shall apply to a person in respect of any defect in any game or agricultural produce if the only supply of the game or produce by that person to another was at a time when it had not undergone an industrial process.

(5) Where two or more persons are liable by virtue of this Part for the same damage, their liability shall be joint and several.

(6) This section shall be without prejudice to any liability arising otherwise than by virtue of this Part.

Meaning of "defect"

3.—(1) Subject to the following provisions of this section, there is a defect in a product for the purposes of this Part if the safety of the product is not such as persons generally are entitled to expect; and for those purposes "safety", in relation to a product, shall include safety with respect to products comprised in that product and safety in the context of risks of damage to property, as well as in the context of risks of death or personal injury.

(2) In determining for the purposes of subsection (1) above what persons generally are entitled to expect in relation to a product all the circumstances shall be taken into account, including—

    (a) the manner in which, and purposes for which, the product has been marketed, its get-up, the use of any mark in relation to the product and any instructions for, or warnings with respect to, doing or refraining from doing anything with or in relation to the product;

    (b) what might reasonably be expected to be done with or in relation to the product; and

    (c) the time when the product was supplied by its producer to another;

and nothing in this section shall require a defect to be inferred from the fact alone that the safety of a product which is supplied after that time is greater than the safety of the product in question.

Defences

4.—(1) In any civil proceedings by virtue of this Part against any person ("the person proceeded against") in respect of a defect in a product it shall be a defence for him to show—

(a) that the defect is attributable to compliance with any requirement imposed by or under any enactment or with any Community obligation; or

(b) that the person proceeded against did not at any time supply the product to another; or

(c) that the following conditions are satisfied, that is to say—

(i) that the only supply of the product to another by the person proceeded against was otherwise than in the course of a business of that person's; and

(ii) that section 2(2) above does not apply to that person or applies to him by virtue only of things done otherwise than with a view to profit; or

(d) that the defect did not exist in the product at the relevant time; or

(e) that the state of scientific and technical knowledge at the relevant time was not such that a producer of products of the same description as the product in question might be expected to have discovered the defect if it had existed in his products while they were under his control; or

(f) that the defect—

(i) constituted a defect in a product ("the subsequent product") in which the product in question had been comprised; and

(ii) was wholly attributable to the design of the subsequent product or to compliance by the producer of the product in question with instructions given by the producer of the subsequent product.

(2) In this section "the relevant time", in relation to electricity, means the time at which it was generated, being a time before it was transmitted or distributed, and in relation to any other product, means—

(a) if the person proceeded against is a person to whom subsection (2) of section 2 above applies in relation to the product, the time when he supplied the product to another;

(b) if that subsection does not apply to that person in relation to the product, the time when the product was last supplied by a person to whom that subsection does apply in relation to the product.

Damage giving rise to liability

5.—(1) Subject to the following provisions of this section, in this Part "damage" means death or personal injury or any loss of or damage to any property (including land).

(2) A person shall not be liable under section 2 above in respect of any defect in a product for the loss of or any damage to the product itself or for the loss of or any damage to the whole or any part of any product which has been supplied with the product in question comprised in it.

(3) A person shall not be liable under section 2 above for any loss of or damage to any property which, at the time it is lost or damaged, is not—

(a) of a description of property ordinarily intended for private use, occupation or consumption; and

(b) intended by the person suffering the loss or damage mainly for his own private use, occupation or consumption.

(4) No damages shall be awarded to any person by virtue of this Part in respect of any loss of or damage to any property if the amount which would fall to be so awarded to that person, apart from this subsection and any liability for interest, does not exceed £275.

(5) In determining for the purposes of this Part who has suffered any loss of or damage to property and when any such loss or damage occurred, the loss or damage shall be regarded as having occurred at the earliest time at which a person with an interest in the property had knowledge of the material facts about the loss or damage.

(6) For the purposes of subsection (5) above the material facts about any loss of or damage to any property are such facts about the loss or damage as would lead a reasonable person with an interest in the property to consider the loss or damage sufficiently serious to justify his instituting proceedings for damages against a defendant who did not dispute liability and was able to satisfy a judgment.

(7) For the purposes of subsection (5) above a person's knowledge includes knowledge which he might reasonably have been expected to acquire—

(a) from facts observable or ascertainable by him; or

(b) from facts ascertainable by him with the help of appropriate expert advice which it is reasonable for him to seek;

but a person shall not be taken by virtue of this subsection to have knowledge of a fact ascertainable by him only with the help of expert advice unless he has failed to take all reasonable steps to obtain (and, where appropriate, to act on) that advice.

(8) Subsections (5) to (7) above shall not extend to Scotland.

Application of certain enactments etc.

6.—(1) Any damage for which a person is liable under section 2 above shall be deemed to have been caused—

(a) for the purposes of the Fatal Accidents Act 1976, by that person's wrongful act, neglect or default;

(b) for the purposes of section 3 of the Law Reform (Miscellaneous Provisions) (Scotland) Act 1940 (contribution among joint wrongdoers), by that person's wrongful act or negligent act or omission;

(c) for the purposes of section 1 of the Damages (Scotland) Act 1976 (rights of relatives of a deceased), by that person's act or omission; and

(d) for the purposes of Part II of the Administration of Justice Act 1982 (damages for personal injuries, etc.—Scotland), by an act or omission giving rise to liability in that person to pay damages.

(2) Where—

(a) a person's death is caused wholly or partly by a defect in a product, or a person dies after suffering damage which has been so caused;

(b) a request such as mentioned in paragraph (a) of subsection (3) of section 2 above is made to a supplier of the product by that person's personal representatives or, in the case of a person whose death is

caused wholly or partly by the defect, by any dependant or relative of
that person; and

(c) the conditions specified in paragraphs (b) and (c) of that subsection
are satisfied in relation to that request,

this Part shall have effect for the purposes of the Law Reform (Miscellaneous
Provisions) Act 1934, the Fatal Accidents Act 1976 and the Damages (Scotland)
Act 1976 as if liability of the supplier to that person under that subsection did
not depend on that person having requested the supplier to identify certain persons or on the said conditions having been satisified in relation to a request
made by that person.

(3) Section 1 of the Congenital Disabilities (Civil Liability) Act 1976 shall
have effect for the purposes of this Part as if—

(a) a person were answerable to a child in respect of an occurrence caused
wholly or partly by a defect in a product if he is or has been liable
under section 2 above in respect of any effect of the occurrence on a
parent of the child, or would be so liable if the occurrence caused a
parent of the child to suffer damage;

(b) the provisions of this Part relating to liability under section 2 above
applied in relation to liability by virtue of paragraph (a) above under
the said section 1; and

(c) subsection (6) of the said section 1 (exclusion of liability) were
omitted.

(4) Where any damage is caused partly by a defect in a product and partly
by the fault of the person suffering the damage, the Law Reform (Contributory
Negligence) Act 1945 and section 5 of the Fatal Accidents Act 1976
(contributory negligence) shall have effect as if the defect were the fault of
every person liable by virtue of this Part for the damage caused by the defect.

(5) In subsection (4) above "fault" has the same meaning as in the said Act
of 1945.

(6) Schedule 1 to this Act shall have effect for the purpose of amending the
Limitation Act 1980 and the Prescription and Limitation (Scotland) Act 1973
in their application in relation to the bringing of actions by virtue of this Part.

(7) It is hereby declared that liability by virtue of this Part is to be treated
as liability in tort for the purposes of any enactment conferring jurisdiction on
any court with respect to any matter.

(8) Nothing in this Part shall prejudice the operation of section 12 of the
Nuclear Installations Act 1965 (rights to compensation for certain breaches of
duties confined to rights under that Act).

Prohibition on exclusions from liability

7.   The liability of a person by virtue of this Part to a person who has suffered
damage caused wholly or partly by a defect in a product, or to a dependant or
relative of such a person, shall not be limited or excluded by any contract term,
by any notice or by any other provision.

Power to modify Part I

8.—(1) Her Majesty may by Order in Council make such modifications of
this Part and of any other enactment (including an enactment contained in the
following Parts of this Act, or in an Act passed after this Act) as appear to Her
Majesty in Council to be necessary or expedient in consequence of any modification of the product liability Directive which is made at any time after the
passing of this Act.

(2) An Order in Council under subsection (1) above shall not be submitted to Her Majesty in Council unless a draft of the Order has been laid before, and approved by a resolution of, each House of Parliament.

Application of Part I to Crown
    9.—(1) Subject to subsection (2) below, this Part shall bind the Crown.
    (2) The Crown shall not, as regards the Crown's liability by virtue of this Part, be bound by this Part further than the Crown is made liable in tort or in reparation under the Crown Proceedings Act 1947, as that Act has effect from time to time.

PART II

CONSUMER SAFETY

The general safety requirement
    10.—(1) A person shall be guilty of an offence if he—
    (a) supplies any consumer goods which fail to comply with the general safety requirement;
    (b) offers or agrees to supply any such goods; or
    (c) exposes or possesses any such goods for supply.
    (2) For the purposes of this section consumer goods fail to comply with the general safety requirement if they are not reasonably safe having regard to all the circumstances, including—
    (a) the manner in which, and purposes for which, the goods are being or would be marketed, the get-up of the goods, the use of any mark in relation to the goods and any instructions or warnings which are given or would be given with respect to the keeping, use or consumption of the goods;
    (b) any standards of safety published by any person either for goods of a description which applies to the goods in question or for matters relating to goods of that description; and
    (c) the existence of any means by which it would have been reasonable (taking into account the cost, likelihood and extent of any improvement) for the goods to have been made safer.
    (3) For the purposes of this section consumer goods shall not be regarded as failing to comply with the general safety requirement in respect of—
    (a) anything which is shown to be attributable to compliance with any requirement imposed by or under any enactment or with any Community obligation;
    (b) any failure to do more in relation to any matter than is required by—
    (i) any safety regulations imposing requirements with respect to that matter;
    (ii) [*Repealed*]
    (iii) any provision of any enactment or subordinate legislation imposing such requirements with respect to that matter as are designated for the purposes of this subsection by any such regulations.
    (4) In any proceedings against any person for an offence under this section in respect of any goods it shall be a defence for that person to show—
    (a) that he reasonably believed that the goods would not be used or consumed in the United Kingdom; or
    (b) that the following conditions are satisfied, that is to say—

(i) that he supplied the goods, offered or agreed to supply them or, as the case may be, exposed or possessed them for supply in the course of carrying on a retail business; and

(ii) that, at the time he supplied the goods or offered or agreed to supply them or exposed or possessed them for supply, he neither knew nor had reasonable grounds for believing that the goods failed to comply with the general safety requirement; or

(c) that the terms on which he supplied the goods or agreed or offered to supply them or, in the case of goods which he exposed or possessed for supply, the terms on which he intended to supply them—

(i) indicated that the goods were not supplied or to be supplied as new goods; and

(ii) provided for, or contemplated, the acquisition of an interest in the goods by the persons supplied or to be supplied.

(5) For the purposes of subsection (4)(b) above goods are supplied in the course of carrying on a retail business if—

(a) whether or not they are themselves acquired for a person's private use or consumption, they are supplied in the course of carrying on a business of making a supply of consumer goods available to persons who generally acquire them for private use or consumption; and

(b) the descriptions of goods the supply of which is made available in the course of that business do not, to a significant extent, include manufactured or imported goods which have not previously been supplied in the United Kingdom.

(6) A person guilty of an offence under this section shall be liable on summary conviction to imprisonment for a term not exceeding six months or to a fine not exceeding level 5 on the standard scale or to both.

(7) In this section "consumer goods" means any goods which are ordinarily intended for private use or consumption, not being—

(a) growing crops or things comprised in land by virtue of being attached to it;

(b) water, food, feeding stuff or fertiliser;

(c) gas which is, is to be or has been supplied by a person authorised to supply it by or under section 6, 7 or 8 of the Gas Act 1986 (authorisation of supply of gas through pipes);

(d) aircraft (other than hang-gliders) or motor vehicles;

(e) controlled drugs or licensed medicinal products;

(f) tobacco.

Safety regulations

11.—(1) The Secretary of State may by regulations under this section ("safety regulations") make such provision as he considers appropriate for the purposes of section 10(3) above and for the purpose of securing—

(a) that goods to which this section applies are safe;

(b) that goods to which this section applies which are unsafe, or would be unsafe in the hands of persons of a particular description, are not made available to persons generally or, as the case may be, to persons of that description; and

(c) that appropriate information is, and inappropriate information is not, provided in relation to goods to which this section applies.

(2) Without prejudice to the generality of subsection (1) above, safety regulations may contain provision—

(a) with respect to the composition or contents, design, construction, finish or packing of goods to which this section applies, with respect to standards for such goods and with respect to other matters relating to such goods;

(b) with respect to the giving, refusal, alteration or cancellation of approvals of such goods, of descriptions of such goods or of standards for such goods;

(c) with respect to the conditions that may be attached to any approval given under the regulations;

(d) for requiring such fees as may be determined by or under the regulations to be paid on the giving or alteration of any approval under the regulations and on the making of an application for such an approval or alteration;

(e) with respect to appeals against refusals, alterations and cancellations of approvals given under the regulations and against the conditions contained in such approvals;

(f) for requiring goods to which this section applies to be approved under the regulations or to conform to the requirements of the regulations or to descriptions or standards specified in or approved by or under the regulations;

(g) with respect to the testing or inspection of goods to which this section applies (including provision for determining the standards to be applied in carrying out any test or inspection);

(h) with respect to the ways of dealing with goods of which some or all do not satisfy a test required by or under the regulations or a standard connected with a procedure so required;

(i) for requiring a mark, warning or instruction or any other information relating to goods to be put on or to accompany the goods or to be used or provided in some other manner in relation to the goods, and for securing that inappropriate information is not given in relation to goods either by means of misleading marks or otherwise;

(j) for prohibiting persons from supplying, or from offering to supply, agreeing to supply, exposing for supply or possessing for supply, goods to which this section applies and component parts and raw materials for such goods;

(k) for requiring information to be given to any such person as may be determined by or under the regulations for the purpose of enabling that person to exercise any function conferred on him by the regulations.

(3) Without prejudice as aforesaid, safety regulations may contain provision—

(a) for requiring persons on whom functions are conferred by or under section 27 below to have regard, in exercising their functions so far as relating to any provision of safety regulations, to matters specified in a direction issued by the Secretary of State with respect to that provision;

(b) for securing that a person shall not be guilty of an offence under section 12 below unless it is shown that the goods in question do not conform to a particular standard;

(c) for securing that proceedings for such an offence are not brought in England and Wales except by or with the consent of the Secretary of State or the Director of Public Prosecutions;

(d) for securing that proceedings for such an offence are not brought in

Northern Ireland except by or with the consent of the Secretary of State
or the Director of Public Prosecutions for Northern Ireland;

(e) for enabling a magistrates' court in England and Wales or Northern
Ireland to try an information or, in Northern Ireland, a complaint in
respect of such an offence if the information was laid or the complaint
made within twelve months from the time when the offence was
committed;

(f) for enabling summary proceedings for such an offence to be brought
in Scotland at any time within twelve months from the time when the
offence was committed; and

(g) for determining the persons by whom, and the manner in which, anything required to be done by or under the regulations is to be done.

(4) Safety regulations shall not provide for any contravention of the regulations to be an offence.

(5) Where the Secretary of State proposes to make safety regulations it shall
be his duty before he makes them—

(a) to consult such organisations as appear to him to be representative of
interests substantially affected by the proposal;

(b) to consult such other persons as he considers appropriate; and

(c) in the case of proposed regulations relating to goods suitable for use
at work, to consult the Health and Safety Commission in relation to
the application of the proposed regulations to Great Britain;

but the preceding provisions of this subsection shall not apply in the case of
regulations which provide for the regulations to cease to have effect at the end
of a period of not more than twelve months beginning with the day on which
they come into force and which contain a statement that it appears to the Secretary of State that the need to protect the public requires that the regulations
should be made without delay.

(6) The power to make safety regulations shall be exercisable by statutory
instrument subject to annulment in pursuance of a resolution of either House
of Parliament and shall include power—

(a) to make different provision for different cases; and

(b) to make such supplemental, consequential and transitional provision as
the Secretary of State considers appropriate.

(7) This section applies to any goods other than—

(a) growing crops and things comprised in land by virtue of being attached
to it;

(b) water, food, feeding stuff and fertiliser;

(c) gas which is, is to be or has been supplied by a person authorised to
supply it by or under section 6, 7 or 8 of the Gas Act 1986
(authorisation of supply of gas through pipes);

(d) controlled drugs and licensed medicinal products.

Offences against the safety regulations

12.—(1) Where safety regulations prohibit a person from supplying or
offering or agreeing to supply any goods or from exposing or possessing any
goods for supply, that person shall be guilty of an offence if he contravenes the
prohibition.

(2) Where safety regulations require a person who makes or processes any
goods in the course of carrying on a business—

(a) to carry out a particular test or use a particular procedure in connection with the making or processing of the goods with a view to ascertaining whether the goods satisfy any requirements of such regulations; or

(b) to deal or not to deal in a particular way with a quantity of the goods of which the whole or part does not satisfy such a test or does not satisfy standards connected with such a procedure,

that person shall be guilty of an offence if he does not comply with the requirement.

(3) If a person contravenes a provision of safety regulations which prohibits or requires the provision, by means of a mark or otherwise, of information of a particular kind in relation to goods, he shall be guilty of an offence.

(4) Where safety regulations require any person to give information to another for the purpose of enabling that other to exercise any function, that person shall be guilty of an offence if—

(a) he fails without reasonable cause to comply with the requirement; or

(b) in giving the information which is required of him—

(i) he makes any statement which he knows is false in a material particular; or

(ii) he recklessly makes any statement which is false in a material particular.

(5) A person guilty of an offence under this section shall be liable on summary conviction to imprisonment for a term not exceeding six months or to a fine not exceeding level 5 on the standard scale or to both.

Prohibition notices and notices to warn

13.—(1) The Secretary of State may—

(a) serve on any person a notice ("a prohibition notice") prohibiting that person, except with the consent of the Secretary of State, from supplying, or from offering to supply, agreeing to supply, exposing for supply or possessing for supply, any relevant goods which the Secretary of State considers are unsafe and which are described in the notice;

(b) serve on any person a notice ("a notice to warn") requiring that person at his own expense to publish, in a form and manner and on occasions specified in the notice, a warning about any relevant goods which the Secretary of State considers are unsafe, which that person supplies or has supplied and which are described in the notice.

(2) Schedule 2 to this Act shall have effect with respect to prohibition notices and notices to warn; and the Secretary of State may by regulations make provision specifying the manner in which information is to be given to any person under that Schedule.

(3) A consent given by the Secretary of State for the purposes of a prohibition notice may impose such conditions on the doing of anything for which the consent is required as the Secretary of State considers appropriate.

(4) A person who contravenes a prohibition notice or a notice to warn shall be guilty of an offence and liable on summary conviction to imprisonment for a term not exceeding six months or to a fine not exceeding level 5 on the standard scale or to both.

(5) The power to make regulations under subsection (2) above shall be exercisable by statutory instrument subject to annulment in pursuance of a resolution of either House of Parliament and shall include power—

(a) to make different provision for different cases; and

(b) to make such supplemental, consequential and transitional provision as the Secretary of State considers appropriate.

(6) In this section "relevant goods" means—
    (a) in relation to a prohibition notice, any goods to which section 11 above applies; and
    (b) in relation to a notice to warn, any goods to which that section applies or any growing crops or things comprised in land by virtue of being attached to it.

Suspension notices

14.—(1) Where an enforcement authority has reasonable grounds for suspecting that any safety provision has been contravened in relation to any goods, the authority may serve a notice ("a suspension notice") prohibiting the person on whom it is served, for such period ending not more than six months after the date of the notice as is specified therein, from doing any of the following things without the consent of the authority, that is to say, supplying the goods, offering to supply them, agreeing to supply them or exposing them for supply.

(2) A suspension notice served by an enforcement authority in respect of any goods shall—
    (a) describe the goods in a manner sufficient to identify them;
    (b) set out the grounds on which the authority suspects that a safety provision has been contravened in relation to the goods; and
    (c) state that, and the manner in which, the person on whom the notice is served may appeal against the notice under section 15 below.

(3) A suspension notice served by an enforcement authority for the purpose of prohibiting a person for any period from doing the things mentioned in subsection (1) above in relation to any goods may also require that person to keep the authority informed of the whereabouts throughout that period of any of those goods in which he has an interest.

(4) Where a suspension notice has been served on any person in respect of any goods, no further such notice shall be served on that person in respect of the same goods unless—
    (a) proceedings against that person for an offence in respect of a contravention in relation to the goods of a safety provision (not being an offence under this section); or
    (b) proceedings for the forfeiture of the goods under section 16 or 17 below,
are pending at the end of the period specified in the first-mentioned notice.

(5) A consent given by an enforcement authority for the purposes of subsection (1) above may impose such conditions on the doing of anything for which the consent is required as the authority considers appropriate.

(6) Any person who contravenes a suspension notice shall be guilty of an offence and liable on summary conviction to imprisonment for a term not exceeding six months or to a fine not exceeding level 5 on the standard scale or to both.

(7) Where an enforcement authority serves a suspension notice in respect of any goods, the authority shall be liable to pay compensation to any person having an interest in the goods in respect of any loss or damage caused by reason of the service of the notice if—
    (a) there has been no contravention in relation to the goods of any safety provision; and
    (b) the exercise of the power is not attributable to any neglect or default by that person.

(8) Any disputed question as to the right to or the amount of any compensa-

tion payable under this section shall be determined by arbitration or, in Scotland, by a single arbiter appointed, failing agreement between the parties, by the sheriff.

Appeals against suspension notices

15.—(1) Any person having an interest in any goods in respect of which a suspension notice is for the time being in force may apply for an order setting aside the notice.

(2) An application under this section may be made—

    (a) to any magistrates' court in which proceedings have been brought in England and Wales or Northern Ireland—

        (i) for an offence in respect of a contravention in relation to the goods of any safety provision; or

        (ii) for the forfeiture of the goods under section 16 below;

    (b) where no such proceedings have been so brought, by way of complaint to a magistrates' court; or

    (c) in Scotland, by summary application to the sheriff.

(3) On an application under this section to a magistrates' court in England and Wales or Northern Ireland the court shall make an order setting aside the suspension notice only if the court is satisfied that there has been no contravention in relation to the goods of any safety provision.

(4) On an application under this section to the sheriff he shall make an order setting aside the suspension notice only if he is satisfied that at the date of making the order—

    (a) proceedings for an offence in respect of a contravention in relation to the goods of any safety provision; or

    (b) proceedings for the forfeiture of the goods under section 17 below,

have not been brought or, having been brought, have been concluded.

(5) Any person aggrieved by an order made under this section by a magistrates' court in England and Wales or Northern Ireland, or by a decision of such a court not to make such an order, may appeal against that order or decision—

    (a) in England and Wales, to the Crown Court;

    (b) in Northern Ireland, to the county court;

and an order so made may contain such provision as appears to the court to be appropriate for delaying the coming into force of the order pending the making and determination of any appeal (including any application under section 111 of the Magistrates' Courts Act 1980 or Article 146 of the Magistrates' Courts (Northern Ireland) Order 1981 (statement of case)).

Forfeiture: England and Wales and Northern Ireland

16.—(1) An enforcement authority in England and Wales or Northern Ireland may apply under this section for an order for the forfeiture of any goods on the grounds that there has been a contravention in relation to the goods of a safety provision.

(2) An application under this section may be made—

    (a) where proceedings have been brought in a magistrates' court for an offence in respect of a contravention in relation to some or all of the goods of any safety provision, to that court;

    (b) where an application with respect to some or all of the goods has been made to a magistrates' court under section 15 above or section 33 below, to that court; and

    (c) where no application for the forfeiture of the goods has been made under paragraph (a) or (b) above, by way of complaint to a magistrates' court.

(3) On an application under this section the court shall make an order for the forfeiture of any goods only if it is satisfied that there has been a contravention in relation to the goods of a safety provision.

(4) For the avoidance of doubt it is declared that a court may infer for the purposes of this section that there has been a contravention in relation to any goods of a safety provision if it is satisfied that any such provision has been contravened in relation to goods which are representative of those goods (whether by reason of being of the same design or part of the same consignment or batch or otherwise).

(5) Any person aggrieved by an order made under this section by a magistrates' court, or by a decision of such a court not to make such an order, may appeal against that order or decision—

(a) in England and Wales, to the Crown Court;

(b) in Northern Ireland, to the county court;

and an order so made may contain such provision as appears to the court to be appropriate for delaying the coming into force of the order pending the making and determination of any appeal (including any application under section 111 of the Magistrates' Courts Act 1980 or Article 146 of the Magistrates' Courts (Northern Ireland) Order 1981 (statement of case)).

(6) Subject to subsection (7) below, where any goods are forfeited under this section they shall be destroyed in accordance with such directions as the court may give.

(7) On making an order under this section a magistrates' court may, if it considers it appropriate to do so, direct that the goods to which the order relates shall (instead of being destroyed) be released, to such person as the court may specify, on condition that that person—

(a) does not supply those goods to any person otherwise than as mentioned in section 46(7)(a) or (b) below; and

(b) complies with any order to pay costs or expenses (including any order under section 35 below) which has been made against that person in the proceedings for the order for forfeiture.

Forfeiture: Scotland

17.—(1) In Scotland a sheriff may make an order for forfeiture of any goods in relation to which there has been a contravention of a safety provision—

(a) on an application by the procurator-fiscal made in the manner specified in section 310 of the Criminal Procedure (Scotland) Act 1975; or

(b) where a person is convicted of any offence in respect of any such contravention, in addition to any other penalty which the sheriff may impose.

(2) The procurator-fiscal making an application under subsection (1)(a) above shall serve on any person appearing to him to be the owner of, or otherwise to have an interest in, the goods to which the application relates a copy of the application, together with a notice giving him the opportunity to appear at the hearing of the application to show cause why the goods should not be forfeited.

(3) Service under subsection (2) above shall be carried out, and such service may be proved, in the manner specified for citation of an accused in summary proceedings under the Criminal Procedure (Scotland) Act 1975.

(4) Any person upon whom notice is served under subsection (2) above and any other person claiming to be the owner of, or otherwise to have an interest

in, goods to which an application under this section relates shall be entitled to appear at the hearing of the application to show cause why the goods should not be forfeited.

(5) The sheriff shall not make an order following an application under subsection (1)(a) above—

    (a) if any person on whom notice is served under subsection (2) above does not appear, unless service of the notice on that person is proved; or

    (b) if no notice under subsection (2) above has been served, unless the court is satisfied that in the circumstances it was reasonable not to serve notice on any person.

(6) The sheriff shall make an order under this section only if he is satisfied that there has been a contravention in relation to those goods of a safety provision.

(7) For the avoidance of doubt it is declared that the sheriff may infer for the purposes of this section that there has been a contravention in relation to any goods of a safety provision if he is satisfied that any such provision has been contravened in relation to any goods which are representative of those goods (whether by reason of being of the same design or part of the same consignment or batch or otherwise).

(8) Where an order for the forfeiture of any goods is made following an application by the procurator-fiscal under subsection (1)(a) above, any person who appeared, or was entitled to appear, to show cause why goods should not be forfeited may, within twenty-one days of the making of the order, appeal to the High Court by Bill of Suspension on the ground of an alleged miscarriage of justice; and section 452(4)(a) to (e) of the Criminal Procedure (Scotland) Act 1975 shall apply to an appeal under this subsection as it applies to a stated case under Part II of that Act.

(9) An order following an application under subsection (1)(a) above shall not take effect—

    (a) until the end of the period of twenty-one days beginning with the day after the day on which the order is made; or

    (b) if an appeal is made under subsection (8) above within that period, until the appeal is determined or abandoned.

(10) An order under subsection (1)(b) above shall not take effect—

    (a) until the end of the period within which an appeal against the order could be brought under the Criminal Procedure (Scotland) Act 1975; or

    (b) if an appeal is made within that period, until the appeal is determined or abandoned.

(11) Subject to subsection (12) below, goods forfeited under this section shall be destroyed in accordance with such directions as the sheriff may give.

(12) If he thinks fit, the sheriff may direct that the goods be released, to such person as he may specify, on condition that that person does not supply those goods to any other person otherwise than as mentioned in section 46(7)(a) or (b) below.

Power to obtain information

18.—(1) If the Secretary of State considers that, for the purpose of deciding whether—

    (a) to make, vary or revoke any safety regulations; or

    (b) to serve, vary or revoke a prohibition notice; or

    (c) to serve or revoke a notice to warn,

he requires information which another person is likely to be able to furnish, the Secretary of State may serve on the other person a notice under this section.

(2) A notice served on any person under this section may require that person—

    (a) to furnish to the Secretary of State, within a period specified in the notice, such information as is so specified;

    (b) to produce such records as are specified in the notice at a time and place so specified and to permit a person appointed by the Secretary of State for the purpose to take copies of the records at that time and place.

(3) A person shall be guilty of an offence if he—

    (a) fails, without reasonable cause, to comply with a notice served on him under this section; or

    (b) in purporting to comply with a requirement which by virtue of paragraph (a) of subsection (2) above is contained in such a notice—

        (i) furnishes information which he knows is false in a material particular; or

        (ii) recklessly furnishes information which is false in a material particular.

(4) A person guilty of an offence under subsection (3) above shall—

    (a) in the case of an offence under paragraph (a) of that subsection, be liable on summary conviction to a fine not exceeding level 5 on the standard scale; and

    (b) in the case of an offence under paragraph (b) of that subsection be liable—

        (i) on conviction on indictment, to a fine;

        (ii) on summary conviction, to a fine not exceeding the statutory maximum.

Interpretation of Part II

19.—(1) In this Part—

"controlled drug" means a controlled drug within the meaning of the Misuse of Drugs Act 1971;

"feeding stuff" and "fertiliser" have the same meanings as in Part IV of the Agriculture Act 1970;

"food" does not include anything containing tobacco but, subject to that, has the same meaning as in the Food Safety Act 1990 or, in relation to Northern Ireland, the same meaning as in the Food (Northern Ireland) Order 1991;

"licensed medicinal product" means—

    (a) any medicinal product within the meaning of the Medicines Act 1968 in respect of which a product licence within the meaning of that Act is for the time being in force; or

    (b) any other article or substance in respect of which any such licence is for the time being in force in pursuance of an order under section 104 or 105 of that Act (application of Act to other articles and substances);

"safe", in relation to any goods, means such that there is no risk, or no risk apart from one reduced to a minimum, that any of the following will (whether immediately or after a definite or indefinite period) cause the death of, or any personal injury to, any person whatsoever, that is to say—

    (a) the goods;

    (b) the keeping, use or consumption of the goods;

    (c) the assembly of any of the goods which are, or are to be, supplied unassembled;

(d) any emission or leakage from the goods or, as a result of the keeping, use or consumption of the goods, from anything else; or

(e) reliance on the accuracy of any measurement, calculation or other reading made by or by means of the goods,

and "safer" and "unsafe" shall be construed accordingly;

"tobacco" includes any tobacco product within the meaning of the Tobacco Products Duty Act 1979 and any article or substance containing tobacco and intended for oral or nasal use.

(2) In the definition of "safe" in subsection (1) above, references to the keeping, use or consumption of any goods are references to—

(a) the keeping, use or consumption of the goods by the persons by whom, and in all or any of the ways or circumstances in which, they might reasonably be expected to be kept, used or consumed; and

(b) the keeping, use or consumption of the goods either alone or in conjunction with other goods in conjunction with which they might reasonably be expected to be kept, used or consumed.

PART III

MISLEADING PRICE INDICATIONS

Offence of giving misleading indication

20.—(1) Subject to the following provisions of this Part, a person shall be guilty of an offence if, in the course of any business of his, he gives (by any means whatever) to any consumers an indication which is misleading as to the price at which any goods, services, accommodation or facilities are available (whether generally or from particular persons).

(2) Subject as aforesaid, a person shall be guilty of an offence if—

(a) in the course of any business of his, he has given an indication to any consumers which, after it was given, has become misleading as mentioned in subsection (1) above; and

(b) some or all of those consumers might reasonably be expected to rely on the indication at a time after it has become misleading; and

(c) he fails to take all such steps as are reasonable to prevent those consumers from relying on the indication.

(3) For the purposes of this section it shall be immaterial—

(a) whether the person who gives or gave the indication is or was acting on his own behalf or on behalf of another;

(b) whether or not that person is the person, or included among the persons, from whom the goods, services, accommodation or facilities are available; and

(c) whether the indication is or has become misleading in relation to all the consumers to whom it is or was given or only in relation to some of them.

(4) A person guilty of an offence under subsection (1) or (2) above shall be liable—

(a) on conviction on indictment, to a fine;

(b) on summary conviction, to a fine not exceeding the statutory maximum.

(5) No prosecution for an offence under subsection (1) or (2) above shall be brought after whichever is the earlier of the following, that is to say—

(a) the end of the period of three years beginning with the day on which the offence was committed; and

(b) the end of the period of one year beginning with the day on which the person bringing the prosecution discovered that the offence had been committed.

(6) In this Part—

"consumer"—

    (a) in relation to any goods, means any person who might wish to be supplied with the goods for his own private use or consumption;

    (b) in relation to any services or facilities, means any person who might wish to be provided with the services or facilities otherwise than for the purposes of any business of his; and

    (c) in relation to any accommodation, means any person who might wish to occupy the accommodation otherwise than for the purposes of any business of his;

"price", in relation to any goods, services, accommodation or facilities, means—

    (a) the aggregate of the sums required to be paid by a consumer for or otherwise in respect of the supply of the goods or the provision of the services, accommodation or facilities; or

    (b) except in section 21 below, any method which will be or has been applied for the purpose of determining that aggregate.

Meaning of "misleading"

21.—(1) For the purposes of section 20 above an indication given to any consumers is misleading as to a price if what is conveyed by the indication, or what those consumers might reasonably be expected to infer from the indication or any omission from it, includes any of the following, that is to say—

    (a) that the price is less than in fact it is;

    (b) that the applicability of the price does not depend on facts or circumstances on which its applicability does in fact depend;

    (c) that the price covers matters in respect of which an additional charge is in fact made;

    (d) that a person who in fact has no such expectation—

        (i) expects the price to be increased or reduced (whether or not at a particular time or by a particular amount); or

        (ii) expects the price, or the price as increased or reduced, to be maintained (whether or not for a particular period); or

    (e) that the facts or circumstances by reference to which the consumers might reasonably be expected to judge the validity of any relevant comparison made or implied by the indication are not what in fact they are.

(2) For the purposes of section 20 above, an indication given to any consumers is misleading as to a method of determining a price if what is conveyed by the indication, or what those consumers might reasonably be expected to infer from the indication or any omission from it, includes any of the following, that is to say—

    (a) that the method is not what in fact it is;

    (b) that the applicability of the method does not depend on facts or circumstances on which its applicability does in fact depend;

    (c) that the method takes into account matters in respect of which an additional charge will in fact be made;

    (d) that a person who in fact has no such expectation—

    (i) expects the method to be altered (whether or not at a particular time or in a particular respect); or

    (ii) expects the method, or that method as altered, to remain unaltered (whether or not for a particular period); or

(e) that the facts or circumstances by reference to which the consumers might reasonably be expected to judge the validity of any relevant comparison made or implied by the indication are not what in fact they are.

(3) For the purposes of subsections (1)(e) and (2)(e) above a comparison is a relevant comparison in relation to a price or method of determining a price if it is made between that price or that method, or any price which has been or may be determined by that method, and—

(a) any price or value which is stated or implied to be, to have been or to be likely to be attributed or attributable to the goods, services, accommodation or facilities in question or to any other goods, services, accommodation or facilities; or

(b) any method, or other method, which is stated or implied to be, to have been or to be likely to be applied or applicable for the determination of the price or value of the goods, services, accommodation or facilities in question or of the price or value of any other goods, services, accommodation or facilities.

Application to provision of services and facilities

22.—(1) Subject to the following provisions of this section, references in this Part to services or facilities are references to any services or facilities whatever including, in particular—

(a) the provision of credit or of banking or insurance services and the provision of facilities incidental to the provision of such services;

(b) the purchase or sale of foreign currency;

(c) the supply of electricity;

(d) the provision of a place, other than on a highway, for the parking of a motor vehicle;

(e) the making of arrangements for a person to put or keep a caravan on any land other than arrangements by virtue of which that person may occupy the caravan as his only or main residence.

(2) References in this Part to services shall not include references to services provided to an employer under a contract of employment.

(3) References in this Part to services or facilities shall not include references to services or facilities which are provided by an authorised person or appointed representative in the course of the carrying on of an investment business.

(4) In relation to a service consisting in the purchase or sale of foreign currency, references in this Part to the method by which the price of the service is determined shall include references to the rate of exchange.

(5) In this section—

"appointed representative", "authorised person" and "investment business" have the same meanings as in the Financial Services Act 1986;

"caravan" has the same meaning as in the Caravan Sites and Control of Development Act 1960;

"contract of employment" and "employer" have the same meanings as in the Employment Protection (Consolidation) Act 1978;

"credit" has the same meaning as in the Consumer Credit Act 1974.

Application to provision of accommodation etc.

23.—(1) Subject to subsection (2) below, references in this Part to accommodation or facilities being available shall not include references to accommodation or facilities being available to be provided by means of the creation or disposal of an interest in land except where—

(a) the person who is to create or dispose of the interest will do so in the course of any business of his; and

(b) the interest to be created or disposed of is a relevant interest in a new dwelling and is to be created or disposed of for the purpose of enabling that dwelling to be occupied as a residence, or one of the residences, of the person acquiring the interest.

(2) Subsection (1) above shall not prevent the application of any provision of this Part in relation to—

(a) the supply of any goods as part of the same transaction as any creation or disposal of an interest in land; or

(b) the provision of any services or facilities for the purposes of, or in connection with, any transaction for the creation or disposal of such an interest.

(3) In this section—

"new dwelling" means any building or part of a building in Great Britain which—

(a) has been constructed or adapted to be occupied as a residence; and

(b) has not previously been so occupied or has been so occupied only with other premises or as more than one residence,

and includes any yard, garden, out-houses or appurtenances which belong to that building or part or are to be enjoyed with it;

"relevant interest"—

(a) in relation to a new dwelling in England and Wales, means the freehold estate in the dwelling or a leasehold interest in the dwelling for a term of years absolute of more than twenty-one years, not being a term of which twenty-one years or less remains unexpired;

(b) in relation to a new dwelling in Scotland, means the *dominium utile* of the land comprising the dwelling, or a leasehold interest in the dwelling where twenty-one years or more remains unexpired.

Defences

24.—(1) In any proceedings against a person for an offence under subsection (1) or (2) of section 20 above in respect of any indication it shall be a defence for that person to show that his acts or omissions were authorised for the purposes of this subsection by regulations made under section 26 below.

(2) In proceedings against a person for an offence under subsection (1) or (2) of section 20 above in respect of an indication published in a book, newspaper, magazine, or film or in a programme included in a programme service (within the meaning of the Broadcasting Act 1990), it shall be a defence for that person to show that the indication was not contained in an advertisement.

(3) In proceedings against a person for an offence under subsection (1) or (2) of section 20 above in respect of an indication published in an advertisement it shall be a defence for that person to show that—

(a) he is a person who carries on a business of publishing or arranging for the publication of advertisements;

(b) he received the advertisement for publication in the ordinary course of that business; and

    (c) at the time of publication he did not know and had no grounds for suspecting that the publication would involve the commission of the offence.

(4) In any proceedings against a person for an offence under subsection (1) of section 20 above in respect of any indication, it shall be a defence for that person to show that—

    (a) the indication did not relate to the availability from him of any goods, services, accommodation or facilities;

    (b) a price had been recommended to every person from whom the goods, services, accommodation or facilities were indicated as being available;

    (c) the indication related to that price and was misleading as to that price only by reason of a failure by any person to follow the recommendation; and

    (d) it was reasonable for the person who gave the indication to assume that the recommendation was for the most part being followed.

(5) The provisions of this section are without prejudice to the provisions of section 39 below.

(6) In this section—

"advertisement" includes a catalogue, a circular and a price list;

[*Remainder repealed*]

Code of practice

25.—(1) The Secretary of State may, after consulting the Director General of Fair Trading and such other persons as the Secretary of State considers it appropriate to consult, by order approve any code of practice issued (whether by the Secretary of State or another person) for the purpose of—

    (a) giving practical guidance with respect to any of the requirements of section 20 above; and

    (b) promoting what appear to the Secretary of State to be desirable practices as to the circumstances and manner in which any person gives an indication as to the price at which any goods, services, accommodation or facilities are available or indicates any other matter in respect of which any such indication may be misleading.

(2) A contravention of a code of practice approved under this section shall not of itself give rise to any criminal or civil liability, but in any proceedings against any person for an offence under section 20(1) or (2) above—

    (a) any contravention by that person of such a code may be relied on in relation to any matter for the purpose of establishing that that person committed the offence or of negativing any defence; and

    (b) compliance by that person with such a code may be relied on in relation to any matter for the purpose of showing that the commission of the offence by that person has not been established or that that person has a defence.

(3) Where the Secretary of State approves a code of practice under this section he may, after such consultation as is mentioned in subsection (1) above, at any time by order—

    (a) approve any modification of the code; or

    (b) withdraw his approval;

and references in subsection (2) above to a code of practice approved under this section shall be construed accordingly.

(4) The power to make an order under this section shall be exercisable by

statutory instrument subject to annulment in pursuance of a resolution of either House of Parliament.[2]

Power to make regulations

26.—(1) The Secretary of State may, after consulting the Director General of Fair Trading and such other persons as the Secretary of State considers it appropriate to consult, by regulations make provision—

 (a) for the purpose of regulating the circumstances and manner in which any person—
  (i) gives any indication as to the price at which any goods, services, accommodation or facilities will be or are available or have been supplied or provided; or
  (ii) indicates any other matter in respect of which any such indication may be misleading;
 (b) for the purpose of facilitating the enforcement of the provisions of section 20 above or of any regulations made under this section.

(2) The Secretary of State shall not make regulations by virtue of subsection (1)(a) above except in relation to—

 (a) indications given by persons in the course of business; and
 (b) such indications given otherwise than in the course of business as—
  (i) are given by or on behalf of persons by whom accommodation is provided to others by means of leases or licences; and
  (ii) relate to goods, services or facilities supplied or provided to those others in connection with the provision of the accommodation.

(3) Without prejudice to the generality of subsection (1) above, regulations under this section may—

 (a) prohibit an indication as to a price from referring to such matters as may be prescribed by the regulations;
 (b) require an indication as to a price or other matter to be accompanied or supplemented by such explanation or such additional information as may be prescribed by the regulations;
 (c) require information or explanations with respect to a price or other matter to be given to an officer of an enforcement authority and to authorise such an officer to require such information or explanations to be given;
 (d) require any information or explanation provided for the purposes of any regulations made by virtue of paragraph (b) or (c) above to be accurate;
 (e) prohibit the inclusion in indications as to a price or other matter of statements that the indications are not to be relied upon;
 (f) provide that expressions used in any indication as to a price or other matter shall be construed in a particular way for the purposes of this Part;
 (g) provide that a contravention of any provision of the regulations shall constitute a criminal offence punishable—
  (i) on conviction on indictment, by a fine;
  (ii) on summary conviction, by a fine not exceeding the statutory maximum;

---

[2] The Consumer Protection (Code of Practice for Traders on Price Indications) Approval Order 1988 (S.I. 1988 No. 2078) has been made under section 25. The Order, together with the Code of Practice set out in the Schedule thereto, is printed below at p. 291.

(h) apply any provision of this Act which relates to a criminal offence to an offence created by virtue of paragraph (g) above.

(4) The power to make regulations under this section shall be exercisable by statutory instrument subject to annulment in pursuance of a resolution of either House of Parliament and shall include power—

(a) to make different provision for different cases; and

(b) to make such supplemental, consequential and transitional provision as the Secretary of State considers appropriate.

(5) In this section "lease" includes a sub-lease and an agreement for a lease and a statutory tenancy (within the meaning of the Landlord and Tenant Act 1985 or the Rent (Scotland) Act 1984).

PART IV

ENFORCEMENT OF PARTS II AND III

Enforcement

27.—(1) Subject to the following provisions of this section—

(a) it shall be the duty of every weights and measures authority in Great Britain to enforce within their area the safety provisions and the provisions made by or under Part III of this Act; and

(b) it shall be the duty of every district council in Northern Ireland to enforce within their area the safety provisions.

(2) The Secretary of State may by regulations—

(a) wholly or partly transfer any duty imposed by subsection (1) above on a weights and measures authority or a district council in Northern Ireland to such other person who has agreed to the transfer as is specified in the regulations;

(b) relieve such an authority or council of any such duty so far as it is exercisable in relation to such goods as may be described in the regulations.

(3) The power to make regulations under subsection (2) above shall be exercisable by statutory instrument subject to annulment in pursuance of a resolution of either House of Parliament and shall include power—

(a) to make different provision for different cases; and

(b) to make such supplemental, consequential and transitional provision as the Secretary of State considers appropriate.

(4) Nothing in this section shall authorise any weights and measures authority, or any person on whom functions are conferred by regulations under subsection (2) above, to bring proceedings in Scotland for an offence.

Test purchases

28.—(1) An enforcement authority shall have power, for the purpose of ascertaining whether any safety provision or any provision made by or under Part III of this Act has been contravened in relation to any goods, services, accommodation or facilities—

(a) to make, or to authorise an officer of the authority to make, any purchase of any goods; or

(b) to secure, or to authorise an officer of the authority to secure, the provision of any services, accommodation or facilities.

(2) Where—

(a) any goods purchased under this section by or on behalf of an enforcement authority are submitted to a test; and

(b) the test leads to—

    (i) the bringing of proceedings for an offence in respect of a contravention in relation to the goods of any safety provision or of any provision made by or under Part III of this Act or for the forfeiture of the goods under section 16 or 17 above; or

    (ii) the serving of a suspension notice in respect of any goods; and

(c) the authority is requested to do so and it is practicable for the authority to comply with the request,

the authority shall allow the person from whom the goods were purchased or any person who is a party to the proceedings or has an interest in any goods to which the notice relates to have the goods tested.

(3) The Secretary of State may by regulations provide that any test of goods purchased under this section by or on behalf of an enforcement authority shall—

(a) be carried out at the expense of the authority in a manner and by a person prescribed by or determined under the regulations; or

(b) be carried out either as mentioned in paragraph (a) above or by the authority in a manner prescribed by the regulations.

(4) The power to make regulations under subsection (3) above shall be exercisable by statutory instrument subject to annulment in pursuance of a resolution of either House of Parliament and shall include power—

(a) to make different provision for different cases; and

(b) to make such supplemental, consequential and transitional provision as the Secretary of State considers appropriate.

(5) Nothing in this section shall authorise the acquisition by or on behalf of an enforcement authority of any interest in land.

Powers of search etc.

29.—(1) Subject to the following provisions of this Part, a duly authorised officer of an enforcement authority may at any reasonable hour and on production, if required, of his credentials exercise any of the powers conferred by the following provisions of this section.

(2) The officer may, for the purpose of ascertaining whether there has been any contravention of any safety provision or of any provision made by or under Part III of this Act, inspect any goods and enter any premises other than premises occupied only as a person's residence.

(3) The officer may, for the purpose of ascertaining whether there has been any contravention of any safety provision, examine any procedure (including any arrangements for carrying out a test) connected with the production of any goods.

(4) If the officer has reasonable grounds for suspecting that any goods are manufactured or imported goods which have not been supplied in the United Kingdom since they were manufactured or imported he may—

(a) for the purpose of ascertaining whether there has been any contravention of any safety provision in relation to the goods, require any person carrying on a business, or employed in connection with a business, to produce any records relating to the business;

(b) for the purpose of ascertaining (by testing or otherwise) whether there has been any such contravention, seize and detain the goods;

(c) take copies of, or of any entry in, any records produced by virtue of paragraph (a) above.

(5) If the officer has reasonable grounds for suspecting that there has been a contravention in relation to any goods of any safety provision or of any provision made by or under Part III of this Act, he may—

    (a) for the purpose of ascertaining whether there has been any such contravention, require any person carrying on a business, or employed in connection with a business, to produce any records relating to the business;

    (b) for the purpose of ascertaining (by testing or otherwise) whether there has been any such contravention, seize and detain the goods;

    (c) take copies of, or of any entry in, any records produced by virtue of paragraph (a) above.

(6) The officer may seize and detain—

    (a) any goods or records which he has reasonable grounds for believing may be required as evidence in proceedings for an offence in respect of a contravention of any safety provision or of any provision made by or under Part III of this Act;

    (b) any goods which he has reasonable grounds for suspecting may be liable to be forfeited under section 16 or 17 above.

(7) If and to the extent that it is reasonably necessary to do so to prevent a contravention of any safety provision or of any provision made by or under Part III of this Act, the officer may, for the purpose of exercising his power under subsection (4), (5) or (6) above to seize any goods or records—

    (a) require any person having authority to do so to open any container or to open any vending machine; and

    (b) himself open or break open any such container or machine where a requirement made under paragraph (a) above in relation to the container or machine has not been complied with.

Provisions supplemental to s. 29

30.—(1) An officer seizing any goods or records under section 29 above shall inform the following persons that the goods or records have been so seized, that is to say—

    (a) the person from whom they are seized; and

    (b) in the case of imported goods seized on any premises under the control of the Commissioners of Customs and Excise, the importer of those goods (within the meaning of the Customs and Excise Management Act 1979).

(2) If a justice of the peace—

    (a) is satisfied by any written information on oath that there are reasonable grounds for believing either—

        (i) that any goods or records which any officer has power to inspect under section 29 above are on any premises and that their inspection is likely to disclose evidence that there has been a contravention of any safety provision or of any provision made by or under Part III of this Act; or

        (ii) that such a contravention has taken place, is taking place or is about to take place on any premises; and

    (b) is also satisfied by any such information either—

        (i) that admission to the premises has been or is likely to be refused and that notice of intention to apply for a warrant under this subsection has been given to the occupier; or

(ii) that an application for admission, or the giving of such a notice, would defeat the object of the entry or that the premises are unoccupied or that the occupier is temporarily absent and it might defeat the object of the entry to await his return,

the justice may by warrant under his hand, which shall continue in force for a period of one month, authorise any officer of an enforcement authority to enter the premises, if need be by force.

(3) An officer entering any premises by virtue of section 29 above or a warrant under subsection (2) above may take with him such other persons and such equipment as may appear to him necessary.

(4) On leaving any premises which a person is authorised to enter by a warrant under subsection (2) above, that person shall, if the premises are unoccupied or the occupier is temporarily absent, leave the premises as effectively secured against trespassers as he found them.

(5) If any person who is not an officer of an enforcement authority purports to act as such under section 29 above or this section he shall be guilty of an offence and liable on summary conviction to a fine not exceeding level 5 on the standard scale.

(6) Where any goods seized by an officer under section 29 above are submitted to a test, the officer shall inform the persons mentioned in subsection (1) above of the result of the test and, if—

(a) proceedings are brought for an offence in respect of a contravention in relation to the goods of any safety provision or of any provision made by or under Part III of this Act or for the forfeiture of the goods under section 16 or 17 above, or a suspension notice is served in respect of any goods; and

(b) the officer is requested to do so and it is practicable to comply with the request,

the officer shall allow any person who is a party to the proceedings or, as the case may be, has an interest in the goods to which the notice relates to have the goods tested.

(7) The Secretary of State may by regulations provide that any test of goods seized under section 29 above by an officer of an enforcement authority shall—

(a) be carried out at the expense of the authority in a manner and by a person prescribed by or determined under the regulations; or

(b) be carried out either as mentioned in paragraph (a) above or by the authority in a manner prescribed by the regulations.

(8) The power to make regulations under subsection (7) above shall be exercisable by statutory instrument subject to annulment in pursuance of a resolution of either House of Parliament and shall include power—

(a) to make different provision for different cases; and

(b) to make such supplemental, consequential and transitional provision as the Secretary of State considers appropriate.

(9) In the application of this section to Scotland, the reference in subsection (2) above to a justice of the peace shall include a reference to a sheriff and the references to written information on oath shall be construed as references to evidence on oath.

(10) In the application of this section to Northern Ireland, the references in subsection (2) above to any information on oath shall be construed as references to any complaint on oath.

Power of customs officer to detain goods

31.—(1) A customs officer may, for the purpose of facilitating the exercise by an enforcement authority or officer of such an authority of any functions conferred on the authority or officer by or under Part II of this Act, or by or under this Part in its application for the purposes of the safety provisions, seize any imported goods and detain them for not more than two working days.

(2) Anything seized and detained under this section shall be dealt with during the period of its detention in such manner as the Commissioners of Customs and Excise may direct.

(3) In subsection (1) above the reference to two working days is a reference to a period of forty-eight hours calculated from the time when the goods in question are seized but disregarding so much of any period as falls on a Saturday or Sunday or on Christmas Day, Good Friday or a day which is a bank holiday under the Banking and Financial Dealings Act 1971 in the part of the United Kingdom where the goods are seized.

(4) In this section and section 32 below "customs officer" means any officer within the meaning of the Customs and Excise Management Act 1979.

Obstruction of authorised officer

32.—(1) Any person who—

(a) intentionally obstructs any officer of an enforcement authority who is acting in pursuance of any provision of this Part or any customs officer who is so acting; or

(b) intentionally fails to comply with any requirement made of him by any officer of an enforcement authority under any provision of this Part; or

(c) without reasonable cause fails to give any officer of an enforcement authority who is so acting any other assistance or information which the officer may reasonably require of him for the purposes of the exercise of the officer's functions under any provision of this Part,

shall be guilty of an offence and liable on summary conviction to a fine not exceeding level 5 on the standard scale.

(2) A person shall be guilty of an offence if, in giving any information which is required of him by virtue of subsection (1)(c) above—

(a) he makes any statement which he knows is false in a material particular; or

(b) he recklessly makes a statement which is false in a material particular.

(3) A person guilty of an offence under subsection (2) above shall be liable—

(a) on conviction on indictment, to a fine;

(b) on summary conviction, to a fine not exceeding the statutory maximum.

Appeals against detention of goods

33.—(1) Any person having an interest in any goods which are for the time being detained under any provision of this Part by an enforcement authority or by an officer of such an authority may apply for an order requiring the goods to be released to him or to another person.

(2) An application under this section may be made—

(a) to any magistrates' court in which proceedings have been brought in England and Wales or Northern Ireland—

(i) for an offence in respect of a contravention in relation to the goods of any safety provision or of any provision made by or under Part III of this Act; or

       (ii) for the forfeiture of the goods under section 16 above;
   (b) where no such proceedings have been so brought, by way of complaint to a magistrates' court; or
   (c) in Scotland, by summary application to the sheriff.

(3) On an application under this section to a magistrates' court or to the sheriff, an order requiring goods to be released shall be made only if the court or sheriff is satisfied—
   (a) that proceedings—
       (i) for an offence in respect of a contravention in relation to the goods of any safety provision or of any provision made by or under Part III of this Act; or
       (ii) for the forfeiture of the goods under section 16 or 17 above,
have not been brought or, having been brought, have been concluded without the goods being forfeited; and
   (b) where no such proceedings have been brought, that more than six months have elapsed since the goods were seized.

(4) Any person aggrieved by an order made under this section by a magistrates' court in England and Wales or Northern Ireland, or by a decision of such a court not to make such an order, may appeal against that order or decision—
   (a) in England and Wales, to the Crown Court;
   (b) in Northern Ireland, to the county court;
and an order so made may contain such provision as appears to the court to be appropriate for delaying the coming into force of the order pending the making and determination of any appeal (including any application under section 111 of the Magistrates' Courts Act 1980 or Article 146 of the Magistrates' Courts (Northern Ireland) Order 1981 (statement of case)).

Compensation for seizure and detention

34.—(1) Where an officer of an enforcement authority exercises any power under section 29 above to seize and detain goods, the enforcement authority shall be liable to pay compensation to any person having an interest in the goods in respect of any loss or damage caused by reason of the exercise of the power if—
   (a) there has been no contravention in relation to the goods of any safety provision or of any provision made by or under Part III of this Act; and
   (b) the exercise of the power is not attributable to any neglect or default by that person.

(2) Any disputed question as to the right to or the amount of any compensation payable under this section shall be determined by arbitration or, in Scotland, by a single arbiter appointed, failing agreement between the parties, by the sheriff.

Recovery of expenses of enforcement

35.—(1) This section shall apply where a court—
   (a) convicts a person of an offence in respect of a contravention in relation to any goods of any safety provision or of any provision made by or under Part III of this Act; or
   (b) makes an order under section 16 or 17 above for the forfeiture of any goods.

(2) The court may (in addition to any other order it may make as to costs or expenses) order the person convicted or, as the case may be, any person having

an interest in the goods to reimburse an enforcement authority for any expenditure which has been or may be incurred by that authority—

    (a) in connection with any seizure or detention of the goods by or on behalf of the authority; or

    (b) in connection with any compliance by the authority with directions given by the court for the purposes of any order for the forfeiture of the goods.

PART V

MISCELLANEOUS AND SUPPLEMENTAL

Amendments of Part I of the Health and Safety at Work etc. Act 1974

36. Part I of the Health and Safety at Work etc. Act 1974 (which includes provision with respect to the safety of certain articles and substances) shall have effect with the amendments specified in Schedule 3 to this Act; and, accordingly, the general purposes of that Part of that Act shall include the purpose of protecting persons from the risks protection from which would not be afforded by virtue of that Part but for those amendments.

Power of Commissioners of Customs and Excise to disclose information

37.—(1) If they think it appropriate to do so for the purpose of facilitating the exercise by any person to whom subsection (2) below applies of any functions conferred on that person by or under Part II of this Act, or by or under Part IV of this Act in its application for the purposes of the safety provisions, the Commissioners of Customs and Excise may authorise the disclosure to that person of any information obtained for the purposes of the exercise by the Commissioners of their functions in relation to imported goods.

(2) This subsection applies to an enforcement authority and to any officer of an enforcement authority.

(3) A disclosure of information made to any person under subsection (1) above shall be made in such manner as may be directed by the Commissioners of Customs and Excise and may be made through such persons acting on behalf of that person as may be so directed.

(4) Information may be disclosed to a person under subsection (1) above whether or not the disclosure of the information has been requested by or on behalf of that person.

Restrictions on disclosure of information

38.—(1) Subject to the following provisions of this section, a person shall be guilty of an offence if he discloses any information—

    (a) which was obtained by him in consequence of its being given to any person in compliance with any requirement imposed by safety regulations or regulations under section 26 above;

    (b) which consists in a secret manufacturing process or a trade secret and was obtained by him in consequence of the inclusion of the information—

        (i) in written or oral representations made for the purposes of Part I or II of Schedule 2 to this Act; or

        (ii) in a statement of a witness in connection with any such oral representations;

   (c) which was obtained by him in consequence of the exercise by the Secretary of State of the power conferred by section 18 above;

   (d) which was obtained by him in consequence of the exercise by any person of any power conferred by Part IV of this Act; or

   (e) which was disclosed to or through him under section 37 above.

(2) Subsection (1) above shall not apply to a disclosure of information if the information is publicised information or the disclosure is made—

   (a) for the purpose of facilitating the exercise of a relevant person's functions under this Act or any enactment or subordinate legislation mentioned in subsection (3) below;

   (b) for the purposes of compliance with a Community obligation; or

   (c) in connection with the investigation of any criminal offence or for the purposes of any civil or criminal proceedings.

(3) The enactments and subordinate legislation referred to in subsection (2)(a) above are—

   (a) the Trade Descriptions Act 1968;

   (b) Parts II and III and section 125 of the Fair Trading Act 1973;

   (c) the relevant statutory provisions within the meaning of Part I of the Health and Safety at Work etc. Act 1974 or within the meaning of the Health and Safety at Work (Northern Ireland) Order 1978;

   (d) the Consumer Credit Act 1974;

   (e) the Restrictive Trade Practices Act 1976;

   (f) the Resale Prices Act 1976;

   (g) the Estate Agents Act 1979;

   (h) the Competition Act 1980;

   (i) the Telecommunications Act 1984;

   (j) the Airports Act 1986;

   (k) the Gas Act 1986;

   (l) any subordinate legislation made (whether before or after the passing of this Act) for the purpose of securing compliance with the Directive of the Council of the European Communities, dated 10th September 1984 (No. 84/450/EEC) on the approximation of the laws, regulations and administrative provisions of the member States concerning misleading advertising.

   (m) the Electricity Act 1989;

  (mm) Part IV of the Airports (Northern Ireland) Order 1994;

   (n) the Electricity (Northern Ireland) Order 1992;

   (o) the Railways Act 1993

(4) In subsection (2)(a) above the reference to a person's functions shall include a reference to any function of making, amending or revoking any regulations or order.

(5) A person guilty of an offence under this section shall be liable—

   (a) on summary conviction, to a fine not exceeding the statutory maximum;

   (b) on conviction on indictment, to imprisonment for a term not exceeding two years or to a fine or to both.

(6) In this section—

"publicised information" means any information which has been disclosed in any civil or criminal proceedings or is or has been required to be contained in a warning published in pursuance of a notice to warn; and

"relevant person" means any of the following, that is to say—

   (a) a Minister of the Crown, Government department or Northern Ireland department;

(b) the Monopolies and Mergers Commission, the Director General of Fair Trading, the Director General of Telecommunications or the Director General of Gas Supply or the Director General of Electricity Supply or the Director General of Electricity Supply for Northern Ireland or the Rail Regulator;

(c) the Civil Aviation Authority;

(d) any weights and measures authority, any district council in Northern Ireland or any person on whom functions are conferred by regulations under section 27(2) above;

(e) any person who is an enforcing authority for the purposes of Part I of the Health and Safety at Work etc. Act 1974 or for the purposes of Part II of the Health and Safety at Work (Northern Ireland) Order 1978.

Defence of due diligence

39.—(1) Subject to the following provisions of this section, in proceedings against any person for an offence to which this section applies it shall be a defence for that person to show that he took all reasonable steps and exercised all due diligence to avoid committing the offence.

(2) Where in any proceedings against any person for such an offence the defence provided by subsection (1) above involves an allegation that the commission of the offence was due—

(a) to the act or default of another; or

(b) to reliance on information given by another,

that person shall not, without the leave of the court, be entitled to rely on the defence unless, not less than seven clear days before the hearing of the proceedings, he has served a notice under subsection (3) below on the person bringing the proceedings.

(3) A notice under this subsection shall give such information identifying or assisting in the identification of the person who committed the act or default or gave the information as is in the possession of the person serving the notice at the time he serves it.

(4) It is hereby declared that a person shall not be entitled to rely on the defence provided by subsection (1) above by reason of his reliance on information supplied by another, unless he shows that it was reasonable in all the circumstances for him to have relied on the information, having regard in particular—

(a) to the steps which he took, and those which might reasonably have been taken, for the purpose of verifying the information; and

(b) to whether he had any reason to disbelieve the information.

(5) This section shall apply to an offence under section 10, 12(1), (2) or (3), 13(4), 14(6) or 20(1) above.

Liability of persons other than principal offender

40.—(1) Where the commission by any person of an offence to which section 39 above applies is due to an act or default committed by some other person in the course of any business of his, the other person shall be guilty of the offence and may be proceeded against and punished by virtue of this subsection whether or not proceedings are taken against the first-mentioned person.

(2) Where a body corporate is guilty of an offence under this Act (including where it is so guilty by virtue of subsection (1) above) in respect of any act or

default which is shown to have been committed with the consent or connivance of, or to be attributable to any neglect on the part of, any director, manager, secretary or other similar officer of the body corporate or any person who was purporting to act in any such capacity he, as well as the body corporate, shall be guilty of that offence and shall be liable to be proceeded against and punished accordingly.

(3) Where the affairs of a body corporate are managed by its members, subsection (2) above shall apply in relation to the acts and defaults of a member in connection with his functions of management as if he were a director of the body corporate.

Civil proceedings

41.—(1) An obligation imposed by safety regulations shall be a duty owed to any person who may be affected by a contravention of the obligation and, subject to any provision to the contrary in the regulations and to the defences and other incidents applying to actions for breach of statutory duty, a contravention of any such obligation shall be actionable accordingly.

(2) This Act shall not be construed as conferring any other right of action in civil proceedings, apart from the right conferred by virtue of Part I of this Act, in respect of any loss or damage suffered in consequence of a contravention of a safety provision or of a provision made by or under Part III of this Act.

(3) Subject to any provision to the contrary in the agreement itself, an agreement shall not be void or unenforceable by reason only of a contravention of a safety provision or of a provision made by or under Part III of this Act.

(4) Liability by virtue of subsection (1) above shall not be limited or excluded by any contract term, by any notice or (subject to the power contained in subsection (1) above to limit or exclude it in safety regulations) by any other provision.

(5) Nothing in subsection (1) above shall prejudice the operation of section 12 of the Nuclear Installations Act 1965 (rights to compensation for certain breaches of duties confined to rights under that Act).

(6) In this section "damage" includes personal injury and death.

Reports etc.

42.—(1) It shall be the duty of the Secretary of State at least once in every five years to lay before each House of Parliament a report on the exercise during the period to which the report relates of the functions which under Part II of this Act, or under Part IV of this Act in its application for the purposes of the safety provisions, are exercisable by the Secretary of State, weights and measures authorities, district councils in Northern Ireland and persons on whom functions are conferred by regulations made under section 27(2) above.

(2) The Secretary of State may from time to time prepare and lay before each House of Parliament such other reports on the exercise of those functions as he considers appropriate.

(3) Every weights and measures authority, every district council in Northern Ireland and every person on whom functions are conferred by regulations under subsection (2) of section 27 above shall, whenever the Secretary of State so directs, make a report to the Secretary of State on the exercise of the functions exercisable by that authority or council under that section or by that person by virtue of any such regulations.

(4) A report under subsection (3) above shall be in such form and shall contain such particulars as are specified in the direction of the Secretary of State.

(5) The first report under subsection (1) above shall be laid before each House of Parliament not more than five years after the laying of the last report under section 8(2) of the Consumer Safety Act 1978.

Financial provisions

43.—(1) There shall be paid out of money provided by Parliament—

(a) any expenses incurred or compensation payable by a Minister of the Crown or Government department in consequence of any provision of this Act; and

(b) any increase attributable to this Act in the sums payable out of money so provided under any other Act.

(2) Any sums received by a Minister of the Crown or Government department by virtue of this Act shall be paid into the Consolidated Fund.

Service of documents etc.

44.—(1) Any document required or authorised by virtue of this Act to be served on a person may be so served—

(a) by delivering it to him or by leaving it at his proper address or by sending it by post to him at that address; or

(b) if the person is a body corporate, by serving it in accordance with paragraph (a) above on the secretary or clerk of that body; or

(c) if the person is a partnership, by serving it in accordance with that paragraph on a partner or on a person having control or management of the partnership business.

(2) For the purposes of subsection (1) above, and for the purposes of section 7 of the Interpretation Act 1978 (which relates to the service of documents by post) in its application to that subsection, the proper address of any person on whom a document is to be served by virtue of this Act shall be his last known address except that—

(a) in the case of service on a body corporate or its secretary or clerk, it shall be the address of the registered or principal office of the body corporate;

(b) in the case of service on a partnership or a partner or a person having the control or management of a partnership business, it shall be the principal office of the partnership;

and for the purposes of this subsection the principal office of a company registered outside the United Kingdom or of a partnership carrying on business outside the United Kingdom is its principal office within the United Kingdom.

(3) The Secretary of State may by regulations make provision for the manner in which any information is to be given to any person under any provision of Part IV of this Act.

(4) Without prejudice to the generality of subsection (3) above regulations made by the Secretary of State may prescribe the person, or manner of determining the person, who is to be treated for the purposes of section 28(2) or 30 above as the person from whom any goods were purchased or seized where the goods were purchased or seized from a vending machine.

(5) The power to make regulations under subsection (3) or (4) above shall be exercisable by statutory instrument subject to annulment in pursuance of a resolution of either House of Parliament and shall include power—

(a) to make different provision for different cases; and

(b) to make such supplemental, consequential and transitional provision as the Secretary of State considers appropriate.

Interpretation

45.—(1) In this Act, except in so far as the context otherwise requires—

"aircraft" includes gliders, balloons and hovercraft;

"business" includes a trade or profession and the activities of a professional or trade association or of a local authority or other public authority;

"conditional sale agreement", "credit-sale agreement" and "hire-purchase agreement" have the same meanings as in the Consumer Credit Act 1974 but as if in the definitions in that Act "goods" had the same meaning as in this Act;

"contravention" includes a failure to comply and cognate expressions shall be construed accordingly;

"enforcement authority" means the Secretary of State, any other Minister of the Crown in charge of a Government department, any such department and any authority, council or other person on whom functions under this Act are conferred by or under section 27 above;

"gas" has the same meaning as in Part I of the Gas Act 1986;

"goods" includes substances, growing crops and things comprised in land by virtue of being attached to it and any ship, aircraft or vehicle;

"information" includes accounts, estimates and returns;

"magistrates' court", in relation to Northern Ireland, means a court of summary jurisdiction;

"modifications" includes additions, alterations and omissions, and cognate expressions shall be construed accordingly;

"motor vehicle" has the same meaning as in the Road Traffic Act 1988;

"notice" means a notice in writing;

"notice to warn" means a notice under section 13(1)(b) above;

"officer", in relation to an enforcement authority, means a person authorised in writing to assist the authority in carrying out its functions under or for the purposes of the enforcement of any of the safety provisions or of any of the provisions made by or under Part III of this Act;

"personal injury" includes any disease and any other impairment of a person's physical or mental condition;

"premises" includes any place and any ship, aircraft or vehicle;

"prohibition notice" means a notice under section 13(1)(a) above;

"records" includes any books or documents and any records in non-documentary form;

"safety provision" means the general safety requirement in section 10 above or any provision of safety regulations, a prohibition notice or a suspension notice;

"safety regulations" means regulations under section 11 above;

"ship" includes any boat and any other description of vessel used in navigation;

"subordinate legislation" has the same meaning as in the Interpretation Act 1978;

"substance" means any natural or artificial substance, whether in solid, liquid or gaseous form or in the form of a vapour, and includes substances that are comprised in or mixed with other goods;

"supply" and cognate expressions shall be construed in accordance with section 46 below;

"suspension notice" means a notice under section 14 above.

(2) Except in so far as the context otherwise requires, references in this Act to a contravention of a safety provision shall, in relation to any goods, include references to anything which would constitute such a contravention if the goods were supplied to any person.

(3) References in this Act to any goods in relation to which any safety provision has been or may have been contravened shall include references to any goods which it is not reasonably practicable to separate from any such goods.

Meaning of "supply"

46.—(1) Subject to the following provisions of this section, references in this Act to supplying goods shall be construed as references to doing any of the following, whether as principal or agent, that is to say—

(a) selling, hiring out or lending the goods;

(b) entering into a hire-purchase agreement to furnish the goods;

(c) the performance of any contract for work and materials to furnish the goods;

(d) providing the goods in exchange for any consideration (including trading stamps) other than money;

(e) providing the goods in or in connection with the performance of any statutory function; or

(f) giving the goods as a prize or otherwise making a gift of the goods;

and, in relation to gas or water, those references shall be construed as including references to providing the service by which the gas or water is made available for use.

(2) For the purposes of any reference in this Act to supplying goods, where a person ("the ostensible supplier") supplies goods to another person ("the customer") under a hire-purchase agreement, conditional sale agreement or credit-sale agreement or under an agreement for the hiring of goods (other than a hire-purchase agreement) and the ostensible supplier—

(a) carries on the business of financing the provision of goods for others by means of such agreements; and

(b) in the course of that business acquired his interest in the goods supplied to the customer as a means of financing the provision of them for the customer by a further person ("the effective supplier"),

the effective supplier and not the ostensible supplier shall be treated as supplying the goods to the customer.

(3) Subject to subsection (4) below, the performance of any contract by the erection of any building or structure on any land or by the carrying out of any other building works shall be treated for the purposes of this Act as a supply of goods in so far as, but only in so far as, it involves the provision of any goods to any person by means of their incorporation into the building, structure or works.

(4) Except for the purposes of, and in relation to, notices to warn or any provision made by or under Part III of this Act, references in this Act to supplying goods shall not include references to supplying goods comprised in land where the supply is effected by the creation or disposal of an interest in the land.

(5) Except in Part I of this Act references in this Act to a person's supplying goods shall be confined to references to that person's supplying goods in the course of a business of his, but for the purposes of this subsection it shall be immaterial whether the business is a business of dealing in the goods.

(6) For the purposes of subsection (5) above goods shall not be treated as supplied in the course of a business if they are supplied, in pursuance of an obligation arising under or in connection with the insurance of the goods, to the person with whom they were insured.

(7) Except for the purposes of, and in relation to, prohibition notices or suspension notices, references in Parts II to IV of this Act to supplying goods shall not include—

    (a) references to supplying goods where the person supplied carries on a business of buying goods of the same description as those goods and repairing or reconditioning them;

    (b) references to supplying goods by a sale of articles as scrap (that is to say, for the value of materials included in the articles rather than for the value of the articles themselves).

(8) Where any goods have at any time been supplied by being hired out or lent to any person, neither a continuation or renewal of the hire or loan (whether on the same or different terms) nor any transaction for the transfer after that time of any interest in the goods to the person to whom they were hired or lent shall be treated for the purposes of this Act as a further supply of the goods to that person.

(9) A ship, aircraft or motor vehicle shall not be treated for the purposes of this Act as supplied to any person by reason only that services consisting in the carriage of goods or passengers in that ship, aircraft or vehicle, or in its use for any other purpose, are provided to that person in pursuance of an agreement relating to the use of the ship, aircraft or vehicle for a particular period or for particular voyages, flights or journeys.

Savings for certain privileges

47.—(1) Nothing in this Act shall be taken as requiring any person to produce any records if he would be entitled to refuse to produce those records in any proceedings in any court on the grounds that they are the subject of legal professional privilege or, in Scotland, that they contain a confidential communication made by or to an advocate or solicitor in that capacity, or as authorising any person to take possession of any records which are in the possession of a person who would be so entitled.

(2) Nothing in this Act shall be construed as requiring a person to answer any question or give any information if to do so would incriminate that person or that person's spouse.

Minor and consequential amendments and repeals

48.—(1) The enactments mentioned in Schedule 4 to this Act shall have effect subject to the amendments specified in that Schedule (being minor amendments and amendments consequential on the provisions of this Act).

(2) The following Acts shall cease to have effect, that is to say—

    (a) the Trade Descriptions Act 1972; and

    (b) the Fabrics (Misdescription) Act 1913.

(3) The enactments mentioned in Schedule 5 to this Act are hereby repealed to the extent specified in the third column of that Schedule.

Northern Ireland

49.—(1) This Act shall extend to Northern Ireland with the exception of—

    (a) the provisions of Parts I and III;

(b) any provision amending or repealing an enactment which does not so extend; and

(c) any other provision so far as it has effect for the purposes of, or in relation to, a provision falling within paragraph (a) or (b) above.

(2) Subject to any Order in Council made by virtue of subsection (1)(a) of section 3 of the Northern Ireland Constitution Act 1973, consumer safety shall not be a transferred matter for the purposes of that Act but shall for the purposes of subsection (2) of that section be treated as specified in Schedule 3 to that Act.

(3) An Order in Council under paragraph 1(1)(b) of Schedule 1 to the Northern Ireland Act 1974 (exercise of legislative functions for Northern Ireland) which states that it is made only for purposes corresponding to any of the provisions of this Act mentioned in subsection (1)(a) to (c) above—

(a) shall not be subject to paragraph 1(4) and (5) of that Schedule (affirmative resolution procedure and procedure in cases of urgency); but

(b) shall be subject to annulment in pursuance of a resolution of either House of Parliament.

Short title, commencement and transitional provision

50.—(1) This Act may be cited as the Consumer Protection Act 1987.

(2) This Act shall come into force on such day as the Secretary of State may by order made by statutory instrument appoint, and different days may be so appointed for different provisions or for different purposes.

(3) The Secretary of State shall not make an order under subsection (2) above bringing into force the repeal of the Trade Descriptions Act 1972, a repeal of any provision of that Act or a repeal of that Act or of any provision of it for any purposes, unless a draft of the order has been laid before, and approved by a resolution of, each House of Parliament.

(4) An order under subsection (2) above bringing a provision into force may contain such transitional provision in connection with the coming into force of that provision as the Secretary of State considers appropriate.

(5) Without prejudice to the generality of the power conferred by subsection (4) above, the Secretary of State may by order provide for any regulations made under the Consumer Protection Act 1961 or the Consumer Protection Act (Northern Ireland) 1965 to have effect as if made under section 11 above and for any such regulations to have effect with such modifications as he considers appropriate for that purpose.

(6) The power of the Secretary of State by order to make such provision as is mentioned in subsection (5) above, shall, in so far as it is not exercised by an order under subsection (2) above, be exercisable by statutory instrument subject to annulment in pursuance of a resolution of either House of Parliament.

(7) Nothing in this Act or in any order under subsection (2) above shall make any person liable by virtue of Part I of this Act for any damage caused wholly or partly by a defect in a product which was supplied to any person by its producer before the coming into force of Part I of this Act.[3]

(8) Expressions used in subsection (7) above and in Part I of this Act have the same meanings in that subsection as in that Part.

---

[3] The Consumer Protection Act 1987 (Commencement No. 1) Order 1987 (S.I. 1987 No. 1680) brought Part I into force on March 1, 1988.

SCHEDULES

SCHEDULE 1

LIMITATION OF ACTIONS UNDER PART I

*   *   *   *   *

SCHEDULE 2

PROHIBITION NOTICES AND NOTICES TO WARN

PART I

PROHIBITION NOTICES

1. A prohibition notice in respect of any goods shall—
  (a) state that the Secretary of State considers that the goods are unsafe;
  (b) set out the reasons why the Secretary of State considers that the goods are unsafe;
  (c) specify the day on which the notice is to come into force; and
  (d) state that the trader may at any time make representations in writing to the Secretary of State for the purpose of establishing that the goods are safe.

2.—(1) If representations in writing about a prohibition notice are made by the trader to the Secretary of State, it shall be the duty of the Secretary of State to consider whether to revoke the notice and—
  (a) if he decides to revoke it, to do so;
  (b) in any other case, to appoint a person to consider those representations, any further representations made (whether in writing or orally) by the trader about the notice and the statements of any witnesses examined under this Part of this Schedule.

(2) Where the Secretary of State has appointed a person to consider representations about a prohibition notice, he shall serve a notification on the trader which—
  (a) states that the trader may make oral representations to the appointed person for the purpose of establishing that the goods to which the notice relates are safe; and
  (b) specifies the place and time at which the oral representations may be made.

(3) The time specified in a notification served under sub-paragraph (2) above shall not be before the end of the period of twenty-one days beginning with the day on which the notification is served, unless the trader otherwise agrees.

(4) A person on whom a notification has been served under sub-paragraph (2) above or his representative may, at the place and time specified in the notification—
  (a) make oral representations to the appointed person for the purpose of establishing that the goods in question are safe; and
  (b) call and examine witnesses in connection with the representations.

3.—(1) Where representations in writing about a prohibition notice are made by the trader to the Secretary of State at any time after a person has been appointed to consider representations about that notice, then, whether or not the appointed person has made a report to the Secretary of State, the following provisions of this paragraph shall apply instead of paragraph 2 above.

(2) The Secretary of State shall, before the end of the period of one month beginning with the day on which he receives the representations, serve a notification on the trader which states—

(a) that the Secretary of State has decided to revoke the notice, has decided to vary it or, as the case may be, has decided neither to revoke nor to vary it; or

(b) that, a person having been appointed to consider representations about the notice, the trader may, at a place and time specified in the notification, make oral representations to the appointed person for the purpose of establishing that the goods to which the notice relates are safe.

(3) The time specified in a notification served for the purposes of subparagraph (2)(b) above shall not be before the end of the period of twenty-one days beginning with the day on which the notification is served, unless the trader otherwise agrees or the time is the time already specified for the purposes of paragraph 2(2)(b) above.

(4) A person on whom a notification has been served for the purposes of subparagraph (2)(b) above or his representative may, at the place and time specified in the notification—

(a) make oral representations to the appointed person for the purpose of establishing that the goods in question are safe; and

(b) call and examine witnesses in connection with the representations.

4.—(1) Where a person is appointed to consider representations about a prohibition notice, it shall be his duty to consider—

(a) any written representations made by the trader about the notice, other than those in respect of which a notification is served under paragraph 3(2)(a) above;

(b) any oral representations made under paragraph 2(4) or 3(4) above; and

(c) any statements made by witnesses in connection with the oral representations,

and, after considering any matters under this paragraph, to make a report (including recommendations) to the Secretary of State about the matters considered by him and the notice.

(2) It shall be the duty of the Secretary of State to consider any report made to him under sub-paragraph (1) above and, after considering the report, to inform the trader of his decision with respect to the prohibition notice to which the report relates.

5.—(1) The Secretary of State may revoke or vary a prohibition notice by serving on the trader a notification stating that the notice is revoked or, as the case may be, is varied as specified in the notification.

(2) The Secretary of State shall not vary a prohibition notice so as to make the effect of the notice more restrictive for the trader.

(3) Without prejudice to the power conferred by section 13(2) of this Act, the service of a notification under sub-paragraph (1) above shall be sufficient to satisfy the requirement of paragraph 4(2) above that the trader shall be informed of the Secretary of State's decision.

PART II

NOTICES TO WARN

6.—(1) If the Secretary of State proposes to serve a notice to warn on any person in respect of any goods, the Secretary of State, before he serves the notice, shall serve on that person a notification which—

    (a) contains a draft of the proposed notice;

    (b) states that the Secretary of State proposes to serve a notice in the form of the draft on that person;

    (c) states that the Secretary of State considers that the goods described in the draft are unsafe;

    (d) sets out the reasons why the Secretary of State considers that those goods are unsafe; and

    (e) states that that person may make representations to the Secretary of State for the purpose of establishing that the goods are safe if, before the end of the period of fourteen days beginning with the day on which the notification is served, he informs the Secretary of State—

        (i) of his intention to make representations; and

        (ii) whether the representations will be made only in writing or both in writing and orally.

(2) Where the Secretary of State has served a notification containing a draft of a proposed notice to warn on any person, he shall not serve a notice to warn on that person in respect of the goods to which the proposed notice relates unless—

    (a) the period of fourteen days beginning with the day on which the notification was served expires without the Secretary of State being informed as mentioned in sub-paragraph (1)(e) above;

    (b) the period of twenty-eight days beginning with that day expires without any written representations being made by that person to the Secretary of State about the proposed notice; or

    (c) the Secretary of State has considered a report about the proposed notice by a person appointed under paragraph 7(1) below.

7.—(1) Where a person on whom a notification containing a draft of a proposed notice to warn has been served—

    (a) informs the Secretary of State as mentioned in paragraph 6 (1)(e) above before the end of the period of fourteen days beginning with the day on which the notification was served; and

    (b) makes written representations to the Secretary of State about the proposed notice before the end of the period of twenty-eight days beginning with that day,

the Secretary of State shall appoint a person to consider those representations, any further representations made by that person about the draft notice and the statements of any witnesses examined under this Part of this Schedule.

(2) Where—

    (a) the Secretary of State has appointed a person to consider representations about a proposed notice to warn; and

    (b) the person whose representations are to be considered has informed the Secretary of State for the purposes of paragraph 6(1)(e) above that the representations he intends to make will include oral representations,

the Secretary of State shall inform the person intending to make the representations of the place and time at which oral representations may be made to the appointed person.

(3) Where a person on whom a notification containing a draft of a proposed notice to warn has been served is informed of a time for the purposes of sub-paragraph (2) above, that time shall not be—

    (a) before the end of the period of twenty-eight days beginning with the day on which the notification was served; or

    (b) before the end of the period of seven days beginning with the day on which that person is informed of the time.

(4) A person who has been informed of a place and time for the purposes of sub-paragraph (2) above or his representative may, at that place and time—

    (a) make oral representations to the appointed person for the purpose of establishing that the goods to which the proposed notice relates are safe; and

    (b) call and examine witnesses in connection with the representations.

8.—(1) Where a person is appointed to consider representations about a proposed notice to warn, it shall be his duty to consider—

    (a) any written representations made by the person on whom it is proposed to serve the notice; and

    (b) in a case where a place and time has been appointed under paragraph 7(2) above for oral representations to be made by that person or his representative, any representations so made and any statements made by witnesses in connection with those representations,

and, after considering those matters, to make a report (including recommendations) to the Secretary of State about the matters considered by him and the proposal to serve the notice.

(2) It shall be the duty of the Secretary of State to consider any report made to him under sub-paragraph (1) above and, after considering the report, to inform the person on whom it was proposed that a notice to warn should be served of his decision with respect to the proposal.

(3) If at any time after serving a notification on a person under paragraph 6 above the Secretary of State decides not to serve on that person either the proposed notice to warn or that notice with modifications, the Secretary of State shall inform that person of the decision; and nothing done for the purposes of any of the preceding provisions of this Part of this Schedule before that person was so informed shall—

    (a) entitle the Secretary of State subsequently to serve the proposed notice or that notice with modifications; or

    (b) require the Secretary of State, or any person appointed to consider representations about the proposed notice, subsequently to do anything in respect of, or in consequence of, any such representations.

(4) Where a notification containing a draft of a proposed notice to warn is served on a person in respect of any goods, a notice to warn served on him in consequence of a decision made under sub-paragraph (2) above shall either be in the form of the draft or shall be less onerous than the draft.

9. The Secretary of State may revoke a notice to warn by serving on the person on whom the notice was served a notification stating that the notice is revoked.

PART III

GENERAL

10.—(1) Where in a notification served on any person under this Schedule the Secretary of State has appointed a time for the making of oral representations or the examination of witnesses, he may, by giving that person such notification as the Secretary of State considers appropriate, change that time to a later time or appoint further times at which further representations may be made or the examination of witnesses may be continued; and paragraphs 2(4), 3(4) and 7(4) above shall have effect accordingly.

(2) For the purposes of this Schedule the Secretary of State may appoint a person (instead of the appointed person) to consider any representations or statements, if the person originally appointed, or last appointed under this subparagraph, to consider those representations or statements has died or appears to the Secretary of State to be otherwise unable to act.

11.   In this Schedule—
"the appointed person" in relation to a prohibition notice or a proposal to serve a notice to warn, means the person for the time being appointed under this Schedule to consider representations about the notice or, as the case may be, about the proposed notice;
"notification" means a notification in writing;
"trader", in relation to a prohibition notice, means the person on whom the notice is or was served.

*   *   *   *   *

Consumer Arbitration Agreements Act 1988

(c. 21)

An Act to extend to consumers certain rights as regards agreements to refer future differences to arbitration and for purposes connected therewith.

[28th June 1988]

England, Wales and Northern Ireland

Arbitration agreements

1.—(1) Where a person (referred to in section 4 below as "the consumer") enters into a contract as a consumer, an agreement that future differences arising between parties to the contract are to be referred to arbitration cannot be enforced against him in respect of any cause of action so arising to which this section applies except—

(a) with his written consent signified after the differences in question have arisen; or

(b) where he has submitted to arbitration in pursuance of the agreement, whether in respect of those or any other differences; or

(c) where the court makes an order under section 4 below in respect of that cause of action.

(2) This section applies to a cause of action—

(a) if proceedings in respect of it would be within the jurisdiction of a county court; or

(b) if it satisfies such other conditions as may be prescribed for the purposes of this paragraph in an order under section 5 below.

(3) Neither section 4(1) of the Arbitration Act 1950 nor section 4 of the Arbitration Act (Northern Ireland) 1937 (which provide for the staying of court proceedings where an arbitration agreement is in force) shall apply to an arbitration agreement to the extent that it cannot be enforced by virtue of this section.

Exclusions

2. Section 1 above does not affect—

(a) the enforcement of an arbitration agreement to which section 1 of the Arbitration Act 1975 applies, that is, an arbitration agreement other than a domestic arbitration agreement within the meaning of that section;

(b) the resolution of differences arising under any contract so far as it is, by virtue of section 1(2) of, and Schedule 1 to, the Unfair Contract Terms Act 1977 ("the Act of 1977"), excluded from the operation of section 2, 3, 4 or 7 of that Act.

Contracting "as a consumer"

3.—(1) For the purposes of section 1 above a person enters into a contract "as a consumer" if—

(a) he neither makes the contract in the course of a business nor holds himself out as doing so; and

(b) the other party makes the contract in the course of a business; and

(c) in the case of a contract governed by the law of sale of goods or

253

hire-purchase, or by section 7 of the Act of 1977, the goods passing under or in pursuance of the contract are of a type ordinarily supplied for private use or consumption;

but on a sale by auction or by competitive tender the buyer is not in any circumstances to be regarded as entering into the contract as a consumer.

(2) In subsection (1) above—

"business" includes a profession and the activities of any government department, Northern Ireland department or local or public authority; and

"goods" has the same meaning as in the Sale of Goods Act 1979.

(3) It is for those claiming that a person entered into a contract otherwise than as a consumer to show that he did so.

Power of court to disapply section 1 where no detriment to consumer

4.—(1) The High Court or a county court may, on an application made after the differences in question have arisen, order that a cause of action to which this section applies shall be treated as one to which section 1 above does not apply.

(2) Before making an order under this section the court must be satisfied that it is not detrimental to the interests of the consumer for the differences in question to be referred to arbitration in pursuance of the arbitration agreement instead of being determined by proceedings before a court.

(3) In determining for the purposes of subsection (2) above whether a reference to arbitration is or is not detrimental to the interests of the consumer, the court shall have regard to all factors appearing to be relevant, including, in particular, the availability of legal aid and the relative amount of any expense which may result to him—

(a) if the differences in question are referred to arbitration in pursuance of the arbitration agreement; and

(b) if they are determined by proceedings before a court.

(4) This section applies to a cause of action—

(a) if proceedings in respect of it would be within the jurisdiction of a county court and would not fall within the small claims limit; or

(b) if it satisfies the conditions referred to in section 1(2)(b) above and the order under section 5 below prescribing the conditions in question provides for this section to apply to causes of action which satisfy them.

(5) For the purposes of subsection (4)(a) above proceedings "fall within the small claims limit"—

(a) in England and Wales, if in a county court they would stand referred to arbitration (without any order of the court) under rules made by virtue of section 64(1)(a) of the County Courts Act 1984;

(b) in Northern Ireland, if in a county court the action would be dealt with by way of arbitration by a circuit registrar by virtue of Article 30(3) of the County Courts (Northern Ireland) Order 1980.

(6) Where the consumer submits to arbitration in consequence of an order under this section, he shall not be regarded for the purposes of section 1(1)(b) above as submitting to arbitration in pursuance of the agreement there mentioned.

Orders adding to the causes of action to which section 1 applies

5.—(1) Orders under this section may prescribe the conditions referred to in section 1(2)(b) above; and any such order may provide that section 4 above shall apply to a cause of action which satisfies the conditions so prescribed.

(2) Orders under this section may make different provision for different cases and for different purposes.

(3) The power to make orders under this section for England and Wales shall be exercisable by statutory instrument made by the Secretary of State with the concurrence of the Lord Chancellor; but no such order shall be made unless a draft of it has been laid before, and approved by resolution of, each House of Parliament.

(4) The power to make orders under this section for Northern Ireland shall be exercisable by the Department of Economic Development for Northern Ireland with the concurrence of the Lord Chancellor; and any such order—

    (a) shall be a statutory rule for the purposes of the Statutory Rules (Northern Ireland) Order 1979; and

    (b) shall be subject to affirmative resolution, within the meaning of section 41(4) of the Interpretation Act (Northern Ireland) 1954.

Scotland

Arbitration agreements: Scotland

6.—(1) In the case of a consumer contract to which, by virtue of subsections (2) to (4) of section 15 of the Act of 1977 (scope of Part II of that Act), sections 16 to 18 of that Act apply, an agreement to refer future differences arising out of the contract to arbitration cannot, if it is a domestic arbitration agreement, be enforced against the consumer in respect of a relevant difference so arising except—

    (a) with his written consent given after that difference has arisen; or

    (b) where, subject to subsection (2) below, he has submitted to arbitration in pursuance of the agreement (whether or not the arbitration was in respect of that difference); or

    (c) by virtue of an order under section 7 below in respect of that difference.

(2) In determining for the purposes of subsection (1)(b) above whether the consumer has submitted to arbitration, any arbitration which takes place in consequence of an order of the court under section 7 below shall be disregarded.

Power of court to disapply section 6 where no detriment to consumer

7.—(1) Subject to subsection (4) below, the Court of Session or the sheriff ("the court") may, on an application made after a relevant difference has arisen, order that section 6 above shall not apply as respects that difference.

(2) No such order shall be made unless the court is satisfied that it would not be detrimental to the interests of the consumer were the difference to be referred to arbitration in pursuance of the arbitration agreement.

(3) In determining for the purposes of subsection (2) above whether there would be any detriment to the consumer's interests, the court shall have regard to all factors appearing to be relevant, including, in particular, the availability of legal aid and the relative amounts of any expenses which he might incur—

    (a) if the difference is referred to arbitration; and

    (b) if it is determined by proceedings before a court.

(4) No order shall be made under subsection (1) above where, if (disregarding the arbitration agreement) the difference were to be resolved by civil proceedings in the sheriff court, the form of summary cause process to be used for the purposes of those proceedings would be that of a small claim.

Construction of sections 6 and 7

8.—(1) In sections 6 and 7 above "consumer" and "consumer contract" have the meanings assigned to those expressions by section 25(1) of the Act of 1977 and "domestic arbitration agreement" has the same meaning as in section 1 of the Arbitration Act 1975.

(2) For the purposes of sections 6 and 7 above a difference is "relevant" where, if (disregarding the arbitration agreement) it were to be resolved by civil proceedings in the sheriff court—

    (a) the form of process to be used for the purposes of those proceedings would be that of a summary cause; or

    (b) the proceedings would come within such description of proceedings as may, by order, be specified by the Secretary of State for the purposes of this paragraph.

(3) The power to make an order under paragraph (b) of subsection (2) above shall be exercisable by statutory instrument made with the concurrence of the Lord Advocate; but no order shall be so made unless a draft has been laid before, and approved by resolution of, each House of Parliament.

Supplementary

Short title, commencement, interpretation and extent

9.—(1) This Act may be cited as the Consumer Arbitration Agreements Act 1988.

(2) This Act shall have effect in relation to contracts made on or after such day as the Secretary of State may by order made by statutory instrument appoint; and different days may be so appointed for different provisions and different purposes.

(3) In this Act "the Act of 1977" means the Unfair Contract Terms Act 1977.

(4) Sections 1 to 5 above do not extend to Scotland, sections 6 to 8 extend to Scotland only, and this Act, apart from sections 6 to 8, extends to Northern Ireland.

Food Safety Act 1990

(c. 16)

* * * * *

Food safety

Rendering food injurious to health

7.—(1) Any person who renders any food injurious to health by means of any of the following operations, namely—

(a) adding any article or substance to the food;

(b) using any article or substance as an ingredient in the preparation of the food;

(c) abstracting any constituent from the food; and

(d) subjecting the food to any other process or treatment,

with intent that it shall be sold for human consumption, shall be guilty of an offence.

(2) In determining for the purposes of this section and section 8(2) below whether any food is injurious to health, regard shall be had—

(a) not only to the probable effect of that food on the health of a person consuming it; but

(b) also to the probable cumulative effect of food of substantially the same composition on the health of a person consuming it in ordinary quantities.

(3) In this Part "injury", in relation to health, includes any impairment, whether permanent or temporary, and "injurious to health" shall be construed accordingly.

Selling food not complying with food safety requirements

8.—(1) Any person who—

(a) sells for human consumption, or offers, exposes or advertises for sale for such consumption, or has in his possession for the purpose of such sale or of preparation for such sale; or

(b) deposits with, or consigns to, any other person for the purpose of such sale or of preparation for such sale,

any food which fails to comply with food safety requirements shall be guilty of an offence.

(2) For the purposes of this Part food fails to comply with food safety requirements if—

(a) it has been rendered injurious to health by means of any of the operations mentioned in section 7(1) above;

(b) it is unfit for human consumption; or

(c) it is so contaminated (whether by extraneous matter or otherwise) that would not be reasonable to expect it to be used for human consumption in that state;

and references to such requirements or to food complying with such requirements shall be construed accordingly.

(3) Where any food which fails to comply with food safety requirements is part of a batch, lot of consignment of food of the same class or description, it shall be presumed for the purposes of this section and section 9 below, until the contrary is proved, that all of the food in that batch, lot or consignment falls to comply with those requirements.

(4) For the purposes of this Part, any part of, or product derived wholly or partly from, an animal—

(a) which has been slaughtered in a knacker's yard, or of which the carcase has been brought into a knacker's yard; or

(b) in Scotland, which has been slaughtered otherwise than in a slaughterhouse,

shall be deemed to be unfit for human consumption.

(5) In subsection (4) above, in its application to Scotland, "animal" means any description of cattle, sheep, goat, swine, horse, ass or mule; and paragraph (b) of that subsection shall not apply where accident, illness or emergency affecting the animal in question required it to be slaughtered as mentioned in that paragraph.

*   *   *   *   *

Consumer protection

Selling food not of the nature or substance or quality demanded

14.—(1) Any person who sells to the purchaser's prejudice any food which is not of the nature or substance or quality demanded by the purchaser shall be guilty of an offence.

(2) In subsection (1) above the reference to sale shall be construed as a reference to sale for human consumption; and in proceedings under that subsection it shall not be a defence that the purchaser was not prejudiced because he bought for analysis or examination.

Falsely describing or presenting food

15.—(1) Any person who gives with any food sold by him, or displays with any food offered or exposed by him for sale or in his possession for the purpose of sale, a label, whether or not attached to or printed on the wrapper or container, which—

(a) falsely describes the food; or

(b) is likely to mislead as to the nature or substance or quality of the food,

shall be guilty of an offence.

(2) Any person who publishes, or is a party to the publication of, an advertisement (not being such a label given or displayed by him as mentioned in subsection (1) above) which—

(a) falsely describes any food; or

(b) is likely to mislead as to the nature or substance or quality of any food,

shall be guilty of an offence.

(3) Any person who sells, or offers or exposes for sale, or has in his possession for the purpose of sale, any food the presentation of which is likely to mislead as to the nature or substance or quality of the food shall be guilty of an offence.

(4) In proceedings for an offence under subsection (1) or (2) above, the fact

that a label or advertisement in respect of which the offence is alleged to have been committed contained an accurate statement of the composition of the food shall not preclude the court from finding that the offence was committed.

(5) In this section references to sale shall be construed as references to sale for human consumption.

* * * * *

Defences etc.

Offences due to fault of another person

20. Where the commission by any person of an offence under any of the preceding provisions of this Part is due to an act or default of some other person, that other person shall be guilty of the offence; and a person may be charged with and convicted of the offence by virtue of this section whether or not proceedings are taken against the first-mentioned person.

Defence of due diligence

21.—(1) In any proceedings for an offence under any of the preceding provisions of this Part (in this section referred to as "the relevant provision"), it shall, subject to subsection (5) below, be a defence for the person charged to prove that he took all reasonable precautions and exercised all due diligence to avoid the commission of the offence by himself or by a person under his control.

(2) Without prejudice to the generality of subsection (1) above, a person charged with an offence under section 8, 14 or 15 above who neither—

(a) prepared the food in respect of which the offence is alleged to have been committed; nor

(b) imported it into Great Britain,

shall be taken to have established the defence provided by that subsection if he satisfies the requirements of subsection (3) or (4) below.

(3) A person satisfies the requirements of this subsection if he proves—

(a) that the commission of the offence was due to an act or default of another person who was not under his control, or to reliance on information supplied by such a person;

(b) that he carried out all such checks of the food in question as were reasonable in all the circumstances, or that it was reasonable in all the circumstances for him to rely on checks carried out by the person who supplied the food to him; and

(c) that he did not know and had no reason to suspect at the time of the commission of the alleged offence that his act or omission would amount to an offence under the relevant provision.

(4) A person satisfies the requirements of this subsection if he proves—

(a) that the commission of the offence was due to an act or default of another person who was not under his control, or to reliance on information supplied by such a person;

(b) that the sale or intended sale of which the alleged offence consisted was not a sale or intended sale under his name or mark; and

(c) that he did not know, and could not reasonably have been expected to know. at the time of the commission of the alleged offence that his act or omission would amount to an offence under the relevant provision.

(5) If in any case the defence provided by subsection (1) above involves the allegation that the commission of the offence was due to an act or default of another person, or to reliance on information supplied by another person, the person charged shall not, without leave of the court, be entitled to rely on that defence unless—

    (a) at least seven clear days before the hearing; and

    (b) where he has previously appeared before a court in connection with the alleged offence, within one month of his first such appearance,

he has served on the prosecutor a notice in writing giving such information identifying or assisting in the identification of that other person as was then in his possession.

(6) In subsection (5) above any reference to appearing before a court shall be construed as including a reference to being brought before a court.

Defence of publication in the course of business

22. In proceedings for an offence under any of the preceding provisions of this Part consisting of the advertisement for sale of any food, it shall be a defence for the person charged to prove—

    (a) that he is a person whose business it is to publish or arrange for the publication of advertisements; and

    (b) that he received the advertisement in the ordinary course of business and did not know and had no reason to suspect that its publication would amount to an offence under that provision.

* * * * *

Property Misdescriptions Act 1991

(c. 29)

An Act to prohibit the making of false or misleading statements about property matters in the course of estate agency business and property development business. [27th June 1991]

Offence of property misdescription

1.—(1) Where a false or misleading statement about a prescribed matter is made in the course of an estate agency business or a property development business, otherwise than in providing conveyancing services, the person by whom the business is carried on shall be guilty of an offence under this section.

(2) Where the making of the statement is due to the act or default of an employee the employee shall be guilty of an offence under this section; and the employee may be proceeded against and punished whether or not proceedings are also taken against his employer.

(3) A person guilty of an offence under this section shall be liable—

    (a) on summary conviction, to a fine not exceeding the statutory maximum, and

    (b) on conviction on indictment, to a fine.

(4) No contract shall be void or unenforceable, and no right of action in civil proceedings in respect of any loss shall arise, by reason only of the commission of an offence under this section.

(5) For the purposes of this section—

    (a) "false" means false to a material degree,

    (b) a statement is misleading if (though not false) what a reasonable person may be expected to infer from it, or from any omission from it, is false,

    (c) a statement may be made by pictures or any other method of signifying meaning as well as by words and, if made by words, may be made orally or in writing,

    (d) a prescribed matter is any matter relating to land which is specified in an order made by the Secretary of State,

    (e) a statement is made in the course of an estate agency business if (but only if) the making of the statement is a thing done as mentioned in subsection (1) of section 1 of the Estate Agents Act 1979 and that Act either applies to it or would apply to it but for subsection (2)(a) of that section (exception for things done in course of profession by practising solicitor or employee),

    (f) a statement is made in the course of a property development business if (but only if) it is made—

        (i) in the course of a business (including a business in which the person making the statement is employed) concerned wholly or substantially with the development of land, and

        (ii) for the purpose of, or with a view to, disposing of an interest in land consisting of or including a building, or a part of a building, constructed or renovated in the course of the business, and

    (g) "conveyancing services" means the preparation of any transfer, conveyance, writ, contract or other document in connection with the disposal or acquisition of an interest in land, and services ancillary to that, but does not include anything done as mentioned in section 1(1)(a) of the Estate Agents Act 1979.

(6) For the purposes of this section any reference in this section or section 1 of the Estate Agents Act 1979 to disposing of or acquiring an interest in land—

    (a) in England and Wales and Northern Ireland shall be construed in accordance with section 2 of that Act, and

    (b) in Scotland is a reference to the transfer or creation of an "interest in land" as defined in section 28(1) of the Land Registration (Scotland) Act 1979.

(7) An order under this section may—

    (a) make different provision for different cases, and

    (b) include such supplemental, consequential and transitional provisions as the Secretary of State considers appropriate;

and the power to make such an order shall be exercisable by statutory instrument which shall be subject to annulment in pursuance of a resolution of either House of Parliament.[1]

Due diligence defence

2.—(1) In proceedings against a person for an offence under section 1 above it shall be a defence for him to show that he took all reasonable steps and exercised all due diligence to avoid committing the offence.

(2) A person shall not be entitled to rely on the defence provided by subsection (1) above by reason of his reliance on information given by another unless he shows that it was reasonable in all the circumstances for him to have relied on the information, having regard in particular—

    (a) to the steps which he took, and those which might reasonably have been taken, for the purpose of verifying the information, and

    (b) to whether he had any reason to disbelieve the information.

(3) Where in any proceedings against a person for an offence under section 1 above the defence provided by subsection (1) above involves an allegation that the commission of the offence was due—

    (a) to the act or default of another, or

    (b) to reliance on information given by another,

the person shall not, without the leave of the court, be entitled to rely on the defence unless he has served a notice under subsection (4) below on the person bringing the proceedings not less than seven clear days before the hearing of the proceedings or, in Scotland, the diet of trial.

(4) A notice under this subsection shall give such information identifying or assisting in the identification of the person who committed the act or default, or gave the information, as is in the possession of the person serving the notice at the time he serves it.

Enforcement

3. The Schedule to this Act (which makes provision about the enforcement of this Act) shall have effect.

---

[1] The Property Misdescriptions (Specified Matters) Order 1992 (S.I. 1992 No. 2834) has been made under section 1 of the 1991 Act, and is printed below at p. 310.

Bodies corporate and Scottish partnerships

4.—(1) Where an offence under this Act committed by a body corporate is proved to have been committed with the consent or connivance of, or to be attributable to neglect on the part of, a director, manager, secretary or other similar officer of the body corporate or a person who was purporting to act in such a capacity, he (as well as the body corporate) is guilty of the offence and liable to be proceeded against and punished accordingly.

(2) Where the affairs of a body corporate are managed by its members, subsection (1) above applies in relation to the acts and defaults of a member in connection with his functions of management as if he were a director of the body corporate.

(3) Where an offence under this Act committed in Scotland by a Scottish partnership is proved to have been committed with the consent or connivance of, or to be attributable to neglect on the part of, a partner, he (as well as the partnership) is guilty of the offence and liable to be proceeded against and punished accordingly.

Prosecution time limit

5.—(1) No proceedings for an offence under section 1 above or paragraph 5(3), 6 or 7 of the Schedule to this Act shall be commenced after—

(a) the end of the period of three years beginning with the date of the commission of the offence, or

(b) the end of the period of one year beginning with the date of the discovery of the offence by the prosecutor,

whichever is the earlier.

(2) For the purposes of this section a certificate signed by or on behalf of the prosecutor and stating the date on which the offence was discovered by him shall be conclusive evidence of that fact; and a certificate stating that matter and purporting to be so signed shall be treated as so signed unless the contrary is proved.

Financial provision

6. There shall be paid out of money provided by Parliament any increase attributable to this Act in the sums payable out of such money under any other Act.

Short title and extent

7.—(1) This Act may be cited as the Property Misdescriptions Act 1991.

(2) This Act extends to Northern Ireland.

SCHEDULE

ENFORCEMENT

Enforcement authority

1.—(1) Every local weights and measures authority in Great Britain shall be an enforcement authority for the purposes of this Act, and it shall be the duty of each such authority to enforce the provisions of this Act within their area.

(2) The Department of Economic Development in Northern Ireland shall be an enforcement authority for the purposes of this Act, and it shall be the duty of the Department to enforce the provisions of this Act within Northern Ireland.

Prosecutions

2.—(1) In section 130(1) of the Fair Trading Act 1973 (notice to Director General of Fair Trading of intended prosecution by local weights and measures authority in England and Wales), after the words "the Consumer Protection Act 1987," there shall be inserted the words "or for an offence under section 1 of, or paragraph 6 of the Schedule to, the Property Misdescriptions Act 1991,".

(2) Nothing in paragraph 1 above shall authorise a local weights and measures authority to bring proceedings in Scotland for an offence.

Powers of officers of enforcement authority

3.—(1) If a duly authorised officer of an enforcement authority has reasonable grounds for suspecting that an offence under section 1 of this Act has been committed, he may—

(a) require a person carrying on or employed in a business to produce any book or document relating to the business, and take copies of it or any entry in it, or

(b) require such a person to produce in a visible and legible documentary form any information so relating which is contained in a computer, and take copies of it,

for the purpose of ascertaining whether such an offence has been committed.

(2) Such an officer may inspect any goods for the purpose of ascertaining whether such an offence has been committed.

(3) If such an officer has reasonable grounds for believing that any documents or goods may be required as evidence in proceedings for such an offence, he may seize and detain them.

(4) An officer seizing any documents or goods in the exercise of his power under sub-paragraph (3) above shall inform the person from whom they are seized.

(5) The powers of an officer under this paragraph may be exercised by him only at a reasonable hour and on production (if required) of his credentials.

(6) Nothing in this paragraph—

(a) requires a person to produce a document if he would be entitled to refuse to produce it in proceedings in a court on the ground that it is the subject of legal professional privilege or, in Scotland, that it contains a confidential communication made by or to an advocate or a solicitor in that capacity, or

(b) authorises the taking possession of a document which is in the possession of a person who would be so entitled.

4.—(1) A duly authorised officer of an enforcement authority may, at a reasonable hour and on production (if required) of his credentials, enter any premises for the purpose of ascertaining whether an offence under section 1 of this Act has been committed.

(2) If a justice of the peace, or in Scotland a justice of the peace or a sheriff, is satisfied—

(a) that any relevant books, documents or goods are on, or that any relevant information contained in a computer is available from, any premises, and that production or inspection is likely to disclose the commission of an offence under section 1 of this Act, or

    (b) that such an offence has been, is being or is about to be committed on any premises,

and that any of the conditions specified in sub-paragraph (3) below is met, he may by warrant under his hand authorise an officer of an enforcement authority to enter the premises, if need be by force.

    (3) The conditions referred to in sub-paragraph (2) above are—

    (a) that admission to the premises has been or is likely to be refused and that notice of intention to apply for a warrant under that sub-paragraph has been given to the occupier,

    (b) that an application for admission, or the giving of such a notice, would defeat the object of the entry,

    (c) that the premises are unoccupied, and

    (d) that the occupier is temporarily absent and it might defeat the object of the entry to await his return.

    (4) In sub-paragraph (2) above "relevant", in relation to books, documents, goods or information, means books, documents, goods or information which, under paragraph 3 above, a duly authorised officer may require to be produced or may inspect.

    (5) A warrant under sub-paragraph (2) above may be issued only if—

    (a) in England and Wales, the justice of the peace is satisfied as required by that sub-paragraph by written information on oath,

    (b) in Scotland, the justice of the peace or sheriff is so satisfied by evidence on oath, or

    (c) in Northern Ireland, the justice of the peace is so satisfied by complaint on oath.

    (6) A warrant under sub-paragraph (2) above shall continue in force for a period of one month.

    (7) An officer entering any premises by virtue of this paragraph may take with him such other persons as may appear to him necessary.

    (8) On leaving premises which he has entered by virtue of a warrant under subparagraph (2) above, an officer shall, if the premises are unoccupied or the occupier is temporarily absent, leave the premises as effectively secured against trespassers as he found them.

    (9) In this paragraph "premises" includes any place (including any vehicle, ship or aircraft) except premises used only as a dwelling.

Obstruction of officers

5.—(1) A person who—

    (a) intentionally obstructs an officer of an enforcement authority acting in pursuance of this Schedule,

    (b) without reasonable excuse fails to comply with a requirement made of him by such an officer under paragraph 3(1) above, or

    (c) without reasonable excuse fails to give an officer of an enforcement authority acting in pursuance of this Schedule any other assistance or information which the officer may reasonably require of him for the purpose of the performance of the officer's functions under this Schedule,

shall be guilty of an offence.

    (2) A person guilty of an offence under sub-paragraph (1) above shall be liable on summary conviction to a fine not exceeding level 5 on the standard scale.

(3) If a person, in giving any such information as is mentioned in sub-paragraph (1)(c) above,—

  (a) makes a statement which he knows is false in a material particular, or
  (b) recklessly makes a statement which is false in a material particular, he shall be guilty of an offence.

(4) A person guilty of an offence under sub-paragraph (3) above shall be liable—

  (a) on summary conviction, to a fine not exceeding the statutory maximum, and
  (b) on conviction on indictment, to a fine.

Impersonation of officers

6.—(1) If a person who is not a duly authorised officer of an enforcement authority purports to act as such under this Schedule he shall be guilty of an offence.

(2) A person guilty of an offence under sub-paragraph (1) above shall be liable—

  (a) on summary conviction, to a fine not exceeding the statutory maximum, and
  (b) on conviction on indictment, to a fine.

Disclosure of information

7.—(1) If a person discloses to another any information obtained by him by virtue of this Schedule he shall be guilty of an offence unless the disclosure was made—

  (a) in or for the purpose of the performance by him or any other person of any function under this Act, or
  (b) for a purpose specified in section 38(2)(a), (b) or (c) of the Consumer Protection Act 1987.

(2) A person guilty of an offence under sub-paragraph (1) above shall be liable—

  (a) on summary conviction, to a fine not exceeding the statutory maximum, and
  (b) on conviction on indictment, to a fine.

Privilege against self-incrimination

8. Nothing in this Schedule requires a person to answer any question or give any information if to do so might incriminate him.

Sunday Trading Act 1994

(c. 20)

An Act to reform the law of England and Wales relating to Sunday trading; to make provision as to the rights of shop workers under the law of England and Wales in relation to Sunday working; and for connected purposes.

[5 July 1994]

Reform of law relating to Sunday trading

1.—(1) Schedules 1 and 2 to this Act shall come into force on such day as the Secretary of State may by order made by statutory instrument appoint (in this section referred to as "the appointed day").

(2) Sections 47 to 66 of, and Schedules 5, 6 and 7 to, the Shops Act 1950 shall cease to have effect on the appointed day.[1]

Loading and unloading at large shops on Sunday morning

2.—(1) A local authority may by resolution designate their area as a loading control area for the purposes of this section with effect from a date specified in the resolution which must be a date at least one month after the date on which the resolution is passed.

(2) A local authority may by resolution revoke any designation made by them under subsection (1) above.

(3) It shall be the duty of a local authority, before making or revoking any designation under subsection (1) above, to consult persons appearing to the local authority to be likely to be affected by the proposed designation or revocation (whether as the occupiers of shops or as local residents) or persons appearing to the local authority to represent such persons.

(4) Where a local authority make or revoke a designation under this section, they shall publish notice of the designation or revocation in such manner as they consider appropriate.

(5) Schedule 3 to this Act (which imposes restrictions on loading and unloading on Sunday before 9 am at large shops in loading control areas) shall have effect.

Construction of certain leases and agreements

3.—(1) Where any lease or agreement (however worded) entered into before the commencement of this section has the effect of requiring the occupier of a shop to keep the shop open for the serving of retail customers—

(a) during normal business hours, or

(b) during hours to be determined otherwise than by or with the consent of the occupier,

that lease or agreement shall not be regarded as requiring, or as enabling any person to require, the occupier to open the shop on Sunday for the serving of retail customers.

(2) Subsection (1) above shall not affect any lease or agreement—

(a) to the extent that it relates specifically to Sunday and would (apart

---

[1] The appointed day is August 26, 1994 (S.I. 1994 No. 1841).

from this section) have the effect of requiring Sunday trading of a kind which before the commencement of this section would have been lawful by virtue of any provision of Part IV of the Shops Act 1950, or

(b) to the extent that it is varied by agreement after the commencement of this section.

(3) In this section "retail customer" and "shop" have the same meaning as in Schedule 1 to this Act.

Rights of shop workers as respects Sunday working

4. Schedule 4 to this Act shall have effect.

5. [*Repealed by the Deregulation and Contracting Out Act 1994, s. 81 and Sched. 17.*]

Consequential repeal or amendment of local Acts

6.—(1) The Secretary of State may by order made by statutory instruyment—

(a) repeal any provision of a local Act passed before or in the same Session as this Act if it appears to him that the provision is inconsistent with or has become unnecessary in consequence of any provision of this Act, and

(b) amend any provision of such a local Act if it appears to him that the provision requires amendment in consequence of any provision of this Act or any repeal made by virtue of paragraph (a) above.

(2) It shall be the duty of the Secretary of State, before he makes an order under subsection (1) above repealing or amending any provision of a local Act, to consult each local authority which he considers would be affected by the repeal or amendment of that provision.

(3) A statutory instrument containing an order under subsection (1) above shall be subject to annulment in pursuance of a resolution of either House of Parliament.

Expenses

7. There shall be paid out of money provided by Parliament any increase attributable to this Act in the sums payable out of such money under any other Act.

Meaning of "local authority"

8.—(1) In this Act "local authority" means any unitary authority or any district council so far as they are not a unitary authority.

(2) In subsection (1) above "unitary authority" means—

(a) the council of any county so far as they are the council for an area for which there are no district councils,

(b) the council of any district comprised in an areas for which there is no county council,

(c) a county borough council,

(d) a London borough council,

(e) the Common Council of the City of London, or

(f) the Council of the Isles of Scilly.

(3) Until 1st April 1996, the definition of "unitary authority" in subsection (2) above shall have effect with the omission of paragraph (c).

Short title, repeals, commencement and extent

9.—(1) This Act may be cited as the Sunday Trading Act 1994.

(2) The enactments mentioned in Schedule 5 to this Act are hereby repealed to the extent specified in the third column of that Schedule.

(3) The following provisions of this Act—

sections 2 to 5,

subsection (2) of this section, and

Schedules 3, 4 and 5,

shall not come into force until the appointed day (as defined in section 1 above).

(4) This Act extends to England and Wales only.

SCHEDULES

SCHEDULE 1

RESTRICTIONS ON SUNDAY OPENING OF LARGE SHOPS

Interpretation

1. In this Schedule—

"intoxicating liquor" has the same meaning as in the Licensing Act 1964,

"large shop" means a shop which has a relevant floor area exceeding 280 square metres

"medicinal product" and "registered pharmacy" have the same meaning as in the Medicines Act 1968,

"relevant floor area", in relation to a shop, means the internal floor area of so much of the shop as consists of or is comprised in a building, but excluding any part of the shop which, throughout the week ending with the Sunday in question is, used neither for the serving of customers in connection with the sale of goods nor for the display of goods,

"retail customer" means a person who purchases goods retail,

"retail sale" means any sale other than a sale for use or resale in the course of a trade or business, and references to retail purchase shall be construed accordingly,

"sale of goods" does not include—

(a) the sale of meals, refreshments or intoxicating liquor for consumption on the premises on which they are sold, or

(b) the sale of meals or refreshments prepared to order for immediate consumption off those premises,

"shop" means any premises where there is carried on a trade or business consisting wholly or mainly of the sale of goods, and

"stand", in relation to an exhibition, means any platform, structure, space or other area provided for exhibition purposes.

Large shops not to open on Sunday except in accordance with notice to local authority

2.—(1) Subject to sub-paragraphs (2) and (3) below, a large shop shall not be open on Sunday for the serving of retail customers.

(2) Sub-paragraph (1) above does not apply in relation to—

(a) any of the shops mentioned in paragraph 3(1) below, or

(b) any shop in respect of which a notice under paragraph 8(1) of Schedule

2 to this Act (shops occupied by persons observing the Jewish Sabbath) has effect.

(3) Where a notice under paragraph 4 below has effect in relation to a shop, sub-paragraph (1) above does not apply in relation to the shop during the permitted Sunday opening hours specified in the notice, but this sub-paragraph has effect subject to sub-paragraph (4) below.

(4) The exemption conferred by sub-paragraph (3) above does not apply where the Sunday is Easter Day or Christmas Day.

Exemptions

3.—(1) The shops referred to in paragraph 2(2)(a) above are—

    (a) any shop which is at a farm and where the trade or business carried on consists wholly or mainly of the sale of produce from that farm,

    (b) any shop where the trade or business carried on consists wholly or mainly of the sale of intoxicating liquor,

    (c) any shop where the trade or business carried on consists wholly or mainly of the sale of any one or more of the following—

        (i) motor supplies and accessories, and

        (ii) cycle supplies and accessories,

    (d) any shop which—

        (i) is a registered pharmacy, and

        (ii) is not open for the retail sale of any goods other than medicinal products and medical and surgical appliances.

    (e) any shop at a designated airport which is situated in a part of the airport to which sub-paragraph (3) below applies,

    (f) any shop in a railway station,

    (g) any shop at a service area within the meaning of the Highways Act 1980,

    (h) any petrol filling station,

    (j) any shop which is not open for the retail sale of any goods other than food, stores or other necessaries required by any person for a vessel or aircraft on its arrival at, or immediately before its departure from, a port, harbour or airport, and

    (k) any stand used for the retail sale of goods during the course of an exhibition.

(2) In determining whether a shop falls within sub-paragraph (1)(a), (b) or (c) above, regard shall be had to the nature of the trade or business carried on there on weekdays as well as to the nature of the trade or business carried on there on Sunday.

(3) This sub-paragraph applies to every part of a designated airport, except any part which is not ordinarily used by persons travelling by air to or from the airport.

(4) In this paragraph "designated airport" means an airport designated for the purposes of this paragraph by an order made by the Secretary of State, as being an airport at which there appears to him to be a substantial amount of international passenger traffic.

(5) The power to make an order under sub-paragraph (4) above shall be exercisable by statutory instrument.

(6) Any order made under section 1(2) of the Shops (Airports) Act 1962 and in force at the commencement of this Schedule shall, so far as it relates to England and Wales, have effect as if made also under sub-paragraph (4) above,

and may be amended or revoked as it has effect for the purposes of this paragraph by an order under sub-paragraph (4) above.

Notice of proposed Sunday opening

4.—(1) A person who is, or proposes to become, the occupier of a large shop may give notice to the local authority for the area in which the shop is situated—
  (a) stating that he proposes to open the shop on Sunday for the serving of retail customers, and
  (b) specifying a continuous period of six hours, beginning no earlier than 10 am and ending no later than 6 pm, as the permitted Sunday opening hours in relation to the shop.

(2) The occupier of a shop in respect of which notice has been given under sub-paragraph (1) above may, by a subsequent notice—
  (a) specify permitted Sunday opening hours that could be specified under sub-paragraph (1)(b) above but are different from those specified in the earlier notice, or
  (b) cancel the earlier notice.

(3) A notice under this paragraph shall not take effect until the end of the period of 14 days beginning with the day on which it is given, unless the local authority agree that it is to take effect at the end of a shorter period.

(4) A notice under this paragraph shall cease to have effect when superseded by a subsequent notice or cancelled as mentioned in sub-paragraph (2)(b) above.

Register of shops

5.—(1) Every local authority shall keep a register of shops in respect of which a notice under paragraph 4 above has effect.

(2) In relation to every such shop, the register shall contain particulars of—
  (a) the name (if any) and address of the shop, and
  (b) the permitted Sunday opening hours specified in the notice under paragraph 4 above.

(3) Any register kept under this paragraph—
  (a) shall be open to inspection by members of the public at all reasonable times, and
  (b) may be kept by means of a computer.

Duty to display notice

6. At any time when—
  (a) a large shop is open on Sunday for the serving of retail customers, and
  (b) the prohibition in sub-paragraph (1) of paragraph 2 above is excluded only by sub-paragraph (3) of that paragraph,
a notice specifying the permitted Sunday opening hours specified in the notice under paragraph 4 above shall be displayed in a conspicuous position inside and outside the shop.

Offences

7.—(1) If paragraph 2(1) above is contravened in relation to a shop, the occupier of the shop shall be liable on summary conviction to a fine not exceeding £50,000.

(2) If paragraph 6 above is contravened in relation to a shop, the occupier of the shop shall be liable on summary conviction to a fine not exceeding level 2 on the standard scale.

8.   Where a person is charged with having contravened paragraph 2(1) above, in relation to a large shop which was permitted to be open for the serving of retail customers on the Sunday in question during the permitted Sunday opening hours specified in a notice under paragraph 4 above, by reason of his having served a retail customer after the end of those hours, it shall be a defence to prove that the customer was in the shop before that time and left not later than half an hour after that time.

Transitional provision

9.   Any notice given for the purposes of paragraph 4(1) above after the passing of this Act but before the commencement of this Schedule shall, notwithstanding paragraph 4(3) above, take effect on that commencement.

Schedule 2

Supplementary Provisions

Part I

General Enforcement Provisions

Duty to enforce Act

1.   It shall be the duty of every local authority to enforce within their area the provisions of Schedules 1 and 3 to this Act and Part II of this Schedule.

Inspectors

2.   For the purposes of their duties under paragraph 1 above it shall be the duty of every local authority to appoint inspectors.

Powers of entry

3.   An inspector appointed by a local authority under paragraph 2 above shall, on producing if so required some duly authenticated document showing his authority, have a right at all reasonable hours—

    (a) to enter any premises within the area of the local authority, with or without a constable, for the purpose of ascertaining whether there is or has been on the premises any contravention of the provisions of Schedules 1 and 3 to this Act,

    (b) to require the production of, inspect and take copies of any records (in whatever form they are held) relating to any business carried on on the premises which appear to him to be relevant for the purpose mentioned in paragraph (a) above,

    (c) where those records are kept by means of a computer, to require the records to be produced in a form in which they may be taken away, and

(d) to take such measurements and photographs as he considers necessary for the purpose mentioned in paragraph (a) above.

Obstruction of inspectors

4. Any person who intentionally obstructs an inspector appointed under paragraph 2 above acting in the execution of his duty shall be liable on summary conviction to a fine not exceeding level 3 on the standard scale.

Offences due to fault of other person

5. Where the commission by any person of an offence under this Act is due to the act or default of some other person, that other person shall be guilty of the offence, and a person may be charged with and convicted of the offence by virtue of this paragraph whether or not proceeding are taken against the first-mentioned person.

Offences by bodies corporate

6.—(1) Where an offence under this Act committed by a body corporate is proved to have been committed with the consent or connivance of, or to be attributable to any neglect on the part of, any director, manager, secretary or other similar officer of the body corporate, or any person who was purporting to act in any such capacity, he as well as the body corporate shall be guilty of the offence and shall be liable to be proceeded against and punished accordingly.

(2) Where the affairs of a body corporate are managed by its members, sub-paragraph (1) above shall apply in relation to the acts and defaults of a member in connection with his functions of management as if he were a director of the body corporate.

Defence of due diligence

7.—(1) In any proceedings for an offence under this Act it shall, subject to sub-paragraph (2) below, be a defence for the person charged to prove that he took all reasonable precautions and exercised all due diligence to avoid the commission of the offence by himself or by a person under his control.

(2) If in any case the defence provided by sub-paragraph (1) above involves the allegation that the commission of the offence was due to the act or default of another person, the person charged shall not, without leave of the court, be entitled to rely on that defence unless, at least seven clear days before the hearing, he has served on the prosecutor a notice in writing giving such information identifying or assisting in the identification of that other person as was then in his possession.

PART II

SHOPS OCCUPIED BY PERSONS OBSERVING THE JEWISH SABBATH

* * * * *

The Mail Order Transactions (Information) Order 1976[1]

(S.I. 1976 No. 1812)

1. This Order may be cited as the Mail Order Transactions (Information) Order 1976 and shall come into operation on 1st January 1977.

2. The Interpretation Act 1889 shall apply for the interpretation of this Order as it applies for the interpretation of an Act of Parliament.

3.—(1) A communication to which this Article applies is an advertisement, circular, catalogue or other communication which fulfils the following conditions, that is to say—

  (i) it describes goods;
  (ii) it contains an invitation (express or implied) to persons to order goods of that description by post, and the invitation is not expressly limited to persons who are not consumers;
  (iii) it states, or from its terms it is reasonable to infer, that a payment is to be made before the goods are dispatched;
  (iv) it is not an advertisement made by way of a sound or television broadcast or an exhibition of a film.

(2) Subject to paragraph (3) below, a person shall not, in the course of a business, publish, distribute or furnish or cause to be published, distributed or furnished a communication to which this Article applies unless the communication contains in legible characters the true name or registered business name of the person carrying on the business in the course of which orders sent by post pursuant to the invitation contained in that communication are to be fulfilled and the address at which that business is managed.

(3) Nothing in paragraph (2) above shall require any address of a body corporate to be given in a document which is required to comply—

  (a) with subsection (7) of section 9 of the European Communities Act 1972 or with that subsection as extended by virtue of subsection (8) of that section; or
  (b) with Article 7 of the Companies (European Communities) Order (Northern Ireland) 1972, or with that Article as extended by virtue of Article 8 thereof,

and which mentions the address of the registered office of the body corporate in compliance therewith.

(4) In this Article—

"true name" means, in the case of an individual, his true surname with or without the addition of christian names or forenames or the initials thereof and, in the case of a body corporate, its corporate name; and

"registered business name" means a name registered under the Registration of Business Names Act 1916.

---

[1] Made in exercise of the powers conferred by the Fair Trading Act 1973, s. 22, printed above at p. 48.

The Consumer Transactions (Restrictions on Statements) Order 1976[1]

(S.I. 1976 No. 1813)

1.   This Order may be cited as the Consumer Transactions (Restrictions on Statements) Order 1976 and shall come into operation as respects—
   (a) this Article, Article 2 and Article 3(a), at the expiry of the period of 1 month beginning with the date on which this Order is made;
   (b) the remainder of Article 3, at the expiry of the period of 12 months beginning with that date; and
   (c) the remainder of this Order, at the expiry of the period of 2 years beginning with that date.

2.—(1) In this Order—
"advertisement" includes a catalogue and a circular;
"consumer" means a person acquiring goods otherwise than in the course of a business but does not include a person who holds himself out as acquiring them in the course of a business;
"consumer transaction" means—
   (a) a consumer sale, that is a sale of goods (other than an excepted sale) by a seller where the goods—
      (i) are of a type ordinarily bought for private use or consumption, and
      (ii) are sold to a person who does not buy or hold himself out as buying them in the course of a business.
For the purposes of this paragraph an excepted sale is a sale by auction, a sale by competitive tender and a sale arising by virtue of a contract for the international sale of goods as originally defined in section 62(1) of the Sale of Goods Act 1893 as amended by the Supply of Goods (Implied Terms) Act 1973;
   (b) a hire-purchase agreement (within the meaning of section 189(1) of the Consumer Credit Act 1974) where the owner makes the agreement in the course of a business and the goods to which the agreement relates—
      (i) are of a type ordinarily supplied for private use or consumption, and
      (ii) are hired to a person who does not hire or hold himself out as hiring them in the course of a business;
   (c) an agreement for the redemption of trading stamps under a trading stamp scheme within section 10(1) of the Trading Stamps Act 1964 or, as the case may be, within section 9 of the Trading Stamps Act (Northern Ireland) 1965;
"container" includes any form of packaging of goods whether by way of wholly or partly enclosing the goods or by way of attaching the goods to, or winding the goods round, some other article, and in particular includes a wrapper or confining band;
"statutory rights" means the rights arising by virtue of sections 13 to 15 of

---

[1] Made in exercise of the powers conferred by the Fair Trading Act 1973, s. 22, printed above at p. 48. Amendments made by the Consumer Transactions (Restrictions on Statements) (Amendment) Order 1978 (S.I. 1978 No. 127) are incorporated herein.

the Sale of Goods Act 1893 as amended by the Act of 1973, sections 9 to 11 of the Act of 1973, or section 4(1)(*c*) of the Trading Stamps Act 1964 or section 4(1)(*c*) of the Trading Stamps Act (Northern Ireland) 1965 both as amended by the Act of 1973.

(2) The Interpretation Act 1889 shall apply for the interpretation of this Order as it applies for the interpretation of an Act of Parliament.

3. A person shall not, in the course of a business—
     (a) display, at any place where consumer transactions are effected (whether wholly or partly), a notice containing a statement which purports to apply, in relation to consumer transactions effected there, a term which would—
          (i) be void by virtue of section 6 or 20 of the Unfair Contract Terms Act 1977 or
          (ii) be inconsistent with a warranty (in Scotland a stipulation) implied by section 4(1)(c) of the Trading Stamps Act 1964 or section 4(1)(c) of the Trading Stamps Act (Northern Ireland) 1965 both as amended by the Act of 1973,
if applied to some or all such consumer transactions;
     (b) publish or cause to be published any advertisement which is intended to induce persons to enter into consumer transactions and which contains a statement purporting to apply in relation to such consumer transactions such a term as is mentioned in paragraph (a)(i) or (ii), being a term which would be void by virtue of, or as the case may be, inconsistent with, the provisions so mentioned if applied to some or all of those transactions;
     (c) supply to a consumer pursuant to a consumer transaction goods bearing, or goods in a container bearing, a statement which is a term of that consumer transaction and which is void by virtue of, or inconsistent with, the said provisions, or if it were a term of that transaction, would be so void or inconsistent;
     (d) furnish to a consumer in connection with the carrying out of a consumer transaction or to a person likely, as a consumer, to enter into such a transaction, a document which includes a statement which is a term of that transaction and is void or inconsistent as aforesaid, or, if it were a term of that transaction, or were to become a term of a prospective transaction, would be so void or inconsistent.

4. A person shall not in the course of a business—
     (i) supply to a consumer pursuant to a consumer transaction goods bearing, or goods in a container bearing, a statement about the rights that the consumer has against that person or about the obligations to the consumer accepted by that person in relation to the goods (whether legally enforceable or not), being rights or obligations that arise if the goods are defective or are not fit for a purpose or do not correspond with a description;
     (ii) furnish to a consumer in connection with the carrying out of a consumer transaction or to a person likely, as a consumer, to enter into such a transaction with him or through his agency a document containing a statement about such rights and obligations,
unless there is in close proximity to any such statement another statement which

is clear and conspicuous and to the effect that the first-mentioned statement does not or will not affect the statutory rights of a consumer.

5.—(1) This Article applies to goods which are supplied in the course of a business by one person ("the supplier") to another where, at the time of the supply, the goods were intended by the supplier to be, or might reasonably be expected by him to be, the subject of a subsequent consumer transaction.

(2) A supplier shall not—

    (a) supply goods to which this Article applies if the goods bear, or are in a container bearing, a statement which sets out or describes or limits obligations (whether legally enforceable or not) accepted or to be accepted by him in relation to the goods; or

    (b) furnish a document in relation to the goods which contains such a statement,

unless there is in close proximity to any such statement another statement which is clear and conspicuous and to the effect that the first-mentioned statement does not or will not affect the statutory rights of a consumer.

(3) A person does not contravene paragraph (2) above—

    (i) in a case to which sub-paragraph (a) of that paragraph applies, unless the goods have become the subject of a consumer transaction;

    (ii) in a case to which sub-paragraph (b) applies, unless the document has been furnished to a consumer in relation to goods which were the subject of a consumer transaction, or to a person likely to become a consumer pursuant to such a transaction; or

    (iii) by virtue of any statement if before the date on which this Article comes into operation the document containing, or the goods or container bearing, the statement has ceased to be in his possession.

The Business Advertisements (Disclosure) Order 1977[1]

(S.I. 1977 No. 1918)

1.—(1) This Order may be cited as the Business Advertisements (Disclosure) Order 1977 and shall come into operation on 1st January 1978.

(2) The Interpretation Act 1978 shall apply for the interpretation of this Order as it applies for the interpretation of an Act of Parliament.

2.—(1) Subject to paragraphs (2) and (3) below, a person who is seeking to sell goods that are being sold in the course of a business shall not publish or cause to be published an advertisement—

(a) which indicates that the goods are for sale, and

(b) which is likely to induce consumers to buy the goods,

unless it is reasonably clear whether from the contents of the advertisement, its format or size, the place or manner of its publication or otherwise that the goods are to be sold in the course of a business.

(2) Paragraph (1) applies whether the person who is seeking to sell the goods is acting on his own behalf or that of another, and where he is acting as agent, whether he is acting in the course of a business carried on by him or not; but the reference in that paragraph to a business does not include any business carried on by the agent.

(3) Paragraph (1) above shall not apply in relation to advertisements—

(a) which are concerned only with sales by auction or competitive tender, or

(b) which are concerned only with the sale of flowers, fruit or vegetables, eggs or dead animals, fish or birds, gathered, produced or taken by the person seeking to sell the goods.

---

[1] Made in exercise of the powers conferred by the Fair Trading Act 1973, s. 22, printed above at p. 48.

The Consumer Protection (Cancellation of Contracts Concluded away from Business Premises) Regulations 1987[1]

(S.I. 1987 No. 2117)

Citation and commencement

1. These Regulations may be cited as the Consumer Protection (Cancellation of Contracts Concluded away from Business Premises) Regulations 1987 and shall come into force on 1st July 1988.

Interpretation

2.—(1) In these Regulations—

"business" includes a trade or profession;

"consumer" means a person, other than a body corporate, who, in making a contract to which these Regulations apply, is acting for purposes which can be regarded as outside his business;

"goods" has the meaning given by section 61(1) of the Sale of Goods Act 1979;

"land mortgage" includes any security charged on land and in relation to Scotland includes any heritable security;

"notice of cancellation" has the meaning given by regulation 4(5) below;

"security" in relation to a contract means a mortgage, charge, pledge, bond, debenture, indemnity, guarantee, bill, note or other right provided by the consumer, or at his request (express or implied), to secure the carrying out of his obligations under the contract;

"signed" has the same meaning as in the Consumer Credit Act 1974; and

"trader" means a person who, in making a contract to which these Regulations apply, is acting for the purposes of his business, and anyone acting in the name or on behalf of such a person.

(2) In Scotland any provision in these Regulations requiring a document to be signed shall be complied with by a body corporate if the document is properly executed in accordance with the law of Scotland.

Contracts to which the Regulations apply

3.—(1) These Regulations apply to a contract, other than an excepted contract, for the supply by a trader of goods or services to a consumer which is made—

    (a) during an unsolicited visit by a trader—

        (i) to the consumer's home or to the home of another person; or

        (ii) to the consumer's place of work;

    (b) during a visit by a trader as mentioned in paragraph (a)(i) or (ii) above at the express request of the consumer where the goods or services to which the contract relates are other than those concerning which the consumer requested the visit of the trader, provided that when the visit was requested the consumer did not know, or could not reasonably have known, that the supply of those other goods or services formed part of the trader's business activities;

---

[1] Made in exercise of the powers conferred by the European Communities Act 1972, s 2(2). These Regulations implement Council Directive 85/577/EEC, printed below at p. 352.

(c) after an offer was made by the consumer in respect of the supply by a trader of the goods or services in the circumstances mentioned in paragraph (a) or (b) above or (d) below; or

(d) during an excursion organised by the trader away from premises on which he is carrying on any business (whether on a permanent or temporary basis).

(2) For the purposes of this regulation an excepted contract means

(a) any contract—

(i) for the sale or other disposition of land, or for a lease or land mortgage;

(ii) to finance the purchase of land;

(iii) for a bridging loan in connection with the purchase of land; or

(iv) for the construction or extension of a building or other erection on land:

Provided that these Regulations shall apply to a contract for the supply of goods and their incorporation in any land or a contract for the repair or improvement of a building or other erection on land, where the contract is not financed by a loan secured by a land mortgage;

(b) any contract for the supply of food, drink or other goods intended for current consumption by use in the household and supplied by regular roundsmen;

(c) any contract for the supply of goods or services which satisfies all the following conditions, namely—

(i) terms of the contract are contained in a trader's catalogue which is readily available to the consumer to read in the absence of the trader or his representative before the conclusion of the contract;

(ii) the parties to the contract intend that there shall be maintained continuity of contact between the trader or his representative and the consumer in relation to the transaction in question or any subsequent transaction; and

(iii) both the catalogue and the contract contain or are accompanied by a prominent notice indicating that the consumer has a right to return to the trader or his representative goods supplied to him within the period of not less than 7 days from the day on which the goods are received by the consumer and otherwise to cancel the contract within that period without the consumer incurring any liability, other than any liability which may arise from the failure of the consumer to take reasonable care of the goods while they are in his possession;

(d) contracts of insurance to which the Insurance Companies Act 1982 applies;

(e) investment agreements within the meaning of the Financial Services Act 1986, and agreements for the making of deposits within the meaning of the Banking Act 1987 in respect of which Regulations have been made for regulating the making of unsolicited calls under section 34 of that Act;

(f) any contract not falling within sub-paragraph (g) below under which the total payments to be made by the consumer do not exceed £35; and

(g) any contract under which credit within the meaning of the Consumer Credit Act 1974 is provided not exceeding £35 other than a hire-purchase or conditional sale agreement.

(3) In this regulation "unsolicited visit" means a visit by a trader, whether or not he is the trader who supplies the goods or services, which does not take place at the express request of the consumer and includes a visit which takes place after a trader telephones the consumer (otherwise than at his express request) indicating expressly or by implication that he is willing to visit the consumer.

Cancellation of Contract

4.—(1) No contract to which these Regulations apply shall be enforceable against the consumer unless the trader has delivered to the consumer notice in writing in accordance with paragraphs (3) and (4) below indicating the right of the consumer to cancel the contract within the period of 7 days mentioned in paragraph (5) below containing both the information set out in Part I of the Schedule to these Regulations and a Cancellation Form in the form set out in Part II of the Schedule and completed in accordance with the footnotes.

(2) Paragraph (1) above does not apply to a cancellable agreement within the meaning of the Consumer Credit Act 1974 or to an agreement which may be cancelled by the consumer in accordance with terms of the agreement conferring upon him similar rights as if the agreement were such a cancellable agreement.

(3) The information to be contained in the notice under paragraph (1) above shall be easily legible and if incorporated in the contract or other document shall be afforded no less prominence than that given to any other information in the document apart from the heading to the document and the names of the parties to the contract and any information inserted in handwriting.

(4) The notice shall be dated and delivered to the consumer—

  (a) in the cases mentioned in regulation 3(1)(a), (b) and (d) above, at the time of the making of the contract; and

  (b) in the case mentioned in regulation 3(1)(c) above, at the time of the making of the offer by the consumer.

(5) If within the period of 7 days following the making of the contract the consumer serves a notice in writing (a "notice of cancellation") on the trader or any other person specified in a notice referred to in paragraph (1) above as a person to whom notice of cancellation may be given which, however expressed and whether or not conforming to the cancellation form set out in Part II of the Schedule to these Regulations, indicates the intention of the consumer to cancel the contract, the notice of cancellation shall operate to cancel the contract.

(6) Except as otherwise provided under these Regulations, a contract cancelled under paragraph (5) above shall be treated as if it had never been entered into by the consumer.

(7) Notwithstanding anything in section 7 of the Interpretation Act 1978, a notice of cancellation sent by post by a consumer shall be deemed to have been served at the time of posting, whether or not it is actually received.

Recovery of money paid by consumer

5.—(1) Subject to regulation 7(2) below, on the cancellation of a contract under regulation 4 above, any sum paid by or on behalf of the consumer under or in contemplation of the contract shall become repayable.

(2) If under the terms of the cancelled contract the consumer or any person on his behalf is in possession of any goods, he shall have a lien on them for any sum repayable to him under paragraph (1) above.

(3) Where any security has been provided in relation to the cancelled contract, the security, so far as it is so provided, shall be treated as never having had

effect and any property lodged with the trader solely for the purposes of the security as so provided shall be returned by him forthwith.

Repayment of credit

6.—(1) Notwithstanding the cancellation of a contract regulation 4 above under which credit is provided, the contract shall continue in force so far as it relates to repayment of credit and payment of interest.

(2) If, following the cancellation of the contract, the consumer repays the whole or a portion of the credit—

(a) before the expiry of one month following service of the notice of cancellation, or

(b) in the case of a credit repayable by instalments, before the date on which the first instalment is due,

no interest shall be payable on the amount repaid.

(3) If the whole of a credit repayable by instalments is not repaid on or before the date specified in paragraph (2)(b) above, the consumer shall not be liable to repay any of the credit except on receipt of a request in writing signed by the trader stating the amounts of the remaining instalments (recalculated by the trader as nearly as may be in accordance with the contract and without extending the repayment period), but excluding any sum other than principal and interest.

(4) Repayment of a credit, or payment of interest, under a cancelled contract shall be treated as duly made if it is made to any person on whom, under regulation 4(5) above, a notice of cancellation could have been served.

(5) Where any security has been provided in relation to the contract, the duty imposed on the consumer by this regulation shall not be enforceable before the trader has discharged any duty imposed on him by regulation 5(3) above.

(6) In this regulation, the following expressions have the meanings hereby assigned to them:—

"cash" includes money in any form;

"credit" means a cash loan and any facility enabling the consumer to overdraw on a current account;

"current account" means an account under which the customer may, by means of cheques or similar orders payable to himself or to any other person, obtain or have the use of money held or made available by the person with whom the account is kept and which records alterations in the financial relationship between the said person and the customer; and

"repayment", in relation to credit, means the repayment of money—

(a) paid to a consumer before the cancellation of the contract; or

(b) to the extent that he has overdrawn on his current account before the cancellation.

Return of goods by consumer after cancellation

7.—(1) Subject to paragraph (2) below, a consumer who has before cancelling a contract under regulation 4 above acquired possession of any goods by virtue of the contract shall be under a duty, subject to any lien, on the cancellation to restore the goods to the trader in accordance with this regulation, and meanwhile to retain possession of the goods and take reasonable care of them.

(2) The consumer shall not be under a duty to restore—

(i) perishable goods;

(ii) goods which by their nature are consumed by use and which, before the cancellation, were so consumed;

(iii) goods supplied to meet an emergency; or

(iv) goods which, before the cancellation, had become incorporated in any land or thing not comprised in the cancelled contract,

but he shall be under a duty to pay in accordance with the cancelled contract for the supply of the goods and for the provision of any services in connection with the supply of the goods before the cancellation.

(3) The consumer shall not be under any duty to deliver the goods except at his own premises and in pursuance of a request in writing signed by the trader and served on the consumer either before, or at the time when, the goods are collected from those premises.

(4) If the consumer—

(i) delivers the goods (whether at his own premises or elsewhere) to any person on whom, under regulation 4(5) above, a notice of cancellation could have been served; or

(ii) sends the goods at his own expense to such a person,

he shall be discharged from any duty to retain possession of the goods or restore them to the trader.

(5) Where the consumer delivers the goods as mentioned in paragraph (4)(i) above, his obligation to take care of the goods shall cease; and if he send the goods as mentioned in paragraph (4)(ii) above, he shall be under a duty to take reasonable care to see that they are received by the trader and not damaged in transit, but in other respects his duty to take care of the goods shall cease.

(6) Where, at any time during the period of 21 days following the cancellation, the consumer receives such a request as is mentioned in paragraph (3) above and unreasonably refuses or unreasonably fails to comply with it, his duty to retain possession and take reasonable care of the goods shall continue until he delivers or sends the goods as mentioned in paragraph (4) above, but if within that period he does not receive such a request his duty to take reasonable care of the goods shall cease at the end of that period.

(7) Where any security has been provided in relation to the cancelled contract, the duty imposed on the consumer to restore goods by this regulation shall not be enforceable before the trader has discharged any duty imposed on him by regulation 5(3) above.

(8) Breach of a duty imposed by this regulation on a consumer is actionable as a breach of statutory duty.

Goods given in part-exchange

8.—(1) This regulation applies on the cancellation of a contract under regulation 4 above where the trader agreed to take goods in part-exchange (the "part-exchange goods") and those goods have been delivered to him.

(2) Unless, before the end of the period of ten days beginning with the date of cancellation, the part-exchange goods are returned to the consumer in a condition substantially as good as when they were delivered to the trader, the consumer shall be entitled to recover from the trader a sum equal to the part-exchange allowance.

(3) During the period of ten days beginning with the date of cancellation, the consumer, if he is in possession of goods to which the cancelled contract relates, shall have a lien on them for—

(a) delivery of the part-exchange goods in a condition substantially as good as when they were delivered to the trader; or

(b) a sum equal to the part-exchange allowance;

and if the lien continues to the end of that period it shall thereafter subsist only as a lien for a sum equal to the part-exchange allowance.

(4) In this regulation the part-exchange allowance means the sum agreed as such in the cancelled contract, or if no such sum was agreed, such sum as it would have been reasonable to allow in respect of the part-exchange goods if no notice of cancellation had been served.

Amendment of the Consumer Credit Act 1974

9. [*Amends section 74(2) and is incorporated therein.*]

No contracting-out

10.—(1) A term contained in a contract to which these Regulations apply is void if, and to the extent that, it is inconsistent with a provision for the protection of the consumer contained in these Regulations.

(2) Where a provision of these Regulations specifies the duty or liability of the consumer in certain circumstances a term contained in a contract to which these Regulations apply is inconsistent with that provision if it purports to impose, directly or indirectly, an additional duty or liability on him in those circumstances.

Service of documents

11.—(1) A document to be served under these Regulations on a person may be so served—

(a) by delivering it to him, or by sending it by post to him, or by leaving it with him, at his proper address addressed to him by name;

(b) if the person is a body corporate, by serving it in accordance with paragraph (a) above on the secretary or clerk of that body; or

(c) if the person is a partnership, by serving it in accordance with paragraph (a) above on a partner or on a person having the control or management of the partnership business.

(2) For the purposes of these Regulations, a document sent by post to, or left at, the address last known to the server of the document as the address of a person shall be treated as sent by post to, or left at, his proper address.

SCHEDULE

PART I

INFORMATION TO BE CONTAINED IN NOTICE OF CANCELLATION RIGHTS

1.   The name of the trader.

2.   The trader's reference number, code or other details to enable the contract or offer to be identified.

3.   A statement that the consumer has a right to cancel the contract if he wishes and that this right can be exercised by sending or taking a written notice of cancellation to the person mentioned in paragraph 4 within the period of 7 days following the making of the contract.

4.   The name and address of a person to whom notice of cancellation may be given.

5.   A statement that the consumer can use the cancellation form provided if he wishes.

PART II

CANCELLATION FORM TO BE INCLUDED IN NOTICE OF CANCELLATION RIGHTS

(Complete, detach and return this form ONLY IF YOU WISH TO CANCEL THE CONTRACT.)

To: 1

I/We* hereby give notice that I/we* wish to cancel my/our* contract
      2

Signed

Date

*Delete as appropriate

Notes:

   1. Trader to insert name and address of person to whom notice may be given.

   2. Trader to insert reference number, code or other details to enable the contract or offer to be identified. He may also insert the name and address of the consumer.

The Control of Misleading Advertisements Regulations 1988[1]

(S.I. 1988 No. 915)

Citation and commencement

1. These Regulations may be cited as the Control of Misleading Advertisements Regulations 1988 and shall come into force on 20th June 1988.

Interpretation

2.—(1) In these Regulations—

"advertisement" means any form of representation which is made in connection with a trade, business, craft or profession in order to promote the supply or transfer of goods or services, immovable property, rights or obligations;

"the Commission" means the Independent Television Commission;

"court", in relation to England and Wales and Northern Ireland, means the High Court, and, in relation to Scotland, the Court of Session;

"Director" means the Director General of Fair Trading;

"licensed service" means—

    (a) in relation to a complaint made to the Commission, a service in respect of which the Commission have granted a licence under Part I or II of the Broadcasting Act 1990; and

    (b) in relation to a complaint made to the Radio Authority, a service in respect of which the Radio Authority have granted a licence under Part III of that Act and "licensed local delivery service" means a service in respect of which the Commission have granted a licence under Part II of that Act;

"publication" in relation to an advertisement means the dissemination of that advertisement whether to an individual person or a number of persons and whether orally or in writing or in any other way whatsoever, and "publish" shall be construed accordingly

"relevant body" means the Commission or the Radio Authority;

"on S4C" has the same meaning as in Part I of the Broadcasting Act 1990;

"the Welsh Authority" has the same meaning as in that Act.

(2) For the purposes of these Regulations an advertisement is misleading if in any way, including its presentation, it deceives or is likely to deceive the persons to whom it is addressed or whom it reaches and if, by reason of its deceptive nature, it is likely to affect their economic behaviour or, for those reasons, injures or is likely to injure a competitor of the person whose interests the advertisement seeks to promote.

(3) In the application of these Regulations to Scotland for references to an injunction or an interlocutory injunction there shall be substituted references to an interdict or an interim interdict respectively.

Application

3.—(1) These Regulations do not apply to—

    (a) the following advertisements issued or caused to be issued by or on

---

[1] Made in exercise of the powers conferred by the European Communities Act 1972, s. 2(2). These regulations implement Council Directive 84/450/EEC: [1984] O.J. L.250, set out below at p. 341.

behalf of an authorised person or appointed representative, that is to say—

  (i) investment advertisements; and

  (ii) any other advertisements in respect of investment business, except where any such advertisements relate exclusively to any matter in relation to which the authorised person in question is an exempted person; and

 (b) advertisements of a description referred to in section 58(1)(d) of the Financial Services Act 1986, except where any such advertisements consist of or any part of the matters referred to in section 58(1)(d)(ii) of that Act as being required or permitted to be published by an approved exchange under Part V of that Act.

(2) In this regulation "appointed representative", "approved exchange", "authorised person", "exempted person", "investment advertisement" and "investment business" have the same meanings as in the Financial Services Act 1986.

Complaints to the Director

4.—(1) Subject to paragraphs (2) and (3) below, it shall be the duty of the Director to consider any complaint made to him that an advertisement is misleading, unless the complaint appears to the Director to be frivolous or vexatious.

(2) The Director shall not consider any complaint which these Regulations require or would require, leaving aside any question as to the frivolous or vexatious nature of the complaint, the Commission, the Radio Authority or the Welsh Authority to consider.

(3) Before considering any complaint under paragraph (1) above the Director may require the person making the complaint to satisfy him that—

 (a) there have been invoked in relation to the same or substantially the same complaint about the advertisement in question such established means of dealing with such complaints as the Director may consider appropriate, having regard to all the circumstances of the particular case;

 (b) a reasonable opportunity has been allowed for those means to deal with the complaint in question; and

 (c) those means have not dealt with the complaint adequately.

(4) In exercising the powers conferred on him by these Regulations the Director shall have regard to—

 (a) all the interests involved and in particular the public interest; and

 (b) the desirability of encouraging the control, by self-regulatory bodies, of advertisements.

Applications to the Court by the Director

5.—(1) If, having considered a complaint about an advertisement pursuant to regulation 4 (1) above, he considers that the advertisement is misleading, the Director may, if he thinks it appropriate to do so, bring proceedings for an injunction (in which proceedings he may also apply for an interlocutory injunction) against any person appearing to him to be concerned or likely to be concerned with the publication of the advertisement.

(2) The Director shall give reasons for his decision to apply or not to apply, as the case may be, for an injunction in relation to any complaint which these Regulations require him to consider.

Functions of the Court

6.—(1) The court on an application by the Director may grant an injunction on such terms as it may think fit but (except where it grants an interlocutory injunction) only if the court is satisfied that the advertisement to which the application relates is misleading. Before granting an injunction the court shall have regard to all the interests involved and in particular the public interest.

(2) An injunction may relate not only to a particular advertisement but to any advertisement in similar terms or likely to convey a similar impression.

(3) In considering an application for an injunction the court may, whether or not on the application of any party to the proceedings, require any person appearing to the court to be responsible for the publication of the advertisement to which the application relates to furnish the court with evidence of the accuracy of any factual claim made in the advertisement. The court shall not make such a requirement unless it appears to the court to be appropriate in the circumstances of the particular case, having regard to the legitimate interests of the person who would be the subject of or affected by the requirement and of any other person concerned with the advertisement.

(4) If such evidence is not furnished to it following a requirement made by it under paragraph (3) above or if it considers such evidence inadequate, the court may decline to consider the factual claim mentioned in that paragraph accurate.

(5) The court shall not refuse to grant an injunction for lack of evidence that—

> (a) the publication of the advertisement in question has given rise to loss or damage to any person; or
>
> (b) the person responsible for the advertisement intended it to be misleading or failed to exercise proper care to prevent its being misleading.

(6) An injunction may prohibit the publication or the continued or further publication of an advertisement.

Powers of the Director to obtain and disclose information and disclosure of information generally

7.—(1) For the purpose of facilitating the exercise by him of any functions conferred on him by these Regulations, the Director may, by notice in writing signed by him or on his behalf, require any person to furnish to him such information as may be specified or described in the notice or to produce to him any documents so specified or described.

(2) A notice under paragraph (1) above may—

> (a) specify the way in which and the time within which it is to be complied with; and
>
> (b) be varied or revoked by a subsequent notice.

(3) Nothing in this regulation compels the production or furnishing by any person of a document or of information which he would in an action in a court be entitled to refuse to produce or furnish on grounds of legal professional privilege or, in Scotland, on the grounds of confidentiality as between client and professional legal adviser.

(4) If a person makes default in complying with a notice under paragraph (1) above the court may, on the application of the Director, make such order as the court thinks fit for requiring the default to be made good, and any such order may provide that all the costs or expenses of and incidental to the application shall be borne by the person in default or by any officers of a company or other association who are responsible for its default.

(5) Subject to any provision to the contrary made by or under any enactment, where the Director considers it appropriate to do so for the purpose of controlling misleading advertisements, he may refer to any person any complaint (including any related documentation) about an advertisement or disclose to any person any information (whether or not obtained by means of the exercise of the power conferred by paragraph (1) above).

(6) For the purpose of enabling information obtained under certain enactments to be used for facilitating the performance of functions under these Regulations, the following amendments shall be made in provisions respecting disclosure of information, that is to say—[2]

* * * * *

(7) Subject to paragraph (5) above, any person who knowingly discloses, otherwise than for the purposes of any legal proceedings or of a report of such proceedings or the investigation of any criminal offence, any information obtained by means of the exercise of the power conferred by paragraph (1) above without the consent either of the person to whom the information relates, or, if the information relates to a business, the consent of the person for the time being carrying on that business, shall be guilty of an offence and liable on summary conviction to imprisonment for a term not exceeding 3 months or to a fine not exceeding Level 5 on the standard scale or to both.

(8) The Director may arrange for the dissemination in such form and manner as he considers appropriate of such information and advice concerning the operation of these Regulations as may appear to him to be expedient to give to the public and to all persons likely to be affected by these Regulations.

Complaints to the Commission and the Radio Authority

8.—(1) Subject to paragraph (2) below, it shall be the duty of a relevant body to consider any complaint made to it that any advertisement included or proposed to be included in a licensed service is misleading, unless the complaint appears to the body to be frivolous or vexatious.

(2) The Commission shall not consider any complaint about an advertisement included or proposed to be included in a licensed local delivery service by the reception and immediate re-transmission of broadcasts made by the British Broadcasting Corporation.

(3) A relevant body shall give reasons for its decisions.

(4) In exercising the powers conferred on it by these Regulations a relevant body shall have regard to all the interests involved and in particular the public interest.

Control by the Commission and the Radio Authority of misleading advertisements

9.—(1) If, having considered a complaint about an advertisement pursuant to regulation 8(1) above, it considers that the advertisement is misleading, a relevant body may, if it thinks it appropriate to do so, exercise in relation to the advertisement the power conferred on it—

---

[2] The list of amendments is omitted; they are incorporated elsewhere in this work where relevant.

(a) where the relevant body is the Commission, by section 9(6) of the Broadcasting Act 1990 (power of Commission to give directions about advertisements), or

(b) where the relevant body is the Radio Authority, by section 93(6) of that Act (power of Radio Authority to give directions about advertisements).

(2) A relevant body may require any person appearing to it to be responsible for an advertisement which the body believes may be misleading to furnish it with evidence as to the accuracy of any factual claim made in the advertisement. In deciding whether or not to make such a requirement the body shall have regard to the legitimate interests of any person who would be the subject of or affected by the requirement.

(3) If such evidence is not furnished to it following a requirement made by it under paragraph (2) above or if it considers such evidence inadequate, a relevant body may consider the factual claim inaccurate.

Complaints to the Welsh Authority

10.—(1) Subject to paragraph (2) below, it shall be the duty of the Welsh Authority to consider any complaint made to them that any advertisement broadcast or proposed to be broadcast on S4C is misleading, unless the complaint appears to the Authority to be frivolous or vexatious.

(2) The Welsh Authority shall not consider any complaint about an advertisement broadcast or proposed to be broadcast on S4C by the reception and immediate re-transmission of broadcasts made by the British Broadcasting Corporation.

(3) The Welsh Authority shall give reasons for their decisions.

(4) In exercising the powers conferred on them by these Regulations the Welsh Authority shall have regard to all the interests involved and in particular the public interest.

Control by the Welsh Authority of misleading advertisements

11.—(1) If having considered a complaint about an advertisement pursuant to regulation 10(1) above, they consider that the advertisement is misleading, the Welsh Authority may, if they think it appropriate to do so, refuse to broadcast the advertisement.

(2) The Welsh Authority may require any person appearing to them to be responsible for an advertisement which the Authority believe may be misleading to furnish them with evidence as to the accuracy of any factual claim made in the advertisement. In deciding whether or not to make such a requirement the Authority shall have regard to the legitimate interests of any person who would be the subject of or affected by the requirement.

(3) If such evidence is not furnished to them following a requirement made by them under paragraph (2) above or if they consider such evidence inadequate, the Welsh Authority may consider the factual claim inaccurate.

The Consumer Protection (Code of Practice for Traders on Price Indications) Approval Order 1988[1]

(S.I. 1988 No. 2078)

1.   This Order may be cited as the Consumer Protection (Code of Practice for Traders on Price Indications) Approval Order 1988 and shall come into force on 1 March 1989.

2.   The code of practice, as set out in the Schedule to this Order, issued by the Secretary of State for the purpose of—
   (a) giving practical guidance with respect to the requirements of section 20 of the Consumer Protection Act 1987; and
   (b) promoting what appear to the Secretary of State to be desirable practices as to the circumstances and manner in which a person gives an indication as to the price at which goods, services, accommodation or facilities are available or indicates any other matter in respect of which any such indication may be misleading—
is hereby approved.

SCHEDULE

CODE OF PRACTICE FOR TRADERS ON PRICE INDICATIONS
NOVEMBER 1988

INTRODUCTION

The Consumer Protection Act
The Consumer Protection Act 1987 makes it a criminal offence to give consumers a misleading price indication about goods, services, accommodation (including the sale of new homes) or facilities. It applies however you give the price indication—whether in a TV or press advertisement, in a catalogue or leaflet, on notices, price tickets or shelf-edge marking in stores, or if you give it orally, for example on the telephone. The term "price indication" includes price comparisons as well as indications of a single price.

2.   This code of practice is approved under section 25 of the Act which gives the Secretary of State power to approve codes of practice to give practical guidance to traders. It is addressed to traders and sets out what is good practice to follow in giving price indications in a wide range of different circumstances, so as to avoid giving misleading price indications. But the Act does not require you to do as this code tells you. You may still give price indications which do not accord with this code, provided they are not misleading. "Misleading" is defined in section 21 of the Act.

The definition covers indications about any conditions attached to a price, about what you expect to happen to a price in future and what you say in price comparisons, as well as indications about the actual price the consumer will have to

---

[1] Made in exercise of the powers conferred by the Consumer Protection Act 1987, s. 25, printed above at p. 231.

pay. It also applies in the same way to any indications you give about the way in which a price will be calculated.

Price comparisons

3.   If you want to make price comparisons, you should do so only if you can show that they are accurate and valid. Indications which give only the price of the product are unlikely to be misleading if they are accurate and cover the total charge you will make. Comparisons with prices which you can show have been or are being charged for the same or similar goods, services, accommodation or facilities and have applied for a reasonable period are also unlikely to be misleading. Guidance on these matters is contained in this code.

Enforcement

4.   Enforcement of the Consumer Protection Act 1987 is the responsibility of officers of the local weights and measures authority (in Northern Ireland, the Department of Economic Development)—usually called Trading Standards Officers. If a Trading Standards Officer has reasonable grounds to suspect that you have given a misleading price indication, the Act gives the Officer power to require you to produce any records relating to your business and to seize and detain goods or records which the Officer has reasonable grounds for believing may be required as evidence in court proceedings.

5.   It may only be practicable for Trading Standards Officers to obtain from you the information necessary to carry out their duties under the Act. In these circumstances the Officer may seek information and assistance about both the claim and the supporting evidence from you. Be prepared to cooperate with Trading Standards Officers and respond to reasonable requests for information and assistance. The Act makes it an offence to obstruct a Trading Standards Officer intentionally or to fail (without good cause) to give any assistance or information the Officer may reasonably require to carry out duties under the Act.

Court proceedings

6.   If you are taken to court for giving a misleading price indication, the court can take into account whether or not you have followed the code. If you have done as the code advises, that will not be an absolute defence but it will tend to show that you have not committed an offence. Similarly if you have done something the code advises against doing it may tend to show that the price indication was misleading. If you do something which is not covered by the code, your price indication will need to be judged only against the terms of the general offence. The Act provides for a defence of due diligence, that is, that you have taken all reasonable steps to avoid committing the offence of giving a misleading price indication, but failure to follow the code of practice may make it difficult to show this.

Regulations

7.   The Act also provides power to make regulations about price indications and you should ensure that your price indications comply with any such regulations. There are none at present.

Other legislation

8.   This code deals only with the requirements of Part III of the Consumer Protection Act 1987. In some sectors there will be other relevant legislation.

For example, price indications about credit terms must comply with the Consumer Credit Act 1974 and the regulations made under it, as well as with the Consumer Protection Act 1987.

Definitions

In this code:

Accommodation includes hotel and other holiday accommodation and new homes for sale freehold or on a lease of over 21 years but does not include rented homes.

Consumer means anyone who might want the goods, services, accommodation or facilities, other than for business use.

Price means both the total amount the consumer will have to pay to get the goods, services, accommodation or facilities and any method which has been or will be used to calculate that amount.

Price comparison means any indication given to consumers that the price at which something is offered to consumers is less than or equal to some other price.

Product means goods, services, accommodation and facilities (but not credit facilities, except where otherwise specified).

Services and Facilities means any services or facilities whatever (including credit, banking and insurance services, purchase or sale of foreign currency, supply of electricity, off-street car parking and caravan sites) *except* those provided by a person who is an authorised person or appointed representative under the Financial Services Act 1986 in the course of an investment business, services provided by an employee to his employer and facilities for a caravan which is the occupier's main or only home.

Shop means any shop, store, stall or other place (including a vehicle or the consumer's home) at which goods, services, accommodation or facilities are offered to consumers.

Trader means anyone (retailers, manufacturers, agents, service providers and others) who is acting in the course of a business.

PART 1: PRICE COMPARISONS

1.1 Price comparisons generally

1.1.1 Always make the meaning of price indications clear. Do not leave consumers to guess whether or not a price comparison is being made. If no price comparison is intended, do not use words or phrases which, in their normal, everyday use and in the context in which they are used, are likely to give your customers the impression that a price comparison is being made.

1.1.2 Price comparisons should always state the higher price as well as the price you intend to charge for the product (goods, services, accommodation or facilities). Do not make statements like "sale price £5" or "reduced to £39" without quoting the higher price to which they refer.

1.1.3 It should be clear what sort of price the higher price is. For example, comparisons with something described by words like "regular price", "usual price" or "normal price" should say whose regular, usual or normal price it is (eg "our normal price"). Descriptions like "reduced from" and crossed out higher prices should be used only if they refer to your own previous price.

Words should not be used in price indications other than with their normal everyday meanings.

1.1.4   Do not use initials or abbreviations to describe the higher price in a comparison, except for the initials "RRP" to describe a recommended retail price or the abbreviation "man. rec. price" to describe a manufacturer's recommended price (see paragraph 1.6.2 below).

1.1.5   Follow the part of the code (sections 1.2 to 1.6 as appropriate) which applies to the type of comparison you intend to make.

1.2   Comparisons with the trader's own previous price

General

1.2.1   In any comparison between your present selling price and another price at which you have in the past offered the product, you should state the previous price as well as the new lower price.

1.2.2   In any comparison with your own previous price:
- (a) the previous price should be the *last* price at which the product was available to consumers in the previous 6 months;
- (b) the product should have been available to consumers at that price for at least 28 consecutive days in the previous 6 months; and
- (c) the previous price should have applied (as above) for that period at the *same* shop where the reduced price is now being offered.

The 28 days at (b) above may include bank holidays, Sundays or other days of religious observance when the shop was closed; and up to 4 days when, for reasons beyond your control, the product was not available for supply. The product must not have been offered at a different price between that 28 day period and the day when the reduced price is first offered.

1.2.3   If the previous price in a comparison does not meet one or more of the conditions set out in paragraph 1.2.2 above:
- (i) the comparison should be fair and meaningful; and
- (ii) give a clear and positive explanation of the period for which and the circumstances in which that higher price applied.

For example "these goods were on sale here at the higher price from 1 February to 26 February" or "these goods were on sale at the higher price in 10 of our 95 stores only". Display the explanation clearly, and as prominently as the price indication. You should *not* use general disclaimers saying for example that the higher prices used in comparisons have not necessarily applied for 28 consecutive days.

Food, drink and perishable goods

1.2.4   For any food and drink, you need not give a positive explanation if the previous price in a comparison has not applied for 28 consecutive days, *provided* it was the last price at which the goods were on sale in the previous 6 months and applied in the same shop where the reduced price is now being offered. This also applies to non-food perishables, if they have a shelf-life of less than 6 weeks.

Catalogue and Mail order traders

1.2.5   Where products are sold only through a catalogue, advertisement or leaflet, any comparison with a previous price should be with the price in your own last catalogue, advertisement or leaflet. If you sell the same products both in shops and through catalogues etc, the previous price should be the last price at which you offered the product. You should also follow the guidance in paragraphs 1.2.2 (a) and (b). If your price comparison does not meet these conditions, you should follow the guidance in paragraph 1.2.3.

Making a series of reductions

1.2.6   If you advertise a price reduction and then want to reduce the price further during the same sale or special offer period, the intervening price (or prices) need not have applied for 28 days. In these circumstances unless you use a positive explanation (paragraph 1.2.3):
the highest price in the series must have applied for 28 consecutive days in the last 6 months at the same shop: and
you must show the highest price, the intervening price(s) and the current selling price (eg "£40, £20, £10, £5").

1.3   Introductory offers, after-sale or after-promotion prices

Introductory Offers

1.3.1   Do not call a promotion an introductory offer unless you intend to continue to offer the product for sale after the offer period is over and to do so at a higher price.
1.3.2   Do not allow an offer to run on so long that it becomes misleading to describe it as an introductory or other special offer. What is a reasonable period will depend on the circumstances (but, depending on the shelf-life of the product, it is likely to be a matter of weeks, not months). An offer is unlikely to be misleading if you state the date the offer will end and keep to it. If you then extend the offer period, make it clear that you have done so.

Quoting a future price

1.3.3   If you indicate an after-sale or after-promotion price, do so only if you are certain that, subject only to circumstances beyond your control, you will continue to offer identical products at that price for at least 28 days in the 3 months after the end of the offer period or after the offer stocks run out.
1.3.4   If you decide to quote a future price, write what you mean in full. Do not use initials to describe it (eg "ASP", "APP"). The description should be clearly and prominently displayed, with the price indication.

1.4   Comparisons with prices related to different circumstances
1.4.1   This section covers comparisons with prices:
(a) for different quantities (eg "15p each, 4 for 50p");
(b) for goods in a different condition (eg "seconds £20, when perfect £30");
(c) for a different availability (eg "price £50, price when ordered specially £60").

(d) for goods in a totally different state (eg "price in kit form £50, price ready-assembled £70"); or

(e) for special groups of people (eg "senior citizens' price £2.50, others £5").

General

1.4.2   Do not make such comparisons unless the product is available in the different quantity, conditions etc at the price you quote. Make clear to consumers the different circumstances which apply and show them prominently with the price indication. Do not use initials (eg "RAP" for "ready-assembled price") to describe the different circumstances, but write what you mean in full.

"When perfect" comparisons

1.4.3   If you do not have the perfect goods on sale in the same shop:

(a) follow section 1.2 if the "when perfect" price is your own previous price for the goods;

(b) follow section 1.5 if the "when perfect" price is another trader's price; or

(c) follow section 1.6 if the "when perfect" price is one recommended by the manufacturer or supplier.

Goods in a different state

1.4.4   Only make comparisons with goods in a totally different state if:

(a) a reasonable proportion (say a third (by quantity)) of your stock of those goods is readily available for sale to consumers in that different state (for example, ready assembled) at the quoted price and from the shop where the price comparison is made; *or*

(b) another trader is offering those goods in that state at the quoted price and you follow section 1.5 below.

Prices for special groups of people

1.4.5   If you want to compare different prices which you charge to different groups of people (eg one price for existing customers and another for new customers, or one price for people who are members of a named organisation (other than the trader) and another for those who are not), do not use words like "our normal" or "our regular" to describe the higher price, unless it applies to at least half your customers.

1.5   Comparisons with another trader's prices

1.5.1   Only compare your prices with another trader's price if:

(a) you know that his price which you quote is accurate and up-to-date;

(b) you give the name of the other trader clearly and prominently, with the price comparison;

(c) you identify the shop where the other trader's price applies, if that other trader is a retailer; and

(d) the other trader's price which you quote applies to the same products— or to substantially similar products and you state any differences clearly.

1.5.2 Do not make statements like "if you can buy this product elsewhere for less, we will refund the difference" about your "own brand" products which other traders do not stock, unless your offer will also apply to other traders' equivalent goods. If there are any conditions attached to the offer (eg it only applies to goods on sale in the same town) you should show them clearly and prominently, with the statement.

1.6 Comparisons with "Recommended Retail Price" or similar

General

1.6.1 This Section covers comparisons with recommended retail prices, manufacturers' recommended prices, suggested retail prices, suppliers' suggested retail prices and similar descriptions. It also covers prices given to cooperative and voluntary group organisations by their wholesalers or headquarters organisations.

1.6.2 Do not use initials or abbreviations to describe the higher price in a comparison *unless*:
  (a) you use the initials "RRP" to describe a recommended retail price; or
  (b) you use the abbreviation "man. rec. price" to describe a manufacturer's recommended price.
Write all other descriptions out in full and show them clearly and prominently with the price indication.

1.6.3 Do not use a recommended price in a comparison unless:
  (a) it has been recommended to you by the manufacturer or supplier as a price at which the product might be sold to consumers;
  (b) you deal with that manufacturer or supplier on normal commercial terms. (This will generally be the case for members of cooperative or voluntary group organisations in relation to their wholesalers or headquarters organisations); and
  (c) the price is not significantly higher than prices at which the product is generally sold at the time you first make that comparison.

1.7 Pre-printed prices
1.7.1 Make sure you pass on to consumers any reduction stated on the manufacturer's packaging (eg "flash packs" such as "10p off RRP").

1.7.2 You are making a price comparison if goods have a clearly visible price already printed on the packaging which is higher than the price you will charge for them. Such pre-printed prices are, in effect, recommended prices (except for retailers' own label goods) and you should follow paragraphs 1.6.1 to 1.6.4. You need not state that the price is a recommended price.

1.8 References to value or worth
1.8.1 Do not compare your prices with an amount described only as "worth" or "value".

1.8.2 Do not present general advertising slogans which refer to "value" or "worth" in a way which is likely to be seen by consumers as a price comparison.

1.9   Sales or special events

1.9.1   If you have bought in items specially for a sale, and you make this clear, you should not quote a higher price when indicating that they are special purchases. Otherwise, your price indications for individual items in the sale which are reduced should comply with section 1.1 of the code and whichever of sections 1.2 to 1.6 applies to the type of comparison you are making.

1.9.2   If you just have a general notice saying, for example, that all products are at "half marked price", the marked price on the individual items should be your own previous price and you should follow section 1.2 of the code.

1.9.3   Do not use general notices saying, eg "up to 50% off" unless the maximum reduction quoted applies to at least 10% (by quantity) of the range of products on offer.

1.10   Free offers

1.10.1   Make clear to consumers, at the time of the offer for sale, exactly what they will have to buy to get the "free offer".

1.10.2   If you give any indication of the monetary value of the "free offer", and that sum is not your own present price for the product, follow whichever of sections 1.2 to 1.6 covers the type of price it is.

1.10.3   If there are any conditions attached to the "free offer", give at least the main points of those conditions with the price indication and make clear to consumers where, before they are committed to buy, they can get full details of the conditions.

1.10.4   Do not claim that an offer is free if:
  (a) you have imposed additional charges that you would not normally make;
  (b) you have inflated the price of any product the consumer must buy or the incidental charges (for example, postage) the consumer must pay to get the "free offer"; or
  (c) you will reduce the price to consumers who do not take it up.

Part 2: Actual price to consumer

2.1   Indicating two different prices

2.1.1   The Consumer Protection Act makes it an offence to indicate a price for goods or services which is lower than the one that actually applies, for example, showing one price in an advertisement, window display, shelf marking or on the item itself, and then charging a higher price at the point of sale or checkout.

2.2   Incomplete information and non-optional extras

2.2.1   Make clear in your price indications the full price consumers will have to pay for the product. Some examples of how to do so in particular circumstances are set out below.

Limited availability of product

2.2.2 Where the price you are quoting for products only applies to a limited number of, say, orders, sizes or colours, you should make this clear in your price indication (eg "available in other colours or sizes at additional cost").

Prices relating to differing forms of products

2.2.3 If the price you are quoting for particular products does not apply to the products in the form they are displayed or advertised, say so clearly in your price indication. For example, advertisements for self-assembly furniture and the like should make it clear that the price refers to a kit of parts.

Postage, packing and delivery charges

2.2.4 If you sell by mail order, make clear any additional charges for postage, packing or delivery on the order form or similar document, so that consumers are fully aware of them before being committed to buying. Where you cannot determine these charges in advance, show clearly on the order form how they will be calculated (eg "Post Office rates apply"), or the place in the catalogue etc where the information is given.

2.2.5 If you sell goods from a shop and offer a delivery service for certain items, make it clear whether there are any separate delivery charges (eg for delivery outside a particular area) and what those charges are, before the consumer is committed to buying.

Value Added Tax

(i) Price indications to consumers
2.2.6 All price indications you give to private consumers, by whatever means, should include VAT.

(ii) Price indications to business customers
2.2.7 Prices may be indicated exclusive of VAT in shops where or advertisements from which most of your business is with business customers. If you also carry out business with private consumers at those shops or from those advertisements you should make clear that the prices exclude VAT and:
>　(i) display VAT-inclusive prices with equal prominence,
>　　or
>　(ii) display prominent statements that on top of the quoted price customers will also have to pay VAT at 15% (or the current rate).

(iii) Professional fees
2.2.8 Where you indicate a price (including estimates) for a professional fee, make clear what it covers. The price should generally include VAT. In cases where the fee is based on an as-yet-unknown sum of money (for example, the sale price of a house), either:
>　(i) quote a fee which includes VAT; or
>　(ii) make it clear that in additon to your fee the consumer would have to pay VAT at the current rate (eg "fee of $1\frac{1}{2}$% of purchase price, plus VAT at 15%).

Make sure that whichever method you choose is used for both estimates and final bills.

(iv) Building work

2.2.9 In estimates for building work, either include VAT in the price indication or indicate with equal prominence the amount or rate of VAT payable in addition to your basic figure. If you give a separate amount for VAT, make it clear that if any provisional sums in estimates vary then the amount of VAT payable would also vary.

Service, cover and minimum charges in hotels, restaurants and similar establishments

2.2.10 If your customers in hotels, restaurants or similar places must pay a non-optional extra charge, eg a "service charge":
  (i) incorporate the charge within fully inclusive prices wherever practicable; and
  (ii) display the fact clearly on any price list or priced menu, whether displayed inside or outside (eg by using statements like "all prices include service").
Do not include suggested optional sums, whether for service or any other item, in the bill presented to the customer.

2.2.11 It will not be practical to include some non-optional extra charges in a quoted price; for instance, if you make a flat charge per person or per table in a restaurant (often referred to as a "cover charge") or a minimum charge. In such cases the charge should be shown as prominently as other prices on any list or menu, whether displayed inside or outside.

Holiday and travel prices

2.2.12 If you offer a variety of prices to give consumers a choice, (for example, paying more or less for a holiday depending on the time of year or the standard of accommodation), make clear in your brochure—or any other price indication—what the basic price is and what it covers. Give details of any optional additional charges and what those charges cover, or of the place where this information can be found, clearly and close to the basic price.

2.2.13 Any non-optional extra charges which are for fixed amounts should be included in the basic price and not shown as additions, unless they are only payable by some consumers. In that case you should specify, near to the details of the basic price, either what the amounts are and the circumstances in which they are payable, or where in the brochure etc the information is given.

2.2.14 Details of non-optional extra charges which may vary, (such as holiday insurance) or of where in the brochure etc the information is given should be made clear to consumers near to the basic price.

2.2.15 If you reserve the right to increase prices after consumers have made their booking, state this clearly with all indications of prices, and include prominently in your brochure full information on the circumstances in which a surcharge is payable.

Ticket prices

2.2.16 If you sell tickets, whether for sporting events, cinema, theatre etc and your prices are higher than the regular price that would be charged to the public at the box office, ie higher than the "face value", you should make clear in any price indication what the "face value" of the ticket is.

Call-out charges

2.2.17 If you make a minimum call-out charge or other flat-rate charge (for example, for plumbing, gas or electrical appliance repairs etc carried out in consumers' homes), ensure that the consumer is made aware of the charge and whether the actual price may be higher (eg if work takes longer than a specific time) before being committed to using your services.

Credit facilities

2.2.18 Price indications about consumer credit should comply with the relevant requirements of regulations under the Consumer Credit Act 1974 governing the form and content of advertisements.

Insurance

2.2.19 Where actual premium rates for a particular consumer or the availability of insurance cover depend on an individual assessment, this should be made clear when any indication of the premium or the method of determining it is given to consumers.

PART 3: PRICE INDICATIONS WHICH BECOME MISLEADING AFTER
THEY HAVE BEEN GIVEN

3.1 General
3.1.1 The Consumer Protection Act makes it an offence to give a price indication which, although correct at the time, becomes misleading after you have given it, if:
      (i) consumers could reasonably be expected still to be relying on it; and
      (ii) you do not take reasonable steps to prevent them doing so.
Clearly it will not be necessary or even possible in many instances to inform all those who may have been given the misleading price indication. However, you should always make sure consumers are given the correct information before they are committed to buying a product and be prepared to cancel any transaction which a consumer has entered into on the basis of a price indication which has become misleading.

3.1.2 Do not give price indications which you know or intend will only apply for a limited period, without making this fact clear in the advertisement or price indication.

3.1.3 The following paragraphs set out what you should do in some particular circumstances.

3.2   Newspaper and magazine advertisements

3.2.1   If the advertisement does not say otherwise, the price indication should apply for a reasonable period (as a general guide, at least 7 days or until the next issue of the newspaper or magazine in which the advertisement was published, whichever is longer). If the price indication becomes misleading within this period make sure consumers are given the correct information before they are committed to buying the product.

3.3   Mail order advertisements, catalogues and leaflets

3.3.1   Paragraph 3.2.1 above also applies to the time for which price indications in mail order advertisements and in regularly published catalogues or brochures should apply. If a price indication becomes misleading within this period, make the correct price indication clear to anyone who orders the product to which it relates. Do so before the consumer is committed to buying the product and, wherever practicable, before the goods are sent to the consumer.

3.4   Selling through agents

Holiday brochures and travel agents

3.4.1   Surcharges are covered in paragraph 2.2.15. If a price indication becomes misleading for any other reason, tour operators who sell direct to consumers should follow paragraph 3.3.1 above; and tour operators who sell through travel agents should follow paragraphs 3.4.2 and 3.4.3 below.

3.4.2   If a price indication becomes misleading while your brochure is still current, make this clear to the travel agents to whom you distributed the brochure. Be prepared to cancel any holiday bookings consumers have made on the basis of a misleading price indication.

3.4.3   In the circumstances set out in paragraph 3.4.2, travel agents should ensure that the correct price indication is made clear to consumers before they make a booking.

Insurance and independent intermediaries

3.4.4   Insurers who sell their products through agents or independent intermediaries should take all reasonable steps to ensure that all such agents who are known to hold information on the insurer's premium rates and terms of the cover provided are told clearly of any changes in those rates or terms.

3.4.5   Agents, independent intermediaries and providers of quotation systems should ensure that they act on changes notified to them by an insurer.

3.5   Changes in the rate of value added tax

3.5.1   If your price indications become misleading because of a change in the general rate of VAT, or other taxes paid at point of sale, make the correct price indication clear to any consumers who order products. Do so before the consumer is committed to buying the product and, wherever practicable, before the goods are sent to the consumer.

PART 4: SALE OF NEW HOMES

4.1 A "new home" is any building, or part of a building to be used only as a private dwelling which is either:
  (i) a newly-built house or flat, or
  (ii) a newly-converted existing building which has not previously been used in that form as a private home.

4.2 The Consumer Protection Act and this code apply to new homes which are either for sale freehold or covered by a long lease, ie with more than 21 years to run. In this context the term "trader" covers not only a business vendor, such as a developer, but also an estate agent acting on behalf of such a vendor.

4.3 You should follow the relevant provision of Part 1 of the code if:
  (i) you want to make a comparison between the price at which you offer new homes for sale and any other price;
  (ii) you offer an inclusive price for new homes which also covers such items as furnishings, domestic appliances and insurance and you compare their value with, for example, High Street prices for similar items.

4.4 Part 2 of the code gives details of the provisions you should follow if:
  (i) the new houses you are selling, or any goods or services which apply to them, are only available in limited numbers or range;
  (ii) the sale price you give does not apply to the houses as displayed; or
  (iii) there are additional non-optional charges payable.

The Consumer Credit (Exempt Agreements) Order 1989[1]

(S.I. 1989 No. 869)

Citation, commencement, interpretation and revocation

1.—(1) This Order may be cited as the Consumer Credit (Exempt Agreements) Order 1989 and shall come into force on 19th June 1989.

(2) In this Order—

"the Act" means the Consumer Credit Act 1974;

"business premises" means premises for occupation for the purposes of a business (including any activity carried on by a body of persons, whether corporate or unincorporate) or for those and other purposes;

and references to the total charge for credit and the rate thereof are respectively references to the total charge for credit and the rate thereof calculated in accordance with the Consumer Credit (Total Charge for Credit) Regulations 1980.

(3) The Orders specified in Schedule 2 to this Order are hereby revoked.

Exemption of certain consumer credit agreements secured on land

2.—(1) The Act shall not regulate a consumer credit agreement which falls within section 16(2) of the Act, being an agreement to which this paragraph applies.

(2) Where the creditor is a body specified in Part I of Schedule 1 to this Order, or a building society authorised under the Building Societies Act 1986, or an authorised institution under the Banking Act 1987 or a wholly-owned subsidiary of such an institution, paragraph (1) above applies only to—

    (a) a debtor-creditor-supplier agreement falling within section 16(2)(a) or (c) of the Act;

    (b) a debtor-creditor agreement secured by any land mortgage to finance—

        (i) the purchase of land; or

        (ii) the provision of dwellings or business premises on any land; or

        (iii) subject to paragraph (3) below, the alteration, enlarging, repair or improvement of a dwelling or business premises on any land;

    (c) a debtor-creditor agreement secured by any land mortgage to refinance any existing indebtedness of the debtor, whether to the creditor or another person, under any agreement by which the debtor was provided with credit for any of the purposes specified in heads (i) to (iii) of sub-paragraph (b) above.

(3) Head (iii) of sub-paragraph (b) of paragraph (2) above applies only—

    (i) where the creditor is the creditor under—

    (a) an agreement (whenever made) by which the debtor is provided with credit for any of the purposes specified in head (i) and head (ii) of that sub-paragraph; or

---

[1] Made in exercise of the powers conferred by the Consumer Credit Act 1974, ss. 16(1), (4)–(6) and 182(2), (4).

This Order is printed incorporating amendments up to the Consumer Credit (Exempt Agreements) (Amendment) Order 1995 (S.I. 1995 No. 1250).

(b) an agreement (whenever made) refinancing an agreement under which the debtor is provided with credit for any of the said purposes,
being, in either case, an agreement relating to the land referred to in the said head (iii) and secured by a land mortgage on that land; or

    (ii) where a debtor-creditor agreement to finance the alteration, enlarging, repair or improvement of a dwelling, secured by a land mortgage on that dwelling, is made as a result of any such services as are described in section 4(3)(e) of the Housing Associations Act 1985 which are certified as having been provided by—

(a) a local authority;

(b) a housing association within the meaning of section 1 of the Housing Associations Act 1985 or Article 3 of the Housing (Northern Ireland) Order 1992;

(c) a body established by such a housing association for the purpose of providing such services as are described in the said section 4(3)(e);

(d) a charity;

(e) the National Home Improvement Council; or

(f) the Northern Ireland Housing Executive.

(g) a body, or a body of any description, that has been approved by the Secretary of State under section 169(4)(c) of the Local Government and Housing Act 1989 or the Department of the Environment for Northern Ireland under article 103(4)(c) of the Housing (Northern Ireland) Order 1992.

(4) Where the creditor is a body specified in Part II of Schedule 1 to this Order, paragraph (1) above applies only to an agreement of a description specified in that Part in relation to that body and made pursuant to an enactment or for a purpose so specified.

(5) Where the creditor is a body specified in Part III of Schedule 1 to this Order, paragraph (1) above applies only to an agreement of a description falling within Article 2(2)(a) to (c) above, being an agreement advancing money on the security of a dwelling-house.

Exemption of certain consumer credit agreements by reference to the number of payments to be made by the debtor

3.—(1) The Act shall not regulate a consumer credit agreement which is an agreement of one of the following descriptions, that is to say—

(a) a debtor-creditor-supplier agreement being either—

    (i) an agreement for fixed-sum credit under which the total number of payments to be made by the debtor does not exceed four, and those payments are required to be made within a period not exceeding 12 months beginning with the date of the agreement; or

    (ii) an agreement for running-account credit which provides for the making of payments by the debtor in relation to specified periods and requires that the number of payments to be made by the debtor in repayment of the whole amount of the credit provided in each such period shall not exceed one;

not being, in either case, an agreement of a description specified in paragraph (2) below; and in this sub-paragraph, "payment" means a payment comprising an amount in respect of credit with or without any other amount;

(b) a debtor-creditor-supplier agreement financing the purchase of land being an agreement under which the number of payments to be made by the debtor does not exceed four; and in this sub-paragraph, "payment" means a payment comprising or including an amount in respect of credit or the total charge for credit (if any);

(c) a debtor-creditor-supplier agreement for fixed-sum credit to finance a premium under a contract of insurance relating to any land or to anything thereon where—

    (i) the creditor is the creditor under an agreement secured by a land mortgage on that land which either is an exempt agreement by virtue of section 16(1) of the Act or of article 2 above, or is a personal credit agreement which would be an exempt agreement by virtue of either of those provisions if the credit provided were not to exceed £15,000;

    (ii) the amount of the credit is to be repaid within the period to which the premium relates, not being a period exceeding 12 months; and

    (iii) there is no charge forming part of the total charge for credit under the agreement other than interest at a rate not exceeding the rate of interest from time to time payable under the agreement mentioned in head (i) above,

and the number of payments to be made by the debtor does not exceed twelve; and in this sub-paragraph "payment" has the same meaning as it has in paragraph (1)(b) above; and

(d) a debtor-creditor-supplier agreement for fixed-sum credit where—

    (i) the creditor is the creditor under an agreement secured by a land mortgage on any land which either is an exempt agreement by virtue of section 16(1) of the Act or of article 2 above, or is a personal credit agreement which would be an exempt agreement by virtue of either of those provisions if the credit provided were not to exceed £15,000;

    (ii) the agreement is to finance a premium under a contract of life insurance which provides, in the event of the death before the credit under the agreement referred to in head (i) above has been repaid of the person on whose life the contract is effected, for payment of a sum not exceeding the amount sufficient to defray the sums which, immediately after that credit has been advanced, would be payable to the creditor in respect of that credit and of the total charge for that credit; and

    (iii) there is no charge forming part of the total charge for credit under the agreement other than interest at a rate not exceeding the rate of interest from time to time payable under the agreement referred to in head (i) above,

and the number of payments to be made by the debtor does not exceed twelve; and in this sub-paragraph, "payment" has the same meaning as it has in sub-paragraph (1)(b) above.

(2) The descriptions of agreement referred to in sub-paragraph (a) of paragraph (1) above and to which accordingly that sub-paragraph does not apply are—

(a) agreements financing the purchase of land;

(b) agreements which are conditional sale agreements or hire-purchase agreements; and

(c) agreements secured by a pledge (other than a pledge of documents of title or of bearer bonds).

Exemption of certain consumer credit agreements by reference to the rate of the total charge for credit

4.—(1) The Act shall not regulate a consumer credit agreement which is an agreement of one of the following descriptions, that is to say—

(a) subject to paragraphs (2), (3) and (4) below, any debtor-creditor agreement in respect of which the rate of the total charge for credit does not exceed the rate referred to in paragraph (5) below;

(b) subject to paragraph (4) below, a debtor-creditor-supplier agreement for fixed-sum credit where—

(i) the creditor is the creditor under an agreement secured by a land mortgage on any land which either is an exempt agreement by virtue of section 16(1) of the Act or of article 2 above, or is a personal credit agreement which would be an exempt agreement by virtue of either of those provisions if the credit provided were not to exceed £15,000;

(ii) the agreement is to finance a premium under a contract of life insurance which provides, in the event of the death before the credit under the agreement referred to in head (i) above has been repaid of the person on whose life the contract is effected, for payment of a sum not exceeding the amount sufficient to defray the sums which, immediately after that credit has been advanced, would be payable to the creditor in respect of that credit and of the total charge for that credit; and

(iii) there is no charge forming part of the total charge for credit under the agreement other than interest at a rate not exceeding the rate of interest from time to time payable under the agreement referred to in head (i) above,

and in respect of which the rate of the total charge for credit does not exceed the rate referred to in paragraph (5) below;

(c) subject to paragraph (4) below, a debtor-creditor agreement in respect of which the only amount included in the total charge for credit is interest which cannot under the agreement at any time exceed the higher of the following, that is to say—

(i) the sum of one per cent and the highest of any base rates published by the banks named in paragraph (6) below, being the latest rates in operation on the date 28 days before any such time; and

(ii) 13 per cent;

and for the purposes of this sub-paragraph, "interest" means interest at a rate determined in accordance with the formula set out in paragraph (1) of regulation 7 of the Consumer Credit (Total Charge for Credit) Regulations 1980, and in that formula as applied by this paragraph "period rate of charge" has the meaning assigned to it in paragraph (2) of that regulation.

(2) Subject to paragraph (3) below, sub-paragraph (a) of paragraph (1) above does not apply to agreements which provide for an increase in, or permit the creditor to increase, the rate or amount of any item which—

(a) is included in the total charge for credit; or

(b) would fall to be so included, apart from the operation of regulation 15 of the Consumer Credit (Total Charge for Credit) Regulations 1980,

after the relevant date of the agreement within the meaning of regulation 1(2) of those Regulations.

(3) Sub-paragraph (a) of paragraph (1) above does apply to agreements—

(a) in relation to which the debtor, or any one of two or more debtors where each debtor is a relative of the other debtor or of one of the other debtors, is an employee of the creditor or of an associate of his and which provide for an increase in, or permit the creditor to increase, the rate or amount of any item such as is mentioned in paragraph (2) above on the termination of such employment with the creditor or such associate, as the case may be; or

(b) under which the rate or amount of any such item falls to be ascertained throughout the duration of the agreement by reference to the level of any index or other factor in accordance with any formula specified in the agreement;

and which do not provide for an increase in, or permit the creditor to increase, the rate or amount of any item mentioned in paragraph (2) above in any way other than those permitted by either or both of sub-paragraphs (a) or (b) of this paragraph.

(4) Paragraph (1) above does not apply to agreements under which the total amount to be repaid by the debtor to discharge his indebtedness in respect of the amount of credit provided may vary according to any formula specified in the agreement having effect by reference to movements in the level of any index or to any other factor.

(5) The rate mentioned in sub-paragraphs (a) and (b) of paragraph (1) above is the higher of the following, that is to say—

(a) the sum of one per cent and the highest of any base rates published by the banks named in paragraph (6) below, being the latest rates in operation on the date 28 days before the date on which the agreement is made; and

(b) 13 per cent.

(6) The banks referred to in paragraphs (1)(c) and (5)(a) above are—

Bank of England
Bank of Scotland
Barclays Bank PLC
Clydesdale Bank PLC
Co-operative Bank Public Limited Company
Coutts & Co.
Lloyds Bank PLC
Midland Bank Public Limited Company
National Westminster Bank Public Limited Company
The Royal Bank of Scotland p.l.c.
TSB Bank PLC

Exemption of certain consumer credit agreements having a connection with a country outside the United Kingdom

5. The Act shall not regulate a consumer credit agreement made—

(a) in connection with trade in goods or services between the United Kingdom and a country outside the United Kingdom or within a country or between countries outside the United Kingdom, being an agreement under which credit is provided to the debtor in the course of a business carried on by him; or

(b) between a creditor listed in Part IV of Schedule 1 to this Order and a debtor who is—

(i) a member of any of the armed forces of the United States of America;

(ii) an employee not habitually resident in the United Kingdom of any of those forces; or

(iii) any such member's or employee's wife or husband or any other person (whether or not a child of his) whom he wholly or partly maintains and treats as a child of the family.

Exemption of certain consumer hire agreements

6. The Act shall not regulate a consumer hire agreement where the owner is a body corporate authorised by or under any enactment to supply gas, electricity or water and the subject of the agreement is a meter or metering equipment used or to be used in connection with the supply of gas, electricity or water, as the case may be.[2]

---

[2] Schedule 1 (listing bodies whose agreements of the specified description are exempt agreements) and Schedule 2 (Orders revoked) are both omitted.

The Property Misdescriptions (Specified Matters) Order 1992

(S.I. 1992 No. 2834)[1]

1. This Order may be cited as the Property Misdescriptions (Specified Matters) Order 1992 and shall come into force on 4th April 1993.

2. The matters contained in the Schedule to this Order are hereby specified to the extent described in that Schedule for the purposes of section 1(1) of the Property Misdescriptions Act 1991.

SCHEDULE

SPECIFIED MATTERS

1. Location or address.

2. Aspect, view, outlook or environment.

3. Availability and nature of services, facilities or amenities.

4. Proximity to any services, places, facilities or amenities.

5. Accommodation, measurements or sizes.

6. Fixtures and fittings.

7. Physical or structural characteristics, form of construction or condition.

8. Fitness for any purpose or strength of any buildings or other structures on land or of land itself.

9. Treatments, processes, repairs or improvements or the effects thereof.

10. Conformity or compliance with any scheme, standard, test or regulations or the existence of any guarantee.

11. Survey, inspection, investigation, valuation or appraisal by any person or the results thereof.

12. The grant or giving of any award or prize for design or construction.

13. History, including the age, ownership or use of land or any building or fixture and the date of any alterations thereto.

14. Person by whom any building, (or part of any building), fixture or component was designed, constructed, built, produced, treated, processed, repaired, reconditioned or tested.

15. The length of time during which land has been available for sale either generally or by or through a particular person.

16. Price (other than the price at which accommodation or facilities are

---

[1] Made in exercise of the powers conferred by the Property Misdescriptions Act 1991, s. 1, printed above at p. 261.

available and are to be provided by means of the creation or disposal of an interest in land in the circumstances specified in section 23(1)(a) and (b) of the Consumer Protection Act 1987 or Article 16(1)(a) and (b) of the Consumer Protection (NI) Order 1987 (which relate to the creation or disposal of certain interests in new dwellings)) and previous price.

17. Tenure or estate.

18. Length of any lease or of the unexpired term of any lease and the terms and conditions of a lease (and, in relation to land in Northern Ireland, any fee farm grant creating the relation of landlord and tenant shall be treated as a lease).

19. Amount of any ground-rent, rent or premium and frequency of any review.

20. Amount of any rent-charge.

21. Where all or any part of any land is let to a tenant or is subject to a licence, particulars of the tenancy or licence, including any rent, premium or other payment due and frequency of any review.

22. Amount of any service or maintenance charge or liability for common repairs.

23. Council tax payable in respect of a dwelling within the meaning of section 3, or in Scotland section 72, of the Local Government Finance Act 1992 or the basis or any part of the basis on which that tax is calculated.

24. Rates payable in respect of a non-domestic hereditament within the meaning of section 64 of the Local Government Finance Act 1988 or, in Scotland, in respect of lands and heritages shown on a valuation roll or the basis or any part of the basis on which those rates are calculated.

25. Rates payable in respect of a hereditament within the meaning of the Rates (Northern Ireland) Order 1977 or the basis or any part of the basis on which those rates are calculated.

26. Existence or nature of any planning permission or proposals for development, construction or change of use.

27. In relation to land in England and Wales, the passing or rejection of any plans of proposed building work in accordance with section 16 of the Building Act 1984 and the giving of any completion certificate in accordance with regulation 15 of the Building Regulations 1991.

28. In relation to land in Scotland, the granting of a warrant under section 6 of the Building (Scotland) Act 1959 or the granting of a certificate of completion under section 9 of that Act.

29. In relation to land in Northern Ireland, the passing or rejection of any plans of proposed building work in accordance with Article 13 of the Building Regulations (Northern Ireland) Order 1979 and the giving of any completion certificate in accordance with building regulations made under that Order.

30. Application of any statutory provision which restricts the use of land or which requires it to be preserved or maintained in a specified manner.

31. Existence or nature of any restrictive covenants, or of any restrictions on resale, restrictions on use, or pre-emption rights and, in relation to land in Scotland, (in addition to the matters mentioned previously in this paragraph) the existence or nature of any reservations or real conditions.

32.   Easements, servitudes or wayleaves.

33.   Existence and extent of any public or private right of way.

The Package Travel, Package Holidays and Package Tours Regulations 1992

(S.I. 1992 No. 3282)[1]

Citation and commencement

1. These Regulations may be cited as the Package Travel, Package Holidays and Package Tours Regulations 1992 and shall come into force on the day after the day on which they are made.[2]

Interpretation

2.—(1) In these Regulations—

"brochure" means any brochure in which packages are offered for sale;

"contract" means the agreement linking the consumer to the organiser or to the retailer, or to both, as the case may be;

"the Directive" means Council Directive 90/314/EEC on package travel, package holidays and package tours;

"member State" means a member State of the European Community or another State in the European Economic Area;

"offer" includes an invitation to treat whether by means of advertising or otherwise, and cognate expressions shall be construed accordingly;

"organiser" means the person who, otherwise than occasionally, organises packages and sells or offers them for sale, whether directly or through a retailer;

"the other party to the contract" means the party, other than the consumer, to the contract, that is, the organiser or the retailer, or both, as the case may be;

"package" means the pre-arranged combination of at least two of the following components when sold or offered for sale at an inclusive price and when the service covers a period of more than twenty-four hours or includes overnight accommodation:—

    (a) transport;

    (b) accommodation;

    (c) other tourist services not ancillary to transport or accommodation and accounting for a significant proportion of the package,

and

    (i) the submission of separate accounts for different components shall not cause the arrangements to be other than a package;

    (ii) the fact that a combination is arranged at the request of the consumer and in accordance with his specific instructions (whether modified or not) shall not of itself cause it to be treated as other than pre-arranged;

and

"retailer" means the person who sells or offers for sale the package put together by the organiser.

(2) In the definition of "contract" in paragraph (1) above, "consumer"

---

[1] Made in exercise of the powers conferred by the European Communities Act 1972, s. 2(2).

   These Regulations implement Council Directive 90/314/EEC, printed below at p. 356.

[2] The Regulations came into force on December 23, 1992.

means the person who takes or agrees to take the package ("the principal contractor") and elsewhere in these Regulations "consumer" means, as the context requires, the principal contractor, any person on whose behalf the principal contractor agrees to purchase the package ("the other beneficiaries") or any person to whom the principal contractor or any of the other beneficiaries transfers the package ("the transferee").

Application of Regulations

3.—(1) These Regulations apply to packages sold or offered for sale in the territory of the United Kingdom.

(2) Regulations 4 to 15 apply to packages so sold or offered for sale on or after 31st December 1992.

(3) Regulations 16 to 22 apply to contracts which, in whole or part, remain to be performed on 31st December 1992

Descriptive matter relating to packages must not be misleading

4.—(1) No organiser or retailer shall supply to a consumer any descriptive matter concerning a package, the price of a package or any other conditions applying to the contract which contains any misleading information.

(2) If an organiser or retailer is in breach of paragraph (1) he shall be liable to compensate the consumer for any loss which the consumer suffers in consequence.

Requirements as to brochures

5.—(1) Subject to paragraph (4) below, no organiser shall make available a brochure to a possible consumer unless it indicates in a legible, comprehensible and accurate manner the price and adequate information about the matters specified in Schedule 1 to these Regulations in respect of the packages offered for sale in the brochure to the extent that those matters are relevant to the packages so offered.

(2) Subject to paragraph (4) below, no retailer shall make available to a possible consumer a brochure which he knows or has reasonable cause to believe does not comply with the requirements of paragraph (1).

(3) An organiser who contravenes paragraph (1) of this regulation and a retailer who contravenes paragraph (2) thereof shall be guilty of an offence and liable:—

  (a) on summary conviction, to a fine not exceeding level 5 on the standard scale;
      and
  (b) on conviction on indictment, to a fine.

(4) Where a brochure was first made available to consumers generally before 31st December 1992 no liability shall arise under this regulation in respect of an identical brochure being made available to a consumer at any time.

Circumstances in which particulars in brochure are to be binding

6.—(1) Subject to paragraphs (2) and (3) of this regulation, the particulars in the brochure (whether or not they are required by regulation 5(1) above to be included in the brochure) shall constitute implied warranties (or, as regards Scotland, implied terms) for the purposes of any contract to which the particulars relate.

(2) Paragraph (1) of this regulation does not apply—

(a) in relation to information required to be included by virtue of paragraph 9 of Schedule 1 to these Regulations; or

(b) where the brochure contains an express statement that changes may be made in the particulars contained in it before a contract is concluded and changes in the particulars so contained are clearly communicated to the consumer before a contract is concluded.

(3) Paragraph (1) of this regulation does not apply when the consumer and the other party to the contract agree after the contract has been made that the particulars in the brochure, or some of those particulars, should not form part of the contract.

Information to be provided before contract is concluded

7.—(1) Before a contract is concluded, the other party to the contract shall provide the intending consumer with the information specified in paragraph (2) below in writing or in some other appropriate form.

(2) The information referred to in paragraph (1) is:—

(a) general information about passport and visa requirements which apply to British Citizens who purchase the package in question, including information about the length of time it is likely to take to obtain the appropriate passports and visas;

(b) information about health formalities required for the journey and the stay; and

(c) the arrangements for security for the money paid over and (where applicable) for the repatriation of the consumer in the event of insolvency.

(3) If the intending consumer is not provided with the information required by paragraph (1) in accordance with that paragraph the other party to the contract shall be guilty of an offence and liable:—

(a) on summary conviction, to a fine not exceeding level 5 on the standard scale; and

(b) on conviction on indictment, to a fine.

Information to be provided in good time

8.—(1) The other party to the contract shall in good time before the start of the journey provide the consumer with the information specified in paragraph (2) below in writing or in some other appropriate form.

(2) The information referred to in paragraph (1) is the following:—

(a) the times and places of intermediate stops and transport connections and particulars of the place to be occupied by the traveller (for example, cabin or berth on ship, sleeper compartment on train);

(b) the name, address and telephone number—

(i) of the representative of the other party to the contract in the locality where the consumer is to stay,

or, if there is no such representative,

(ii) of an agency in that locality on whose assistance a consumer in difficulty would be able to call,

or, if there is no such representative or agency, a telephone number or other information which will enable the consumer to contact the other party to the contract during the stay; and

(c) in the case of a journey or stay abroad by a child under the age of 16 on the day when the journey or stay is due to start, information enabling direct contact to be made with the child or the person responsible at the place where he is to stay; and

(d) except where the consumer is required as a term of the contract to take out an insurance policy in order to cover the cost of cancellation by the consumer or the cost of assistance, including repatriation, in the event of accident or illness, information about an insurance policy which the consumer may, if he wishes, take out in respect of the risk of those costs being incurred.

(3) If the consumer is not provided with the information required by paragraph (1) in accordance with that paragraph the other party to the contract shall be guilty of an offence and liable:—

(a) on summary conviction, to a fine not exceeding level 5 on the standard scale; and

(b) on conviction on indictment, to a fine.

Contents and form of contract

9.—(1) The other party to the contract shall ensure that—

(a) depending on the nature of the package being purchased, the contract contains at least the elements specified in Schedule 2 to these Regulations;

(b) subject to paragraph (2) below, all the terms of the contract are set out in writing or such other form as is comprehensible and accessible to the consumer and are communicated to the consumer before the contract is made; and

(c) a written copy of these terms is supplied to the consumer.

(2) Paragraph (1)(b) above does not apply when the interval between the time when the consumer approaches the other party to the contract with a view to entering into a contract and the time of departure under the proposed contract is so short that it is impracticable to comply with the sub-paragraph.

(3) It is an implied condition (or, as regards Scotland, and implied term) of the contract that the other party to the contract complies with the provisions of paragraph (1).

(4) In Scotland, any breach of the condition implied by paragraph (3) above shall be deemed to be a material breach justifying rescission of the contract.

Transfer of bookings

10.—(1) In every contract there is an implied term that where the consumer is prevented from proceeding with the package the consumer may transfer his booking to a person who satisfies all the conditions applicable to the package, provided that the consumer gives reasonable notice to the other party to the contract of his intention to transfer before the date when departure is due to take place.

(2) Where a transfer is made in accordance with the implied term set out in paragraph (1) above, the transferor and the transferee shall be jointly and severally liable to the other party to the contract for payment of the price of the package (or, if part of the price has been paid, for payment of the balance) and for any additional costs arising from such transfer.

Price revision

11.—(1) Any term in a contract to the effect that the prices laid down in the contract may be revised shall be void and of no effect unless the contract provides for the possibility of upward or downward revision and satisfies the conditions laid down in paragraph (2) below.

(2) The conditions mentioned in paragraph (1) are that—

    (a) the contract states precisely how the revised price is to be calculated;

    (b) the contract provides that price revisions are to be made solely to allow for variations in:—

        (i) transportation costs, including the cost of fuel,

        (ii) dues, taxes or fees chargeable for services such as landing taxes or embarkation or disembarkation fees at ports and airports, or

        (iii) the exchange rates applied to the particular package; and

(3) Notwithstanding any terms of a contract,

        (i) no price increase may be made in a specified period which may not be less than 30 days before the departure date stipulated; and

        (ii) as against an individual consumer liable under the contract, no price increase may be made in respect of variations which would produce an increase of less than 2%, or such greater percentage as the contract may specify, (''non-eligible variations'') and that the non-eligible variations shall be left out of account in the calculation.

Significant alterations to essential terms

12. In every contract there are implied terms to the effect that—

    (a) where the organiser is constrained before the departure to alter significantly an essential term of the contract, such as the price (so far as regulation 11 permits him to do so), he will notify the consumer as quickly as possible in order to enable him to take appropriate decisions and in particular to withdraw from the contract without penalty or to accept a rider to the contract specifying the alterations made and their impact on the price; and

    (b) the consumer will inform the organiser or the retailer of his decision as soon as possible.

Withdrawal by consumer pursuant to regulation 12 and cancellation by organiser

13.—(1) The terms set out in paragraphs (2) and (3) below are implied in every contract and apply where the consumer withdraws from the contract pursuant to the term in it implied by virtue of regulation 12(a), or where the organiser, for any reason other than the fault of the consumer, cancels the package before the agreed date of departure.

(2) The consumer is entitled—

    (a) to take a substitute package of equivalent or superior quality if the other party to the contract is able to offer him such a substitute; or

    (b) to take a substitute package of lower quality if the other party to the contract is able to offer him one and to recover from the organiser the difference in price between the price of the package purchased and that of the substitute package; or

    (c) to have repaid to him as soon as possible all the monies paid by him under the contract.

(3) The consumer is entitled, if appropriate, to be compensated by the organiser for non-performance of the contract except where—

    (a) the package is cancelled because the number of persons who agree to take it is less than the minimum number required and the consumer is informed of the cancellation, in writing, within the period indicated in the description of the package; or

(b) the package is cancelled by reason of unusual and unforeseeable circumstances beyond the control of the party by whom this exception is pleaded, the consequences of which could not have been avoided even if all due care had been exercised.

(4) Overbooking shall not be regarded as a circumstance falling within the provisions of sub-paragraph (b) of paragraph (3) above.

Significant proportion of services not provided

14.—(1) The terms set out in paragraphs (2) and (3) below are implied in every contract and apply where, after departure, a significant proportion of the services contracted for is not provided or the organiser becomes aware that he will be unable to procure a significant proportion of the services to be provided.

(2) The organiser will make suitable alternative arrangements, at no extra cost to the consumer, for the continuation of the package and will, where appropriate, compensate the consumer for the difference between the services to be supplied under the contract and those supplied.

(3) If it is impossible to make arrangements as described in paragraph (2), or these are not accepted by the consumer for good reasons, the organiser will, where appropriate, provide the consumer with equivalent transport back to the place of departure or to another place to which the consumer has agreed and will, where appropriate, compensate the consumer.

Liability of other party to the contract for proper performance of obligations under contract

15.—(1) The other party to the contract is liable to the consumer for the proper performance of the obligations under the contract, irrespective of whether such obligations are to be performed by that other party or by other suppliers of services but this shall not affect any remedy or right of action which that other party may have against those other suppliers of services.

(2) The other party to the contract is liable to the consumer for any damage caused to him by the failure to perform the contract or the improper performance of the contract unless the failure or the improper performance is due neither to any fault of that other party nor to that of another supplier of services, because—

(a) the failures which occur in the performance of the contract are attributable to the consumer;

(b) such failures are attributable to a third party unconnected with the provision of the services contracted for, and are unforeseeable or unavoidable; or

(c) such failures are due to—

(i) unusual and unforeseeable circumstances beyond the control of the party by whom this exception is pleaded, the consequences of which could not have been avoided even if all due care had been exercised; or

(ii) an event which the other party to the contract or the supplier of services, even with all due care, could not foresee or forestall.

(3) In the case of damage arising from the non-performance or improper performance of the services involved in the package, the contract may provide for compensation to be limited in accordance with the international conventions which govern such services.

(4) In the case of damage other than personal injury resulting from the non-performance or improper performance of the services involved in the package, the contract may include a term limiting the amount of compensation which will be paid to the consumer, provided that the limitation is not unreasonable.

(5) Without prejudice to paragraph (3) and paragraph (4) above, liability under paragraphs (1) and (2) above cannot be excluded by any contractual term.

(6) The terms set out in paragraphs (7) and (8) below are implied in every contract.

(7) In the circumstances described in paragraph (2)(b) and (c) of this regulation, the other party to the contract will give prompt assistance to a consumer in difficulty.

(8) If the consumer complains about a defect in the performance of the contract, the other party to the contract, or his local representative, if there is one, will make prompt efforts to find appropriate solutions.

(9) The contract must clearly and explicitly oblige the consumer to communicate at the earliest opportunity, in writing or any other appropriate form, to the supplier of the services concerned and to the other party to the contract any failure which he perceives at the place where the services concerned are supplied.

Security in event of insolvency—requirements and offences

16.—(1) The other party to the contract shall at all times be able to provide sufficient evidence of security for the refund of money paid over and for the repatriation of the consumer in the event of insolvency.

(2) Without prejudice to paragraph (1) above, and subject to paragraph (4) below, save to the extent that—

    (a) the package is covered by measures adopted or retained by the member State where he is established for the purpose of implementing Article 7 of the Directive; or

    (b) the package is one in respect of which he is required to hold a licence under the Civil Aviation (Air Travel Organisers' Licensing) Regulations 1972 or the package is one that is covered by the arrangements he has entered into for the purposes of those Regulations,

the other party to the contract shall at least ensure that there are in force arrangements as described in regulations 17, 18, 19 or 20 or, if that party is acting otherwise than in the course of business, as described in any of those regulations or in regulation 21.

(3) Any person who contravenes paragraph (1) or (2) of this regulation shall be guilty of an offence and liable:—

    (a) on summary conviction to a fine not exceeding level 5 on the standard scale; and

    (b) on conviction on indictment, to a fine.

(4) A person shall not be guilty of an offence under paragraph (3) above by reason only of the fact that arrangements such as are mentioned in paragraph (2) above are not in force in respect of any period before 1 April 1993 unless money paid over is not refunded when it is due or the consumer is not repatriated in the event of insolvency.

(5) For the purposes of regulations 17 to 21 below a contract shall be treated as having been fully performed if the package or, as the case may be, the part of the package has been completed irrespective of whether the obligations under the contract have been properly performed for the purposes of regulation 15.

Bonding

17.—(1) The other party to the contract shall ensure that a bond is entered into by an authorised institution under which the institution binds itself to pay to an approved body of which that other party is a member a sum calculated in accordance with paragraph (3) below in the event of the insolvency of that other party.

(2) Any bond entered into pursuant to paragraph (1) above shall not be expressed to be in force for a period exceeding eighteen months.

(3) The sum referred to in paragraph (1) above shall be such sum as may reasonably be expected to enable all monies paid over by consumers under or in contemplation of contracts for relevant packages which have not been fully performed to be repaid and shall not in any event be a sum which is less than the minimum sum calculated in accordance with paragraph (4) below.

(4) The minimum sum for the purposes of paragraph (3) above shall be a sum which represents:—

    (a) not less than 25% of all the payments which the other party to the contract estimates that he will receive under or in contemplation of contracts for relevant packages in the twelve month period from the date of entry into force of the bond referred to in paragraph (1) above; or

    (b) the maximum amount of all the payments which the other party to the contract expects to hold at any one time, in respect of contracts which have not been fully performed,

whichever sum is the smaller.

(5) Before a bond is entered into pursuant to paragraph (1) above, the other party to the contract shall inform the approved body of which he is a member of the minimum sum which he proposes for the purposes of paragraphs (3) and (4) above and it shall be the duty of the approved body to consider whether such sum is sufficient for the purpose mentioned in paragraph (3) and, if it does not consider that this is the case, it shall be the duty of the approved body so to inform the other party to the contract and to inform him of the sum which, in the opinion of the approved body, is sufficient for that purpose.

(6) Where an approved body has informed the other party to the contract of a sum pursuant to paragraph (5) above, the minimum sum for the purposes of paragraphs (3) and (4) above shall be that sum.

(7) In this regulation–

''approved body'' means a body which is for the time being approved by the Secretary of State for the purposes of this regulation;

'authorised institution'' means a person authorised under the law of a member State, of the Channel Islands or of the Isle of Man to carry on the business of entering into bonds of the kind required by this regulation.

Bonding where approved body has reserve fund or insurance

18.—(1) The other party to the contract shall ensure that a bond is entered into by an authorised institution, under which the institution agrees to pay to an approved body of which that other party is a member a sum calculated in accordance with paragraph (3) below in the event of the insolvency of that other party.

(2) Any bond entered into pursuant to paragraph (1) above shall not be expressed to be in force for a period exceeding eighteen months.

(3) The sum referred to in paragraph (1) above shall be such sum as may be specified by the approved body as representing the lesser of–

(a) the maximum amount of all the payments which the other party to the contract expects to hold at any one time in respect of contracts which have not been fully performed; or

(b) the minimum sum calculated in accordance with paragraph (4) below.

(4) The minimum sum for the purposes of paragraph (3) above shall be a sum which represents not less than 10% of all the payments which the other party to the contract estimates that he will receive under or in contemplation of contracts for relevant packages in the twelve month period from the date of entry referred to in paragraph (1) above.

(5) In this regulation "approved body" means a body which is for the time being approved by the Secretary of State for the purposes of this regulation and no such approval shall be given unless the conditions mentioned in paragraph (6) below are satisfied in relation to it.

(6) A body may not be approved for the purposes of this regulation unless—

(a) it has a reserve fund or insurance cover with an insurer authorised in respect of such business in a member State, the Channel Islands or the Isle of Man of an amount in each case which is designed to enable all monies paid over to a member of the body of consumers under or in contemplation of contracts for relevant packages which have not been fully performed to be repaid to those consumers in the event of the insolvency of the member; and

(b) where it has a reserve fund, it agrees that the fund will be held by persons and in a manner approved by the Secretary of State.

(7) In this regulation, authorised institution has the meaning given to that expression by paragraph (7) of regulation 17.

Insurance

19.—(1) The other party to the contract shall have insurance under one or more appropriate policies with an insurer authorised in respect of such business in a member State under which the insurer agrees to indemnify consumers, who shall be insured persons under the policy, against the loss of money paid over by them under or in contemplation of contracts for packages in the event of the insolvency of the contractor.

(2) The other party to the contract shall ensure that it is a term of every contract with a consumer that the consumer acquires the benefit of a policy of a kind mentioned in paragraph (1) above in the event of the insolvency of the other party to the contract.

(3) In this regulation:

"appropriate policy" means one which does not contain a condition which provides (in whatever terms) that no liability shall arise under the policy, or that any liability so arising shall cease:—

(i) in the event of some specified thing being done or omitted to be done after the happening of the event giving rise to a claim under the policy;

(ii) in the event of the policy holder not making payments under or in connection with other policies; or

(iii) unless the policy holder keeps specified records or provides the insurer with or makes available to him information therefrom.

Monies in trust

20.—(1) The other party to the contract shall ensure that all monies paid over by a consumer under or in contemplation of a contract for a relevant package are held in the United Kingdom by a person as trustee for the consumer until the contract has been fully performed or any sum of money paid by the consumer in respect of the contract has been repaid to him or has been forfeited on cancellation by the consumer.

(2) The costs of administering the trust mentioned in paragraph (1) above shall be paid for by the other party to the contract.

(3) Any interest which is earned on the monies held by the trustee pursuant to paragraph (1) shall be held for the other party to the contract and shall be payable to him on demand.

(4) Where there is produced to the trustee a statement signed by the other party to the contract to the effect that—

    (a) a contract for a package the price of which is specified in that statement has been fully performed;

    (b) the other party to the contract has repaid to the consumer a sum of money specified in that statement which the consumer had paid in respect of a contract for a package; or

    (c) the consumer has on cancellation forfeited a sum of money specified in that statement which he had paid in respect of a contract for a relevant package,

the trustee shall (subject to paragraph (5) below) release to the other party to the contract the sum specified in the statement.

(5) Where the trustee considers it appropriate to do so, he may require the other party to the contract to provide further information or evidence of the matters mentioned in sub-paragraph (a), (b) or (c) of paragraph (4) above before he releases any sum to that other party pursuant to that paragraph.

(6) Subject to paragraph (7) below, in the event of the insolvency of the other party to the contract the monies held in trust by the trustee pursuant to paragraph (1) of this regulation shall be applied to meet the claims of consumers who are creditors of that other party in respect of contracts for packages in respect of which the arrangements were established and which have not been fully performed and, if there is a surplus after those claims have been met, it shall form part of the estate of that insolvent other party for the purposes of insolvency law.

(7) If the monies held in trust by the trustee pursuant to paragraph (1) of this regulation are insufficient to meet the claims of consumers as described in paragraph (6), payments to those consumers shall be made by the trustee on a pari passu basis.

Monies in trust where other party to contract is acting otherwise than in the course of business

21.—(1) The other party to the contract shall ensure that all monies paid over by a consumer under or in contemplation of a contract for a relevant package are held in the United Kingdom by a person as trustee for the consumer for the purpose of paying for the consumer's package.

(2) The costs of administering the trust mentioned in paragraph (1) shall be paid for out of the monies held in trust and the interest earned on those monies.

(3) Where there is produced to the trustee a statement signed by the other party to the contract to the effect that—

    (a) the consumer has previously paid over a sum of money specified in that statement in respect of a contract for a package and that sum is required for the purpose of paying for a component (or part of a component) of the package;

    (b) the consumer has previously paid over a sum of money specified in that statement in respect of a contract for a package and the other party to the contract has paid that sum in respect of a component (or part of a component) of the package;

(c) the consumer requires the repayment to him of a sum of money specified in that statement which was previously paid over by the consumer in respect of a contract for a package; or

(d) the consumer has on cancellation forfeited a sum of money specified in that statement which he had paid in respect of a contract for a package,

the trustee shall (subject to paragraph (4) below) release to the other party to the contract the sum specified in the statement.

(4) Where the trustee considers it appropriate to do so, he may require the other party to the contract to provide further information or evidence of the matters mentioned in sub-paragraph (a), (b), (c) or (d) of paragraph (3) above before he releases to that other party any sum from the monies held in trust for the consumer.

(5) Subject to paragraph (6) below, in the event of the insolvency of the other party to the contract and of contracts for packages not being fully performed (whether before or after the insolvency) the monies held in trust by the trustee pursuant to paragraph (1) of this regulation shall be applied to meet the claims of consumers who are creditors of that other party in respect of amounts paid over by them and remaining in the trust fund after deductions have been made in respect of amounts released to that other party pursuant to paragraph (3) and, if there is a surplus after those claims have been met, it shall be divided amongst those consumers pro rata.

(6) If the monies held in trust by the trustee pursuant to paragraph (1) of this regulation are insufficient to meet the claims of consumers as described in paragraph (5) above, payments to those consumers shall be made by the trustee on a pari passu basis.

(7) Any sums remaining after all the packages in respect of which the arrangements were established have been fully performed shall be dealt with as provided in the arrangements or, in default of such provision, may be paid to the other party to the contract.

Offences arising from breach of regulations 20 and 21

22.—(1) If the other party to the contract makes a false statement under paragraph (4) of regulation 20 or paragraph (3) of regulation 21 he shall be guilty of an offence.

(2) If the other party to the contract applies monies released to him on the basis of a statement made by him under regulation 21(3)(a) or (c) for a purpose other than that mentioned in the statement he shall be guilty of an offence.

(3) If the other party to the contract is guilty of an offence under paragraph (1) or (2) of this regulation shall be liable—

(a) on summary conviction to a fine not exceeding level 5 on the standard scale; and

(b) on conviction on indictment, to a fine.

Enforcement

23. Schedule 3 to these Regulations (which makes provision about the enforcement of regulations 5, 7, 8, 16 and 22 of these Regulations) shall have effect.

Due diligence defence

24.—(1) Subject to the following provisions of this regulation, in proceedings against any person for an offence under regulation 5, 7, 8, 16 or 22 of these Regulations, it shall be a defence for that person to show that he took all reasonable steps and exercised all due diligence to avoid committing the offence.

(2) Where in any proceedings against any person for such an offence the defence provided by paragraph (1) above involves an allegation that the commission of the offence was due—

(a) to the act or default of another; or

(b) to reliance on information given by another,

that person shall not, without the leave of the court, be entitled to rely on the defence unless, not less than seven clear days before the hearing of the proceedings, or, in Scotland, the trial diet, he has served a notice under paragraph (3) below on the person bringing the proceedings.

(3) A notice under this paragraph shall give such information identifying or assisting in the identification of the person who committed the act or default or gave the information as is in the possession of the person serving the notice at the time he serves it.

(4) It is hereby declared that a person shall not be entitled to rely on the defence provided by paragraph (1) above by reason of his reliance on information supplied by another, unless he shows that it was reasonable in all the circumstances for him to have relied on the information, having regard in particular—

(a) to the steps which he took, and those which might reasonably have been taken, for the purpose of verifying the information; and

(b) to whether he had any reason to disbelieve the information.

Liability of persons other than principal offender

25.—(1) Where the commission by any person of an offence under regulation 5, 7, 8, 16 or 22 of these Regulations is due to an act or default committed by some other person in the course of any business of his, the other person shall be guilty of the offence and may be proceeded against and punished by virtue of this paragraph whether or not proceedings are taken against the first-mentioned person.

(2) Where a body corporate is guilty of an offence under any of the provisions mentioned in paragraph (1) above (including where it is so guilty by virtue of the said paragraph (1)) in respect of any act or default which is shown to have been committed with the consent or connivance of, or to be attributable to any neglect on the part of, any director, manager, secretary or other similar officer of the body corporate or any person who was purporting to act in any such capacity he, as well as the body corporate, shall be guilty of that offence and shall be liable to be proceeded against and punished accordingly.

(3) Where the affairs of a body corporate are managed by its members, paragraph (2) above shall apply in relation to the acts and defaults of a member in connection with his functions of management as if he were a director of the body corporate.

(4) Where an offence under any of the provisions mentioned in paragraph (1) above committed in Scotland by a Scottish partnership is proved to have been committed with the consent or connivance of, or to be attributable to neglect on the part of, a partner, he (as well as the partnership) is guilty of the offence and liable to be proceeded against and punished accordingly.

(5) On proceedings for an offence under regulation 5 by virtue of paragraph

(1) above committed by the making available of a brochure it shall be a defence for the person charged to prove that he is a person whose business it is to publish or arrange for the publication of brochures and that he received the brochure for publication in the ordinary course of business and did not know and had no reason to suspect that its publication would amount to an offence under these Regulations.

Prosecution time limit

26.—(1) No proceedings for an offence under regulation 5, 7, 8, 16 or 22 of these Regulations or under paragraphs 5(3), 6 or 7 of Schedule 3 thereto shall be commenced after–

    (a) the end of the period of three years beginning within the date of the commission of the offence; or

    (b) the end of the period of one year beginning with the date of the discovery of the offence by the prosecutor,

whichever is the earlier.

(2) For the purposes of this regulation a certificate signed by or on behalf of the prosecutor and stating the date on which the offence was discovered by him shall be conclusive evidence of that fact; and a certificate stating that matter and purporting to be so signed shall be treated as so signed unless the contrary is proved.

(3) In relation to proceedings in Scotland, subsection (3) of section 331 of the Criminal Procedure (Scotland) Act 1975 (date of commencement of proceedings) shall apply for the purposes of this regulation as it applies for the purposes of that section.

Saving for civil consequences

27. No contract shall be void or unenforceable, and no right of action in civil proceedings in respect of any loss shall arise, by reason only of the commission of an offence under regulations 5, 7, 8, 16 or 22 of these Regulations.

Terms implied in contract

28. Where it is provided in these Regulations that a term (whether so described or whether described as a condition or warranty) is implied in the contract it is so implied irrespective of the law which governs the contract.

SCHEDULE 1

Information to be included (in addition to the price) in brochures where relevant to packages offered

1. The destination and the means, characteristics and categories of transport used.

2. The type of accommodation, its location, category or degree of comfort and its main features and, where the accommodation is to be provided in a member State, its approval or tourist classification under the rules of that member State.

3. The meals which are included in the package.

4. The itinerary.

5. General information about passport and visa requirements which apply for British citizens and health formalities required for the journey and the stay.

6. Either the monetary amount or the percentage of the price which is to be paid on account and the timetable for payment of the balance.

7. Whether a minimum number of persons is required for the package to take place and, if so, the deadline for informing the consumer in the event of cancellation.

8. The arrangements (if any) which apply if consumers are delayed at the outward or homeward points of departure.

9. The arrangements for security for money paid over and for the repatriation of the consumer in the event of insolvency.

SCHEDULE 2

Elements to be included in the contract if relevant to the particular package

1. The travel destination(s) and, where periods of stay are involved, the relevant periods, with dates.

2. The means, characteristics and categories of transport to be used and the dates, times and points of departure and return.

3. Where the package includes accommodation, its location, its tourist category or degree of comfort, its main features and, where the accommodation is to be provided in a member State, its compliance with the rules of that member State.

4. The meals which are included in the package.

5. Whether a minimum number of persons is required for the package to take place and, if so, the deadline for informing the consumer in the event of cancellation.

6. The itinerary.

7. Visits, excursions or other services which are included in the total price agreed for the package.

8. The name and address of the organiser, the retailer and, where appropriate, the insurer.

9. The price of the package, if the price may be revised in accordance with the term which may be included in the contract under regulation 11, an indication of the possibility of such price revisions, and an indication of any dues, taxes or fees chargeable for certain services (landing, embarkation or disembarkation fees at ports and airports and tourist taxes) where such costs are not included in the package.

10. The payment schedule and method of payment.

11. Special requirements which the consumer has communicated to the organiser or retailer when making the booking and which both have accepted.

12. The periods within which the consumer must make any complaint about the failure to perform or the inadequate performance of the contract.

SCHEDULE 3

ENFORCEMENT

Enforcement authority

1.—(1) Every local weights and measures authority in Great Britain shall be an enforcement authority for the purposes of regulations 5, 7, 8, 16 and 22 of these Regulations ("the relevant regulations"), and it shall be the duty of each such authority to enforce those provisions within their area.

(2) The Department of Economic Development in Northern Ireland shall be an enforcement authority for the purposes of the relevant regulations, and it shall be the duty of the Department to enforce those provisions within Northern Ireland.

Prosecutions

2.—(1) Where an enforcement authority in England or Wales proposes to institute proceedings for an offence under any of the relevant regulations, it shall as between the enforcement authority and the Director General of Fair Trading be the duty of the enforcement authority to give to the Director General of Fair Trading notice of the intended proceedings, together with a summary of the facts on which the charges are to be founded, and to postpone institution of the proceedings until either—

    (a) twenty-eight days have elapsed since the giving of that notice; or

    (b) the Director General of Fair Trading has notified the enforcement authority that he has received the notice and the summary of the facts.

(2) Nothing in paragraph 1 above shall authorise a local weights and measures authority to bring proceedings in Scotland for an offence.

Powers of officers of enforcement authority

3.—(1) If a duly authorised officer of an enforcement authority has reasonable grounds for suspecting that an offence has been committed under any of the relevant regulations, he may—

    (a) require a person whom he believes on reasonable grounds to be engaged in the organisation or retailing of packages to produce any book or document relating to the activity and take copies of it or any entry in it, or

    (b) require such a person to produce in a visible and legible documentary form any information so relating which is contained in a computer, and take copies of it,

for the purpose of ascertaining whether such an offence has been committed.

(2) Such an officer may inspect any goods for the purpose of ascertaining whether such an offence has been committed.

(3) If such an officer has reasonable grounds for believing that any documents or goods may be required as evidence in proceedings for such an offence, he may seize and detain them.

(4) An officer seizing any documents or goods in the exercise of his power under sub-paragraph (3) above shall inform the person from whom they are seized.

(5) The powers of an officer under this paragraph may be exercised by him only at a reasonable hour and on production (if required) of his credentials.

(6) Nothing in this paragraph—

    (a) requires a person to produce a document if he would be entitled to refuse to produce it in proceedings in a court on the ground that it is the subject of legal professional privilege or, in Scotland, that it contains a confidential communication made by or to an advocate or a solicitor in that capacity; or

(b) authorises the taking possession of a document which is in the possession of a person who would be so entitled.

4.—(1) A duly authorised officer of an enforcement authority may, at a reasonable hour and on production (if required) of his credentials, enter any premises for the purpose of ascertaining whether an offence under any of the relevant regulations has been committed.

(2) If a justice of the peace, or in Scotland a justice of the peace or a sheriff, is satisfied—

(a) that any relevant books, documents or goods are on, or that any relevant information contained in a computer is available from, any premises, and that production or inspection is likely to disclose the commission of an offence under the relevant regulations; or

(b) that any such an offence has been, is being or is about to be committed on any premises,

and that any of the conditions specified in sub-paragraph (3) below is met, he may by warrant under his hand authorise an officer of an enforcement authority to enter the premises, if need be by force.

(3) The conditions referred to in sub-paragraph (2) above are—

(a) that admission to the premises has been or is likely to be refused and that notice of intention to apply for a warrant under that sub-paragraph has been given to the occupier;

(b) that an application for admission, or the giving of such a notice, would defeat the object of the entry;

(c) that the premises are unoccupied; and

(d) that the occupier is temporarily absent and it might defeat the object of the entry to await his return.

(4) In sub-paragraph (2) above "relevant", in relation to books, documents, goods or information, means books, documents, goods or information which, under paragraph 3 above, a duly authorised officer may require to be produced or may inspect.

(5) A warrant under sub-paragraph (2) above may be issued only if—

(a) in England and Wales, the justice of the peace is satisfied as required by that sub-paragraph by written information on oath;

(b) in Scotland, the justice of the peace or sheriff is so satisfied by evidence on oath; or

(c) in Northern Ireland, the justice of the peace is so satisfied by complaint on oath.

(6) A warrant under sub-paragraph (2) above shall continue in force for a period of one month.

(7) An officer entering any premises by virtue of this paragraph may take with him such other persons as may appear to him necessary.

(8) On leaving premises which he has entered by virtue of a warrant under sub-paragraph (2) above, an officer shall, if the premises are unoccupied or the occupier is temporarily absent, leave the premises as effectively secured against trespassers as he found them.

(9) In this paragraph "premises" includes any place (including any vehicle, ship or aircraft) except premises used only as a dwelling.

Obstruction of officers

5.—(1) A person who—
- (a) intentionally obstructs an officer of an enforcement authority acting in pursuance of this Schedule;
- (b) without reasonable excuse fails to comply with a requirement made of him by such an officer under paragraph 3(1) above; or
- (c) without reasonable excuse fails to give an officer of an enforcement authority acting in pursuance of this Schedule any other assistance or information which the officer may reasonably require of him for the purpose of the performance of the officer's functions under this Schedule.

shall be guilty of an offence.

(2) A person guilty of an offence under sub-paragraph (1) above shall be liable on summary conviction to a fine not exceeding level 5 on the standard scale.

(3) If a person, in giving any such information as is mentioned in sub-paragraph (1)(c) above,—
- (a) makes a statement which he knows is false in a material particular; or
- (b) recklessly makes a statement which is false in a material particular,

he shall be guilty of an offence.

(4) A person guilty of an offence under sub-paragraph (3) above shall be liable—
- (a) on summary conviction, to a fine not exceeding level 5 on the standard scale; and
- (b) on conviction on indictment, to a fine.

Impersonation of officers

6.—(1) If a person who is not a duly authorised officer of an enforcement authority purports to act as such under this Schedule he shall be guilty of an offence.

(2) A person guilty of an offence under sub-paragraph (1) above shall be liable—
- (a) on summary conviction, to a fine not exceeding level 5 on the standard scale; and
- (b) on conviction on indictment, to a fine.

Disclosure of information

7.—(1) If a person discloses to another any information obtained by him by virtue of this Schedule he shall be guilty of an offence unless the disclosure was made—
- (a) in or for the purpose of the performance by him or any other person of any function under the relevant regulations; or
- (b) for a purpose specified in section 38(2)(a), (b) or (c) of the Consumer Protection Act 1987.

(2) A person guilty of an offence under sub-paragraph (1) above shall be liable—
- (a) on summary conviction, to a fine not exceeding level 5 on the standard scale; and
- (b) on conviction on indictment, to a fine.

Privilege against self-incrimination

8. Nothing in this Schedule requires a person to answer any question or give any information if to do so might incriminate him.

The General Product Safety Regulations 1994[1]

(S.I. 1994 No. 2328)

Citation and commencement

1. (1) These Regulations may be cited as the General Product Safety Regulations 1994 and shall come into force on 3rd October 1994.

(2) Nothing in these Regulations applies to a medicinal product for human use to which the Medicines for Human Use (Marketing Authorizations Etc.) Regulations 1994 apply.

Interpretation

2.— (1) In these Regulations—

"the 1968 Act" means the Medicines Act 1968;

"the 1987 Act" means the Consumer Protection Act 1987;

"the 1990 Act" means the Food Safety Act 1990;

"commercial activity" includes a business and a trade;

"consumer" means a consumer acting otherwise than in the course of a commercial activity;

"dangerous product" means any product other than a safe product;

"distributor" means any professional in the supply chain whose activity does not affect the safety properties of a product;

"enforcement authority" means the Secretary of State, any other Minister of the Crown in charge of a Goverment Department, any such department and any authority, council and other person on whom functions under these Regulations are imposed by or under regulation 11;

"general safety requirement" means the requirement in regulation 7;

"the GPS Directive" means Council Directive 92/59/EEC on general product safety;

"the 1991 Order" means the Food Safety (Northern Ireland) Order 1991;

"producer" means

   (a) the manufacturer of the product, when he is established in the Community, and includes any person presenting himself as the manufacturer by affixing to the product his name, trade mark or other distinctive mark, or the person who reconditions the product;

   (b) when the manufacturer is not established in the Community—
       (i) if the manufacturer does not have a representative established in the Community, the importer of the product;
       (ii) in all other cases, the manufacturer's representative; and

   (c) other professionals in the supply chain, insofar as their activities may affect the safety properties of a product placed on the market;

"product" means any product intended for consumers or likely to be used by consumers, supplied whether for consideration or not in the course of a commercial activity and whether new, used or reconditioned; provided, however, a product which is used exclusively in the context of a commercial activity even if it is used for or by a consumer shall not be regarded as a product for the purposes of these Regulations provided always and for the

---

[1] Made in exercise of the powers conferred by the European Communities Act 1972, s. 2(2). These Regulations implement Council Directive 92/59/EEC, printed below at p. 364.

avoidance of doubt this exception shall not extend to the supply of such a product to a consumer;

"safe product" means any product which, under normal or reasonably fore-seeable conditions of use, including duration, does not present any risk or only the minimum risks compatible with the product's use, considered as acceptable and consistent with a high level of protection for the safety and health of persons, taking into account in particular—

(a) the characteristics of the product, including its composition, packaging, instructions for assembly and maintenance;

(b) the effect on other products, where it is reasonably foreseeable that it will be used with other products;

(c) the presentation of the product, the labelling, any instructions for its use and disposal and any other indication or information provided by the producer; and

(d) the categories of consumers at serious risk when using the product, in particular children,

and the fact that higher levels of safety may be obtained or other products presenting a lesser degree of risk may be available shall not of itself cause the product to be considered other than a safe product.

(2) References in these Regulations to the "Community" are references to the European Economic Area established under the Agreement signed at Oporto on 2nd May 1992 as adjusted by the Protocol signed at Brussels on 17th March 1993.

Application and revocation

3. These Regulations do not apply to—

(a) second-hand products which are antiques;

(b) products supplied for repair or reconditioning before use, provided the supplier clearly informs the person to whom he supplies the product to that effect; or

(c) any product where there are specific provisions in rules of Community law governing all aspects of the safety of the product.

4. The requirements of these Regulations apply to a product where the product is the subject of provisions of Community law other than the GPS Directive insofar as those provisions do not make specific provision governing an aspect of the safety of the product.

5. For the purposes of these Regulations the provisions of section 10 of the 1987 Act to the extent that they impose general safety requirements which must be complied with if products are to be—

(i) placed on the market, offered or agreed to be placed on the market or exposed or possessed to be placed on the market by producers; or

(ii) supplied, offered or agreed to be supplied or exposed or possessed to be supplied by distributors,

are hereby disapplied.

6.—(1) Sub-paragraph (ii) of paragraph (b) of sub-section (3) of section 10 of the 1987 Act is hereby repealed.

(2) The Approval of Safety Standards Regulations 1987 are hereby revoked.

General safety requirement

7.   No producer shall place a product on the market unless the product is a safe product.

Requirement as to information

8.—(1) Within the limits of his activity, a producer shall—

    (a) provide consumers with the relevant information to enable them to assess the risks inherent in a product throughout the normal or reasonably foreseeable period of its use, where such risks are not immediately obvious without adequate warnings, and to take precautions against those risks; and

    (b) adopt measures commensurate with the characteristics of the products which he supplies, to enable him to be informed of the risks which these products might present and to take appropriate action, including, if necessary, withdrawing the product in question from the market to avoid those risks.

(2) The measures referred to in sub-paragraph (b) of paragraph (1) above may include, whenever appropriate—

    (i) marking of the products or product batches in such a way that they can be identified;

    (ii) sample testing of marketed products;

    (iii) investigating complaints; and

    (iv) keeping distributors informed of such monitoring.

Requirements of distributors

9.   A distributor shall act with due care in order to help ensure compliance with the requirements of regulation 7 above and, in particular, without limiting the generality of the foregoing—

    (a) a distributor shall not supply products to any person which he knows, or should have presumed, on the basis of the information in his possession and as a professional, are dangerous products; and

    (b) within the limits of his activities, a distributor shall participate in monitoring the safety of products placed on the market, in particular by passing on information on the product risks and cooperating in the action taken to avoid those risks.

Presumption of conformity and product assessment

10.—(1) Where in relation to any product such product conforms to the specific rules of the law of the United Kingdom laying down the health and safety requirements which the product must satisfy in order to be marketed there shall be a presumption that, until the contrary is proved, the product is a safe product.

(2) Where no specific rules as are mentioned or referred to in paragraph (1) exist, the conformity of a product to the general safety requirement shall be assessed taking into account—

    (i) voluntary national standards of the United Kingdom giving effect to a European standard; or

    (ii) Community technical specifications; or

    (iii) if there are no such voluntary national standards of the United Kingdom or Community technical specifications—

        (aa) standards drawn up in the United Kingdom; or

        (bb) the codes of good practice in respect of health and safety in the product sector concerned; or (cc) the state of the art and technology

and the safety which consumers may reasonably expect.

Enforcement

11. For the purposes of providing for the enforcement of these Regulations—

(a) section 13 of the 1987 Act (prohibition notices and notices to warn) shall (to the extent that it does not already do so) apply to products as it applies to relevant goods under that section;

(b) the requirements of these Regulations shall constitute safety provisions for the purposes of sections 14 (suspension notices), 15 (appeals against suspension notices), 16 (forfeiture: England, Wales and Northern Ireland), 17 (forfeiture: Scotland) and 18 (power to obtain information) of the 1987 Act;

(c) (i) subject to paragraph (ii) below a weights and measures authority in Great Britain and a district council in Northern Ireland shall have the same duty to enforce these Regulations as they have in relation to Part II of the 1987 Act, and Part IV, sections 37 and 38 and subsections (3) and (4) of section 42 of that Act shall apply accordingly;

(ii) without prejudice to the provisions of paragraphs (a) and (b) above and subparagraph (i) above, insofar as these Regulations apply:—

(aa) to products licensed in accordance with the provisions of the 1968 Act or which are the subject of a marketing authorization within the meaning of the Medicines for Human Use (Marketing Authorization Etc.) Regulations 1994, it shall be the duty of the enforcement authority as defined in section 132(1) of the 1968 Act to enforce or to secure the enforcement of these Regulations and sections 108 to 115 and section 119 of and Schedule 3 to that Act shall apply accordingly as if these Regulations were regulations made under the said Act;

(bb) in relation to food within the meaning of section 1 of the 1990 Act, it shall be the duty of each food authority as defined in section 5 of the 1990 Act to enforce or to secure the enforcement of these Regulations, within its area, in Great Britain and sections 9, 29, 30 and 32 of that Act shall apply accordingly as if these Regulations were food safety requirements made under the said Act and section 10 of that Act shall apply as if these Regulations were regulations made under Part II of that Act; and

(cc) in relation to food within the meaning of article 2 of the 1991 Order, it shall be the duty of the relevant enforcement authority as provided for in article 26 of that Order to enforce or to secure enforcement of these Regulations in Northern Ireland and articles 8, 29, 30, 31 and 33 of that Order shall apply accordingly as if these Regulations were food safety requirements made under that Order and article 9 of that Order shall apply as if these Regulations were regulations made under Part II of that Order;

(d) in sections 13(4) and 14(6) of the 1987 Act for the words "six months" there shall be substituted "three months"; and

(e) nothing in this regulation shall authorise any enforcement authority to bring proceedings in Scotland for an offence.

Offences and preparatory acts

12. Any person who contravenes regulation 7 or 9(a) shall be guilty of an offence.

13. No producer or distributor shall—
   (a) offer or agree to place on the market any dangerous product or expose or possess any such product for placing on the market; or
   (b) offer or agree to supply any dangerous product or expose or possess any such product for supply,

and any person who contravenes the requirements of this regulation shall be guilty of an offence.

Defence of due diligence

14.—(1) Subject to the following paragraphs of this regulation, in proceedings against any person for an offence under these Regulations it shall be a defence for that person to show that he took all reasonable steps and exercised all due diligence to avoid committing the offence.

(2) Where in any proceedings against any person for such an offence the defence provided by paragraph (1) above involves an allegation that the commission of the offence was due—
   (a) to the act or default of another, or
   (b) to reliance on information given by another,

that person shall not, without leave of the court, be entitled to rely on the defence unless, not less than seven days before, in England, Wales and Northern Ireland, the hearing of the proceedings or, in Scotland, the trial diet, he has served a notice under paragraph (3) below on the person bringing the proceedings.

(3) A notice under this paragraph shall give such information identifying or assisting in the identification of the person who committed the act or default or gave the information as is in the possession of the person serving the notice at the time he serves it.

(4) It is hereby declared that a person shall not be entitled to rely on the defence provided in paragraph (1) above by reason of his reliance on information supplied by another, unless he shows that it was reasonable in all the circumstances for him to have relied on the information, having regard in particular—
   (a) to the steps which he took, and those which might reasonably have been taken, for the purpose of verifying the information; and
   (b) to whether he had any reason to disbelieve the information.

(5) It is hereby declared that a person shall not be entitled to rely on the defence provided by paragraph (1) above or by section 39(1) of the 1987 Act (defence of due diligence) if he has contravened regulation 9(b).

Liability of persons other than principal offender

15.—(1) Where the commission by any person of an offence to which regulation 14 above applies is due to the act or default committed by some other person in the course of a commercial activity of his, the other person shall be guilty of an offence and may be proceeded against and punished by virtue of this paragraph whether or not proceedings are taken against the first-mentioned person.

(2) Where a body corporate is guilty of an offence under these Regulations (including where it is so guilty by virtue of paragraph (1) above) in respect of any act or default which is shown to have been committed with the consent or connivance of, or to be attributable to any neglect on the part of any director,

manager, secretary or other similar officer of the body corporate or any person who was purporting to act in any such capacity he, as well as the body corporate, shall be guilty of that offence and shall be liable to be proceeded against and punished accordingly.

(3) Where the affairs of a body corporate are managed by its members, paragraph (2) above shall apply in relation to the acts and defaults of a member in connection with his functions of management as if he were a director of the body corporate.

(4) Where a Scottish partnership is guilty of an offence under regulation 14 above (including where it is so guilty by virtue of paragraph (1) above) in respect of any act or default which is shown to have been committed with the consent or connivance of, or to be attributable to any neglect on the part of, a partner in the partnership, he, as well as the partnership, shall be guilty of that offence and shall be liable to be proceeded against and punished accordingly.

Extension of the time for bringing summary proceedings

16.—(1) Notwithstanding section 127 of the Magistrates' Courts Act 1980 and article 19 of the Magistrates' Courts (Northern Ireland) Order 1981, in England, Wales and Northern Ireland a magistrates' court may try an information (in the case of England and Wales) or a complaint (in the case of Northern Ireland) in respect of proceedings for an offence under regulation 12 or 13 above if (in the case of England and Wales) the information is laid or (in the case of Northern Ireland) the complaint is made within twelve months from the date of the offence.

(2) Notwithstanding section 331 of the Criminal Procedure (Scotland) Act 1975, in Scotland summary proceedings for an offence under regulation 12 or 13 above may be commenced at any time within twelve months from the date of the offence.

(3) For the purposes of paragraph (2) above, section 331(3) of the Criminal Procedure (Scotland) Act 1975 shall apply as it applies for the purposes of that section.

Penalties

17. A person guilty of an offence under regulation 12 or 13 above shall be liable on summary conviction to—

    (a) imprisonment for a term not exceeding three months; or

    (b) a fine not exceeding level 5 on the standard scale;

or to both.

Duties of enforcement authorities

18.—(1) Every enforcement authority shall give immediate notice to the Secretary of State of any action taken by it to prohibit or restrict the supply of any product or forfeit or do any other thing in respect of any product for the purposes of these Regulations.

(2) The requirements of paragraph (1) above shall not apply in the case of any action taken in respect of any second-hand product.

The Unfair Terms in Consumer Contracts Regulations 1994[1]

(S.I. 1994 No. 3159)

Citation and commencement

1.   These Regulations may be cited as the Unfair Terms in Consumer Contracts Regulations 1994 and shall come into force on 1st July 1995.

Interpretation

2.—(1) In these Regulations—

"business" includes a trade or profession and the activities of any government department or local or public authority;

"the Community" means the European Economic Community and the other States in the European Economic Area;

"consumer" means a natural person who, in making a contract to which these Regulations apply, is acting for purposes which are outside his business;

"court" in relation to England and Wales and Northern Ireland means the High Court, and in relation to Scotland, the Court of Session;

"Director" means the Director General of Fair Trading;

"EEA Agreement" means the Agreement on the European Economic Area signed at Oporto on 2 May 1992 as adjusted by the protocol signed at Brussels on 17 March 1993;

"member State" shall mean a State which is a contracting party to the EEA Agreement but until the EEA Agreement comes into force in relation to Liechtenstein does not include the State of Liechtenstein;

"seller" means a person who sells goods and who, in making a contract to which these Regulations apply, is acting for purposes relating to his business; and

"supplier" means a person who supplies goods or services and who, in making a contract to which these Regulations apply, is acting for purposes relating to his business.

(2) In the application of these Regulations to Scotland for references to an "injunction" or an "interlocutory injunction" there shall be substituted references to an "interdict" or "interim interdict" respectively.

Terms to which these Regulations apply

3.—(1) Subject to the provisions of Schedule 1, these Regulations apply to any term in a contract concluded between a seller or supplier and a consumer where the said term has not been individually negotiated.

(2) In so far as it is in plain, intelligible language, no assessment shall be made of the fairness of any term which—

   (a) defines the main subject matter of the contract, or
   (b) concerns the adequacy of the price or remuneration, as against the goods or services sold or supplied.

---

[1] Made in exercise of the powers conferred by the European Communities Act 1972, s. 2(2). These Regulations implement Council Directive 93/13/EEC, printed below at p. 374.

(3) For the purposes of these Regulations, a term shall always be regarded as not having been individually negotiated where it has been drafted in advance and the consumer has not been able to influence the substance of the term.

(4) Notwithstanding that a specific term or certain aspects of it in a contract has been individually negotiated, these Regulations shall apply to the rest of a contract if an overall assessment of the contract indicates that it is a pre-formulated standard contract.

(5) It shall be for any seller or supplier who claims that a term was individually negotiated to show that it was.

Unfair terms

4.—(1) In these Regulations, subject to paragraphs (2) and (3) below, "unfair term" means any term which contrary to the requirement of good faith causes a significant imbalance in the parties' rights and obligations under the contract to the detriment of the consumer.

(2) An assessment of the unfair nature of a term shall be made taking into account the nature of the goods or services for which the contract was concluded and referring, as at the time of the conclusion of the contract, to all circumstances attending the conclusion of the contract and to all the other terms of the contract or of another contract on which it is dependent.

(3) In determining whether a term satisfies the requirement of good faith, regard shall be had in particular to the matters specified in Schedule 2 to these Regulations.

(4) Schedule 3 to these Regulations contains an indicative and non-exhaustive list of the terms which may be regarded as unfair.

Consequence of inclusion of unfair terms in contracts

5.—(1) An unfair term in a contract concluded with a consumer by a seller or supplier shall not be binding on the consumer.

(2) The contract shall continue to bind the parties if it is capable of continuing in existence without the unfair term.

Construction of written contracts

6. A seller or supplier shall ensure that any written term of a contract is expressed in plain, intelligible language, and if there is doubt about the meaning of a written term, the interpretation most favourable to the consumer shall prevail.

Choice of law clauses

7. These Regulations shall apply notwithstanding any contract term which applies or purports to apply the law of a non member State, if the contract has a close connection with the territory of the member States.

Prevention of continued use of unfair terms

8.—(1) It shall be the duty of the Director to consider any complaint made to him that any contract term drawn up for general use is unfair, unless the complaint appears to the Director to be frivolous or vexatious.

(2) If having considered a complaint about any contract term pursuant to paragraph (1) above the Director considers that the contract term is unfair he may, if he considers it appropriate to do so, bring proceedings for an injunction (in which proceedings he may also apply for an interlocutory injunction) against

any person appearing to him to be using or recommending use of such a term in contracts concluded with consumers.

(3) The Director may, if he considers it appropriate to do so, have regard to any undertakings given to him by or on behalf of any person as to the continued use of such a term in contracts concluded with consumers.

(4) The Director shall give reasons for his decision to apply or not to apply, as the case may be, for an injunction in relation to any complaint which these Regulations require him to consider.

(5) The court on an application by the Director may grant an injunction on such terms as it thinks fit.

(6) An injunction may relate not only to use of a particular contract term drawn up for general use but to any similar term, or a term having like effect, used or recommended for use by any party to the proceedings.

(7) The Director may arrange for the dissemination in such form and manner as he considers appropriate of such information and advice concerning the operation of these Regulations as may appear to him to be expedient to give to the public and to all persons likely to be affected by these Regulations.

Schedule 1

Contracts and Particular Terms Excluded from the Scope of these Regulations

These Regulations do not apply to—
- (a) any contract relating to employment;
- (b) any contract relating to succession rights;
- (c) any contract relating to rights under family law;
- (d) any contract relating to the incorporation and organisation of companies or partnerships; and
- (e) any term incorporated in order to comply with or which reflects—
  - (i) statutory or regulatory provisions of the United Kingdom; or
  - (ii) the provisions or principles of international conventions to which the member States or the Community are party.

Schedule 2

Assessment of Good Faith

In making an assessment of good faith, regard shall be had in particular to—
- (a) the strength of the bargaining positions of the parties;
- (b) whether the consumer had an inducement to agree to the term;
- (c) whether the goods or services were sold or supplied to the special order of the consumer, and
- (d) the extent to which the seller or supplier has dealt fairly and equitably with the consumer.

Schedule 3

Indicative and Illustrative List of Terms Which may be Regarded as Unfair

1. Terms which have the object or effect of—

(a) excluding or limiting the legal liability of a seller or supplier in the event of the death of a consumer or personal injury to the latter resulting from an act or omission of that seller or supplier;

(b) inappropriately excluding or limiting the legal rights of the consumer vis-à-vis the seller or supplier or another party in the event of total or partial non-performance or inadequate performance by the seller or supplier of any of the contractual obligations, including the option of offsetting a debt owed to the seller or supplier against any claim which the consumer may have against him;

(c) making an agreement binding on the consumer whereas provision of services by the seller or supplier is subject to a condition whose realisation depends on his own will alone;

(d) permitting the seller or supplier to retain sums paid by the consumer where the latter decides not to conclude or perform the contract, without providing for the consumer to receive compensation of an equivalent amount from the seller or supplier where the latter is the party cancelling the contract;

(e) requiring any consumer who fails to fulfil his obligation to pay a disproportionately high sum in compensation;

(f) authorising the seller or supplier to dissolve the contract on a discretionary basis where the same facility is not granted to the consumer, or permitting the seller or supplier to retain the sums paid for services not yet supplied by him where it is the seller or supplier himself who dissolves the contract;

(g) enabling the seller or supplier to terminate a contract of indeterminate duration without reasonable notice except where there are serious grounds for doing so;

(h) automatically extending a contract of fixed duration where the consumer does not indicate otherwise, when the deadline fixed for the consumer to express this desire not to extend the contract is unreasonably early;

(i) irrevocably binding the consumer to terms with which he had no real opportunity of becoming acquainted before the conclusion of the contract;

(j) enabling the seller or supplier to alter the terms of the contract unilaterally without a valid reason which is specified in the contract;

(k) enabling the seller or supplier to alter unilaterally without a valid reason any characteristics of the product or service to be provided;

(l) providing for the price of goods to be determined at the time of delivery or allowing a seller of goods or supplier of services to increase their price without in both cases giving the consumer the corresponding right to cancel the contract if the final price is too high in relation to the price agreed when the contract was concluded;

(m) giving the seller or supplier the right to determine whether the goods or services supplied are in conformity with the contract, or giving him the exclusive right to interpret any term of the contract;

(n) limiting the seller's or supplier's obligation to respect commitments undertaken by his agents or making his commitments subject to compliance with a particular formality;

(o) obliging the consumer to fulfil all his obligations where the seller or supplier does not perform his;

(p) giving the seller or supplier the possibility of transferring his rights and obligations under the contract, where this may serve to reduce the guarantees for the consumer, without the latter's agreement;

(q) excluding or hindering the consumer's right to take legal action or exercise any other legal remedy, particularly by requiring the consumer to take disputes exclusively to arbitration not covered by legal provisions, unduly restricting the evidence available to him or imposing on him a burden of proof which, according to the applicable law, should lie with another party to the contract.

2. Scope of subparagraphs 1(g), (j) and (l)

(a) Subparagraph 1(g) is without hindrance to terms by which a supplier of financial services reserves the right to terminate unilaterally a contract of indeterminate duration without notice where there is a valid reason, provided that the supplier is required to inform the other contracting party or parties thereof immediately.

(b) Subparagraph 1(j) is without hindrance to terms under which a supplier of financial services reserves the right to alter the rate of interest payable by the consumer or due to the latter, or the amount of other charges for financial services without notice where there is a valid reason, provided that the supplier is required to inform the other contracting party or parties thereof at the earliest opportunity and that the latter are free to dissolve the contract immediately.

Subparagraph 1(j) is also without hindrance to terms under which a seller or supplier reserves the right to alter unilaterally the conditions of a contract of indeterminate duration, provided that he is required to inform the consumer with reasonable notice and that the consumer is free to dissolve the contract.

(c) Subparagraphs 1(g), (j) and (l) do not apply to:

—transactions in transferable securities, financial instruments and other products or services where the price is linked to fluctuations in a stock exchange quotation or index or a financial market rate that the seller or supplier does not control;

—contracts for the purchase or sale of foreign currency, traveller's cheques or international money orders denominated in foreign currency;

(d) Subparagraph 1(l) is without hindrance to price indexation clauses, where lawful, provided that the method by which prices vary is explicitly described.

EC Directives

Council Directive of 10 September 1984 relating to the approximation of the laws, regulations and administrative provisions of the Member States concerning misleading advertising[1]

(84/450/EEC)

THE COUNCIL OF THE EUROPEAN COMMUNITIES,

Having regard to the Treaty establishing the European Economic Community, and in particular Article 100 thereof,

Having regard to the proposal from the Commission,

Having regard to the opinion of the European Parliament,

Having regard to the opinion of the Economic and Social Committee,

Whereas the laws against misleading advertising now in force in the Member States differ widely; whereas, since advertising reaches beyond the frontiers of individual Member States, it has a direct effect on the establishment and the functioning of the common market;

Whereas misleading advertising can lead to distortion of competition within the common market;

Whereas advertising, whether or not it induces a contract, affects the economic welfare of consumers;

Whereas misleading advertising may cause a consumer to take decisions prejudicial to him when acquiring goods or other property, or using services, and the differences between the laws of the Member States not only lead, in many cases, to inadequate levels of consumer protection, but also hinder the execution of advertising campaigns beyond national boundaries and thus affect the free circulation of goods and provision of services;

Whereas the second programme of the European Economic Community for a consumer protection and information policy provides for appropriate action for the protection of consumers against misleading and unfair advertising;

Whereas it is in the interest of the public in general, as well as that of consumers and all those who, in competition with one another, carry on a trade, business, craft or profession, in the common market, to harmonise in the first instance national provisions against misleading advertising and that, at a second stage, unfair advertising and, as far as necessary, comparative advertising should be dealt with, on the basis of appropriate Commission proposals;

Whereas minimum and objective criteria for determining whether advertising is misleading should be established for this purpose;

Whereas the laws to be adopted by Member States against misleading advertising must be adequate and effective;

Whereas persons or organisations regarded under national law as having a legitimate interest in the matter must have facilities for initiating proceedings against misleading advertising, either before a court or before an administrative

---

[1] This Directive (84/450/EEC) has been implemented in the United Kingdom by the Control of Misleading Advertisements Regulations 1988 (S.I. 1988 No. 915), printed above at p. 286.

authority which is competent to decide upon complaints or to initiate appropriate legal proceedings;

Whereas it should be for each Member State to decide whether to enable the courts or administrative authorities to require prior recourse to other established means of dealing with the complaint;

Whereas the courts or administrative authorities must have powers enabling them to order or obtain the cessation of misleading advertising;

Whereas in certain cases it may be desirable to prohibit misleading advertising even before it is published; whereas, however, this in no way implies that Member States are under an obligation to introduce rules requiring the systematic prior vetting of advertising;

Whereas provision should be made for accelerated procedures under which measures with interim or definitive effect can be taken;

Whereas it may be desirable to order the publication of decisions made by courts or administrative authorities or of corrective statements in order to eliminate any continuing effects of misleading advertising;

Whereas administrative authorities must be impartial and the exercise of their powers must be subject to judicial review;

Whereas the voluntary control exercised by self-regulatory bodies to eliminate misleading advertising may avoid recourse to administrative or judicial action and ought therefore to be encouraged;

Whereas the advertiser should be able to prove, by appropriate means, the material accuracy of the factual claims he makes in his advertising, and may in appropriate cases be required to do so by the court or administrative authority;

Whereas this Directive must not preclude Member States from retaining or adopting provisions with a view to ensuring more extensive protection of consumers, persons carrying on a trade, business, craft or profession, and the general public,

HAS ADOPTED THIS DIRECTIVE:

Article 1
The purpose of this Directive is to protect consumers, persons carrying on a trade or business or practising a craft or profession and the interests of the public in general against misleading advertising and the unfair consequences thereof.

Article 2
For the purposes of this Directive:

1. ''advertising'' means the making of a representation in any form in connection with a trade, business, craft or profession in order to promote the supply of goods or services, including immovable property, rights and obligations;

2. ''misleading advertising'' means any advertising which in any way, including its presentation, deceives or is likely to deceive the persons to whom it is addressed or whom it reaches and which, by reason of its deceptive nature, is likely to affect their economic behaviour or which, for those reasons, injures or is likely to injure a competitor;

3. ''person'' means any natural or legal person.

Article 3
In determining whether advertising is misleading, account shall be taken of all its features, and in particular of any information it contains concerning:

(a) the characteristics of goods or services, such as their availability, nature, execution, composition, method and date of manufacture or provision, fitness for purpose, uses, quantity, specification, geographical or commercial origin or the results to be expected from their use, or the results and material features of tests or checks carried out on the goods or services;

(b) the price or the manner in which the price is calculated, and the conditions on which the goods are supplied or the services provided;

(c) the nature, attributes and rights of the advertiser, such as his identity and assets, his qualifications and ownership of industrial, commercial or intellectual property rights or his awards and distinctions.

Article 4

1. Member States shall ensure that adequate and effective means exist for the control of misleading advertising in the interests of consumers as well as competitors and the general public.

Such means shall include legal provisions under which persons or organisations regarded under national law as having a legitimate interest in prohibiting misleading advertising may:

(a) take legal action against such advertising; and/or

(b) bring such advertising before an administrative authority competent either to decide on complaints or to initiate appropriate legal proceedings.

It shall be for each Member State to decide which of these facilities shall be available and whether to enable the courts or administrative authorities to require prior recourse to other established means of dealing with complaints, including those referred to in Article 5

2. Under the legal provisions referred to in paragraph 1, Member States shall confer upon the courts or administrative authorities powers enabling them, in cases they deem such measures to be necessary taking into account all the interests involved and in particular the public interest:

—to order the cessation of, or to institute appropriate legal proceedings for an order for the cessation of, misleading advertising, or

—if misleading advertising has not yet been published but publication is imminent, to order the prohibition of, or to institute appropriate legal proceedings for an order for the prohibition of, such publication,

even without proof of actual loss or damage or of intention or negligence on the part of the advertiser.

Member States shall also make provision for the measures referred to in the first paragraph to be taken under an accelerated procedure:

—either with interim effect, or

—with definitive effect,

on the understanding that it is for each Member State to decide which of the two options to select.

Furthermore, Member States may confer upon the courts or administrative authorities powers enabling them, with a view to eliminating the continuing effects of misleading advertising the cessation of which has been ordered by a final decision:

—to require publication of that decision in full or in part and in such form as they deem adequate,

—to require in addition the publication of a corrective statement.

3. The administrative authorities referred to in paragraph 1 must:
  (a) be composed so as not to cast doubt on their impartiality;
  (b) have adequate powers, where they decide on complaints, to monitor and enforce the observance of their decisions effectively;
  (c) normally give their reasons for their decisions.

Where the powers referred to in paragraph 2 are exercised exclusively by an administrative authority, reasons for its decisions shall always be given. Furthermore in this case, provision must be made for procedures whereby improper or unreasonable exercise of its powers by the administrative authority or improper or unreasonable failure to exercise the said powers can be the subject of judicial review.

Article 5

This Directive does not exclude the voluntary control of misleading advertising by self-regulatory bodies and recourse to such bodies by the persons or organisations referred to in Article 4 if proceedings before such bodies are in addition to the court or administrative proceedings referred to in that Article.

Article 6

Member States shall confer upon the courts or administrative authorities powers enabling them in the civil or administrative proceedings provided for in Article 4:
  (a) to require the advertiser to furnish evidence as to the accuracy of factual claims in advertising if, taking into account the legitimate interests of the advertiser and any other party to the proceedings, such a requirement appears appropriate on the basis of the circumstances of the particular case; and
  (b) to consider factual claims as inaccurate if the evidence demanded in accordance with (a) is not furnished or is deemed insufficient by the court or administrative authority.

Article 7

This Directive shall not preclude Member States from retaining or adopting provisions with a view to ensuring more extensive protection for consumers, persons carrying on a trade, business, craft or profession, and the general public.

Article 8

Member States shall bring into force the measures necessary to comply with this Directive by 1 October 1986 at the latest. They shall forthwith inform the Commission thereof.

Member States shall communicate to the Commission the text of all provisions of national law which they adopt in the field covered by this Directive.

Article 9

This Directive is addressed to Member States.

Done at Brussels, 10 September 1984.

Council Directive of 25 July 1985 on the approximation of the laws, regulations and administrative provisions of the Member States concerning liability for defective products[1]

(85/374/EEC)

THE COUNCIL OF THE EUROPEAN COMMUNITIES,

Having regard to the Treaty establishing the European Economic Community, and in particular Article 100 thereof,

Having regard to the proposal from the Commission,

Having regard to the opinion of the European Parliament,

Having regard to the opinion of the Economic and Social Committee,

Whereas approximation of the laws of the Member States concerning the liability of the producer for damage caused by the defectiveness of his products is necessary because the existing divergences may distort competition and affect the movement of goods within the common market and entail a differing degree of protection of the consumer against damage caused by a defective product to his health or property;

Whereas liability without fault on the part of the producer is the sole means of adequately solving the problem, peculiar to our age of increasing technicality, of a fair apportionment of the risks inherent in modern technological production;

Whereas liability without fault should apply only to movables which have been industrially produced; whereas, as a result, it is appropriate to exclude liability for agricultural products and game, except where they have undergone a processing of an industrial nature which could cause a defect in these products; whereas the liability provided for in this Directive should also apply to movables which are used in the construction of immovables or are installed in immovables;

Whereas protection of the consumer requires that all producers involved in the production process should be made liable, in so far as their finished product, component part or any raw material supplied by them was defective; whereas, for the same reason, liability should extend to importers of products into the Community and to persons who present themselves as producers by affixing their name, trade mark or other distinguishing feature or who supply a product the producer of which cannot be identified;

Whereas, in situations where several persons are liable for the same damage, the protection of the consumer requires that the injured person should be able to claim full compensation for the damage from any one of them;

Whereas, to protect the physical well-being and property of the consumer, the defectiveness of the product should be determined by reference not to its fitness for use but to the lack of the safety which the public at large is entitled to expect; whereas the safety is assessed by excluding any misuse of the product not reasonable under the circumstances;

Whereas a fair apportionment of risk between the injured person and the producer implies that the producer should be able to free himself from liability if he furnishes proof as to the existence of certain exonerating circumstances;

---

[1] This Directive (85/374/EEC) has been implemented in the United Kingdom by the Consumer Protection Act 1987, Part I, printed above at p. 212.

Whereas the protection of the consumer requires that the liability of the producer remains unaffected by acts or omissions of other persons having contributed to cause the damage; whereas, however, the contributory negligence of the injured person may be taken into account to reduce or disallow such liability;

Whereas the protection of the consumer requires compensation for death and personal injury as well as compensation for damage to property; whereas the latter should nevertheless be limited to goods for private use or consumption and be subject to a deduction of a lower threshold of a fixed amount in order to avoid litigation in an excessive number of cases; whereas this Directive should not prejudice compensation for pain and suffering and other non-material damages payable, where appropriate, under the law applicable to the case;

Whereas a uniform period of limitation for the bringing of an action for compensation is in the interests both of the injured person and of the producer;

Whereas products age in the course of time, higher safety standards are developed and the state of science and technology progresses; whereas, therefore, it would not be reasonable to make the producer liable for an unlimited period for the defectiveness of his product; whereas, therefore, liability should expire after a reasonable length of time, without prejudice to claims pending at law;

Whereas, to achieve effective protection of consumers, no contractual derogation should be permitted as regards the liability of the producer in relation to the injured person;

Whereas under the legal systems of the Member States an injured party may have a claim for damages based on grounds of contractual liability or on grounds of non-contractual liability other than that provided for in this Directive; in so far as these provisions also serve to attain the objective of effective protection of consumers, they should remain unaffected by this Directive; whereas, in so far as effective protection of consumers in the sector of pharmaceutical products is already also attained in a Member State under a special liability system, claims based on this system should similarly remain possible;

Whereas, to the extent that liability for nuclear injury or damage is already covered in all Member States by adequate special rules, it has been possible to exclude damage of this type from the scope of this Directive;

Whereas, since the exclusion of primary agricultural products and game from the scope of this Directive may be felt, in certain Member States, in view of what is expected for the protection of consumers, to restrict unduly such protection, it should be possible for a Member State to extend liability to such products;

Whereas, for similar reasons, the possibility offered to a producer to free himself from liability if he proves that the state of scientific and technical knowledge at the time when he put the product into circulation was not such as to enable the existence of a defect to be discovered may be felt in certain Member States to restrict unduly the protection of the consumer; whereas it should therefore be possible for a Member State to maintain in its legislation or to provide by new legislation that this exonerating circumstance is not admitted; whereas, in the case of new legislation, making use of this derogation should, however, be subject to a Community stand-still procedure, in order to raise, if possible, the level of protection in a uniform manner throughout the Community;

Whereas, taking into account the legal traditions in most of the Member States, it is inappropriate to set any financial ceiling on the producer's liability without fault; whereas, in so far as there are, however, differing traditions, it seems possible to admit that a Member State may derogate from the principle of unlimited lability by providing a limit for the total lability of the producer for damage resulting from a death or personal injury and caused by identical items with the same defect, provided that this limit is established at a level sufficiently high to guarantee adequate protection of the consumer and the correct functioning of the common market;

Whereas the harmonisation resulting from this cannot be total at the present stage, but opens the way towards greater harmonisation, whereas it is therefore necessary that the Council receive at regular intervals, reports from the Commission on the application of this Directive, accompanied, as the case may be, by appropriate proposals;

Whereas it is particularly important in this respect that a re-examination be carried out of those parts of the Directive relating to the derogations open to the Member States, at the expiry of sufficient length to gather practical experience on the effects of these derogations on the protection of consumers and on the functioning of the common market,

HAS ADOPTED THIS DIRECTIVE:

Article 1
The producer shall be liable for damage caused by a defect in his product.

Article 2
For the purpose of this Directive "product" means all movables, with the exception of primary agricultural products and game, even though incorporated into another movable or into an immovable. "Primary agricultural products" means the products of the soil, of stock-farming and of fisheries, excluding products which have undergone initial processing. "Product" includes electricity.

Article 3
1. "Producer" means the manufacturer of a finished product, the producer of any raw material or the manufacturer of a component part and any person who, by putting his name, trade mark or other distinguishing feature on the product presents himself as its producer.

2. Without prejudice to the liability of the producer, any person who imports into the Community a product for sale, hire, leasing or any form of distribution in the course of his business shall be deemed to be a producer within the meaning of this Directive and shall be responsible as a producer.

3. Where the producer of the product cannot be identified, each supplier of the product shall be treated as its producer unless he informs the injured person, within a reasonable time, of the identity of the producer or of the person who supplied him with the product. The same shall apply, in the case of an imported product, if this product does not indicate the identity of the importer referred to paragraph 2, even if the name of the producer is indicated.

Article 4
The injured person shall be required to prove the damage, the defect and the causal relationship between defect and damage.

Article 5
Where, as a result of the provisions of this Directive, two or more persons are liable for the same damage, they shall be liable jointly and severally, without

prejudice to the provisions of national law concerning the rights of contribution or recourse.

Article 6

1. A product is defective when it does not provide the safety which a person is entitled to expect, taking all circumstances into account, including:

(a) the presentation of the product;

(b) the use to which it could reasonably be expected that the product would be put;

(c) the time when the product was put into circulation.

2. A product shall not be considered defective for the sole reason that a better product is subsequently put into circulation.

Article 7

The producer shall not be liable as a result of this Directive if he proves:

(a) that he did not put the product into circulation; or

(b) that, having regard to the circumstances, it is probable that the defect which caused the damage did not exist at the time when the product was put into circulation by him or that this defect came into being afterwards; or

(c) that the product was neither manufactured by him for sale or any form of distribution for economic purpose nor manufactured or distributed by him in the course of his business; or

(d) that the defect is due to compliance of the product with mandatory regulations issued by the public authorities; or

(e) that the state of scientific and technical knowledge at the time when he put the product into circulation was not such as to enable the existence of the defect to be discovered; or

(f) in the case of a manufacturer of a component, that the defect is attributable to the design of the product in which the component has been fitted or to the instructions given by the manufacturer of the product.

Article 8

1. Without prejudice to the provisions of national law concerning the right of contribution or recourse, the liability of the producer shall not be reduced when the damage is caused both by a defect in product and by the act or omission of a third party.

2. The liability of the producer may be reduced or disallowed when, having regard to all the circumstances, the damage is caused both by a defect in the product and by the fault of the injured person or any person for whom the injured person is responsible.

Article 9

For the purpose of Article 1, "damage" means:

(a) damage caused by death or by personal injuries;

(b) damage to, or destruction of, any item of property other than the defective product itself, with a lower threshold of 500 ECU, provided that the item of property:

(i) is of a type ordinarily intended for private use or consumption; and

(ii) was used by the injured person mainly for his own private use or consumption.

This Article shall be without prejudice to national provisions relating to non-material damage.

Article 10
1.   Member States shall provide in their legislation that a limitation period of three years shall apply to proceedings for the recovery of damages as provided for in this Directive. The limitation period shall begin to run from the day on which the plaintiff became aware, or should reasonably have become aware, of the damage, the defect and the identity of the producer.

2.   The laws of the Member States regulating suspension or interruption of the limitation period shall not be affected by this Directive.

Article 11
Member States shall provide in their legislation that the rights conferred upon the injured person pursuant to this Directive shall be extinguished upon the expiry of a period of 10 years from the date on which the producer put into circulation the actual product which caused the damage, unless the injured person has in the meantime instituted proceedings against the producer.

Article 12
The liability of the producer arising from this Directive may not, in relation to the injured person, be limited or excluded by a provision limiting his liability or exempting him from liability.

Article 13
This Directive shall not affect any rights which an injured person may have according to the rules of the law of contractual or non-contractual liability or a special liability system existing at the moment when this Directive is notified.

Article 14
This Directive shall not apply to injury or damage arising from nuclear accidents and covered by international conventions ratified by the Member States.

Article 15
1.   Each Member State may:
    (a) by way of derogation from Article 2, provide in its legislation that within the meaning of Article 1 of this Directive "product" also means primary agricultural products and game;
    (b) by way of derogation from Article 7 (e), maintain or, subject to the procedure set out in paragraph 2 of this Article, provide in this legislation that the producer shall be liable even if he proves that the state of scientific and technical knowledge at the time when he put the product into circulation was not such as to enable the defect to be discovered.

2.   A Member State wishing to introduce the measure specified in paragraph 1 (b) shall communicate the text of the proposed measure to the Commission. The Commission shall inform the other Member States thereof.
The Member State concerned shall hold the proposed measure in abeyance for nine months after the Commission is informed and provided that in the meantime the Commission has not submitted to the Council a proposal amending this Directive on the relevant matter. However, if within three months

of receiving the said information, the Commission does not inform the Member State concerned that it intends submitting such a proposal to the Council, the Member State may take the proposed measure immediately.

If the Commission does submit to the Council such a proposal amending this Directive within the aforementioned nine months, the Member State concerned shall hold the proposed measure in abeyance for a further period of 18 months from the date on which the proposal is submitted.

3. Ten years after the date of notification of this Directive, the Commission shall submit to the Council a report on the effect that rulings by the courts as to the application of Article 7 (e) and of paragraph 1 (b) of this Article have on consumer protection and the functioning of the common market. In the light of this report the Council, acting on a proposal from the Commission and pursuant to the terms of Article 100 of the Treaty, shall decide whether to repeal Article 7 (e).

Article 16
1. Any Member State may provide that a producer's total liability for damage resulting from a death or personal injury and caused by identical items with the same defect shall be limited to an amount which may not be less than 70 million ECU.

2. Ten years after the date of notification of this Directive, the Commission shall submit to the Council a report on the effect on consumer protection and the functioning of the common market of the implementation of the financial limit on liability by those Member States which have used the option provided for in paragraph 1. In the light of this report the Council, acting on a proposal from the Commission and pursuant to the terms of Article 100 of the Treaty, shall decide whether to repeal paragraph 1.

Article 17
This Directive shall not apply to products put into circulation before the date on which the provisions referred to in Article 19 enter into force.

Article 18
1. For the purposes of this Directive, the ECU shall be that defined by Regulation (EEC) No 3180/78, as amended by Regulation (EEC) No 2626/84. The equivalent in national currency shall initially be calculated at the rate obtaining on the date of adoption of this Directive.

2. Every five years the Council, acting on a proposal from the Commission, shall examine and, if need be, revise the amounts in this Directive, in the light of economic and monetary trends in the Community.

Article 19
1. Member States shall bring into force, not later than three years from the notification of this Directive, the laws, regulations and administrative provisions necessary to comply with this Directive. They shall forthwith inform the Commission thereof.

2. The procedure set out in Article 15 (2) shall apply from the date of notification of this Directive.

Article 20
Member States shall communicate to the Commission the texts of the main provisions of national law which they subsequently adopt in the field governed by this Directive.

Article 21
Every five years the Commission shall present a report to the Council on the application of this Directive and, if necessary, shall submit appropriate proposals to it.

Article 22
This Directive is addressed to the Member States.

Done at Brussels, 25 July 1985.

Council Directive of 20 December 1985 to protect the consumer in respect of contracts negotiated away from business premises[1]

(85/577/EEC)

THE COUNCIL OF THE EUROPEAN COMMUNITIES,

Having regard to the Treaty establishing the European Economic Community, and in particular Article 100 thereof,

Having regard to the proposal from the Commission,

Having regard to the opinion of the European Parliament,

Having regard to the opinion of the Economic and Social Committee,

Whereas it is a common form of commercial practice in the Member States for the conclusion of a contract or a unilateral engagement between a trader and consumer to be made away from the business premises of the trader, and whereas such contracts and engagements are the subject of legislation which differs from one Member State to another;

Whereas any disparity between such legislation may directly affect the functioning of the common market; whereas it is therefore necessary to approximate laws in this field;

Whereas the preliminary programme of the European Economic Community for a consumer protection and information policy provides *inter alia*, under paragraphs 24 and 25, that appropriate measures be taken to protect consumers against unfair commercial practices in respect of doorstep selling; whereas the second programme of the European Economic Community for a consumer protection and information policy confirmed that the action and priorities defined in the preliminary programme would be pursued;

Whereas the special feature of contracts concluded away from the business premises of the trader is that as a rule it is the trader who initiates the contract negotiations, for which the consumer is unprepared or which he does not expect; whereas the consumer is often unable to compare the quality and price of the offer with other offers; whereas this surprise element generally exists not only in contracts made at the doorstep but also in other forms of contract concluded by the trader away from his business premises;

Whereas the consumer should be given a right of cancellation over a period of at least seven days in order to enable him to assess the obligations arising under the contract;

Whereas appropriate measures should be taken to ensure that the consumer is informed in writing of this period for reflection;

Whereas the freedom of the Member States to maintain or introduce a total or partial prohibition on the conclusion of contracts away from business premises, inasmuch as they consider this to be in the interest of consumers, must not be affected;

HAS ADOPTED THIS DIRECTIVE:

---

[1] This Directive (85/577/EEC) has been implemented in the United Kingdom by the Consumer Protection (Cancellation of Contracts Concluded away from Business Premises) Regulations 1987 (S.I. 1987 No. 2117), printed above at p. 279.

Article 1

1. This Directive shall apply to contracts under which a trader supplies goods or services to a consumer and which are concluded:
—during an excursion organised by the trader away from his business
—during a visit by a trader
    (i) to the consumer's home or to that of another consumer;
    (ii) to the consumer's place of work;
where the visit does not take place at the express request of the consumer.

2. This Directive shall also apply to contracts for the supply of goods or services other than those concerning which the consumer requested the visit of the trader, provided that when he requested the visit the consumer did not know, or could not reasonably have known, that the supply of those other goods or services formed part of the trader's commercial or professional activities.

3. This Directive shall also apply to contracts in respect of which an offer was made by the consumer under conditions similar to those described in paragraph 1 or paragraph 2 although the consumer was not bound by that offer before its acceptance by the trader.

4. This Directive shall also apply to offers made contractually by the consumer under conditions similar to those described in paragraph 1 or paragraph 2 where the consumer is bound by his offer.

Article 2

For the purposes of this Directive:
"consumer" means a natural person who, in transactions covered by this Directive, is acting for purposes which can be regarded as outside his trade or profession;
"trader" means a natural or legal person who, for the transaction in question, acts in his commercial or professional capacity, and anyone acting in the name or on behalf of a trader.

Article 3

1. The Member States may decide that this Directive shall apply only to contracts for which the payment to be made by the consumer exceeds a specified amount. This amount may not exceed 60 ECU.
The Council, acting on a proposal from the Commission, shall examine and, if necessary, revise this amount for the first time no later than four years after the notification of the Directive and thereafter every two years, taking into account economic and monetary developments in the Community.

2. This Directive shall not apply to:
    (a) contracts for the construction, sale and rental of immovable property or contracts for repairing immovable property or contracts concerning other rights relating to immovable property.
        Contracts for the supply of goods and for their incorporation in immovable property or contracts for repairing immovable property shall fall within the scope of this Directive;
    (b) contracts for the supply of foodstuffs or beverages or other goods intended for current consumption in the household and supplied by regular roundsmen;
    (c) contracts for the supply of goods or services, provided that all three of the following conditions are met:

(i) the contract is concluded on the basis of a trader's catalogue which the consumer has a proper opportunity of reading in the absence of the trader's representative,

(ii) there is intended to be continuity of contract between the trader's representative and the consumer in relation to that or any subsequent transaction,

(iii) both the catalogue and the contract clearly inform the consumer of his right to return goods to the supplier within a period of not less than seven days of receipt or otherwise to cancel the contract within that period without obligation of any kind other than to take reasonable care of the goods;

(d) insurance contracts;

(e) contracts for securities.

3. By way of derogation from Article 1(2), member States may refrain from applying this Directive to contracts for the supply of goods or services having a direct connection with the goods or service concerning which the consumer requested the visit of the trader.

Article 4
In the case of transactions within the scope of Article 1, traders shall be required to give consumers written notice of their right of cancellation within the period laid down in Article 5, together with the name and address of a person against whom that right may be exercised.

Such notice shall be dated and shall state particulars enabling the contract to be identified. It shall be given to the consumer:

(a) in the case of Article 1(1), at the time of conclusion of the contract;

(b) in the case of Article 1(2), not later than the time of conclusion of the contract;

(c) in the case of Article 1(3) and 1(4), when the offer is made by the consumer.

Member States shall ensure that their national legislation lays down appropriate consumer protection measures in cases where the information referred to in this Article is not supplied.

Article 5
1. The consumer shall have the right to renounce the effects of his undertaking by sending notice within a period of not less than seven days from receipt by the consumer of the notice referred to in Article 4, in accordance with the procedure laid down by national law. It shall be sufficient if the notice is dispatched before the end of such period.

2. The giving of the notice shall have effect of releasing the consumer from any obligations under the cancelled contract.

Article 6
The consumer may not waive the rights conferred on him by this Directive.

Article 7
If the consumer exercises his right of renunciation, the legal effects shall be governed by national laws, particularly regarding reimbursement of payments for goods and services provided and the return of goods received.

Article 8
This Directive shall not prevent Member States from adopting or maintaining more favourable provisions to protect consumers in the field in which it covers.

Article 9
1. Member States shall take the measures necessary to comply with this Directive within 24 months of its notification. They shall forthwith inform the Commission thereof.

2. Member States shall ensure that the texts of the main provisions of national law which they adopt in the field covered by this Directive are communicated to the Commission.

Article 10
This Directive is addressed to Member States.

Done at Brussels, 20 December 1985.

Council Directive of 13 June 1990 on
package travel, package holidays and package tours[1]

(90/314/EEC)

THE COUNCIL OF THE EUROPEAN COMMUNITIES,

Having regard to the Treaty establishing the European Economic Community, and in particular Article 100a thereof,

Having regard to the proposal from the Commission,

In co-operation with the European Parliament,

Having regard to the opinion of the Economic and Social Committee,

Whereas one of the main objectives of the Community is to complete the internal market, of which the tourist sector is an essential part;

Whereas the national laws of Member States concerning package travel, package holidays and package tours, hereinafter referred to as "packages," show many disparities and national practices in this field are markedly different, which gives rise to obstacles to the freedom to provide services in respect of packages and distortions of competition amongst operators established in different Member States;

Whereas the establishment of common rules on packages will contribute to the elimination of these obstacles and thereby to the achievement of a common market in services, thus enabling operators established in one Member State to offer their services in other Member States and Community consumers to benefit from comparable conditions when buying a package in any Member State;

Whereas paragraph 36(b) of the Annex to the Council resolution of May 19, 1981 on a second programme of the European Economic Community for a consumer protection and information policy invites the Commission to study, *inter alia*, tourism and, if appropriate, to put forward suitable proposals, with due regard for their significance for consumer protection and the effects of differences in Member States' legislation on the proper functioning of the common market;

Whereas in the resolution on a Community policy on tourism on April 10, 1984 the Council welcomed the Commission's initiative in drawing attention to the importance of tourism and took note of the Commission's initial guidelines for a Community policy on tourism;

Whereas the Commission communication to the Council entitled "A New Impetus for Consumer Protection Policy," which was approved by resolution of the Council on May 6, 1986, lists in paragraph 37, among the measures proposed by the Commission, the harmonisation of legislation on packages;

Whereas tourism plays an increasingly important role in the economies of the Member States; whereas the package system is a fundamental part of tourism; whereas the package travel industry in Member States would be stimulated to greater growth and productivity if at least a minimum of common rules were adopted in order to give it a Community dimension; whereas this would not only produce benefits for Community citizens buying packages organised on

---

[1] This Directive (90/314/EEC) has been implemented in the United Kingdom by the Package Travel, Package Holidays and Package Tours Regulations 1992, printed above at p. 313.

the basis of those rules, but would attract tourists from outside the Community seeking the advantages of guaranteed standards in packages;

Whereas disparities in the rules protecting consumers in different Member States are a disincentive to consumers in one Member State from buying packages in another Member State;

Whereas this disincentive is particularly effective in deterring consumers from buying packages outside their own Member State, and more effective than it would be in relation to the acquisition of other services, having regard to the special nature of the services supplied in a package which generally involve the expenditure of substantial amounts of money in advance and the supply of the services in a State other than that in which the consumer is resident;

Whereas the consumer should have the benefit of the protection introduced by this Directive irrespective of whether he is a direct contracting party, a transferee or a member of a group on whose behalf another person has concluded a contract in respect of a package;

Whereas the organiser of the package and/or the retailer of it should be under obligation to ensure that in descriptive matter relating to packages which they respectively organise and sell, the information which is given is not misleading and brochures made available to consumers contain information which is comprehensible and accurate;

Whereas the consumer needs to have a record of the terms of contract applicable to the package; whereas this can conveniently be achieved by requiring that all the terms of the contract be stated in writing of such other documentary form as shall be comprehensible and accessible to him, and that he be given a copy thereof;

Whereas the consumer should be at liberty in certain circumstances to transfer to a willing third person a booking made by him for a package;

Whereas the price established under the contract should not in principle be subject to revision except where the possibility of upward or downward revision is expressly provided for in the contract; whereas that possibility should nonetheless be subject to certain conditions;

Whereas the consumer should in certain circumstances be free to withdraw before departure from a package travel contract;

Whereas there should be a clear definition of the rights available to the consumer in circumstances where the organiser of the package cancels it before the agreed date of departure;

Whereas if, after the consumer has departed, there occurs a significant failure of performance of the services for which he has contracted or the organiser perceives that he will be unable to procure a significant part of the services to be provided; the organiser should have certain obligations towards the consumer;

Whereas the organiser and/or retailer party to the contract should be liable to the consumer for the proper performance of the obligations arising from the contract; whereas, moreover, the organizer and/or retailer should be liable for the damage resulting for the consumer from failure to perform or improper performance of the contract unless the defects in the performance of the contract are attributable neither to any fault of theirs nor to that of another supplier of services;

Whereas in cases where the organizer and/or retailer is liable for failure to perform or improper performance of the services involved in the package, such liability should be limited in accordance with the international conventions governing such services, in particular the Warsaw Convention of 1929 in International Carriage by Air, the Berne Convention of 1961 on Carriage by Rail, the

Athens Convention of 1974 on Carriage by Sea and the Paris Convention of 1962 on the Liability of Hotel-keepers; whereas, moreover, with regard to damage other than personal injury, it should be possible for liability also to be limited under the package contract provided, however, that such limits are not unreasonable;

Whereas certain arrangements should be made for the information of consumers and the handling of complaints;

Whereas both the consumer and the package travel industry would benefit if organizers and/or retailers were placed under an obligation to provide sufficient evidence of security in the event of insolvency;

Whereas Member States should be at liberty to adopt, or retain, more stringent provisions relating to package travel for the purpose of protecting the consumer,

HAS ADOPTED THIS DIRECTIVE:

Article 1
The purpose of this Directive is to approximate the laws, regulations and administrative provisions of the Member States relating to packages sold or offered for sale in the territory of the Community.

Article 2
For the purposes of this Directive:

1. ''package'' means the pre-arranged combination of not fewer than two of the following when sold or offered for sale at an inclusive price and when the service covers a period of more than twenty-four hours or includes overnight accommodation:
- (a) transport;
- (b) accommodation;
- (c) other tourist services not ancillary to transport or accommodation and accounting for a significant proportion of the package.

The separate billing of various components of the same package shall not absolve the organizer or retailer from the obligations under this Directive;

2. ''organizer'' means the person who, other than occasionally, organizes packages and sells or offers them for sale, whether directly or through a retailer;

3. ''retailer'' means the person who sells or offers for sale the package put together by the organizer;

4. ''consumer'' means the person who takes or agrees to take the package (''the principal contractor''), or any person on whose behalf the principal contractor agrees to purchase the package (''the other beneficiaries'') or any person to whom the principal contractor or any of the other beneficiaries transfers the package (''the transferee'');

5. ''contract'' means the agreement linking the consumer to the organizer and/or the retailer.

Article 3
1. Any descriptive matter concerning a package and supplied by the organizer or the retailer to the consumer, the price of the package and any other conditions applying to the contract must not contain any misleading information.

2. When a brochure is made available to the consumer, it shall indicate in a legible, comprehensible and accurate manner both the price and adequate information concerning:

(a) the destination and the means, characteristics and categories of transport used;

(b) the type of accommodation, its location, category or degree of comfort and its main features, its approval and tourist classification under the rules of the host Member State concerned;

(c) the meal plan;

(d) the itinerary;

(e) general information on passport and visa requirements for nationals of the Member State or States concerned and health formalities required for the journey and the stay;

(f) either the monetary amount or the percentage of the price which is to be paid on account, and the timetable for payment of the balance;

(g) whether a minimum number of persons is required for the package to take place and, if so, the deadline for informing the consumer in the event of cancellation.

The particulars contained in the brochure are binding on the organizer or retailer, unless:

— changes in such particulars have been clearly communicated to the consumer before conclusion of the contract, in which case the brochure shall expressly state so,

— changes are made later following an agreement between the parties to the contract.

Article 4

1.(a) The organizer and/or the retailer shall provide the consumer, in writing or any other appropriate form, before the contract is concluded, with general information on passport and visa requirements applicable to nationals of the Member State or States concerned and in particular on the periods for obtaining them, as well as with information on the health formalities required for the journey and the stay;

(b) The organizer and/or retailer shall also provide the consumer, in writing or any other appropriate form, with the following information in good time before the start of the journey:

(i) the times and places of intermediate stops and transport connections as well as details of the place to be occupied by the traveller, e.g. cabin or berth on ship, sleeper compartment on train;

(ii) the name, address and telephone number of the organizers and/or retailer's local representative or, failing that, of local agencies on whose assistance a consumer in difficulty could call.

Where no such representatives or agencies exist, the consumer must in any case be provided with an emergency telephone number or any other information that will enable him to contact the organizer and/or the retailer;

(iii) in the case of journeys or stays abroad by minors, information enabling direct contact to be established with the child or the person responsible at the child's place of stay;

(iv) information on the optional conclusion of an insurance policy to cover the cost of cancellation by the consumer or the cost of assistance, including repatriation, in the event of accident or illness.

2. Member States shall ensure that in relation to the contract the following principles apply:

> (a) depending on the particular package, the contract shall contain at least the elements listed in the Annex;
>
> (b) all the terms of the contract are set out in writing or such other form as is comprehensible and accessible to the consumer and must be communicated to him before the conclusion of the contract; the consumer is given a copy of these terms;
>
> (c) the provision under (b) shall not preclude the belated conclusion of last-minute reservations or contracts.

3. Where the consumer is prevented from proceeding with the package, he may transfer his booking, having first given the organizer or the retailer reasonable notice of his intention before departure, to a person who satisfied all the conditions applicable to the package. The transferor of the package and the transferee shall be jointly and severally liable to the organizer or retailer party to the contract for payment of the balance due and for any additional costs arising from such transfer.

4.
> (a) The prices laid down in the contract shall not be subject to revision unless the contract expressly provides for the possibility of upward or downward revision and states precisely how the revised price is to be calculated, and solely to allow for variations in:
> - transportation costs, including the cost of fuel,
> - dues, taxes or fees chargeable for certain services, such as landing taxes or embarkation or disembarkation fees at ports and airports,
> - the exchange rates applied to the particular package.
>
> (b) During the twenty days prior to the departure date stipulated, the price stated in the contract shall not be increased.

5. If the organizer finds that before the departure he is constrained to alter significantly any of the essential terms, such as the price, he shall notify the consumer as quickly as possible in order to enable him to take appropriate decisions and in particular:

> - either to withdraw from the contract without penalty,
> - or to accept a rider to the contract specifying the alterations made and their impact on the price.

The consumer shall inform the organizer or the retailer of his decision as soon as possible.

6. If the consumer withdraws from the contract pursuant to paragraph 5, or if, for whatever cause, other than the fault of the consumer, the organizer cancels the package before the agreed date of departure, the consumer shall be entitled;

> (a) either to take a substitute package of equivalent or higher quality where the organizer and/or retailer is able to offer him such a substitute. If the replacement package offered is of lower quality, the organizer shall refund the difference in price to the consumer;
>
> (b) or to be repaid as soon as possible all sums paid by him under the contract.

In such a case, he shall be entitled, if appropriate, to be compensated by either the organizer or the retailer, whichever the relevant Member State's law requires, for non-performance of the contract, except where:

> (i) cancellation is on the grounds that the number of persons enrolled for the package is less than the minimum number required and the con-

sumer is informed of the cancellation, in writing, within the period indicated in the package description; or

(ii) cancellation, excluding overbooking, is for reasons of *force majeure*, i.e. unusual and unforseeable circumstances beyond the control of the party by whom it is pleaded, the consequences of which could not have been avoided even if all due care had been exercised.

7.   Where, after departure, a significant proportion of the services contracted for is not provided or the organizer perceives that he will be unable to procure a significant proportion of the services to be provided, the organizer shall make suitable alternative arrangements, at no extra cost to the consumer, for the continuation of the package, and where appropriate compensate the consumer for the difference between the services offered and those supplied.

If it is impossible to make such arrangements or these are not accepted by the consumer for good reasons, the organizer shall, where appropriate, provide the consumer, at no extra cost, with the equivalent transport back to the place of departure, or to another return-point to which the consumer has agreed and shall, where appropriate, compensate the consumer.

Article 5

1.   Member States shall take the necessary steps to ensure that the organizer and/or retailer party to the contract is liable to the consumer for the proper performance of the obligations arising from the contract, irrespective of whether such obligations are to be performed by that organizer and/or retailer or by other suppliers of services without prejudice to the right of the organizer and/or retailer to pursue those other suppliers of services.

2.   With regard to the damage resulting for the consumer from the failure to perform or the improper performance of the contract, Member States shall take the necessary steps to ensure that the organizer and/or retailer is/are liable unless such failure to perform or improper performance is attributable neither to any fault of theirs nor to that of another supplier of services, because:

— the failures which occur in the performance of the contract are attributable to the consumer,

— such failures are attributable to a third party unconnected with the provision of the services contracted for, and are unforseeable or unavoidable,

— such failures are due to a case of *force majeure* such as that defined in Article 4(6), second subparagraph (ii), or to an event which the organizer and/or retailer or the supplier of services, even with all due care, could not foresee or forestall.

In the cases referred to in the second and third indents, the organizer and/or retailer party to the contract shall be required to give prompt assistance to a consumer in difficulty.

In the matter of damages arising from the non-performance or improper performance of the services involved in the package, the Member States may allow compensation to be limited in accordance with the international conventions governing such services.

In the matter of damage other than personal injury resulting from the non-performance or improper performance of the services involved in the package, the Member States may allow compensation to be limited under the contract. Such limitation shall not be unreasonable.

3. Without prejudice to the fourth subparagraph of paragraph 2, there may be no exclusion by means of a contractual clause from the provisions of paragraphs 1 and 2.

4. The consumer must communicate any failure in the performance of a contract which he perceives on the spot to the supplier of the services concerned and to the organizer and/or retailer in writing or any other appropriate form at the earliest opportunity.

This obligation must be stated clearly and explicitly in the contract

Article 6
In cases of complaint, the organizer and/or retailer or his local representative, if there is one, must make prompt efforts to find appropriate solutions.

Article 7
The organizer and/or retailer party to the contract shall provide sufficient evidence of security for the refund of money paid over and for the repatriation of the consumer in the event of insolvency.

Article 8
Member States may adopt or return more stringent provisions in the field covered by this Directive to protect the consumer.

Article 9
1. Member States shall bring into force the measures necessary to comply with this Directive before 31 December 1992. They shall forthwith inform the Commission thereof.

2. Member States shall communicate to the Commission the texts of the main provisions of national law which they adopt in the field governed by this Directive. The Commission shall inform the other Member States thereof.

Articles 10
This Directive is addressed to the Member States.

Done at Luxembourg, 13 June 1990

ANNEX

Elements to be included in the contract if relevant to the particular package;
- (a) the travel destination(s) and, where periods of stay are involved, the relevant periods, with dates;
- (b) the means, characteristics and categories of transport to be used, the dates, times and points of departure and return;
- (c) where the package includes accommodation, its location, its tourist category or degree of comfort, its main features, its compliance with the rules of the host Member State concerned and the meal plan;
- (d) whether a minimum number of persons is required for the package to take place and, if so, the deadline for informing the consumer in the event of cancellation;
- (e) the itinerary;
- (f) visits, excursions or other services which are included in the total price agreed for the package;

(g) the name and address of the organizer, the retailer and, where appropriate, the insurer;

(h) the price of the package, an indication of the possibility of price revisions under Article 4(4) and an indication of any dues, taxes or fees chargeable for certain services (landing, embarkation fees at ports and airports, tourist taxes) where such costs are not included in the package;

(i) the payment schedule and method of payment;

(j) special requirements which the consumer has communicated to the organizer or retailer when making the booking, and which both have accepted;

(k) periods with which the consumer must make any complaint concerning failure to perform or improper performance of the contract.

Council Directive of 29 June 1992 on general product safety[1]

(92/59/EEC)

THE COUNCIL OF THE EUROPEAN COMMUNITIES

Having regard to the Treaty establishing the European Economic Community, and in particular Article 100a thereof,

Having regard to the proposal from the Commission,

In cooperation with the European Parliament,

Having regard to the opinion of the Economic and Social Committee,

Whereas it is important to adopt measures with the aim of progressively establishing the internal market over a period expiring on 31 December 1992; whereas the internal market is to comprise an area without internal frontiers in which the free movement of goods, persons, services and capital is ensured;

Whereas some Member States have adopted horizontal legislation on product safety, imposing, in particular, a general obligation on economic operators to market only safe products; whereas those legislations differ in the level of protection afforded to persons; whereas such disparities and the absence of horizontal legislation in other Member States are liable to create barriers to trade and distortions of competition within the internal market;

Whereas it is very difficult to adopt Community legislation for every product which exists or may be developed; whereas there is a need for a broadly-based, legislative framework of a horizontal nature to deal with those products, and also to cover lacunae in existing or forthcoming specific legislation, in particular with a view to ensuring a high level of protection of safety and health of persons, as required by Article 100a(3) of the Treaty;

Whereas it is therefore necessary to establish on a Community level a general safety requirement for any product placed on the market that is intended for consumers or likely to be used by consumers; whereas certain second-hand goods should nevertheless be excluded by their nature;

Whereas production equipment, capital goods and other products used exclusively in the context of a trade or business are not covered by this Directive;

Whereas, in the absence of more specific safety provisions, within the framework of Community regulations, covering the products concerned, the provisions of this Directive are to apply;

Whereas when there are specific rules of Community law, of the total harmonization type, and in particular rules adopted on the basis of the new approach, which lay down obligations regarding product safety, further obligations should not be imposed on economic operators as regards the placing on the market of products covered by such rules;

Whereas, when the provisions of specific Community regulations cover only certain aspects of safety or categories of risks in respect of the product concerned, the obligations of economic operators in respect of such aspects are determined solely by those provisions;

Whereas it is appropriate to supplement the duty to observe the general safety requirement by an obligation on economic operators to supply consumers with relevant information and adopt measures commensurate with the characteristics

---

[1] This Directive (92/59/EEC) has been implemented in the United Kingdom by the General Product Safety Regulations 1994 (S.I. 1994 No. 2328), printed above at p. 330.

of the products, enabling them to be informed of the risks that these products might present;

Whereas in the absence of specific regulations, criteria should be defined whereby product safety can be assessed;

Whereas Member States must establish authorities responsible for monitoring product safety and with powers to take the appropriate measures;

Whereas it is necessary in particular for the appropriate measures to include the power for Member States to organize, immediately and efficiently, the withdrawal of dangerous products already placed on the market;

Whereas it is necessary for the preservation of the unity of the market to inform the Commission of any measure restricting the placing on the market of a product or requiring its withdrawal from the market except for those relating to an event which is local in effect and in any case limited to the territory of the Member State concerned; whereas such measures can be taken only in compliance with the provisions of the Treaty, and in particular Articles 30 to 36;

Whereas this Directive applies without prejudice to the notification procedures in Council Directive 83/189/EEC of 28 March 1983 laying down a procedure for the provision of information in the field of technical standards and regulations and in Commission Decision 88/383/EEC of 24 February 1988 providing for the improvement of information on safety, hygiene and health at work;

Whereas effective supervision of product safety requires the setting-up at national and Community levels of a system of rapid exchange of information in emergency situations in respect of the safety of a product and whereas the procedure laid down by Council Decision 89/45/EEC of 21 December 1988 on a Community system for the rapid exchange of information on dangers arising from the use of consumer products should therefore be incorporated into this Directive and the above Decision should be repealed; whereas it is also advisable for this Directive to take over the detailed procedures adopted under the above Decision and to give the Commission, assisted by a committee, power to adapt them;

Whereas, moreover, equivalent notification procedures already exist for pharmaceuticals, which come under Directives 75/319/EEC and 81/851/EEC, concerning animal diseases referred to in Directive 82/894/EEC, for products of animal origin covered by Directive 89/662/EEC, and in the form of the system for the rapid exchange of information in radiological emergencies under Decision 87/600/Euratom;

Whereas it is primarily for Member States, in compliance with the Treaty and in particular with Articles 30 to 36 thereof, to take appropriate measures with regard to dangerous products located within their territory;

Whereas in such a situation the decision taken on a particular product could differ from one Member State to another; whereas such a difference may entail unacceptable disparities in consumer protection and constitute a barrier to intra-Community trade;

Whereas it may be necessary to cope with serious product-safety problems which affect or could affect, in the immediate future, all or a large part of the Community and which, in view of the nature of the safety problem posed by the product cannot be dealt with effectively in a manner commensurate with the urgency of the problem under the procedures laid down in the specific rules of Community law applicable to the products or category of products in question;

Whereas it is therefore necessary to provide for an adequate mechanism allowing, in the last resort, for the adoption of measures applicable throughout the Community, in the form of a decision addressed to the Member States, in order to cope with emergency situations as mentioned above; whereas such a decision is not of direct application to economic operators and must be incorporated into a national instrument; whereas measures adopted under such a procedure can be no more than interim measures that have to be taken by the Commission assisted by a committee of representatives of the Member States; whereas, for reasons of cooperation with the Member States, it is appropriate to provide for a regulatory committee according to procedure III (b) of Decision 87/373/ EEC;

Whereas this Directive does not affect victims' rights within the meaning of Council Directive 85/374/EEC of 25 July 1985 on the approximation of the laws, regulations and administrative provisions of the Member States concerning liability for defective products;

Whereas it is necessary that Member States provide for appropriate means of redress before the competent courts in respect of measures taken by the competent authorities which restrict the placing on the market of a product or require its withdrawal;

Whereas it is appropriate to consider, in the light of experience, possible adaptation of this Directive, particularly as regards extension of its scope and provisions on emergency situations and intervention at Community level;

Whereas, in addition, the adoption of measures concerning imported products with a view to preventing risks to the safety and health of persons must comply with the Community's international obligations,

HAS ADOPTED THIS DIRECTIVE:

TITLE I: Objective—Scope—Definitions

Article 1

1. The purpose of the provisions of this Directive is to ensure that products placed on the market are safe.

2. The provisions of this Directive shall apply in so far as there are no specific provisions in rules of Community law governing the safety of the products concerned.

In particular, where specific rules of Community law contain provisions imposing safety requirements on the products which they govern, the provisions of Articles 2 to 4 of this Directive shall not, in any event, apply to those products.

Where specific rules of Community law contain provisions governing only certain aspects of product safety or categories of risks for the products concerned, those are the provisions which shall apply to the products concerned with regard to the relevant safety aspects or risks.

Article 2

For the purposes of this Directive:

(a) *product* shall mean any product intended for consumers or likely to be used by consumers, supplied whether for consideration or not in the course of a commercial activity and whether new, used or reconditioned.

However, this Directive shall not apply to second-hand products supplied as antiques or as products to be repaired or reconditioned prior to being used, provided that the supplier clearly informs the person to whom he supplies the product to that effect;

(b) *safe product* shall mean any product which, under normal or reasonably foreseeable conditions of use, including duration, does not present any risk or only the minimum risks compatible with the product's use, considered as acceptable and consistent with a high level of protection for the safety and health of persons, taking into account the following points in particular:

—the characteristics of the product, including its composition, packaging, instructions for assembly and maintenance,

—the effect on other products, where it is reasonably foreseeable that it will be used with other products,

—the presentation of the product, the labelling, any instructions for its use and disposal and any other indication or information provided by the producer,

—the categories of consumers at serious risk when using the product, in particular children.

The feasibility of obtaining higher levels of safety or the availability of other products presenting a lesser degree of risk shall not constitute grounds for considering a product to be "unsafe" or "dangerous";

(c) *dangerous product* shall mean any product which does not meet the definition of "safe product" according to point (b) hereof;

(d) *producer* shall mean:

—the manufacturer of the product, when he is established in the Community, and any other person presenting himself as the manufacturer by affixing to the product his name, trade mark or other distinctive mark, or the person who reconditions the product,

—the manufacturer's representative, when the manufacturer is not established in the Community or, if there is no representative established in the Community, the importer of the product,

—other professionals in the supply chain, insofar as their activities may affect the safety properties of a product placed on the market.

(e) *distributor* shall mean any professional in the supply chain whose activity does not affect the safety properties of a product.

TITLE II: General safety requirement

Article 3

1. Producers shall be obliged to place only safe products on the market.

2. Within the limits of their respective activities, producers shall:

—provide consumers with the relevant information to enable them to assess the risks inherent in a product throughout the normal or reasonably foreseeable period of its use, where such risks are not immediately obvious without adequate warnings, and to take precautions against those risks.

Provision of such warnings does not, however, exempt any person from compliance with the other requirements laid down in this Directive,

—adopt measures commensurate with the characteristics of the products which they supply, to enable them to be informed of risks which these products might present and to take appropriate action including, if necessary, withdrawing the product in question from the market to avoid these risks.

The above measures shall for example include, whenever appropriate, marking of the products or product batches in such a way that they can be identified, sample testing of marketed products, investigating complaints made and keeping distributors informed of such monitoring.

   3.   Distributors shall be required to act with due care in order to help to ensure compliance with the general safety requirement, in particular by not supplying products which they know or should have presumed, on the basis of the information in their possession and as professionals, do not comply with this requirement. In particular, within the limits of their respective activities, they shall participate in monitoring the safety of products placed on the market, especially by passing on information on product risks and cooperating in the action taken to avoid these risks.

Article 4

   1.   Where there are no specific Community provisions governing the safety of the products in question, a product shall be deemed safe when it conforms to the specific rules of national law of the Member State in whose territory the product is in circulation, such rules being drawn up in conformity with the Treaty, and in particular Articles 30 and 36 thereof, and laying down the health and safety requirements which the product must satisfy in order to be marketed.

   2.   In the absence of specific rules as referred to in paragraph 1, the conformity of a product to the general safety requirement shall be assessed having regard to voluntary national standards giving effect to a European standard or, where they exist, to Community technical specification, or, failing these, to standards drawn up in the Member State in which the product is in circulation, or to the codes of good practice in respect of health and safety in the sector concerned or to the state of the art and technology and to the safety which consumers may reasonably expect.

   3.   Conformity of a product with the provisions mentioned in paragraphs 1 or 2 shall not bar the competent authorities of the Member States from taking appropriate measures to impose restrictions on its being placed on the market or to require its withdrawal from the market where there is evidence that, despite such conformity, it is dangerous to the health and safety of consumers.

TITLE III: Obligations and powers of the Member States

Article 5

   5.   Member States shall adopt the necessary laws, regulations and administrative provisions to make producers and distributors comply with their obligations under this Directive in such a way that products placed on the market are safe.

In particular, Member States shall establish or nominate authorities to monitor the compliance of products with the obligation to place only safe products on the market and arrange for such authorities to have the necessary powers to take the appropriate measures incumbent upon them under this Directive, including the possibility of imposing suitable penalties in the event of failure to comply with the obligations deriving from this Directive. They shall notify the Commission of the said authorities; the Commission shall pass on the information to the other Member States.

Article 6

1.   For the purposes of Article 5, Member States shall have the necessary powers, acting in accordance with the degree or risk and in conformity with the Treaty, and in particular Articles 30 and 36 thereof, to adopt appropriate measures with a view, *inter alia*, to:

(a) organizing appropriate checks on the safety properties of products, even after their being placed on the market as being safe, on an adequate scale, up to the final stage of use or consumption;

(b) requiring all necessary information from the parties concerned;

(c) taking samples of a product or a product line and subjecting them to safety checks;

(d) subjecting product marketing to prior conditions designed to ensure product safety and requiring that suitable warnings be affixed regarding the risks which the product may present;

(e) making arrangements to ensure that persons who might be exposed to a risk from a product are informed in good time and in a suitable manner of the said risk by, *inter alia*, the publication of special warnings;

(f) temporarily prohibiting, for the period required to carry out the various checks, anyone from supplying, offering to supply or exhibiting a product or product batch, whenever there are precise and consistent indications that they are dangerous;

(g) prohibiting the placing on the market of a product or product batch which has proved dangerous and establishing the accompanying measures needed to ensure that the ban is complied with;

(h) organizing the effective and immediate withdrawal of a dangerous product or product batch already on the market and, if necessary, its destruction under appropriate conditions.

2.   The measures to be taken by the competent authorities of the Member States under this Article shall be addressed, as appropriate, to:

(a) the producer;

(b) within the limits of their respective activities, distributors and in particular the party responsible for the first stage of distribution on the national market;

(c) any other person, where necessary, with regard to cooperation in action taken to avoid risks arising from a product.

TITLE IV: Notification and Exchanges of Information

Article 7

1.   Where a Member State takes measures which restrict the placing of a product or a product batch on the market or require its withdrawal from the market, such as provided for in Article 6(1)(d) to (h), the Member State shall, to the extent that such notification is not required under any specific Community legislation, inform the Commission of the said measures, specifying its reasons for adopting them. This obligation shall not apply where the measures relate to an event which is local in effect and in any case limited to the territory of the Member State concerned.

2.   The Commission shall enter into consultations with the parties concerned as quickly as possible. Where the Commission concludes, after such consultations, that the measure is justified, it shall immediately inform the Member State

which initiated the action and the other Member States. Where the Commission concludes, after such consultations, that the measures are not justified, it shall immediately inform the Member State which initiated the action.

TITLE V: Emergency situations and action at Community level

Article 8

1. Where a Member State adopts or decides to adopt emergency measures to prevent, restrict or impose specific conditions on the possible marketing or use, within its own territory, of a product or product batch by reason of a serious and immediate risk presented by the said product or product batch to the health and safety of consumers, it shall forthwith inform the Commission thereof, unless provision is made for this obligation in procedures of a similar nature in the context of other Community instruments.

This obligation shall not apply if the effects of the risk do not, or cannot, go beyond the territory of the Member State concerned.

Without prejudice to the provisions of the first subparagraph, Member States may pass on to the Commission any information in their possession regarding the existence of a serious and immediate risk before deciding to adopt the measures in question.

2. On receiving this information, the Commission shall check to see whether it complies with the provisions of this Directive and shall forward it to the other Member States, which, in turn, shall immediately inform the Commission of any measures adopted.

3. Detailed procedures for the Community information system described in this Article are set out in the Annex. They shall be adapted by the Commission in accordance with the procedure laid down in Article 11.

Article 9

If the Commission becomes aware, through notification given by the Member States or through information provided by them, in particular under Article 7 or Article 8, of the existence of a serious and immediate risk from a product to the health and safety of consumers in various Member States and if:

 (a) one or more Member States have adopted measures entailing restrictions on the marketing of the product or requiring its withdrawal from the market, such as those provided for in Article 6(1)(d) to (h);

 (b) Member States differ on the adoption of measures to deal with the risk in question;

 (c) the risk cannot be dealt with, in view of the nature of the safety issue posed by the product and in a manner compatible with the urgency of the case, under the other procedures laid down by the specific Community legislation applicable to the product or category of products concerned; and

 (d) the risk can be eliminated effectively only by adopting appropriate measures applicable at Community level, in order to ensure the protection of the health and safety of consumers and the proper functioning of the common market,

the Commission, after consulting the Member States and at the request of at least one of them, may adopt a decision, in accordance with the procedure laid down in Article 11, requiring Member States to take temporary measures from among those listed in Article 6(1)(d) to (h).

Article 10

1. The Commission shall be assisted by a Committee on Product Safety Emergencies, hereinafter referred to as "the Committee", composed of the representatives of the Member States and chaired by a representative of the Commission.

2. Without prejudice to Article 9(c), there shall be close cooperation between the Committee referred to in paragraph 1 and the other Committees established by specific rules of Community law to assist the Commission as regards the health and safety aspects of the product concerned.

Article 11

1. The Commission representative shall submit to the Committee a draft of the measures to be taken. The Committee, having verified that the conditions listed in Article 9 are fulfilled, shall deliver its opinion on the draft within a time limit which the Chairman may lay down according to the urgency of the matter but which may not exceed one month. The opinion shall be delivered by the majority laid down in Article 148(2) of the Treaty for adoption of decisions by the Council on a proposal from the Commission. The votes of the representatives of the Member States within the Committee shall be weighted in the manner set out in that Article. The Chairman shall not vote.

The Commission shall adopt the measures in question, if they are in accordance with the opinion of the Committee. If the measures proposed are not in accordance with the Committee's opinion, or in the absence of an opinion, the Commission shall forthwith submit to the Council a proposal regarding the measures to be taken. The Council shall act by a qualified majority.

If the Council has not acted within 15 days of the date on which the proposal was submitted to it, the measures proposed shall be adopted by the Commission unless the Council has decided against them by a simple majority.

2. Any measure adopted under this procedure shall be valid for no longer than three months. That period may be prolonged under the same procedure.

3. Member States shall take all necessary measures to implement the decisions adopted under this procedure within less than 10 days.

4. The competent authorities of the Member States responsible for carrying out measures adopted under this procedure shall, within one month, give the parties concerned an opportunity to submit their views and shall inform the Commission accordingly.

Article 12

The Member States and the Commission shall take the steps necessary to ensure that their officials and agents are required not to disclose information obtained for the purposes of this Directive which, by its nature, is covered by professional secrecy, except for information relating to the safety properties of a given product which must be made public if circumstances so require, in order to protect the health and safety of persons.

TITLE VI: Miscellaneous and final provisions

Article 13

This Directive shall be without prejudice to Directive 85/374/EEC.

Article 14

1. Any decision adopted under this Directive and involving restrictions on the placing of a product on the market, or requiring its withdrawal from the market, must state the appropriate reasons on which it is based. It shall be notified as soon as possible to the party concerned and shall indicate the remedies available under the provisions in force in the Member State in question and the time limits applying to such remedies.

The parties concerned shall, whenever feasible, be given an opportunity to submit their views before the adoption of the measure. If this has not been done in advance because of the urgency of the measures to be taken, such opportunity shall be given in due course after the measure has been implemented.

Measures requiring the withdrawal of a product from the market shall take into consideration the need to encourage distributors, users and consumers to contribute to the implementation of such measures.

2. Member States shall ensure that any measure taken by the competent authorities involving restrictions on the placing of a product on the market or requiring its withdrawal from the market can be challenged before the competent courts.

3. Any decision taken by virtue of this Directive and involving restrictions on the placing of a product on the market or requiring its withdrawal from the market shall be entirely without prejudice to assessment of the liability of the party concerned, in the light of the national criminal law applying in the case in question.

Article 15

Every two years following the date of adoption, the Commission shall submit a report on the implementation of this Directive to the European Parliament and the Council.

Article 16

Four years from the date referred to in Article 17(1), on the basis of a Commission report on the experience acquired, together with appropriate proposals, the Council shall decide whether to adjust this Directive, in particular with a view to extending its scope as laid down in Article 1(1) and Article 2(a), and whether the provisions of Title V should be amended.

Article 17

Member States shall adopt the laws, regulations and administrative provisions necessary to comply with this Directive by 29 June 1994 at the latest. They shall forthwith inform the Commission thereof. The provisions adopted shall apply with effect from 29 June 1994.

2. When these measures are adopted by the Member States, they shall contain a reference to this Directive or be accompanied by such a reference on the occasion of their official publication. The methods of making such a reference shall be laid down by the Member States.

3. Member States shall communicate to the Commission the text of the provisions of national law which they adopt in the area covered by this Directive.

Article 18

Decision 89/45/EEC is hereby repealed on the date referred to in Article 17(1).

Article 19

This Directive is addressed to the Member States.

Done at Luxembourg, 29 June 1992.

ANNEX

DETAILED PROCEDURES FOR THE APPLICATION OF THE COMMUNITY SYSTEM FOR THE RAPID EXCHANGE OF INFORMATION PROVIDED FOR IN ARTICLE 8.

[*Omitted*]

Council Directive of 5 April 1993 on unfair terms in consumer contracts[1]

(93/13/EEC)

THE COUNCIL OF THE EUROPEAN COMMUNITIES,

Having regard to the Treaty establishing the European Economic Community, and in particular Article 100A thereof,

Having regard to the proposal from the Commission,

In co-operation with the European Parliament,

Having regard to the opinion of the Economic and Social Committee,

Whereas it is necessary to adopt measures with the aim of progressively establishing the internal market before 31 December 1992; whereas the internal market comprises an area without internal frontiers in which goods, persons, services and capital move freely;

Whereas the laws of Member States relating to the terms of contract between the seller of goods or supplier of services, on the one hand, and the consumer of them, on the other hand, show many disparities, with the result that the national markets for the sale of goods and services to consumers differ from each other and that distortions of competition may arise amongst the sellers and suppliers, notably when they sell and supply in other Member States;

Whereas, in particular, the laws of Member States relating to unfair terms in consumer contracts show marked divergences;

Whereas it is the responsibility of the Member States to ensure that contracts concluded with consumers do not contain unfair terms;

Whereas, generally speaking, consumers do not know the rules of law which, in Member States other than their own, govern contracts for the sale of goods or services; whereas this lack of awareness may deter them from direct transactions for the purchase of goods or services in another Member State;

Whereas, in order to facilitate the establishment of the internal market and to safeguard the citizen in his role as consumer when acquiring goods and services under contracts which are governed by the laws of Member States other than his own, it is essential to remove unfair terms from those contracts;

Whereas sellers of goods and suppliers of services will thereby be helped in their task of selling goods and supplying services, both at home and throughout the internal market; whereas competition will thus be stimulated, so contributing to increased choice for Community citizens as consumers;

Whereas the two Community programmes for a consumer protection and information policy underlined the importance of safeguarding consumers in the matter of unfair terms of contract; whereas this protection ought to be provided by laws and regulations which are either harmonised at Community level or adopted directly at that level;

Whereas in accordance with the principle laid down under the heading "Protection of the economic interests of the consumers", as stated in those programmes: "acquirers of goods and services should be protected against the

---

[1] This Directive (93/13/EEC) has been implemented in the United Kingdom by the Unfair Terms in Consumer Contracts Regulations 1994 (S.I. 1994 No. 3159), printed above at p. 336.

abuse of power by the seller or supplier, in particular against one-sided standard contracts and the unfair exclusion of essential rights in contracts'';

Whereas more effective protection of the consumer can be achieved by adopting uniform rules of law in the matter of unfair terms; whereas those rules should apply to all contracts concluded between sellers or suppliers and consumers; whereas as a result *inter alia* contracts relating to employment, contracts relating to succession rights, contracts relating to rights under family law and contracts relating to the incorporation and organisation of companies or partnership agreements must be excluded from this Directive;

Whereas the consumer must receive equal protection under contracts concluded by word of mouth and written contracts regardless, in the latter case, of whether the terms of the contract are contained in one or more documents;

Whereas, however, as they now stand, national laws allow only partial harmonisation to be envisaged; whereas, in particular, only contractual terms which have not been individually negotiated are covered by this Directive; whereas Member States should have the option, with due regard for the Treaty, to afford consumers a higher level of protection through national provisions that are more stringent than those of this Directive;

Whereas the statutory or regulatory provisions of the Member States which directly or indirectly determine the terms of consumer contracts are presumed not to contain unfair terms; whereas, therefore, it does not appear to be necessary to subject the terms which reflect mandatory statutory or regulatory provisions and the principles or provisions of international contraventions to which the Member States or the Community are party; whereas in that respect the wording ''mandatory statutory or regulatory provisions'' in Article 1(2) also covers rules which, according to the law, shall apply between the contracting parties provided that no other arrangements have been established;

Whereas Member States must however ensure that unfair terms are not included, particularly because this Directive also applies to trades, business or professions of a public nature;

Whereas it is necessary to fix in a general way the criteria for assessing the unfair character of contract terms;

Whereas the assessment, according to the general criteria chosen, of the unfair character of terms, in particular in sale or supply activities of a public nature providing collective services which take account of solidarity among users, must be supplemented by a means of making an overall evaluation of the different interests involved; whereas this constitutes the requirement of good faith; whereas, in making an assessment of good faith, particular regard shall be had to the strength of the bargaining positions of the parties, whether the consumer had an inducement to agree to the term and whether the goods or services were sold or supplied to the special order of the consumer; whereas the requirement of good faith may be satisfied by the seller or supplier where he deals fairly and equitably with the other party whose legitimate interests he has to take into account;

Whereas, for the purposes of this Directive, the annexed list of terms can be of indicative value only and, because of the cause of the minimal character of the Directive, the scope of these terms may be the subject of amplification or more restrictive editing by the Member States in their national laws;

Whereas the nature of goods or services should have an influence on assessing the unfairness of contractual terms;

Whereas, for the purposes of this Directive, assessment of unfair character shall not be made of terms which describe the main subject matter of the contract nor the quality/price ratio of the goods or services supplied; whereas the main subject matter of the contract and the price/quality ratio may nevertheless be taken into account in assessing the fairness of other terms; whereas it follows, *inter alia*, that in insurance contracts, the terms which clearly define or circumscribe the insured risk and the insurer's liability shall not be subject to such assessment since these restrictions are taken into account in calculating the premium paid by the consumer;

Whereas contracts should be drafted in plain, intelligible language, the consumer should actually be given an opportunity to examine all the terms and, if in doubt, the interpretation most favourable to the consumer should prevail;

Whereas Member States should ensure that unfair terms are not used in contracts concluded with consumers by a seller or supplier and that if, nevertheless, such terms are so used, they will not bind the consumer, and the contract will continue to bind the parties upon those terms if it is capable of continuing in existence without the unfair provisions;

Whereas there is a risk that, in certain cases, the consumer may be deprived of protection under this Directive by designating the law of a non-Member country as the law applicable to the contract; whereas provisions should therefore be included in this Directive designed to avert this risk;

Whereas persons or organisations, if regarded under the law of a Member State as having a legitimate interest in the matter, must have facilities for initiating proceedings concerning terms of contract drawn up for general use in contracts concluded with consumers, and in particular unfair terms, either before a court or before an administrative authority competent to decide upon complaints or to initiate appropriate legal proceedings; whereas this possibility does not, however, entail prior verification of the general conditions obtaining in individual economic sectors;

Whereas the courts or administrative authorities of the Member States must have at their disposal adequate and effective means of preventing the continued application of unfair terms in consumer contracts,

HAS ADOPTED THIS DIRECTIVE:

Article 1

1. The purpose of this Directive is to approximate the laws, regulations and administrative provisions of the Member States relating to unfair terms in contracts concluded between a seller or supplier and a consumer.

2. The contractual terms which reflect mandatory statutory or regulatory provisions and the provisions or principles of international conventions to which the Member States or the Community are party, particularly in the transport area, shall not be subject to the provisions of this Directive.

Article 2

For the purposes of this Directive:
  (a) "unfair terms" means the contractual terms defined in Article 3;
  (b) "consumer" means any natural person who, in contracts covered by this Directive, is acting for purposes which are outside his trade, business or profession;
  (c) "seller or supplier" means any natural or legal person who, in contracts covered by this Directive, is acting for purposes relating to his

trade, business or profession, whether publicly owned or privately owned.

Article 3

1. A contractual term which has not been individually negotiated shall be regarded as unfair if, contrary to the requirement of good faith, it causes a significant imbalance in the parties' rights and obligations arising under the contract, to the detriment of the consumer.

2. A term shall always be regarded as not individually negotiated where it has been drafted in advance and the consumer has therefore not been able to influence the substance of the term, particularly in the context of a pre-formulated standard contract.

The fact that certain aspects of a term or one specific term have been individually negotiated shall not exclude the application of this Article to the rest of a contract if an overall assessment of the contract indicates that it is nevertheless a pre-formulated standard contract.

Where any seller or supplier claims that a standard term has been individually negotiated, the burden of proof in this respect shall be incumbent on him.

3. The Annex shall contain an indicative and non-exhaustive list of the terms which may be regarded as unfair.

Article 4

1. Without prejudice to Article 7, the unfairness of a contractual term shall be assessed, taking into account the nature of the goods or services for which the contract was concluded and by referring, at the time of conclusion of the contract, to all the circumstances attending the conclusion of the contract and to all the other terms of the contract or of another contract on which it is dependent.

2. Assessment of the unfair nature of the terms shall relate neither to the definition of the main subject matter of the contract nor to the adequacy of the price and remuneration, on the one hand, as against the services or goods supplied in exchange, on the other, in so far as these terms are in plain intelligible language.

Article 5

In the case of contracts where all or certain terms offered to the consumer are in writing, these terms must always be drafted in plain, intelligible language. Where there is doubt about the meaning of a term, the interpretation most favourable to the consumer shall prevail. This rule on interpretation shall not apply in the context of the procedures laid down in Article 7(2).

Article 6

1. Member States shall lay down that unfair terms used in a contract concluded with a consumer by a seller or supplier shall, as provided for under their national law, not be binding on the consumer and that the contract shall continue to bind the parties upon those terms if it is capable of continuing in existence without the unfair terms.

2. Member States shall take the necessary measures to ensure that the consumer does not lose the protection granted by this Directive by virtue of the choice of the law of a non-Member country as the law applicable to the contract if the latter has a close connection with the territory of the Member States.

Article 7
1. Member States shall ensure that, in the interests of consumers and of competitors, adequate and effective means exist to prevent the continued use of unfair terms in contracts concluded with consumers by sellers or suppliers.

2. The means referred to in paragraph 1 shall include provisions whereby persons or organisations, having a legitimate interest under national law in protecting consumers, may take action according to the national law concerned before the courts or before competent administrative bodies for a decision as to whether contractual terms drawn up for general use are unfair, so that they can apply appropriate and effective means to prevent the continued use of such terms.

3. With due regard for national laws, the legal remedies referred to in paragraph 2 may be directed separately or jointly against a number of sellers or suppliers from the same economic sector or their associations which use or recommend the use of the same general contractual terms or similar terms.

Article 8
Member States may adopt or retain the most stringent provisions compatible with the Treaty in the area covered by this Directive, to ensure a maximum degree of protection for the consumer.

Article 9
The Commission shall present a report to the European Parliament and to the Council concerning the application of this Directive five years at the latest after the date in Article 10(1).

Article 10
1. Member States shall bring into force the laws, regulations and administrative provisions necessary to comply with this Directive no later than 31 December 1994. They shall forthwith inform the Commission thereof.
These provisions shall be applicable to all contracts concluded after 31 December 1994.

2. When Member States adopt these measures, they shall contain a reference to this Directive or shall be accompanied by such reference on the occasion of their official publication. The methods of making such a reference shall be laid down by the Member States.

3. Member States shall communicate the main provisions of national law which they adopt in the field covered by this Directive to the Commission.

Article 11
This Directive is addressed to the Member States.

Done at Luxembourg, 5 April 1993.

ANNEX

TERMS REFERRED TO IN ARTICLE 3(3)

Terms which have the object or effect of:
1. (a) excluding or limiting the legal liability of a seller or supplier in the

event of the death of a consumer or personal injury to the latter resulting from an act or omission of that seller or supplier;

(b) inappropriately excluding or limiting the legal rights of the consumer *vis-à-vis* the seller or supplier or another party in the event of total or partial non-performance or inadequate performance by the seller or supplier of any of the contractual obligations, including the option of offsetting a debt owed to the seller or supplier against any claim which the consumer may have against him;

(c) making an agreement binding on the consumer whereas provision of services by the seller or supplier is subject to a condition whose realisation depends on his own will alone;

(d) permitting the seller or supplier to retain sums paid by the consumer where the latter decided not to conclude or perform the contract, without providing for the consumer to receive compensation of an equivalent amount from the seller or supplier where the latter is the party cancelling the contract;

(e) requiring any consumer who fails to fulfil his obligation to pay a disproportionately high sum in compensation;

(f) authorising the seller or supplier to dissolve the contract on a discretionary basis where the same facility is not granted to the consumer, or permitting the seller or supplier to retain the sums paid for services not yet supplied by him where it is the seller or supplier himself who dissolves the contract;

(g) enabling the seller or supplier to terminate a contract of indeterminate duration without reasonable notice except where there are serious grounds for doing so;

(h) automatically extending a contract of fixed duration where the consumer does not indicate otherwise, when the deadline fixed for the consumer to express this desire not to extend the contract is unreasonably early;

(i) irrevocably binding the consumer to terms with which he had no real opportunity of becoming acquainted before the conclusion of the contract;

(j) enabling the seller or supplier to alter the terms of the contract unilaterally without a valid reason which is specified in the contract;

(k) enabling the seller or supplier to alter unilaterally without a valid reason any characteristics of the product or service to be provided;

(l) providing for the price of goods to be determined at the time of delivery or allowing a seller of goods or supplier of services to increase their price without in both cases giving the consumer the corresponding right to cancel the contract if the final price is too high in relation to the price agreed when the contract was concluded;

(m) giving the seller or supplier the right to determine whether the goods or services supplied are in conformity with the contract, or giving him the exclusive right to interpret any term of the contract;

(n) limiting the seller's or supplier's obligation to respect commitments undertaken by his agents or making his commitments subject to compliance with a particular formality;

(o) obliging the consumer to fulfil all his obligations where the seller or supplier does not perform his;

(p) giving the seller or supplier the possibility of transferring his rights and obligations under the contract, where this may serve to reduce the guarantees for the consumer, without the latter's agreement;

(q) excluding or hindering the consumer's right to take legal action or exercise any other legal remedy, particularly by requiring the consumer to take disputes exclusively to arbitration not covered by legal provisions, unduly restricting the evidence available to him or imposing on him a burden of proof which, according to the applicable law, should lie with another party to the contract.

Scope of subparagraphs (g), (j) and (l)

2.—(a) Subparagraph (g) is without hindrance to terms by which a supplier of financial services reserves the right to terminate unilaterally a contract of indeterminate duration without notice where there is a valid reason, provided that the supplier is required to inform the other contracting party or parties thereof immediately.

(b) Subparagraph (j) is without hindrance to terms under which a supplier of financial services reserves the right to alter the rate of interest payable by the consumer or due to the latter, or the amount of other charges for financial services without notice where there is a valid reason, provided that the supplier is required to inform the other contracting party or parties thereof at the earliest opportunity and that the latter are free to dissolve the contract immediately.

Subparagraph (j) is also without hindrance to terms under which a seller or supplier reserves the right to alter unilaterally the conditions of a contract of indeterminate duration, provided that he is required to inform the consumer with reasonable notice and that the consumer is free to dissolve the contract.

(c) Subparagraphs (g), (j) and (l) do not apply to:
— transactions in transferable securities, financial instruments and other products or services where the price is linked to fluctuations in a stock exchange quotation or index or a financial market rate that the seller or supplier does not control;
— contracts for the purchase or sale of foreign currency, traveller's cheques or international money orders denominated in foreign currency;

(d) Subparagraph (l) is without hindrance to price-indexation clauses, where lawful, provided that the method by which prices vary is explicitly described.

INDEX

Index